Ms. Agnes Traylor
5742 Vancourt St.
Detroit, MI 48210-1275

MW01713447

Friday May 4, 2001

# The Resourceful Gardener's Guide

# The Resourceful Gardener's Guide

## Garden Solutions, Hints, and Homemade Gadgets from Gardeners Across the Country

**Edited by Christine Bucks and Fern Marshall Bradley**

RODALE®

RODALE

WE **INSPIRE** AND **ENABLE** PEOPLE TO IMPROVE
THEIR LIVES AND THE WORLD AROUND THEM

© 2001 by Rodale Inc.
Illustrations © 2001 Jason Schneider and John and Linda Gist

All rights reserved. No part of this publication may be reproduced or transmitted in any form or by any means, electronic or mechanical, including photocopy, recording, or any other information storage and retrieval system, without the written permission of the publisher.

The information in this book has been carefully researched, and all efforts have been made to ensure accuracy. Rodale Inc. assumes no responsibility for any injuries suffered or for damages or losses incurred during the use of or as a result of following this information. It is important to study all directions carefully before taking any action based on the information and advice presented in this book. When using any commercial product, *always* read and follow label directions. Where trade names are used, no discrimination is intended and no endorsement by Rodale Inc. is implied.

Printed in the United States of America on acid-free (∞), recycled ♻ paper

LIBRARY OF CONGRESS CATALOGING-IN-PUBLICATION DATA

The resourceful gardener's guide : garden solutions, hints, and homemade gadgets from gardeners across the country / edited by Christine Bucks and Fern Marshall Bradley.
p. cm.
Includes bibliographical references (p. ) and index.
ISBN 0–87596–826–0 (hardcover)
1. Gardening. 2. Organic gardening. 3. Garden tools. 4. Gardening—Equipment and supplies.
I. Bucks, Christine. II. Bradley, Fern Marshall.
III. Title.
SB453 .R46 2001
635—dc21 2001000009

Distributed in the book trade by St. Martin's Press

2 4 6 8 10 9 7 5 3 1 hardcover

Editors: Christine Bucks and Fern Marshall Bradley
Contributing Editors: Karen Bolesta, Erana Bumbardatore, Tony O'Malley, Nancy Ondra, Karen Costello Soltys
Cover and Interior Designer: Marta Mitchell Strait
Contributing Designer: Dale Mack
Interior Illustrators: Jason Schneider (Part 1) John and Linda Gist (Part 2)
Cover Illustrator: Jason Schneider
Layout Designer: Jennifer H. Giandomenico
Researchers: Claudia Curran, Diana Erney, Sarah Wolfgang Heffner
Copy Editors: Stacey A. Follin, Candace B. Levy
Manufacturing Coordinator: Patrick T. Smith
Indexer: Lina Burton
Editorial Assistance: Kerrie A. Cadden

**RODALE ORGANIC GARDENING BOOKS**

Executive Editor: Kathleen DeVanna Fish
Managing Editor: Fern Marshall Bradley
Executive Creative Director: Christin Gangi
Art Director: Patricia Field
Production Manager: Robert V. Anderson Jr.
Studio Manager: Leslie M. Keefe
Copy Manager: Nancy N. Bailey
Book Manufacturing Director: Helen Clogston

We're always happy to hear from you. For questions or comments concerning the editorial content of this book, please write to:

Rodale Book Readers' Service
33 East Minor Street
Emmaus, PA 18098

Look for other Rodale books wherever books are sold. Or call us at (800) 848-4735.

For more information about Rodale Organic Gardening magazine and books, visit us at

**www.organicgardening.com**

# Rodale

**ORGANIC GARDENING STARTS HERE!**

Here at Rodale, we've been gardening organically for more than 50 years—ever since my grandfather J. I. Rodale learned about composting and decided that healthy living starts with healthy soil. In 1940 J. I. started the Rodale Organic Farm to test his theories, and today the nonprofit Rodale Institute Experimental Farm is still at the forefront of organic gardening and farming research. In 1942 J. I. founded *Organic Gardening* magazine to share his discoveries with gardeners everywhere. His son, my father, Robert Rodale, headed *Organic Gardening* until 1990, and today a fourth generation of Rodales is growing up with the magazine. Over the years we've shown millions of readers how to grow bountiful crops and beautiful flowers using nature's own techniques.

In this book, you'll find the latest organic methods and the best gardening advice. We know—because all our authors and editors are passionate about gardening! We feel strongly that our gardens should be safe for our children, pets, and the birds and butterflies that add beauty and delight to our lives and landscapes. Our gardens should provide us with fresh, flavorful vegetables, delightful herbs, and gorgeous flowers. And they should be a pleasure to work in as well as to view.

Sharing the secrets of safe, successful gardening is why we publish books. So come visit us at the Rodale Institute Experimental Farm, where you can tour the gardens every day—we're open year-round. And use this book to create your best garden ever.

Happy gardening!

Maria Rodale

Maria Rodale
Rodale Organic Gardening Books

# Contents



## Part I: Practical Solutions to Garden Problems

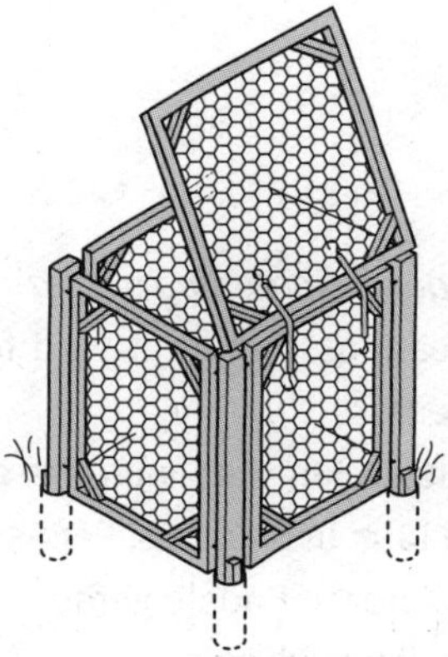

## Part II: Great Garden Gadgets

# Contributors

**Rob Cardillo**, a former editor for *Organic Gardening* magazine, is currently a freelance writer and photographer for a number of publications. His front yard features flowering alliums, unusual shrubs, and a sprinkling of edible greens.

**George DeVault** is the editor of Rodale's Russian-language gardening and farming magazine. He operates a certified organic vegetable farm in Emmaus, Pennsylvania.

**Melanie DeVault**, a frequent contributor to Rodale garden books, raises vegetables and flowers on a certified organic farm in Emmaus, Pennsylvania.

**Nancy Engel** tends a half-acre garden in Putnam County, New York, where she faces the daily challenges of deer, rocks, and roving cats and dogs.

**Mike Ferrara** is a product consultant and spokesperson for major companies in the home improvement market. He currently appears on HGTV and other networks as "The Lazy Homeowner," informing viewers about the latest timesaving tools available.

**Veronica Lorson Fowler** is a freelance garden writer and editor based in Ames, Iowa. She has contributed to various national publications, including *Better Homes and Gardens*, and is also a Master Gardener.

**Linda Harris** is a horticultural writer, desktop designer of Web sites and catalogs, marketing consultant, Master Gardener, and speaker. She's currently working on a book about birds and butterflies.

**Sally McCabe** is an outreach coordinator for the Pennsylvania Horticultural Society's Philadelphia Green. She's also on the board of the American Community Gardening Association. Sally has worked in community gardening for more than 25 years and has recycled 5-gallon buckets for most of that time.

**Pat Michalak** has an M.S. in entomology and a B.S. in crop and soil science from Michigan State University. She's currently an entomologist who works with wholesale greenhouse growers to reduce their pest problems.

**Cass Peterson** is an editor and garden writer. For 17 years, she operated a Pennsylvania farm, growing vegetables, berries, and cutting flowers.

**Barbara Pleasant** lives and gardens in Huntsville, Alabama. She is the author of a dozen gardening books and more magazine articles and newspaper columns than she can remember.

**Melinda Rizzo** is a freelance writer living and gardening in Upper Bucks County, Pennsylvania.

**Sally Roth** is the author of *The Backyard Bird Feeder's Bible, Attracting Butterflies and Hummingbirds to Your Backyard,* and several other books.

**Warren Schultz** is the author of 12 books, including *The Organic Suburbanite* and *A Man's Garden*. Formerly editor-in-chief of *National Gardening*, and features editor of *Garden Design*, he now lives and gardens in South Burlington, Vermont.

**Vicki Webster** is the author of numerous books and magazine articles and has also written extensively for electronic media. She's a former editor at *Country Home* and *Better Homes and Gardens* magazines and is currently a book editor at Storey Books.

# How to Be a Resourceful Gardener

The secrets to successful gardening include practice, patience, luck—as well as a talent for solving problems when they creep up on you. That's because no matter how green your gardening thumb is, you can't control Mother Nature and the potential bugaboos she may unleash in the form of disease, insect, and animals pests, and less-than-stellar weather. But you *can* make the best out of the situation.

And that's where this book comes in. We've gathered tips from gardeners across the country who have to deal with the same problems you do—and who have come up with remarkably resourceful, all-organic solutions for fixing those problems.

In Part I of this book, "Practical Solutions to Garden Problems," you'll find problem-solving secrets, such as how to beat dastardly plant diseases with an oil-and-baking-soda spray, the fastest way to deadhead perennials, and how to hide an ugly heating-oil tank in your landscape. Throughout most chapters in this part, we've called out fast fixes and titled them "Solutions at a Glance." These are quick solutions that don't require a lot of instruction, supplies—or a lot of your time. Also watch for "Pest Detective" charts, which help you figure out what disease or bad bug is at work in your garden and how you can control it organically.

Sometimes you need a particular gadget close at hand to help with your problem-solving situation. Our writers also gathered dozens of ideas for nifty gizmos, recycled doodads, and inventive accessories for nearly every garden task—from making compost and planting seeds to controlling weeds and trellising climbing plants. Part II of this book, "Great Garden Gadgets," holds tons of unique, homemade garden gadgets—here you'll find everything from tool ideas to frost protection contraptions. If the idea of making your own gadgets seems a little intimidating, though, start by searching for the "Recycle It!" logo. That's your clue to fast-and-easy devices and garden helpers you can make using materials that you probably have on hand. If you have a knack for building stuff, watch for the "Build It!" logo throughout this part; each "Build It!" tip offers step-by-step instructions for constructing elaborate creations—such as a tool caddy from boards and dowels.

Ultimately, no matter where you live or how long you've been gardening, *The Resourceful Gardener's Guide* will give you reader-tested information you can use. And the less time you have to spend on solving problems, the more time you'll have to enjoy your beautiful, bountiful garden.

# Part I

# PRACTICAL SOLUTIONS TO GARDEN PROBLEMS

Probably the best part of gardening is the end result, corn so sweet it tastes like candy, roses that smell better than any store-bought fragrance, or a backyard free from eyesores. Of course, getting to that end result often means you have to deal with a few trials and tribulations along the way. And even if you have pretty good success with solving gardening glitches, chances are you've run up against at least a few problems you couldn't figure out.

When you turn the page, however, you'll find a wealth of hints to help you solve those problems for which you thought there were no answers. Learn how to foil deer once and for all, how to grow roses free from powdery mildew, and how to take the itch out of poison ivy. This compilation of smart ideas and clever techniques has been tested by backyard gardeners just like you—with promising results. So try out these solutions in your own backyard—and watch your good garden blossom into a great one.

# Animal Problems

All those lovely vegetables and flowers might constitute a garden to you, but to the two- and four-legged creatures that live nearby, your garden looks like free lunch. Short of growing everything in a greenhouse (and even *that* isn't guaranteed free from furry or feathered beasts), how do you persuade wildlife to look elsewhere for food? Read on for some clever strategies that have worked for other gardeners. Keep in mind that some animals learn quickly, so you may have to switch tactics from time to time to stay ahead of the game.

## Outsmarting Bambi

For most gardeners, deer are the biggest challenge. The low fences that dissuade rabbits and groundhogs are an easy leap for these bounding creatures. And the permanent deer fencing that commercial nurseries and market gardeners use only works if it remains powered all the time. The solution: temporary fencing—which is what Hiu Newcomb, a market gardener in Vienna, Virginia, uses.

The most common kind of temporary fencing has two strands of "hot tape" (ribbon-like material with wire woven into it to carry an electric charge) strung on easily installed fiberglass poles. Temporary fencing works best if you bait it because you want the deer to learn that the fence means business. Peanut butter, which deer adore, is a great bait. Smear some directly on the hot tape every 6 feet or so, or make little peanut butter "sandwiches" by putting a teaspoon of it inside a folded strip of athletic tape, wrapping some foil around the tape, and attaching it to the fence. The deer will stay out, and your garden will stay safe.

*Bait your electric fence with peanut butter to train deer to stay away.*

## Undercover Deer Deterrent

Deer laugh at chicken-wire fencing when it's upright (so easy to jump!)—so lay it flat on the ground around the garden instead. The deer can't see it, and as they approach, they get their hooves entangled in the woven wires. It's easy to install and easy to maintain: Just flip the fence aside occasionally to mow under it so it doesn't become caught in tall grass, and roll it up for storage when the season is over.

## The Not-So-Sweet Smell of Success

Hanging out stuff that smells nasty is another way of keeping deer out of where they don't belong. Deer are naturally mistrustful of unusual or threatening scents, so hanging out cheesecloth bags of human hair, dirty socks, or empty detergent boxes may help deter them. Switching from one aromatic repellent to another every few days keeps the deer off guard.

Commercial deer repellents are available, but they don't always deliver the "antibuck" bang for the buck. Connecticut researchers tested several common deer repellents on nursery trees and shrubs. Their results are in the chart below.

## Tricks of the Trellis

If store-bought fencing isn't an option for keeping deer at bay, why not let trellised vegetables do the job for you? Grow cucumbers, peas, or pole beans on trellises around the perimeter of the garden to protect the veggies within. Deer, being opportunists, will dine on the trellised veggies and leave the produce that they can't get to alone.

## Shine and Shake

When tricks aimed at the deer's nose fail to keep the critter out of your garden, try gambits aimed at the eyes and ears. If there's power nearby,

### Unwelcome Odors

*Surrounding your garden beds with scents deer don't like is one way to pull the welcome mat out from under them. Here's a quick look at five products you can try, their effectiveness, and approximately how much they'll cost.*

| Repellent | Effectiveness | Cost per Acre |
|---|---|---|
| Deer Away (rotten eggs) | 46 percent | $990 |
| Hinder Deer and Rabbit Repellent (ammonium soaps) | 43 percent | $75 |
| Human hair | 34 percent | $24 |
| Magic Circle Deer Repellent (bone tar oil) | 18 percent | $74 |
| Miller Hot Sauce (extract of hot peppers) | 15 percent | $26 |

Note: *Always check the labels of deer repellents to see if they're intended for landscape plants only or for vegetable plants as well.*

spotlight the deer with motion sensor lights. (The lights will discourage raccoons, too.) Deer are also easily spooked by moving shapes—floating row covers on a moonlit night are sometimes enough to send them packing. Or staple plastic trash bags to tomato stakes: The bags look like people and flap in the slightest breeze.

## Crows Out, Seeds In

Birds, especially crows, love to pull seeds and seedlings out of the ground. Here are two ways to keep your young charges safe.

- Protect newly sprouted corn and beans and freshly planted transplants by tying twine to a double row of short bamboo stakes (like miniature telephone wires) and attaching strips of aluminum foil every few feet. The flapping foil will send crows packing.
- Keep crows from dining on newly planted seeds by covering beds with floating row cover or chicken-wire fencing.

*Scare crows away from seedlings and transplants with flapping foil.*

### Solutions at a Glance

**Problem:** Something is eating all your carrot tops.

**Culprit:** Rabbits

**Solve It!** Scare them away with plastic snakes. Cut an old garden hose into serpentlike lengths and place the pieces throughout your garden.

## Bag 'Em

When crows moved in on her new transplants and wild turkeys took a liking to her strawberries, market gardener Sylvia Ehrhardt of Knoxville, Maryland, decided to bag them. "We filled plastic grocery bags with air and tied them shut, and then we put them on top of stakes throughout the garden, every 10 to 15 feet, up and down the row," says Ehrhardt. "The bags move in the breeze and look like people leaning over."

The multicolored bags are more effective than the aluminum pie plates she tried first, Ehrhardt says. "They work well for new transplants, too, which the crows pull up. We take them down when the plants get bigger."

## Bloodmeal Contained

Bloodmeal is an effective repellent for small rodents, but if you simply sprinkle it around your plants, you'll have to reapply it every time it rains. Here's a way to keep it working all season: Put the bloodmeal into empty margarine or yogurt containers (a tablespoon or so per container is plenty). Add a little water and a rock weight so the container doesn't blow away or tip over. Dis-

## Solutions at a Glance

**Problem:** Something is eating your corn.
**Culprit:** Raccoons
**Solve It!** Plant pumpkins or winter squash among the corn. As the squash plants trellis up the cornstalks, they reduce visibility, which makes the raccoons uncomfortable because they like to stand up and look around while they eat.

tribute the containers around your garden. But keep the lids handy so you can cover the containers when you want to work in the garden. Wet bloodmeal puts out a powerful odor.

### Disco Deterrent

Raccoons love sweet corn, but they don't care much for rock music. Put a transistor radio in the corn patch when the corn is ripening, and turn it on each night to your favorite station. (Cover the radio with a plastic bag to protect it from the elements and keep plenty of batteries on hand.) To add to the disco deterrent, string twinkling Christmas lights through the corn. Your garden will be festive, and the lights will keep the raccoons at bay.

### Don't Let Rodents Bite the Bark

Mice, rabbits, and voles love to munch on young trees, but that can mean death for the tree. To protect trees wrap their trunks with commercial tree guards (metal or plastic) or window screen (the openings in chicken wire are too large to keep mice from reaching the bark—they'll slip right through).

If you live in a mild-winter area, a foot or so of trunk protection will be enough to deter mice, rabbits, and voles. If you live in an area where heavy snow is common, make sure the guard extends at least a foot higher than the usual snow depth. Mice and voles will tunnel under the snow to do their nibbling, but rabbits will hop on the top of crusted snow to get at the tender bark higher up.

*Wrap tree trunks high enough to keep rabbits from using snow as a lift to the tender bark.*

### Alternative Eats

Rabbits have to eat, and if your yard and garden look like their favorite restaurant, it may simply be that there isn't much else available in the neighborhood. Letting a few patches of your yard grow up in clovers and wildflowers can help satisfy their hunger and keep them away from your garden. To encourage other wildlife to eat what you want them to, spray the vegetation with a concoction of 1 cup of molasses and 1 tablespoon of salt to 1 gallon of water.

## Grow Unpalatable Fare

One of the tricks to keeping animal pests out of your garden is to grow things they don't like to eat. Some edibles and ornamentals, like rhubarb and foxgloves (*Digitalis* spp.), are repulsive or even toxic to wildlife. Creating a living fence of these plants around your yard can help deter even large animals like deer. See below for some of the things you can grow to keep wildlife at bay.

## Solutions at a Glance

**Problem:** Your lawn is full of tunnels.

**Culprit:** Moles

**Solve It!** Discourage them by shoving prickly twigs of multiflora rose (*Rosa multiflora*) or raspberry canes into their tunnels.

## For the Birds

Birds love fruit, especially berries and cherries. Turn the page for a couple of tips to save these sweet treats from the nibbling beaks.

## Plants Pests Will Pass On

*If you grow these, they won't come. That's right, a few plants, like foxglove and daffodils, are just as vile to some critters as lima beans are to kids.*

| What to Grow | What Doesn't Like It |
|---|---|
| Alliums (*Allium* spp., including ornamental alliums as well as onions and garlic) | Birds, deer, mice, moles, rabbits, voles |
| Artemisias (*Artemisia* spp.) | Deer, mice, moles, rabbits, voles |
| Foxgloves (*Digitalis* spp.) | Deer, mice, rabbits, voles |
| Euphorbias (*Euphorbia* spp.) | Mice, moles |
| Lavenders (*Lavendula* spp.) | Mice, voles |
| Mints (*Mentha* spp.) | Mice, rats |
| Daffodils (*Narcissus* hybrids) | Moles, squirrels |
| Castor beans (*Ricinus communis*) | Moles |
| Siberian squill bulbs (*Scilla siberica*) | Gophers |
| Rhubarbs | Deer, rabbits |

## Solutions at a Glance

**Problem:** Something is eating your shrubs.

**Culprit:** Rabbits? Or deer?

**Solve It!** First you need positive ID on the perpetrator. Has the shrubbery been nibbled off cleanly, as if nipped with pruning shears? That's rabbit damage. Does the damage look ragged? That's the sign of deer munching. Bloodmeal will discourage the rabbit; try hanging soap bars on the shrub if the problem is deer.

---

**Problem:** Your storage shed has squatters.

**Culprit:** Mice

**Solve it!** Traps are your best bet. Bait them with peanut butter, and set a mirror behind each one. Mice are social animals and will approach a trap more readily if they think another mouse is already there.

---

- When cherries start to ripen, hang cut onions in the trees. You can slice the onions into rings, which are easy to hang on branches, but they'll dry out quickly and need to be replaced more often. It's best to cut the onions into halves or quarters, pierce them with a piece of wire, and hang them on the tree like ornaments.
- Birds like chokecherries (*Prunus virginiana*), elderberries (*Sambucus* spp.), and mulberries (*Morus* spp.) as much or more than they like cultivated fruits, so a slightly unkempt fence row may be the best protection for your cultivated fruits. If your fruit is the only game in town, however, you may need netting to keep some of it for yourself. You don't need to use a tight mesh—most birds won't fly into situations that might impede their wings when they're trying to get out. But make sure you aren't inadvertently keeping a mother bird from her nest! Drape the netting loosely over the tree. If the tree is too large to net completely, cover as many of the lower branches as you can.

# Aphids

Aphids are living proof that bad things can come in very small packages. Also known as plant lice or greenbugs, aphids rarely appear in small groups. Instead, you may go to gather some kale that looked perfect only 3 days before and find the leaves nearly covered by swarms of ⅛-inch-long, green-gray, oblong lumps—aphids! Look on the underside of a leaf, and you'll probably find several hundred more. But you don't have to let aphids set up camp in your garden. Read on to find out how to repel these bad bugs with citrus, soap, and water as well as how to help plants with aphid damage.

## Lick 'Em with Lemon "Aid"

Aphids are repelled by limonene and linalool, the two compounds that give lemon, orange, and grapefruit rind their pungent scent. To make an effective aphid remedy that smells good too, mix 1 tablespoon of freshly grated citrus rind with 1 pint of boiling water. Let it steep overnight, strain the mixture through cheesecloth or a coffee filter, and pour the resulting "tea" into a pump spray bottle. Add 3 drops of insecticidal soap or dish-washing liquid to help the lemony mixture stick to plants' leaves and aphids' bodies, then give affected plants a thorough spritz with the spray.

*When life hands you aphids, make lemon "aid." Steep grated citrus peel in boiling water to make a lemon-scented tea that will send aphids packing.*

## Your Pest Defense

Although they're small, aphids can do big damage if they go unchecked for too long. When aphids get out of hand, try these tips to help rid your plants of these pests.

**Start with a stream.** For starters, simply knock the pests from your plants with a strong spray of water from a hose or pressure sprayer. You can repeat this treatment as often as needed to get aphids under control, but don't spray so hard that you harm your plants.

**CUT IT OUT.** Remove plant parts that aren't likely to recover from aphid injury. Pinch off or prune away severely damaged parts of an infested plant. When you find aphids so densely packed on a stem or leaf that they completely cover its surface, get rid of them by picking or pruning off the affected plant part and dropping it into a pail of hot soapy water.

**SCRUB UP WITH (INSECTICIDAL) SOAP.** Treat severe aphid problems by spraying insecticidal soap on infested plants and on plants growing nearby. (Test the spray first to make sure it doesn't do more damage than the aphids. Apply the soap to a few leaves and wait 3 days. If you don't see any signs of damage—leaf browning, spotting, or curling—proceed with the spray.) Make sure you completely cover leaf undersides and other sheltered places. Repeat the application every 5 to 7 days until the aphids are gone. The soap also helps remove deposits of unsightly sooty mold, which commonly forms on the aphids' honeydew. Remember that insecticidal soap also harms beneficial insects, so be sure to use it only when absolutely necessary.

**TAKE A PREVENTIVE APPROACH.** For trees or shrubs that have recurring aphid problems, alternate applications of insecticidal soap and light horticultural oil at weekly intervals beginning in early spring. (Again, test the soap or oil on a few leaves first.) Spray injury becomes more likely at higher temperatures, so be extra careful as spring turns to summer.

## The Aphid-Ant Alliance

The sticky honeydew that aphids excrete is a sugary protein substance that's pure candy for ants. Ants have even been seen protecting aphid colonies from predators to safeguard their treats! If you notice ants lurking near clusters of aphids, douse the affected plant with water to knock the ants to the ground. Then encircle the main stems or trunks with a 1-inch-wide band of a sticky material such as Tanglefoot or Stickem to trap the ants as they try to crawl back up the plants. Without their ant bodyguards, aphids are easier prey for hungry predators.

*Ants actually tend colonies of aphids so they can feed on the sticky sweet honeydew the aphids excrete. Knock the ants off your plants with water, and then use a band of sticky stuff to keep them from coming back.*

# Bean Problems

Beans are some of the easiest and most reliable vegetables to grow, so it's no surprise that they're some of the most popular garden vegetables today. But nothing is foolproof, not even these "easy" vegetables. Coaxing seeds to germinate in cool, spring soil can be tough as can getting seedlings past the tender baby stage when they're so attractive to deer and rabbits. But help is at hand—read on for the secrets to a hearty, healthy bean crop.

## Rx for Healthy Beans

A bumper crop of beans will be easy pickin' if you follow these tips for making beans feel right at home in your garden.

**GET THEM OFF TO A WARM START.** Most veteran gardeners agree that this means waiting until all danger of frost has past—so wait for warm soil and air (both at least 60°F) to plant the beans. If you jump the gun and plant them in cold soil, they'll germinate slowly, and they'll be more vulnerable to rot and soil-borne diseases.

But if you have to have the earliest beans in the neighborhood and the soil temperature is still below 60°F, try these tips: First, for at least 2 weeks before your early target date (slightly before the last expected frost), warm the soil by tightly covering the planting area with black plastic. Second, think purple. Purple varieties tend to be more agreeable to cool soil. (Or check seed catalogs for other early varieties.) Once seedlings emerge, you can use a floating row cover to help protect them from cold temperatures and pests.

**PREPARE THE SOIL.** Beans don't usually need fertilizer if you enrich the soil with a healthy dose of compost before planting. (Also, the microorganisms in compost help suppress diseases.) However, the beans do like a loose soil that encourages germination and root growth, so dig down 8 to 12 inches.

**PREPARE THE BEST SEEDS YOU CAN.** Many expert gardeners soak their bean seeds in water for 30 minutes before planting, or they pregerminate seeds by placing them between two damp paper towels overnight. Whether or not you pregerminate, it's a good idea to inoculate the seed to ensure that beneficial bacteria are present. Some seed companies claim a yield boost of 20 percent with inoculant. (Inoculants help beans, which are legumes, fix nitrogen in their root nodules. Inoculants are available at garden centers and through mail-order catalogs.)

Additionally, Dr. Steve Reiners, associate professor of horticulture at Cornell University, Ithaca, New York, says to check seed packets for the germination percentage (catalogs don't give you this information). "You can learn which seed companies tend to offer higher germination," he says. "If you have a 70 percent germination (weak seed), and plant in 55°F soil, you're setting yourself up for trouble. If you have a choice, go for higher germination (85 percent or more)!"

**PLANT 'EM SNUG.** The biggest disagreement among bean experts is in regard to planting. Traditional wisdom suggests planting seeds 1 inch deep, 2 to 3 inches apart, and then thinning seedlings to 6 inches apart. This strategy is said to increase air circulation and help ward off the spread of disease by removing the weakest plants.

But Reiners says that they've done some amazing studies on bean spacing—and the bottom line is it doesn't really matter whether they're spaced closely or not. You can really crowd those bush bean seeds in there and still get a good crop. "Data collected over a couple of years show it didn't make a difference whether the beans were spaced 2, 3, or even 4 inches apart," he says. And home gardeners can space rows 1½ to 2 feet apart. This denser planting essentially causes the leaves of the plants to grow into a shade-producing canopy that cools the soil and inhibits weeds. So what does this information mean for your garden? Experiment and see what works best for you!

**PROVIDE ADEQUATE MOISTURE AND MULCH.** Beans have shallow root systems, so they'll suffer badly during a drought. Water plants until they're established, and then keep the soil evenly moist. They need at least 1 inch of water a week once they're up and running, but you should let the soil dry out between waterings. Beans don't like to have perpetually wet feet. Mulch can be a big helper, especially if you live where summers are hot and dry. Grass clippings, shredded newspaper, and straw all have their advocates. These mulches don't just keep the soil moist, they keep weeds at bay, which means your beans won't be competing with them for moisture and nutrition.

**PICK, PICK, PICK!** Beans need to be picked often—that is, every 2 to 3 days. If the pods are allowed to mature (to get big and tough), your plants will get Mother Nature's signal that it's fine to slack off on pod production. Picking is the number one way to keep 'em coming.

**STAY OUT OF THE BEAN PATCH WHEN IT'S WET.** If you go trudging through the beans when vines are wet, you're just asking to spread bean diseases like anthracnose or rust.

**ROTATE!** If you have the space to rotate crops, avoid growing beans in the same spot 2 years in a row (some experts even recommend a 3-year rotation). That's because beans are susceptible to a host of diseases that live in the soil, and rotating your bean plantings helps to prevent a buildup of those diseases. If you have a small space garden (which makes

# Pest Detective

*Have a problem with your bean plants but aren't sure who the culprit is? This quick reference chart can help you identify the bad guys and give you organic ways to beat them at their own game.*

| Symptom | Cause | What to Do |
|---|---|---|
| Dark streaks on leaves; sunken spots on pods | Anthracnose | Plant tolerant varieties and destroy infected plants. Don't touch plants when wet, or you may spread the disease. Preventive measures include keeping a clean garden (removing spent plants, weeds, and infected plants regularly) and rotating crops. |
| Mottled, curled leaves; rough spots on pods | Bean mosaic | Avoid touching the plants when wet, or you may spread the disease, and control sucking insects, such as aphids. Destroy infected plants, and plant mosaic-tolerant cultivars. |
| Skeletonized leaves, holes in beans | Mexican bean beetle (yellow larvae, brownish bugs with black spots) | Destroy yellow egg clusters and adults on undersides of leaves, and encourage beneficial insects, such as adult soldier bugs and parasitic wasps. You can purchase the parasitic wasp (*Pediobus foveolatus*) and release it when the first generation of Mexican bean beetle larvae are about half grown. You can also try planting resistant varieties, such as 'Black Valentine'. |
| Reddish brown, orange, or yellow bumps on leaves and pods | Rust | Keep the leaves dry. Destroy any infected leaves, and try planting resistant varieties. |
| Leaves drop or have pale speckles | Spider mites | Use garlic and soap sprays. |
| Warty bumps on pods | Stink bugs | Remove these brown, shield-shape bugs from the plants by shaking them over trays of soapy water; you can also counter them with beneficial insects, such as parasitic wasps and tachinid flies. Spray plants with insecticidal soap, and control weeds around your beans. |

rotating crops difficult), add some compost to your soil before planting—compost helps suppress disease organisms.

*IF YOU WANT THE EARLIEST BEANS ON YOUR BLOCK, WARM UP THE SOIL BY COVERING YOUR PLANTING BED WITH BLACK PLASTIC.*

## SHORT ON SPACE?

No problem, says Weldon Burge, an organic gardener from Newark, Delaware. Probably the biggest myth about beans, he believes, is that you need a lot of garden to grow them. Burge grows all of his beans in a 4 × 8-foot raised bed. He grows six to eight different varieties and supplies his family with ample beans from early summer through late fall. Here's how Burge does it.

He divides his raised beds into 1 × 4-foot-long sections, which he works well to a depth of 8 inches and then mixes in compost and coarse sand. He sows bean seeds in these wide swaths because he believes this not only uses space more efficiently but also boosts bean production by increasing soil moisture and smothering weeds.

He starts planting his early-variety snap beans after the last expected frost in a block at one end of the raised bed. He scatters the seeds so they fall about 1 inch apart, and then he pokes them in about 1 inch deep (he plants them twice that deep in summer). Once plants are established, he makes sure they have adequate water, and he mulches with clean straw to conserve moisture. He does successive plantings every 2 to 3 weeks, moving down the bed, starting with early-season purple varieties ('Royal Burgundy' and 'Purple Teepee' are his favorites), and moving on to mid- and late-season varieties. He sows his final fall crop in August. (Watch the timing in your area to make sure you allow enough time before the first fall frost.)

As each crop finishes heavy production, he cleans the plants out of the foot-wide strip. After he has planted the length of the bed, he returns to these now-empty plots for successive plantings. By removing spent plants, Burge makes room for later plantings and keeps bugs in check. (Despite growing a feast of beans, he reports that he has little problem with Mexican bean beetles.)

*SUCCESSIVE PLANTING IN A RAISED BED CAN GIVE YOU AN AMPLE SUPPLY OF TASTY BEANS WHEN YOU'RE SHORT ON GARDEN SPACE.*

# Berry Problems

Bountiful, beautiful berries are the supreme garden treat, whether you're growing your own perfectly ripened strawberries, luscious raspberries, or plump blueberries. But if you want your share, you'll need to be prepared for freeloaders, especially birds, although many insect pests adore berries as well. Because berries are juicy, sweet, and often soft, they're also prone to mold and mildew problems. Forewarned is forearmed, so read on for solutions.

## Strawberry Weed Woes

Strawberries throw out runners hither and yon, making them difficult to hoe, and they're in the ground for several years—perfect conditions to create a serious problem with perennial weeds. How to prevent weed woes? "You have to start with a clean bed," says market gardener Tony Ricci from Three Springs, Pennsylvania. "Cover-crop the bed you want to grow strawberries in for a year or so. If the weeds start out ahead of you, you'll never catch up."

In established beds, a companion crop that's compatible with the strawberries can help control weeds. Ricci sows oats (*Avena sativa*) between his spring-planted strawberry beds in mid-September, which creates a thick mat between the strawberry plants. This cover crop grows 6 to 8 inches tall and dies in the winter. The next spring the debris from the spent oats suppresses early weeds until about May—then the oats break down completely.

Sylvia Ehrhardt, who specializes in berries at her Knoxville, Maryland, farm, uses straw mulch atop four layers of newspaper between the rows of strawberries and mulches between the plants in the rows with compost or old sawdust. "That keeps weeds down and feeds the plants, too," she says.

Ehrhardt also keeps perennial weeds to a minimum—and renovates her strawberry beds at the same time—by tilling the rows of strawberries to about 1 foot wide every year after harvest. The tilling wipes out weeds between the rows and allows the plants to set new runners every year for maximum yields.

## A Hilly Advantage

If weeding between strawberry runners isn't your cup of tea, try growing strawberries in a hill system. Under this system, the plants aren't allowed to set runners; you snip those off and direct all the plant's energy into the mother plant. The advantage is that the plants are easier to hoe, and you can eliminate weeds entirely by setting the plants into plastic mulch or landscape fabric.

*Say good-bye to strawberry weed woes using the hill system.*

## Saggy Trellis Solution

Keep your blackberry and raspberry trellises from sagging when wet by using *plastic* baling twine between the stakes. One or two strands are all you need, and you can save the twine to use again year after year.

## Outfox Your Feathered Friends

Birds in your blueberries? Here are three ways to put an end to their feast.

**USE SCARE TACTICS.** When the first berries appear on the early ripening varieties at Melanie DeVault's farm in Emmaus, Pennsylvania, she puts up bird scare balloons and bird scare tape. The balloons (many of them metallic with giant eyes printed on them) and Mylar tape (it hums and flutters in the breeze) are readily available in stores, but you can put together your own bird scare arsenal for less money. Just visit your local florist or party-goods store for Mylar balloons, and cut out strips of aluminum foil for bird scare tape.

**PUT UP PLASTIC NETTING.** Plastic bird netting (the holes are about a half-inch in diameter) is available in various sizes at garden centers. You can make the whole job of putting up the netting easier if you erect a permanent wooden frame around your bushes. Then just attach the netting to the frame during berry season. (Staple the top of the netting to the frame, run inexpensive twine through some of the bottom holes in the netting, and tie the twine in a bow. That way, it's easy to untie the twine, lift the netting, and pick the berries.)

**PLANT OTHER BERRIES.** If you have enough space, planting alternative food sources works great for deterring birds. In fact, they prefer mulberries (*Morus* spp.), chokecherry (*Prunus virginiana)*, and elderberries (*Sambucus* spp.) to cultivated berries.

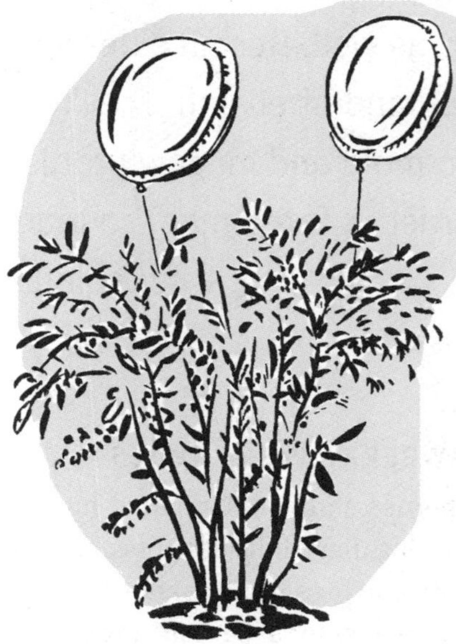

*Create a party atmosphere in your garden and keep birds out of the berries at the same time.*

## Solutions at a Glance

**PROBLEM:** Your berries are rotting.

**CULPRIT:** Fungal diseases

**SOLVE IT!** Take a look at your watering practices. Wet berries invite fungal diseases, so drip irrigation or soaker hoses are better than overhead watering.

---

**PROBLEM:** Something's eating your grapes and raspberries.

**CULPRIT:** Japanese beetles

**SOLVE IT!** Handpick the beetles before 7 A.M., when they're still sluggish.

---

**PROBLEM:** Your strawberries are deformed and seedy.

**CULPRIT:** Tarnished plant bugs

**SOLVE IT!** Rotate the strawberries every 3 years to prevent pests from building up (potatoes are a great rotation crop). Mow the bed and remove debris each year, and cover the berries with a floating row cover until they're in full flower, to prevent adults from laying eggs on the foliage (it's the nymphs that do the damage). Plant fennel or dill nearby to attract beneficial insects, and don't weed out the Queen-Anne's lace.

---

**PROBLEM:** Your blueberry clusters have unwelcome visitors.

**CULPRIT:** Earwigs

**SOLVE IT!** Catch earwigs with a shallow container of vegetable oil, or use toilet-paper tubes coated inside with oil and squashed almost flat. The oiliness and the darkness of the tube will attract the earwigs. Check the traps each morning and dispose of any you've caught.

---

**PROBLEM:** The blueberry foliage is yellowing.

**CULPRIT:** Nutritional deficiency

**SOLVE IT!** Check the soil pH. If it's above 5.2, the problem may be iron deficiency. Add sulfur to acidify the soil. If it's below 5.2, your problem may be calcium deficiency. Add gypsum to provide calcium without raising the pH.

## Sulfur Solutions

*Blueberries love acidic soil, so it's your job to see that their acid requirements are satisfied. After checking your soil's pH, look at the handy chart below to see how much sulfur you need to add to your soil, if any.*

| Current pH | Sandy Soil | Loamy Soil | Clay Soil |
|---|---|---|---|
| 4.5 | 0 | 0 | 0 |
| 5.0 | 0.4 lb. per 100 sq. ft. | 1.2 lb. per 100 sq. ft. | 1.8 lb. per 100 sq. ft. |
| 5.5 | 0.8 lb. per 100 sq. ft. | 2.3 lb. per 100 sq. ft. | 3.5 lb. per 100 sq. ft. |
| 6.0 | 1.2 lb. per 100 sq. ft. | 3.4 lb. per 100 sq. ft. | 5.1 lb. per 100 sq. ft. |
| 6.5 | 1.5 lb. per 100 sq. ft. | 4.5 lb. per 100 sq. ft. | 6.7 lb. per 100 sq. ft. |
| 7.0 | 1.9 lb. per 100 sq. ft. | 5.7 lb. per 100 sq. ft. | 8.5 lb. per 100 sq. ft. |
| 7.5 | 2.2 lb. per 100 sq. ft. | 6.8 lb. per 100 sq. ft. | 10 lb. per 100 sq. ft. |

### Space-Saving Strawberries

Coming up short on garden space? Try growing strawberries with asparagus. "My asparagus bed is a single row along a long end of the vegetable garden," says Lisa Krall, a soil scientist with the USDA's Natural Resources Conservation Service. "Weeding this 3-foot-wide bed for one row seemed like a pain, so I put in the strawberries."

Krall plants berries in rows on either side of the asparagus in her garden in Belgrade, Maine, and directs strawberry runners away from the asparagus.

"I think they're quite compatible," she says. "They occupy different parts of the root zone and seem to like the same treatment. This bed is the only one I water regularly, since both crops seem to respond to an inch a week."

# Bulb Problems

Bulbs . . . just plunk them in the ground, wait a little while, and watch them burst forth into color, right? Well, yes—as long as pesky critters don't gnaw them, viruses don't zap them, the temperatures are just right, and you've planted them correctly.

But you aren't far off. Plant bulbs correctly and foil the pests, and you'll have a dazzling display of color for years to come. And best of all, many bulbs provide color just when you need it the most—early spring. Here's how to make sure you get the most bang from your bulbs.

### Divide and Conquer

Love daffodils and want even more? You can propagate your own by dividing the bulbs.

Daffodil gardener Gene Bauer of Running Springs, California, explains that unlike many perennials, daffodils are capable of multiplying. But they don't necessarily spread on their own—they need a little help.

After a daffodil planting becomes established (say, 7 or 8 years), dig it up in the spring after the flowers have faded and the foliage is browning. Gently break off the little 1-inch or so side bulbs, called the daughters, and set them aside.

Replant the larger bulbs in the regular garden. Then plant the small bulbs in well-marked rows in a nursery bed or in a corner of the vegetable garden. Keep them well watered and fertilize regularly. Don't expect flowers from these small bulbs for at least 2 or 3 years, though. In 3 or 4 years, the bulbs will have grown to about 3 inches, large enough to plant out in the garden where they can fend for themselves.

*Propagate daffodils by breaking off and transplanting "daughter" bulbs.*

## Solutions at a Glance

**Problem:** Critters are destroying all your flower bulbs.

**Culprit:** Voles, moles, and other burrowing animals

**Solve It!** Toss several handfuls of sharp gravel into the planting hole, place your bulbs in the hole and cover with more gravel, then fill in with soil, suggests Connie Cross of Connie Cross Garden Design in Catchogue, New York.

## Companion Cover-Ups

You welcome the color of spring bloomers—daffodils, hyacinths, and tulips. And then you can't stand looking at their unsightly foliage once it starts to fade, right?

Try planting perennials or annuals right on top of them to disguise all of that yellowing and browning. Here's a list of good bulb companion plants that have helpful foliage and modest root systems that won't bother the bulbs.

***Plant on Top of Bulbs***

- Common lady's-mantle (*Alchemilla vulgaris*)
- Columbines (*Aquilegia* spp.)
- Astilbes (*Astilbe* spp.)
- Fringed bleeding heart (*Dicentra eximia*)
- Heucheras (*Heuchera* spp. )
- Ostrich ferns* (*Matteuccia* spp.)
- Tall marigolds, such as the Inca series (*Tagetes* cultivars)
- Pansies (*Viola* × *wittrockiana* cultivars)
- Common periwinkle (*Vinca minor*)

***Plant near Bulbs***

- Flowering spurge (*Euphorbia corollata*)
- Broom (*Genista* spp.)
- English ivy (*Hedera helix*)
- Daylilies (*Hemerocallis* spp.)
- Hostas* (*Hosta* spp.)
- Siberian iris (*Iris sibirica*)
- Prostrate speedwell (*Veronica prostrata*)

* Plant with daffodils or other early-spring-blooming bulbs that will grow under deciduous trees. The area is sunny in early spring, before the trees leaf out, and becomes shady later in the season.

*Use perennials to cover up dying bulb foliage.*

## Buy in Bulk

One of the prettiest ways to plant spring-blooming bulbs is in large drifts, but that can be expensive. Avid daffodil gardener Gene Bauer of Running Springs, California, plants thousands each spring and has found ways to trim her bulb bill.

Bauer discovered that the more you order, the more you save, so seek out catalogs that offer discounts according to quantity. Some companies, for example, might offer substantial savings for ordering 50 or more bulbs of one type and even better savings for ordering 100 bulbs at a time. If you're ordering 100 or more, talk to your local greenhouse or bulb supplier. They may cut a deal. (Beware, however, of too-good-to-be-true-prices. The bulbs may be undersized and poor bloomers.)

Buying in bulk really pays off for bulbs that naturalize well, such as daffodils, grape hyacinths (*Muscari* spp.), crocuses, and snowdrops (*Galanthus* spp.). And because these tough bulbs are going to be around for decades, it's easy to buy many of one variety, adding a new variety each year.

### Solutions at a Glance

**Problem:** Daffodils aren't blooming but their foliage looks great.

**Culprit:** Fertilizer

**Solve It!** Go easy on the fertilizer. Daffodils don't respond well to too much nitrogen. Instead, if it's spring and your daffodils aren't blooming, give them a shot of a low-nitrogen organic fertilizer made for stimulating root development. Or scratch in a little wood ash from the fireplace. These generous amounts of potash will help the bulb replenish itself and come back strong next spring—with plenty of flowers.

## Rx for Healthy Tulips

Tulips, unlike many of their spring-blooming bulb counterparts, aren't reliably perennial. The first spring they come on strong, the second they perform less well, and by the third they may be nothing but a few weak leaves and piddly blooms. Keep your tulips going years longer by doing the following:

**Choose long-lasting species and cultivars.** Bulbs that are described as species or botanical tulips tend to come back better year after year. So do Darwin hybrids. Look for label and catalog descriptions that use the word *perennialize.*

**Give them excellent drainage.** Tulip bulbs need excellent, freely draining soil and benefit from being planted on a slope or in raised beds. "Tossing a little sharp sand directly into the bottom of a tulip planting hole also helps to improve drainage," says gardener Patsy Sadler of Pella, Iowa. "Working plenty of sand into the soil helps too," she notes.

**Deadhead spent blooms.** Each spring, cut off fading flowers so that energy can be diverted from flower and seed production into rejuvenating for next year.

**Leave on the foliage.** Even though it looks awful, bulbs need that ripening foliage left on until it's thoroughly brown and can be removed only with the gentlest of tugs.

**Plant deeply.** Plant tulips 9 inches or deeper. Shallow planting encourages bulbs to split into smaller, nonflowering daughter bulbs earlier, leaving you with bare spots.

## Color Coordinated

Do your spring bulb plantings have a hodgepodge look to them? That willy-nilly appearance might be from the colors you're choosing. Too many people order bulbs randomly, giving

## Pest Detective

*Are your tulips less than perfect? Something nibbling them? The blooms looking piddly? Check out these common tulip problems and how you can help.*

| Symptom | Cause | What to Do |
|---|---|---|
| Edges or tops of leaves have been nibbled | Rabbits | Let your cat (or a neighbor's) have free range of the garden, especially at night, until the tulips start blooming. |
| Bulbs are missing or laying on top of ground | Squirrels or rodents | Plant deep. Even crocuses should be at least 4 inches deep if you have rodent and squirrel problems. Then water well to settle the soil, making it less attractive to these pests. Also, you can temporarily lay a piece of hardware cloth or chicken wire on top of the soil to deter squirrels. And if all else fails, plant rodent-resistant bulbs, such as daffodils, netted iris (*Iris reticulata*), Siberian squill (*Scilla siberica*), ornamental onions (*Allium* spp.), or hyacinths. Also, check out "Solutions at a Glance" on page 20 on planting with gravel. |
| Light and dark spots or extensive gray blotches on leaves and flowers | Botrytis blight | If bulbs are heavily disfigured, dig up to prevent spread of blight to other bulbs. In the fall, prevent blight by planting only healthy bulbs in well-drained soil. If blight recurs a second spring, as a last resort, try treating with an organic fungicide, such as wettable sulfur. |

little thought to how the colors will work together, says Tim Schipper, bulb guru at Colorblends, the color-coordinated Dutch bulb supplier. Just as you would never put together an outfit without considering color, you should never order bulbs without thinking through color schemes.

Schipper suggests using an existing spring-blooming landscape feature—such as a flowering crabapple, redbuds (*Cercis* spp.), or rhododendron—as an inspiration for a color theme. Also, keep in mind not only the color but also the intensity of the color. Most brights, for example, work well with other brights, and most pastels work best with other pastels.

### Speed Planting

Have hundreds of tiny crocus bulbs that you need to get in the ground in a hurry? Use a spading fork. Simply insert the fork about 4 inches into the soil, wiggle it around a bit, remove—and, voilà, four perfect planting holes!

# Cabbage Problems

Everyone, especially gardeners, should get to know and love cabbage. It's low in calories and rich in vitamins A, B, and C; and it's an Easy (yes, *Easy* with a capital E) vegetable for you to grow. Some people don't like "that cabbage smell" while it's cooking, but other than that, this veggie really won't give you many reasons to complain. And we have some nifty new ideas to share with you for fighting off those few common cabbage pests that you may encounter in your garden.

## Rx for Healthy Cabbage

So many varieties of cabbage are available today, it's a wonder cabbage hasn't brought on a gourmet trend like that enjoyed by heirloom tomatoes and baby eggplant. Follow these six tips and you're sure to have success growing early-, mid-, and late-season varieties in a multitude of flavors, shapes, and colors.

**START FROM SEED.** Cabbage is easy to start from seed. Sow seeds ¼ inch deep and 2 inches apart about 2 weeks before the last frost date or in 1 or 1½-inch plug trays about 8 weeks before the last frost date. Transplant them out a month later. (Remember to harden off the seedlings, exposing them to the outdoors gradually for a week before putting them in the garden.) Cabbage seeds aren't fussy about germination temperature—whether it's 50° or 85°F, they're up in a few days. So if you have a small home garden and have had too much of a good thing in the past (like 12 heads of cabbage at once from a nursery pack), why not purchase several packets of seed and try just a few heads of two or three varieties? You can plant more of them in 2 weeks, or save some of the seed for a fall crop (start them in May and transplant them to the garden in July). But don't worry: If you don't want to plant it now, the seed will keep for years in a dark, dry place.

**SPACE FOR SIZE.** When you transplant cabbages outdoors, space them 12 to 18 inches apart in rows 18 to 24 inches apart. Wide spacing produces bigger heads; closer spacing produces smaller heads, which are usually tastier.

**KEEP CABBAGES COVERED.** A simple floating row cover is an easy way to fight some of the worst cabbage pests. Row covers help keep moths away—which keeps them from laying the eggs that give way to several types of worms who love to eat cabbage as much as you do!

**KEEP MOISTURE CONSTANT.** Cabbage doesn't like to be really thirsty one minute and drenched the next. Uneven watering can cause heads to split, and constantly wet leaves, especially in cool weather or high humidity, can encourage disease. Drip irrigation is one solution, and mulch can help keep moisture in the soil. If you don't have an automatic watering system, be vigilant about watering evenly during dry spells.

**COMPOST, PLEASE.** Cabbage plants like a side-dressing of compost a couple of weeks after planting. If leaves start to yellow, try a midseason boost with liquid seaweed fertilizer or compost tea. If plants don't bounce back within 2 weeks, pull and burn them so they don't spread disease.

**ROTATE TO KEEP CABBAGE HEALTHY.** Cabbage crops need to be rotated with noncruciferous crops to fight disease in the garden. They especially like to follow peas, which fix nitrogen in the soil. If you have a small garden and can't rotate crops, add some compost to your bed every year to help suppress disease.

## Cabbage and Clover, Over and Over

An easy way to ensure cabbage health, according to entomologist Geoff Zehnder from Auburn University in Auburn, Alabama, is to seed white clover in fall where you plan to plant cabbage in spring. Then in spring, cultivate strips in the clover and plant your cabbage within those strips. What you'll end up with is cabbage growing in between the flowering clover—which is bringing with it beneficial insects that attack cabbageworms. "We found worms were lower in the areas with the clover all season long. And the clover adds nitrogen to the soil, which benefits the cabbage," Zehnder says.

## Turn Up the Heat on Pests

Science has put an official stamp of approval on what many organic gardeners have known for years: Hot pepper sprays are an effective control for cabbageworms. "We did two seasons of work with it and had good results both times," says entomologist Geoff Zehnder from Auburn University in Auburn, Alabama.

For the study, researchers added 1 tablespoon of ground red pepper (they used McCormick, available in the spice section of the supermarket) to 2 liters of water, plus 6 drops of Ivory dish-washing detergent. They let this mixture sit overnight, stirred to dissolve as much of the pepper as possible, and then sprayed plants once a week. The results showed that the spray was effective in reducing caterpillar populations and insect-feeding damage on cabbage. And damage that did occur was on outer wrapper leaves and didn't affect the head as a whole.

"My feeling is the spray repels the moths. They don't like to lay eggs on the pepper-sprayed leaves. And if you aren't getting the eggs, you aren't getting the worms and the damage," says Zehnder, adding that the spray should be applied early in the season and regularly throughout it.

## Cabbage, Cabbage Everywhere

But what do you do when you don't want to harvest all your cabbage just yet? Here's a great way to delay harvest and keep cabbage from splitting when it's mature. Take a sharp spade and drive it straight into the ground, cutting a semicircle around the plant and severing half of its roots. The remaining roots will pull in just enough moisture to keep the cabbage alive and fresh, but not enough to encourage growth and splitting.

*By severing just half of a mature cabbage's roots with a spade, you can keep the cabbage fresh without splitting.*

## Home Brews Keep Your Cabbage Clean

Entomologist Geoff Zehnder from Auburn University in Auburn, Alabama, says gardeners have a couple of scientifically proven options when it comes to mixing something up to wipe out cabbageworms. He believes BT (*Bacillus thuringiensis*) is very effective for the organic home gardener, as long as the plant is well covered with the spray. Also, a garlic spray—made up of 1 part commercial garlic spray (99 percent garlic concentrate), 1 part fish oil, and 98 parts water—was successful at reducing the number of cabbage pests. (And no, the garlic smell didn't linger or flavor the cabbage.) So brew up a batch and take back the cabbage patch!

## Keep Cool with Chinese Cabbage

Chinese cabbage is finicky: It likes cool weather and has a reputation for bolting in warmer weather (it does better as a fall crop than as a spring crop), plus it doesn't like its roots to be disturbed for transplanting. So try sowing the seeds for fall Chinese cabbage in July. Chinese cabbage that grows under steadily shortening days won't bolt.

Be warned, though: Flea beetles love Chinese cabbage, so you should use row covers if you want to harvest any crop at all. If you can keep your plants from succumbing to the beetle damage, the cabbage will shape up nicely when the weather turns colder and the beetles disappear.

## Cabbageworm Warfare

In her Tennessee Valley garden, Barbara Pleasant, author of *The Gardener's Bug Book*, uses six methods to battle the cabbageworms that come to feed on her favorite cool-season crops. Try any or all of her techniques to keep cabbages and their cousins caterpillar-free in your own garden.

**INTERPLANT RADISHES.** "In spring I stud my cabbage patch with radishes, and allow the radishes to grow tall and flower," Pleasant says. "Don't ask me how this works," she adds, "it just does!"

**EGG PATROL.** "As soon as I see white butterflies, I check leaf undersides for their tiny yel-

# Pest Detective

*Don't let the bad guys get the best of your cabbage crop. Refer to this chart of simple solutions, and you can send pests and diseases packing, leaving heads and heads of cabbage for you and you alone.*

| Symptom | Cause | What to Do |
|---|---|---|
| Holes in leaves make them look like Swiss cheese | Imported cabbageworms | You'll know you have this velvety, pale green, yellow-striped pest if you see dark green pellets of excrement or their yellow eggs. Hand-pick and destroy the worms, and apply hot pepper spray, garlic spray, or BT to the plants. Use row covers and encourage beneficial insects. |
| Round holes in leaves, looks similar to cabbageworm damage | Cabbage looper | Hand-pick and destroy eggs (which are round and greenish white) and adults (which are green with pale stripes down their backs). Apply hot pepper spray, garlic spray, or BT. Use row covers and encourage beneficial insects. |
| Damage similar to cabbageworm and cabbage looper damage, but holes in leaves are smaller | Diamondback moth larvae | Hand-pick these very small worms, use hot pepper or garlic spray, or use BT. Use row covers and encourage beneficial insects. |
| Plants wilt on hot days, or just keel over and die | Cabbage maggot | Prevention is your best bet with these small, blunt-ended, white maggots, so lay a square of tar paper or screening flat on the ground around the stem and dust it with rock phosphate or diatomaceous earth to prevent flies from laying eggs near the cabbage stems. You can also use row covers. And, you can encourage the cabbage maggot's insect predator, the rove beetle. |
| Many tiny holes in leaves | Flea beetle | Cover seedlings with row covers to protect against these black, shiny, striped pests. Plant white clover as a cover crop, or dust with diatomaceous earth. |
| Light-colored, distorted patches on leaves | Cabbage aphids | Protect against these powdery gray insects with row covers, or knock them off with a stream of water. Encourage beneficial insects like lacewings, aphid midges, lady beetles, and parasitic wasps; or apply hot pepper spray, garlic spray, or insecticidal soap. |
| Dark cankers at base of stem; round, brown spots on leaves | Black leg | Rotate crops each season and pull out and destroy diseased plants. |

lowish, bullet-shaped eggs. I scrape them off with my fingernail, or I use a wet cotton swab, if I remember to bring one with me to the garden."

**HAND-PICKING.** "On small seedlings, the little worms like to hide in the new curled leaves of the plants' growing tips," Pleasant explains. "Older cabbageworms often stretch out along the main leaf vein to hide themselves from view. Wherever I find them, I pluck them off and then smash them underfoot."

**GET RED.** "Cabbageworms are easy to spot on red varieties of cabbage or kohlrabi. Hungry birds often find them before I do!"

**FLOATING ROW COVERS.** "When I set out brussels sprouts and broccoli in late summer for harvest in fall and winter, I immediately cover them with a very lightweight row cover, held up over the plants with arches made of white PVC pipe. Otherwise, the seedlings would surely be devoured."

**BTK (*BACILLUS THURINGIENSIS* VAR. *KURSTAKI*).** "In especially bad cabbageworm seasons," Pleasant concludes, "I douse plants with liquid BTK to get rid of small cabbageworms, especially if they're wedged into the ripening heads of broccoli. This biological pesticide is a potent stomach poison when eaten by caterpillars, but it's harmless to beneficial insects." (Because BTK also kills all kinds of butterfly caterpillars, be careful not to get any on flowers or herbs that attract butterflies.)

*RADISHES INTERPLANTED BETWEEN CABBAGE AND ALLOWED TO FLOWER WILL HELP KEEP YOUR PATCH CABBAGEWORM FREE.*

## HARVEST HINTS

You can begin harvesting cabbage as soon as the heads are firm and glossy. If you're not sure if the heads are firm, you can test them by pressing the back of your hand on them. When you harvest early-season cabbage, leave the lower leaves on the plant and small heads will develop for a tasty and tender second harvest. Your fall plantings will taste best if you wait to pick until after a few frosts but before a hard freeze. Late-season cabbage varieties will keep for a long time (up to 3 months!) if you store the heads in plastic wrap at near freezing temperatures in your refrigerator.

# Colorado Potato Beetles

Until Europeans brought vegetables such as eggplant to the New World, Colorado potato beetles had to get by on a diet of weeds. These days only an unlucky few of these striking striped pests are forced to live on horse nettle. The rest find ample dining opportunities in gardens or on farms across most of North America.

A little bit of damage from Colorado potato beetles won't cut into your harvest of potatoes or eggplant, but a few beetles and larvae can quickly grow into a population large enough to strip every leaf off your plants. So here are a few things you can do to help protect your plants—including blocking them out and giving them a little shake, rattle, 'n' roll.

## Three Basic Beetle Blockers

Preventing damage from Colorado potato beetles is as easy as keeping the adult beetles off your plants. And that's not as hard as it might seem. Try any or all of these defensive strategies to block out the beetles before they take their first bites from your precious potato plants:

**MULCH.** As soon as the soil warms up in late spring, place at least 3 inches of mulch around your potato plants. The mulch makes it more difficult and hazardous for adult beetles to make the trip from their underground hiding places to the surface. Ground beetles and other beneficial insects that live under deep mulch may turn the tired beetles into their breakfast.

**COVER.** Use lightweight floating row covers to keep beetles off of your potatoes and eggplant. Check often under the covers to make sure none of these troublemakers has been trapped underneath. Remove the covers by midseason.

**TRENCH.** Dig a trench that's at least 45 degrees steep around your potato (or eggplant) patch and line the trench with plastic. Beetles that emerge from the soil in the spring are too weak to fly to your plants, so they have to walk. When they reach the trench, they fall in and the plastic makes it too slippery for them to escape. Hungry birds will clean out the trenches for you.

## Natural Control

A special strain of BTSD (*Bacillus thuringiensis* var. *san diego*) provides excellent control of potato beetle larvae if you apply it to plants when the critters are young. If you grow a lot of potatoes or eggplants, check the undersides of the leaves often, and apply BTSD at the first sign that eggs have hatched. This handy biological control doesn't harm birds, bees, or other beneficial insects or wildlife. Reapply BTSD after heavy rains to keep beetles at bay.

## Shake Them Out

If an outbreak of beetles catches you by surprise, shake them off of plants into a shallow box. Or, place old sheets over the ground beneath plants, and gently stir the foliage with a broom to send the bugs rolling. You can crush the eggs and larvae or hand-pick the larvae and drown them in a pail of soapy water or dump them on any paved surface far from your garden (where birds will enjoy the beetle larvae buffet).

*Combat Colorado potato beetles by stirring things up a little with a broom. Just make sure you place an old sheet beneath the plants, to catch the beetles when they fall.*

# Compost Problems

Composting is all about building the soil—the foundation of any garden—so that your plants get off to a great start in life. And turning kitchen and garden wastes into black gold doesn't seem very difficult, does it? After all, you just throw everything on a pile, turn it once in a while, make sure it has adequate moisture—and, voilà, compost. Oh, but what about a slimy pile or a smelly pile or a pile that's just too darn hard to turn? Take the following advice from some great decomposers, and you should have no trouble mastering the technique.

## Rx for Healthy Compost

Patrice Kleinberg, who's the compost project director for the Queens Botanical Garden in New York, believes that although there's a science to composting, most gardeners should consider it an art. Here, she shares her tips for creating a compost masterpiece.

**FOR PERFECT COMPOST, SHOOT FOR A CARBON-TO-NITROGEN RATIO OF 30:1.** See "The Compost Construction Crew" on the opposite page for examples of carbon- and nitrogen-providing ingredients. Kleinberg realizes, however, that most home gardeners have an abundance of greens all spring and summer, then an abundance of browns (leaves) in the fall, and hardly any greens in the fall and winter. She suggests stockpiling leaves in the fall and adding them to your pile a layer at a time in spring and summer—and using kitchen scraps for greens in the fall and winter.

**COMPOST FRUIT AND VEGETABLES SCRAPS, PLANT MATERIAL, COFFEE GROUNDS,** tea bags, eggshells, paper towels, cardboard, and newspaper. Avoid composting meat, fish, chicken, bones, oils, fats, dairy products, and waste from Fido or Kitty.

**CHIP, CHOP, OR SHRED BIG PIECES** of stuff into smaller pieces to help them decompose faster.

**GET MICROBES INTO THE PILE WHEN STARTING A NEW ONE FROM SCRATCH.** You can do this, Kleinberg says, by digging a hole and building the pile in the hole. Or, if you're using a bin with a bottom, add a few shovelfuls of earth along with the material you're composting.

**TURN YOUR PILE.** Turning adds oxygen to the pile, stoking it, making it hotter, and helping things break down. You don't have to turn the pile every day; once a week is plenty.

**ADD WATER WHEN NEEDED.** A compost pile shouldn't be dripping wet or bone dry; it should be slightly damp.

**KEEP COMPOSTING DURING THE WINTER.** If you live where it gets really cold and your compost pile freezes, simply add kitchen scraps to bags of leaves you collected in the fall. "Bury the scraps in the middle," says Kleinberg, "and add the whole thing to your compost pile in the spring."

## The Compost Construction Crew

A carbon-to-nitrogen ratio of 30:1 works best for making compost. Here are some examples of each:

| *Carbon* | *Nitrogen* |
|---|---|
| Cardboard bits | Alfalfa |
| Cornstalks | Bloodmeal |
| Dry leaves | Coffee grounds |
| Sawdust | Fresh weeds |
| Shredded paper | Grass clippings |
| Straw | Human hair |
| Wood chips | Kelp meal |
| | Kitchen scraps |
| | Manure |

*TIP THE SCALES IN YOUR FAVOR WHEN CREATING BLACK GOLD BY USING A CARBON-TO-NITROGEN RATIO OF 30:1.*

## Quick Compost

Impatient? Want compost now, not tomorrow, but don't know the road to the fast track? Take a lesson from Renée Beaulieu, who gardens in Waterbury, Connecticut. Here's how she had a pile of hot compost brewing in a mere 2 days.

*WATER IS KEY FOR HOT COMPOST. SO KEEP YOUR PILE COOKING BY ADDING $H_2O$ IF THE INGREDIENTS GET TOO DRY.*

"I bought a bale of straw (not hay, because it contains seeds, which can sprout) and built a pile," says Beaulieu. "The secret, besides layering straw with all the fresh green stuff (spent pea vines, bolted lettuce, coffee grounds, banana peels) was water. I'd read about piles being too wet, but in retrospect, I think mine were always too dry. I kept the hose nearby as I constructed the pile, and watered the debris as I layered it in, so there was plenty of moisture available. I topped off the whole thing with a covering of straw, and the pile was very hot within 2 days."

## A Helping Hand

If you're having trouble turning your pile, take a look at the tool you're using. You might be better off using a manure fork. "The manure fork, with its long handle and much narrower

## Solutions at a Glance

**PROBLEM:** Your compost smells like ammonia.
**CULPRIT:** Too much nitrogen
**SOLVE IT!** Add dry, carbon-rich material like cornstalks, leaves, and wood chips.

---

**PROBLEM:** Your compost pile is really dry.
**CULPRIT:** Drought
**SOLVE IT!** Sprinkle the pile with a watering can or hose nozzle, turning the pile as you water to moisten the whole thing, even the center. When you squeeze a handful of compost, it should feel like a wrung-out sponge, damp but not soggy.

---

**PROBLEM:** Your pile is slimy.
**CULPRIT:** Too much moisture
**SOLVE IT!** Add more dry, carbon-rich material like cornstalks, leaves, and wood chips. Turn the pile as you add the dry stuff so it sops up the excess moisture.

---

**PROBLEM:** Something's picking at your pile.
**CULPRIT:** Rodents
**SOLVE IT!** Make your compost bin rodent resistant by installing ¼-inch wire mesh on the bottom, top, and sides, or consider purchasing a metal barrel compost tumbler. Also, avoid throwing dairy or meat scraps in your pile.

---

**PROBLEM:** Winged insects are flitting around your pile.
**CULPRIT:** Vinegar flies
**SOLVE IT!** Vinegar flies may be a nuisance around piles that have too much fermenting fruits and vegetables. If they bother you, add carbon-rich material like cornstalks, leaves, and wood chips.

tines and bigger head, does a better job lifting and spreading compost than the spading fork I had been using," says gardener Renée Beaulieu from Waterbury, Connecticut. "Hey, I grew up in the city, so what did I know about farm tools?" she adds.

*THE LONG HANDLE AND NARROW TINES OF THIS MANURE FORK TAKE THE TROUBLE OUT OF TURNING A COMPOST PILE.*

## Manure Hot and Cold

Well-aged manure goes a long way toward improving the health and draining power of any soil. Curing your own supply, says Master Gardener Jane Anders from Portland, Oregon, can be easier—and neater—than you might think. Here's how she handles the truckloads she gets from a nearby horse farm.

1. Spread a heavy tarpaulin on the ground.
2. Dump the manure onto the tarp.
3. Fold the tarp up and around the pile.
4. Lay another tarp on top, fold it down around the first one, weight it down, and cut a few slits in the tarps to let some heat escape. The high temperatures generated by the manure will kill most weeds.
5. Let the pile sit for 6 months or so and it'll be cool, weed-free, and ready to add to your garden beds.

"If you have the space," Anders advises, "keep two or three piles going at different stages of cooling. That way you'll always have a ready supply on hand."

## A Little Goes a Long Way

You don't need to bury your garden under truckloads of compost to have bountiful harvests and beautiful flower borders. In most areas of the country, an annual application of a half-inch-thick layer of compost is all you'll need for established garden beds. (In the longer growing seasons of the South and in areas with very high rainfall, double the annual rate to 1 inch.) This will provide enough organic matter and ample nutrients for excellent plant growth. For one-time applications to new garden beds, you can double or triple the annual rate.

# Container Garden Problems

A lack of land shouldn't limit your gardening! If you don't have much in-ground gardening space, move your garden into containers instead. With containers, your deck, patio, rooftop—even your houseboat—can become a great place to grow vegetables, flowers, and more. To succeed with container gardens, the most important steps you can take are to start with the right-size containers and a good soil mix and to be ever mindful of the top problem that container gardeners face: saving plants from dehydration.

### Rx for Luscious Container Gardens

"Anything you can grow in the ground you can grow in a container," says Julie Willimott, whose Portland, Oregon, garden thrives in pots. "I've even raised corn in containers," she says. Here are some of Willimott's tips for container garden success with vegetables.

1. Gather some 15- to 20-gallon pots and wash the pots in a mild bleach solution (1 part bleach to 5 parts water) to kill disease organisms. (If you buy new pots you don't need to wash them out with the bleach solution.) Willimott says she favors black plastic nursery pots. "They attract and hold the sun's heat—and most veggies like warm soil."
2. Add a handful of washed rocks or pot shards for drainage.
3. Stir together a 3:1 mixture of sterilized potting soil and compost (which will help suppress disease), and fill the pot.
4. Plant seeds or transplants in the container. You can plant a single crop or combine crops that are beneficial companions, like tomatoes and basil. (For more ideas, see "Recommended Reading" on page 357 for books on companion planting.) Then, put the container in full sun.
5. Water regularly (when the top couple of inches of soil have dried out). "Moisture is the key," Willimott says. "In pots, roots can't go deep for moisture like they can in the ground."
6. Feed your crops two or three times during the growing season with an organic fertilizer to keep them lush.

## Deeply Does It

To make sure water reaches the whole rootball when you plant a tree or shrub in a pot, container gardener Julie Willimott from Portland, Oregon, offers this advice: "Plant a piece of bamboo or PVC pipe with ⅛-inch holes in it with the tree or shrub. Each time you water, soak the soil *and* fill that reservoir."

*Drill ⅛-inch holes in a piece of PVC pipe, place the pipe in your container, and you'll have an instant water reservoir that will keep thirsty roots happy.*

## A Long Soak Saves Stressed Plants

You forgot to water your container plants, and now they're so dry they won't even take up water. Don't despair—your plants may not be gone for good. When a pot dries out thoroughly, "the soil will form crevices under the surface, where you can't see them," says container specialist Linda Waller, owner of Seattle's Doolittle Gardens. "After that, whenever you water, the water will run right through those little tunnels and out the bottom of the pot." If your plants look stressed even though you water frequently, they're probably the victim of those hidden tunnels. Waller's advice: Soak the soil well. Allow 5 minutes of gentle hosing for a pot 20 inches in diameter and 20 inches deep. Never fear that you'll overwater. Says Waller, "Outdoors in the summer that's all but impossible to do."

## Some Like It Dry

Because the soil in containers dries out faster than the soil in your garden beds, you might opt for drought-tolerant plants for container gardens (especially if you tend to pot things up and then forget about them!). Drought-tolerant ornamental grasses; annuals such as geraniums and marigolds; and perennials like daylilies, sedums, and hardy cacti (*Opuntia* spp.) are good choices. Many herbs are native to hot, dry climates and are also easy to care for—perennials like chives, oregano, sage, and thyme will grow for several years in a large container. And annual herbs like basil and dill are also drought-tolerant.

# Corn Problems

Young, old. Rich, poor. Everyone, it seems, *loves* garden-fresh sweet corn. In fact, some of us can't even wait to get it into the kitchen. We eat it right off the cob—raw—in the middle of the garden. The trouble is, we humans aren't alone in our love of corn. A whole host of pests—deer, raccoons, crows, possums, and insects—get a craving for corn, too. You won't need to go hungry while the garden pests feast, though. Here are some resourceful ways (including using newspaper and soap) to make sure your corn crop is everything you want it to be.

## Rx for Healthy Corn

You're sure to have a high-yield harvest of oh-so-sweet ears if you follow these great tips from market gardener George DeVault, from Emmaus, Pennsylvania. They'll help you choose, grow, and gather corn with ease.

**USE A QUICK-MATURING VARIETY.** At 65 days, 'Kandy Kwik' is the leader of the pack, followed closely by 'Trinity', at 68 days. Scout the seed catalogs for other early or short-season varieties, especially if you garden in the far north.

**PLANT NO CORN BEFORE ITS TIME.** As much as you want to get a jump on the season, you have to wait until soil temperature is warm—at least 65°F— before you plant corn. Waiting until the soil has sufficiently warmed guarantees good, uniform germination and also helps reduce insect and weed problems. Warm soil is especially important when using super-sweet varieties.

**DON'T SKIMP ON THE SEEDS.** You'll need to plant a minimum of two rows of corn (four short rows are better than two long rows) in order to have good pollination and well-filled ears.

**FEED THE SOIL.** Corn is a heavy feeder, particularly when it comes to nitrogen, so make sure your soil has plenty of organic matter. For an early nitrogen boost, work some fish meal into the soil. And add rock phosphate to provide phosphorus, and compost, plant residues, manure, greensand, or granite dust to provide potassium.

Overseeding a nitrogen-fixing legume (like hairy vetch or red clover) between your corn rows in July or August will keep your soil in top condition and provide ample nutrition for future crops. Remove cornstalks as soon as you harvest all the ears to give your cover crop full sun and room to grow. (The cover crop will protect your soil through winter.) Till it into the soil a few weeks before you start your garden the following spring.

**PICK IT WHEN IT'S RIPE.** To get the highest sugar levels and the most old-fashioned corn taste, you absolutely must pick sweet corn on time. Watch for tasseling, and jot down the date when about half of your plants have tassels. Depending on the weather, your corn will be ready for picking 18 to 22 days later. Look for clues like drying and browning silks to help you zero in on the exact date, or pop a few kernels with your thumbnail to make sure they're full and milky. Better yet, pick an ear off the stalk and take a big bite out of it! (If corn is too young to eat, the kernels won't be filled out and it won't have full flavor. If it's past it's prime, the kernels will be tough and chewy and will taste starchy.)

*FIND OUT IF YOUR CORN IS RIGHT FOR THE PICKIN' BY POPPING A FEW KERNELS WITH YOUR THUMBNAIL TO MAKE SURE THEY'RE MILKY.*

**GIVE IT LOTS OF WATER.** Corn is a heavy drinker, too. It needs adequate moisture throughout the season, but especially when setting ears. Super-sweet varieties need twice as much moisture to germinate as regular corn does. For best germination of all varieties, avoid planting corn when the soil is extremely dry, and water the corn regularly during dry spells.

## Pest-Free Corn

Humans aren't the only creatures that think corn on the cob makes a sweet meal on a summer night. Plenty of pests that creep, crawl, and fly like it, too. But here are some super-effective tips to make sure that the only one eating your corn is *you*.

The task of keeping worms out of your corn has been made easy by researchers at the University of Massachusetts and Hampshire College. They reduced earworm damage to corn by 90 to 100 percent by using a mixture of vegetable oil and BTK (*Bacillus thuringiensis* var. *kurstaki*). Just use an oil can or eyedropper to apply 5 drops of an oil and BTK mix to each ear when the silks begin to turn brown.

Birds are another big problem. They'll pluck young corn plants out of the ground as well as pick kernels or corn and damage ears.

You can successfully camouflage your young corn plants by interplanting them with garlic or by mulching around them with fresh grass clippings. "Scare-eye" balloons—15-inch inflatable plastic balls that resemble beach balls—help mimic the eyes of predator birds and can also keep your crop safe.

Raccoons can be crafty little pests, but you can keep them out of ripening corn by spreading newspaper on the ground around the stalks. Raccoons are reluctant to walk across the dry, rustling material, so your young ears will be safe. You can also use netting on the ground to repel these furry foes.

And to keep deer out of your growing corn, hit 'em right in the nose—with a strong scent, that is. Try hanging deodorant soap in net bags from stakes scattered around your corn patch. Fencing helps repel a wide variety of animal pests but must be 8 to 10 feet tall to block deer.

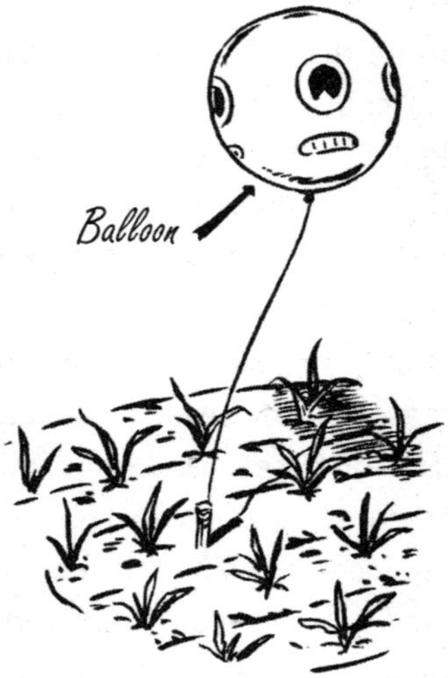


*KEEP YOUR CORN CROP SAFE FROM CRITTERS WITH "SCARE-EYE" BALLOONS.*

## Beat the Winter Corn Blues

Ever get a craving for an ear of sweet, buttered corn right around the end of January? Well, if you plan ahead, you can have the very taste of summer itself. Just stash a few ears in the freezer at the peak of summer's harvest, and you can enjoy delicious corn on the cob year-round. All you need to do is husk the ears, clean off the silk, and blanch the ears in a pot of boiling water for 6 to 8 minutes. Cool the ears quickly (stick them in a sink of cold water), and then pack them in freezer bags and stick them in the freezer.

## Baby Your Corn

You don't have to wait for ears to fully mature to enjoy garden-fresh corn. Any early-maturing variety can be harvested as "baby corn," the tiny ears popular in stir-fries and salads or pickled. Plant your seeds as close as 6 to 8 inches apart. Harvest just as soon as you feel a small bulge inside the little ears, usually about 5 days after silk appears. You can harvest any corn as baby corn, but some varieties (such as 'How Sweet It Is', 'Bodacious', and 'Bonus') are especially tasty.

## Invite the Three Sisters to Your Garden

If you find that your corn is getting snacked on by the local wildlife, try growing the three sisters—a traditional Native American intercropping. This veggie combo of beans, corn, and squash repels critters, naturally!

Beans use the cornstalks as a trellis (make sure you plant a pole bean—and use a corn variety with a strong stalk, such as 'Texas Honey June' or 'Stowell's Evergreen'). The squash vines form a living mulch that conserves soil moisture and helps prevent weeds. But best of all, the prickly squash vines help keep raccoons and deer from snacking on the sisters.

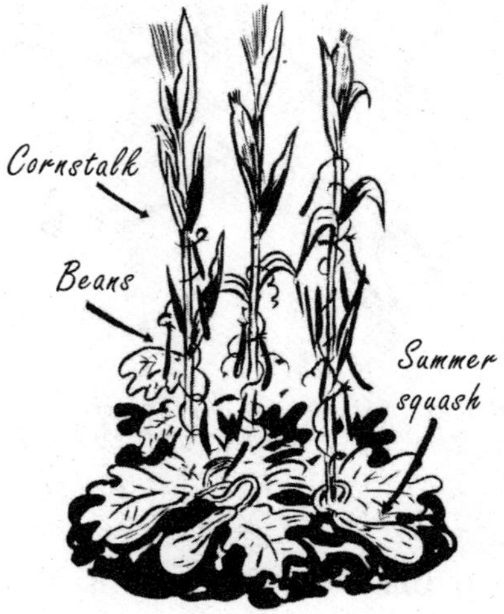


*THE PRICKLY SQUASH VINES IN THE THREE SISTERS COMBINATION HELPS KEEP RACCOONS AND DEER AWAY FROM YOUR CORN.*

# Crop Rotation Problems

Growing the same crop in the same spot every year may lead to problems with pests and diseases. And different veggies use different nutrients, too, so growing the same ones in the same soil year after year may produce malnutrition problems. Although rotating crops in large farm fields isn't too challenging, it can be tough in small backyard gardens. So here are some ways to make the most of crop rotation in smaller spaces and at the same time help to solve some of your other garden problems—like those pesky weeds in the carrots.

## 10 Tips for Successful Rotations

**SEPARATE FEUDING FAMILIES.** Vegetables that belong to the same botanical family—like tomatoes, potatoes, and eggplant (all from the Solanaceae, or nightshade family), or broccoli, cabbage, and cauliflower (all from the Cruciferae, or mustard family)—will attract the same pests and suffer from the same diseases. Minimize contagion by planting them away from each other.

**KEEP FRIENDS TOGETHER.** Some plants grow well together, and should be rotated together. Carrots and tomatoes get along because both dislike too much nitrogen, and they don't share common insect pests or diseases. Cabbage and dill are happy together because when dill flowers, it attracts beneficial insects that feed on aphids and cabbageworms that are attracted to the cabbage plants.

**ROTATE ROOTS, FRUITS, AND GREENS.** Plants that produce edible roots, like carrots and beets, take different nutrients out of the soil than plants that produce fruits (like tomatoes and peppers) or edible greens (like lettuce and spinach). Grow a different edible in the same section of the garden each year to make efficient use of the soil's fertility.

**FERTILIZE WITH ROTATIONS.** Follow a crop that uses a lot of nitrogen, like sweet corn, with a crop that makes its own nitrogen, like peas or beans. Why buy fertilizer if nature will fertilize for you? And you can save your precious compost for the plants that really need it.

**PLOW WITH ROTATIONS.** Market gardener Tony Ricci likes to follow potatoes with garlic on his Three Springs, Pennsylvania, farm because digging the potatoes creates a clean bed for the fall-planted garlic. "When you dig the potatoes, you're really getting the late-germinating weeds out," he says. "The ground is all broken up and just needs to be raked smooth for the garlic." (*Note:* This method works best when the potatoes are growing in hills that you have weeded on a regular basis during the growing season.)

**WEED WITH ROTATIONS.** Have a problem with perennial weeds? Plant a vine crop, like winter squash, to smother them.

**POLLINATE WITH ROTATIONS.** Don't forget flowers or flowering vegetable crops as part of the rotation. For example, plant early-blooming annuals like snapdragons and calendula (*Calendula officinalis*) near summer-

## Starting Up

*If you want to rotate crops but aren't sure what crop should follow what, use this handy chart to help get you started.*

| Crop | Follows | Why? |
|---|---|---|
| Cabbage family crops | Garlic, leeks, onions | Onion family crops thwart parasites and pests that trouble cabbage. |
| Carrots, onions, other root crops | Winter squash or pumpkins | Vining crops smother weeds, making it easier to keep root crops clean. |
| Eggplant, potatoes, tomatoes | Mustard, rape, turnips | Cruciferae crops help cleanse the soil of pathogens that attack Solanaceae crops. |
| Garlic, shallots | Potatoes | Potato harvest results in a clean planting bed for fall-planted crops. |
| Lettuce | Root crops | Roots loosen soil, making penetration easier for shallow-rooted lettuce. |
| Okra | Marigolds | Marigolds exude substances from their roots that deter nematodes, to which okra is sensitive. |
| Peas and beans | Cabbage family crops or corn | Nitrogen-fixing legumes replace nutrients used by heavy-feeding crops. |
| Potatoes | Corn | Corn as a preceding crop increases potato yield. |

bearing cucumbers and squash to attract pollinating insects.

**FIGHT PESTS WITH ROTATIONS.** Farmers have followed onion-family crops with cabbage-family crops for years because the skin of onions exudes a substance that suppresses certain plant parasites. Onions don't attract flea beetles, either, so soil that held onions won't be filled with overwintering flea beetles, which love to feed on cabbage-family plants.

**KEEP THE GARDEN DEBRIS-FREE.** Rotations are tough in small gardens. "I wouldn't worry about it much, as long as you aren't having disease problems," says Ricci. "If you can't rotate your crops, taking out plant debris will help." This means yanking out fusarium-prone plants like basil and tomatoes, roots and all, at the end of the season.

**KEEP RECORDS.** Try this creative method. Draw the garden to scale on a piece of poster board, and permanently ink in perennial crops. Lay a piece of onion-skin paper over the drawing and pencil in where your want to plant annual crops. Next year, lay a new piece of onion-skin paper over last year's—and, voilà, you'll know where not to plant what.

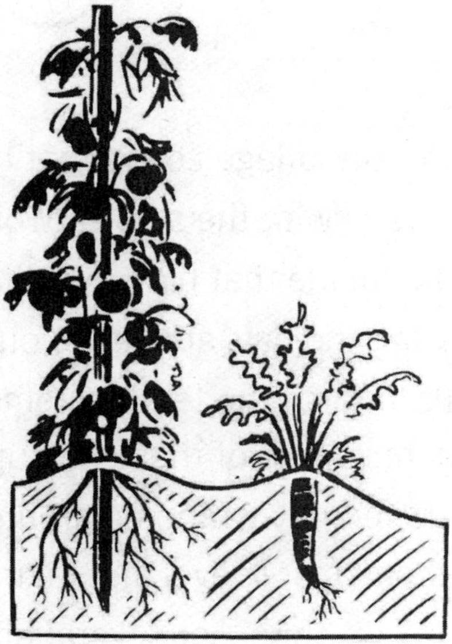

*PRACTICE THE BUDDY SYSTEM WHEN ROTATING CROPS BY KEEPING FRIENDS LIKE CARROTS AND TOMATOES TOGETHER.*

# Cutworms

Dressed in camouflage colors that help them blend in with the soil, cutworms are moth larvae that hide in soil and mulch during the day, and come out at night to taste the tender stems of young plants. Most of these nocturnal nibblers feed by wrapping around a plant's stem at soil level and taking a bite—or several bites.

A few cutworm species climb up onto plants and eat the leaves, but the big heartbreakers are "surface" cutworms that girdle seedling stems and leave behind sad little stumps and felled plants where your garden used to be. Because cutworms work at night, you probably won't spot the culprits that toppled your tender transplants. So use these ideas for providing protective armor, along with tilling hints, to cut off cutworms from their next meal.

## Foil Cutworms with Tilling

You can help cut down on cutworms in your beds by planting a cover crop in the fall, and then, tilling it under in the spring, as soon as you can work the ground. Turning over the top layer of soil will expose cutworms to predators such as birds. Tilling also helps eliminate young weed seedlings, which wipes out easy meals for cutworms.

## Dress Young Plants for Success

To outwit the cutworms that continue to hang around in your garden soil, clothe young plants in armor that protects the lowest 2 inches of stem from cutworm attack. Because seedlings come in different shapes and sizes, tailor your choices from the following list to get a good fit. And don't wait to go on the defensive–install cutworm deterrents when you set out transplants or as soon as seedlings are up. It only takes one night for cutworms to wreak their awful havoc on unprotected plants.

**CIRCULAR COLLARS.** Make collars from cans or paper cups with their bottoms removed, or cut the cardboard rolls from toilet paper or paper towels into 2-inch-long pieces. Place the collars around seedlings, and push them into the soil about 1 inch deep.

**STEM SHEATHS.** Cut plastic drinking straws into 2-inch-long pieces, slit them down the side, and pop them around plant stems. Or, loosely wrap plant stems with small pieces of aluminum foil or double folds of waxed paper.

*PROTECT YOUR YOUNG PLANTS FROM NASTY CUTWORMS WITH AN ARMOR MADE OUT OF PLASTIC DRINKING STRAWS.*

## Solutions at a Glance

**PROBLEM:** Something's damaging your spring garden bed-to-be.

**CULPRIT:** Cutworms

**SOLVE IT!** Mix moistened bran with molasses and BTK (*Bacillus thuringiensis* var. *kurstaki*) and sprinkle it over the soil in your garden about a week before you plan to plant. BTK is a biological control for moth larvae. Cutworms that dine on this sweet treat won't be around in the future to snip off your seedlings and transplants.

## INVITE THE "GOOD GUYS" IN

A number of beneficial insects parasitize cutworm larvae, including many parasitic wasps (Braconid and Ichnuemonid families, and tachinid flies). You can invite them into your garden by providing plants rich in pollen and nectar such as dill, alyssum, yarrow, and cosmos. (Make sure you protect beneficial insects by avoiding the use of any toxic sprays or dust in your garden.)

# Damping-Off

Starting seeds can be a lot of fun and is a great way to grow the varieties you really want to grow, rather than having to choose plants from what might be a limited selection at your local garden center. But how often have seeds that you've started indoors germinated just fine and looked healthy and robust until—yikes!—they started keeling over and dying? The culprit is a fungus that causes a disease called damping-off. A few precautions will keep damping-off from doing in your seedlings.

### Lighter Is Better

Don't be tempted to use garden soil to start your seedlings. Use a sterile seed-starting mix instead, which is not only fungus-free but also lighter in texture. If you use a standard potting soil, it's a good idea to lighten it up with some vermiculite or perlite to improve aeration so those tender roots don't become waterlogged.

### Don't Get Bogged Down

Keep your seed-starting soil moist but not wet because fungus thrives in boggy conditions. Spread a thin layer of milled sphagnum moss on the top of the flat after you've sown the seeds. Because the moss is resistant to moisture, it helps keep the stems and leaves of your fragile seedlings dry. Also, try watering seedling flats from the bottom, rather than sprinkling water over the top. The easiest way to do that is to set the seed pots into a flat that has no holes; then pour the water directly into the flat. The roots get the moisture they need, but the foliage stays dry and is less susceptible to damping-off.

*Water from the bottom to put a damper on damping-off.*

### Foil the Fungus

Got a spot of damping-off anyway? Mix hydrogen peroxide half and half with water, and soak the affected area to kill the damping-off fungus and prevent it from spreading to healthy seedlings.

# Deer Problems

Although they're beautiful animals, deer are a problem for gardeners almost everywhere—except perhaps rooftop gardeners! The growth of the suburbs has left less land for deer to roam and fewer predators to keep their population in check. In most parts of the country, deer drive gardeners crazy by eating their favorite plants, including perennials, annuals, trees, shrubs, and bulbs. In fact, sometimes they nibble so much new growth off of young trees and shrubs that there's nothing left on the plant to grow back—and you're stuck with a bare spot in your yard. You've probably tried a multitude of deterrents, including fencing and deer-resistant plants. Well, we don't want deer to get the best of your garden and landscape, so we've put together some new twists on old solutions, like fencing, in an effort to thwart deer dining tactics.

## Know Their Eating Habits

Try as you might, you can't always predict when deer are going to be chowing down and what they're going to be eating. Seems as if they eat one type of plant in spring and a different type in fall. That's true, says John Van Etten, grounds superintendent of the Mohonk Mountain House in New Paltz, New York. His strategy for foiling hungry deer? Know how deer operate.

Deer eat more herbaceous plants in spring and summer. Toward fall, their digestive systems change and they start gearing up for woody plants. Just knowing this bit of information can help you protect the right plants at the right time. For example, you may want to set up temporary deer fencing or netting around your foundation shrubs after the second killing frost, and leave it in place over the winter until midspring.

### Change the Menu

If you garden in an area that's home to lots of deer and don't have the money or time to put up a fence or to keep replanting the plants they nibble on, all isn't lost. You can still grow a garden—you just have to outsmart the deer by planting things they don't like to eat. John Van Etten came up with a list of plants that deer don't eat, based on his 12 years at the Mohonk Mountain House in New Paltz, New York. So take a look at what they're eating, and then make substitutions where you can based on this list.

***Annuals***

Common snapdragon (*Antirrhinum majus*)
Wax begonias (*Begonia* Semperflorens-Cultorum hybrids)
Strawflower (*Bracteantha bracteata,* also called *Helichrysum bracteatum*)
Snow-on-the-mountain (*Euphorbia marginata*)
Sweet alyssum (*Lobularia maritima*)
Stock (*Matthiola incana*)
Flowering tobacco (*Nicotiana* spp.)
Scented geraniums (*Pelargonium* spp.)
Dusty miller (*Senecio cineraria*)
Marigolds (*Tagetes* spp.)
Nasturtium (*Tropaeolum majus*)
Common zinnia (*Zinnia elegans*)

***Herbaceous Perennials and Bulbs***

Common yarrow (*Achillea millefolium*)
Common monkshood (*Aconitum napellus*)
Stars of Persia (*Allium christophii*)
Meadow saffron (*Colchium autumnale*)
Common bleeding heart (*Dicentra spectabilis*)
Common foxglove (*Digitalis purpurea*)
Coneflower (*Echinacea purpurea*)
Globe thistle (*Echinops* spp.)
Iris (*Iris* spp.)
Lavender (*Lavandula* spp.)
Daffodils (*Narcissus* spp.)
Common peony (*Paoenia lactiflora*)

***Trees and Shrubs***

Bottlebrush buckeye (*Aesculus parviflora*)
Shadblow (*Amelanchier canadensis*)
Red osier dogwood (*Cornus sericea*)
Spruce (*Picea* spp.)
Pine (*Pinus* spp.)
Northern red oak (*Quercus rubra*)
Rugosa rose (*Rosa rugosa*)

*DEER DON'T EAT EVERYTHING, EVEN THOUGH IT SEEMS THAT WAY. YOU CAN PLANT SOME ANNUALS (SUCH AS WAX BEGONIAS) AND HERBACEOUS PERENNIALS (SUCH AS PEONIES), AND DEER WILL LEAVE THEM ALONE.*

## Protect Trunks with Plastic

In the beginning of September, bucks rub their antlers on tree bark to peel off the velvet on their antlers, as well as to mark their territory. If they rub hard enough, though, the rubbing can girdle and eventually kill young trees. And any tree with a straight trunk is a prime target.

Don't let potential deer damage discourage you from planting new trees on your property, however. You can protect young trees by wrapping a plastic spiral tree protector around the trunk, from the ground up to about 5 feet. "This plastic expands when the trees grow," says John Van Etten, grounds superintendent of the Mohonk Mountain House in New Paltz, New York. "I make sure to wrap the trunks by the end of August," he adds.

Hardware cloth also works well for protecting tree trunks, says Tim Steinhoff, who has been gardening for 20 years in New York State. "For a 4½-foot-tall stewartia (*Stewartia* sp.), I use hardware cloth that's 40 inches across, along with a hood of fruit tree netting over the top of the tree," says Steinhoff.

PROTECT THE TRUNKS OF YOUNG TREES FROM THE ANTLERS OF BUCKS BY WRAPPING A PORTION OF THE TRUNK IN HARDWARE CLOTH.

## Change of Screenery

You love your "green screens" of arborvitaes (*Thuja* spp.), rhododendrons, and hemlocks (*Tsuga* spp.). Problem is, deer love them, too. The solution may be as simple, however, as planting different evergreens. Here are some suggestions for evergreen shrubs that deer aren't fond of nibbling.

**BOXWOODS (*BUXUS* SPP.).** Commonly used in formal gardens, this evergreen can also be attractive in natural landscapes.

**SAWARA FALSE CYPRESS (*CHAMAECYPARIS PISIFERA*).** This handsome evergreen tree has a pyramidal form; its cultivars vary in size.

**CAUCASIAN DAPHNE (*DAPHNE CAUCASICA*).** This semievergreen holds its leaves late, finally dropping them in winter before the snow season. (*Note:* This plant is toxic, so you might want to avoid using it if you have small children.)

**AMERICAN HOLLY (*ILEX OPACA*).** Deer leave this evergreen alone because of its spiny leaves.

**JAPANESE PIERIS (*PIERIS JAPONICA*).** This 6- to 8-foot-tall evergreen shrub has fragrant white flowers in spring and should be planted in well-drained soil.

THWART DEER BY SUBSTITUTING JAPANESE PIERIS WHEN PLANTING AN EVERGREEN SCREEN.

## Solutions at a Glance

**Problem:** Four-footed foes are eating all your tulips.

**Culprit:** Deer

**Solve It!** Try a smell repellent. Spray Hinder, an organic product made out of fatty acid soaps, on tulips as soon as the foliage emerges and again 2 weeks later. Hinder is safe for both ornamental and food plants and doesn't burn their foliage. (See "Resources" on page 344.)

### Bring in the Desert

If your landscape is a veritable lunch counter for deer, one way you can make the entrées less appetizing is by changing the offering—that is, changing the style of your landscape. That's what Eve Marx, who gardens in Katonah, New York, did when she decided to xeriscape her property.

"Over the years we've decided to get into xeriscaping, partly because a certain amount of our property closely resembles a high desert, and partly because the deer don't much like yuccas (*Yucca* spp.), ornamental fescues (*Festuca* spp.), zebra grass (*Miscanthus sinensis* 'Zebrinus'), or sedums," says Marx. "We really don't have a lot of problems with the deer now that we've come to terms with the fact that if we want tulips, we'll buy them at the florist," Marx adds.

*Make your garden entrées less appetizing for deer (and cut down on water use at the same time) by xeriscaping and incorporating arid-climate plants such as yuccas.*

### Fight Back with Fencing

Deer are creatures of habit and tend to travel the same paths looking for food. But what do you do if the path is through your backyard? Here's some fencing advice that goes against the norm, from Nancy Engel, who gardens in Cold Spring, New York. Engel's property sits at the edge of a community backing up to 700 acres of posted property—home to a large number of deer.

"My neighborhood was originally a summer community, so the deer were quite used to having the whole place to themselves all winter," Engel explains. "When I bought my house, there was a well-traveled path through my backyard to the lake and the woods beyond. Of course, the deer saw this path as a kind of freeway exit to the diner on my property. So I installed a 6-foot-tall black mesh fence. Although many people insist that a fence must be 10 feet high to keep deer from taking a running start and jumping over it, the deer have not tried to jump this fence once in 15 years."

Engel put up the fence (which she bought in 50-foot rolls from Agway) a full year before she started to plant the backyard. "I got the deer out of the habit of browsing in my yard before it was extra-tempting. Besides, I think deer are lazy, and there are much easier pickings in my neighbors' yards, which aren't fenced," she says.

## Go Electric

Electric fences, although expensive, are one option for keeping deer out of a prized orchard or vegetable patch. Electric fencing provides a sharp electric jolt that doesn't injure deer but convinces them that whatever is on the other side of the fence isn't worth it. To ensure that deer make contact with the wire and get the "keep out" message, put aluminum foil flaps smeared with peanut butter here and there along the electric fence. A number of commercial deer fence products are available, but be sure you understand and follow all of the manufacturer's safety instructions before installing an electric fence. Or have a professional install it for you.

### Solutions at a Glance

**Problem:** Something's eating all your hostas.

**Culprit:** Deer

**Solve It!** Try lining the perimeter of your property with arborvitaes (*Thuja* spp.), three rows deep. Deer love arborvitae and are happy to forgo hostas in favor of it. If your yard is too large to "fence" completely with arborvitaes, try planting a triple-deep hedge along the boundary where deer are most likely to enter your yard.

# Diseases

Detective work is the name of the game when it comes to identifying and controlling garden diseases. That's because plant diseases are caused by microorganisms too tiny to see. However, you can easily learn to recognize the symptoms they cause—and once you diagnose a disease, you may be able to intervene and effectively rid your garden of the problem. But preventing diseases is usually simpler than curing them, so use these expert tips (such as mixing things up) to keep your garden disease-free and growing strong.

## Rx for Healthy Plants

Barbara Pleasant, author of *The Gardener's Guide to Plant Diseases*, suggests four main strategies for preventing disease problems. "They're basic to growing a healthy garden," she says.

**MIX THINGS UP.** Grow a highly diversified garden that includes a number of different plants, and your garden will be naturally resistant to disease. That's because diseases, like insects, are able to damage only specific plants. And once a plant is infected, the disease can spread to other plants that are of the same species or that are closely related. For example, the main disease that causes dark spots to form on the leaves of tomatoes, early blight (*Alternaria solani*), can spread to potatoes but not to beans, corn, or cucumbers. So preserve the peace in your garden, and don't crowd too many family members into your plot together.

**KEEP THINGS MOVING.** Most plant diseases persist from year to year in soil or plant debris, so you can make a big impact on disease problems by rotating where you plant, making sure that you don't grow the same plants in the same soil 2 years in a row. Of course, it's impractical to move long-lived shrubs, trees, and perennials, but you can still deal diseases a huge blow just by gathering up diseased leaves and pruning back withered stems every chance you get. Discard these diseased castoffs—don't compost them—and you'll help avoid spreading plant diseases all around your yard and garden.

**GROW NATURALLY HEALTHY PLANTS.** Seek out disease-resistant varieties whenever you can. Resistant varieties haven't yet been developed for all diseases, but you'll probably find that any variety that shows excellent growth and vigor in your garden will also be a champ at standing up to diseases.

**STOP DISEASES BEFORE THEY START.** You can prevent many soilborne diseases by gardening only in well-drained areas and by enriching your soil with compost or other forms of organic matter at every opportunity. This will help control disease-causing fungi, which multiply by releasing thousands of spores. And fewer spores mean less disease.

## Prevalent Airborne Diseases

The most common diseases in any garden arrive on warm spring breezes, find homes on plant leaves, and flourish through summer as pesky parasites. The three biggies—powdery mildew, early blight, and rose black spot—are all fungi, and they're found almost everywhere! But here are some tips to put the kibosh on these diseases before they put the kibosh on the plants in your garden.

**POWDERY MILDEW.** Your best bet is to grow resistant varieties of the vegetables and flowers known to fall victim to this disease, which makes affected leaves look like they've been lightly dusted with flour. Powdery mildew sucks the life out of leaves and weakens plants, sometimes to the point of death, so you'll need to watch tall garden phlox, monarda, zinnias, and roses closely for early signs of powdery mildew. Early first aid is essential to saving your plants from this disease.

**EARLY BLIGHT.** Your best defense against this disease truly is a good offense. "A little leaf spot can produce hundreds of spores, so I patrol my tomatoes at least once a week and clip off any leaves that show suspicious black spots," says Alabama gardener Barbara Pleasant. "Besides reducing the number of new spores that can infect other leaves, my light clipping gives the plants a better shot at fresh air and sunshine—the biggest enemies of early blight—and it's a lot less messy than spraying."

You can diagnose this disease on potatoes and tomatoes by looking for irregular dark spots with concentric rings around their edges. The spots begin on lower leaves and need damp conditions to flourish and spread. When you see the signs, get clipping!

*USE YOUR OFFENSIVE GAME WHEN IT COMES TO EARLY BLIGHT AND CLIP OFF ANY LEAVES THAT HAVE SUSPICIOUS BLACK SPOTS ON THEM.*

**ROSE BLACK SPOT.** Many new shrub roses show excellent tolerance to this widespread disease, which causes rose leaves to become speckled with black spots that have fringed edges. But even tolerant cultivars may need you to jump in and fight for them when the weather is warm and damp. So pick off badly spotted leaves to limit the number of spores that can infect new ones. Clip off faded blossoms and thin crowded stems so plenty of light and fresh air penetrates the plants. Promote the production of new leaves with regular water and organic fertilizer. By following these steps, you can help keep black spot from weakening or killing your roses.

*HELP YOUR ROSES BEAT BLACK SPOT BY WATERING THEM REGULARLY AND APPLYING ORGANIC FERTILIZER.*

## Be a Smart Shopper

Make shopping for disease resistance a priority when you invest in ornamental shrubs or perennials. Recently, the nursery industry has made huge strides in identifying disease-resistant cultivars, but it's up to you to reward these efforts by choosing only the most disease-tolerant plants for your garden. As gardeners show that disease resistance is important to them, more of these varieties will become available, and that means fewer gardening frustrations for us!

## Fight Fungi with Fungi

Science has finally confirmed what organic gardeners have known for years: Good compost is a banquet of micro-critters that not only help nurture plants but also may suppress diseases.

Scientists at the USDA's Biocontrol of Plant Diseases Laboratory have helped select and evaluate the disease-fighting punch of a beneficial fungus called *Gliocladium virens,* now sold in granulated form as SoilGard. What did they find? The *Glio* guys actually strangulate some disease-causing fungi, proving that putting good fungus head-to-head with bad fungus is great for your garden—and that compost really is your first line of defense against plant diseases!

"I never plant anything without putting compost into the soil first," adds Barbara Pleasant, author of *The Gardener's Guide to Plant Diseases.* "You never know what kind of bad guys might be lurking in the dirt, but by adding compost I figure the troublemakers will have plenty of company that might take away their lunch, or better yet, eat them for dinner!"

## First Aid for Foliar Infections

The fight against foliar infections isn't hopeless—you can fight them off and reclaim your prize plantings. Just follow this expert advice from Barbara Pleasant, who gardens in Huntsville, Alabama.

1. Prune out affected stems, and rake up any diseased leaves that have fallen to the ground. Don't throw them on the compost pile, though; diseased plant parts need to be destroyed.

2. Top-dress with a thin layer of rotted manure or compost. Mix a handful of any good organic fertilizer into the topdressing.
3. Spray plants thoroughly with one of the disease-deterrent sprays below. Then, 1 week later, spray with the other mixture. (Alternating oil- and soap-based sprays will help keep an oily residue from building up on the leaves.)

***Oil and Baking Soda Spray***

1 tablespoon light horticultural oil (such as Sunspray)
1 tablespoon baking soda
1 gallon water

***Soap and Baking Soda Spray***

1 tablespoon insecticidal soap or liquid dishwashing soap
1 tablespoon baking soda
1 gallon water

## Look Out for Your Plants

Plants have to work with the conditions we give them, so it's up to us to make sure they're living in a happy, health-promoting environment. To prevent foliar diseases, follow these four guidelines.

1. Keep leaves as dry as possible because most diseases spread only on wet leaves. Use drip irrigation or water early enough in the day so leaves are completely dry by the time temperatures fall at night.
2. Put mulch to work as a barrier to keep muddy water from splashing on leaves. Use a good straw mulch beneath roses to trap black-spot spores that are washed down with rain. When the mulch dries, the spores will be history!
3. Use balanced organic fertilizers that release nutrients slowly. Plants that are underfed or overfed are more susceptible to diseases.
4. Clean up all old plant debris in winter. Replace old mulches with fresh material by the time spring arrives.

*One of the easiest ways to prevent plant diseases in your garden is to clean up old plant debris at the end of the season.*

## Keep It Clean

Moving your green babies into dirty containers is just asking for trouble, so make a habit of scrubbing out flower pots between uses.

"I do my pot cleaning on a hot day when playing in water is fun," reports Barbara Pleasant, Alabama gardener and author of *The Gardener's Guide to Plant Diseases*. "I put all my dirty flats and pots in a wheelbarrow and fill it with warm water and a tablespoon of granulated dishwasher detergent. After a 10-minute soak, I scrub them with a stiff brush, rinse them clean, and set them in the sun to dry. Besides avoiding disease problems, I always have clean containers ready to use when I want them," Pleasant says.

*A WHEELBARROW MAKES A HANDY SINK IN WHICH TO WASH OUT DIRTY FLATS AND FLOWER POTS.*

## Underground Diseases

You garden soil contains thousands of different microorganisms—meaning dirt is anything but dead. And while most of these life forms help plants by releasing plant nutrients or by supporting other forms of soil life, a few aren't so nice. These tips will help you handle any disease that attacks your plants at their roots.

**DAMPING-OFF.** Growing seedlings in sterile soil that contains no fungi is the safest strategy for preventing this disease that causes young seedlings to suddenly collapse and shrivel. That's why most gardeners used bagged products known as "soilless mixes" to start seedlings. Damping-off is caused by several strains of soilborne fungi, so if you use potting soil you've made yourself or bagged soil that's been open for a while, heat up small batches to kill off those fungi. Just place as much soil as you need in an oven-proof container, sprinkle on some water, and cover it with a lid or aluminum foil. Put it in a 250°F oven for an hour, and all those fungi will be steamed off to fungi heaven!

*HEATING UP SMALL BATCHES OF HOMEMADE POTTING SOIL CAN HELP KILL OFF FUNGI THAT CAUSE DAMPING-OFF.*

**FUSARIUM WILT.** This pervasive disease is the athlete's foot of the plant world, attacking the roots of a number of vegetables and flowers. Hair-thin feeder roots are the first to go, followed by larger roots and the main stem; plant growth usually screeches to a halt, older leaves droop and turn yellow, and the rest of the plant just sits there looking miserable. But don't despair; these strategies will keep your fusarium frustrations at a minimum.

- Grow only resistant varieties of tomatoes, melons, and cabbages.
- Pull out infected plants and throw some compost down the hole to give the fusarium fungi a fight from friendly fungi.
- Plant only in well-drained soil; these fungi thrive in waterlogged soil.
- Prevent fusarium problems with long-lived asparagus, chrysanthemum, and cyclamen by monitoring your soil's pH and adding small amounts of lime (if needed) to keep the pH between 6.5 and 7.0.

*ONE WAY TO BEAT FUSARIUM WILT ON TOMATOES IS TO GROW VARIETIES THAT ARE SPECIFICALLY RESISTANT TO THE DISEASE.*

### Solutions at a Glance

**PROBLEM:** Bruised seedling stems are creating an entry point for damping-off fungi.

**CULPRIT:** Your fingers

**SOLVE IT!** When transplanting young seedlings, handle them only by the seedling leaves—the first ones that pop out when the seeds germinate.

## NUKE THOSE NEMATODES

Nematodes, microscopically small wormlike parasites that infect and clog up plants' roots, can turn any day in the garden sour. But if you know your enemy, there are a few strategies you can try to root these nuisances out.

If you have a plot of soil that you know has nematodes, plant it with French marigolds. Root-knot nematodes—the type gardeners in warm climates tangle with most often—can't abide 'Golden Guardian' and several other French marigold varieties.

You can also cook nematodes to death by harnessing the heat of the summer sun. Cultivate a troubled spot of soil, wet it, and cover it with a sheet of clear plastic for at least a month. Make sure the edges are securely buried so that plenty of heat is trapped under the plastic. Besides killing nematodes, this solarization process will rid the soil of many insects and weed seeds, too. And it'll be ready just in time for fall planting!

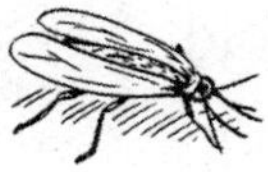

# Evergreen Problems

Evergreen trees and shrubs, with their year-round interest, form the backbone of home gardens. They take center stage during the winter by adding texture, color, and structure to the otherwise brown landscape. And many evergreens add the sparkle of long-lasting flowers in spring and summer. For the rest of the year, they assume more of the role of a supporting cast member.

Most of the time, evergreens are fairly easy to grow and perform their roles year in, year out without complaints. But, just like other plants, they can have problems. And because these hardworking trees and shrubs are usually the most expensive plants in the garden, we all want to nip any problems in the bud. So here's some advice on heading off evergreen problems from deer, cold weather, insect pests, and more.

## Rx for Healthy Pruning

For many of you, pruning ranks right up there with having a tooth filled—you'd prefer to avoid it. Pruning doesn't have to be a pain, however. Here are some tips to follow from John Van Etten, grounds superintendent of Mohonk Mountain House in New Paltz, New York.

**REJUVENATE LEGGY BROAD-LEAVED EVERGREENS (SUCH AS RHODODENDRONS) BY CUTTING THEM BACK** about one-third right after they're finished blooming. This will stimulate new growth from the base of the plant. (Make sure not to remove more than one-third of each plant at one time so the plant doesn't lose its natural shape or the ability to produce its own food.)

*Give your rhododendrons a boost by cutting them back by one-third after they're finished blooming.*

## Solutions at a Glance

**Problem:** Something's eating your evergreens.

**Culprit:** Deer

**Solve It!** Plant evergreens that don't appeal to deer, such as spruces (*Picea* spp.), Scotch pine (*Pinus sylvestris*), and Douglas fir (*Pseudotsuga menziesii*).

---

**Problem:** Evergreens take up a lot of space.

**Culprit:** Limited space

**Solve It!** Look for trees that won't outgrow their space when they're mature. Check what the full size of the tree will be before you buy it and make sure you have enough room to accommodate it.

---

**Problem:** Narrow-leaved evergreens, particularly yews (*Taxus* spp.) and some conifers, are opening up in the middle.

**Culprit:** Snow

**Solve It!** Gently brush the snow off your trees if they aren't too tall. Use a sweeping motion moving from the center to the outer tips of the branches. Or erect tall stakes around the tree and loosely wrap burlap to the stakes and across the tops of them.

---

**Problem:** Your broad-leaved evergreens are rolling up tight.

**Culprit:** Cold weather

**Solve It!** These curled leaves are the plant's defense against the elements. When the leaves curl, water has less surface from which it can evaporate. You can lessen this leaf curling by continuing to water these shrubs in the fall and early winter until the ground freezes. You can also apply an antidessicant in the late fall, to slow down the rate at which the plant loses water.

# Pest Detective

*Something's turning your healthy, vigorous evergreens into sad images of their former selves. Not sure who the culprit is? Check out this chart to find out who's doing the damage and how you can stop it.*

| Symptom | Cause | What to Do |
|---|---|---|
| Brown, cone-shaped galls on Colorado blue spruce (*Picea pungens forma glauca*), Engelmann spruce (*P. engelmannii*), oriental spruce (*P. orientalis*), and Sitka spruce (*P. sitchensis*). The galls look like needles that are curled inward. They're found at the tips of branches and sometimes toward the center of the tree. | Cooley spruce gall adelgid | Early identification is the key to eliminating the Cooley spruce gall adelgid population from your trees. In June, examine your trees for the brown, cone-shaped galls. Hand-pick the galls and burn them before the insects emerge in July and August to lay their eggs. The immature females also like to feed and overwinter on Douglas fir (*Pseudotsuga menziesii*), so keeping Douglas fir and spruce trees separate may help weaken the populations. Insecticidal soap is also effective at stopping galls; apply it in mid- to late April just before the buds open. |
| A dry, woolly substance that looks like white fuzz appears on new hemlock growth (particularly on the undersides of needles) | Woolly adelgid | If woolly adelgids have attacked your hemlocks (*Tsuga* spp.), apply horticultural oil or insecticidal soap in late April or early May, again in late June or late September, and the following year in early June (it's important to thoroughly cover the trees). By improving the tree's overall health and vigor—that is, maintaining good soil, ensuring adequate moisture, and pruning damaged wood—you can help slow down the adelgid. |
| Round notches on the edges of azalea, rhododendron, and yew (*Taxus* spp.) leaves | Black vine weevil | If you don't have too many plants, hand-pick the larvae and adults as you see them. You can also sink small, tuna-size cans in the ground; some of the weevils will inevitably fall off the plants into the cans and will be trapped. You could also apply nematodes to the soil in late spring or fall to take care of the black vine weevil larvae. |
| Leaves or needles are stripped from branches. Larvae live in curious baglike, 2½-inch-long cocoons studded with pieces of leaf and plant debris. Larvae are 1-inch-long, dark brown caterpillars. | Bagworm | Hand-pick the bags during winter. Cut bags away with a knife to avoid leaving a band of silk that could girdle the twig. Spray with *Bacillus thuringiensis* var. *kurstaki* (BTK) every 7 to 10 days from early spring to early summer to kill larvae. |

**GRADUALLY REDUCE THE SURFACE AREA OF NARROW-LEAVED TREES** such as Norway spruce (*Picea abies*) so the trees will be less susceptible to ice, snow damage, and wind. You can do this just before new growth begins on the trees. This selective pruning also creates more air circulation through the trees, improving their health. Also, prune to cut out dead wood, crossed branches, or narrow crotches. (You can prune out dead or diseased wood anytime; prune crossing branches and do other corrective pruning after the "plant's bloom sequence is complete," says Van Etten.)

**TRIM THE TIPS OF YEWS (*TAXUS* SPP.) AND HEDGE PLANTS ONCE EACH SPRING** to encourage bud growth. Take care not to cut more than 2 or 3 inches of foliage during pruning.

## Where Are the Berries?

You have some lovely holly bushes in your yard; the problem is they flower, but they never produce berries. What are you doing wrong?

The problem could be that you have either all male or all female holly bushes. Although both sexes will flower, only females will fruit. And the only way you'll get berries is if you have a female plant and a male plant *of the same species* within half a mile of it. With the help of bees, one male plant is sufficient to pollinate several females. If you aren't sure if your holly plants are male or female, look at the flowers. Male holly flowers have pronounced stamen covered with pollen. Female flowers have nubby stamen and a developed pistil, which is the swollen sack inside the plant's flower.

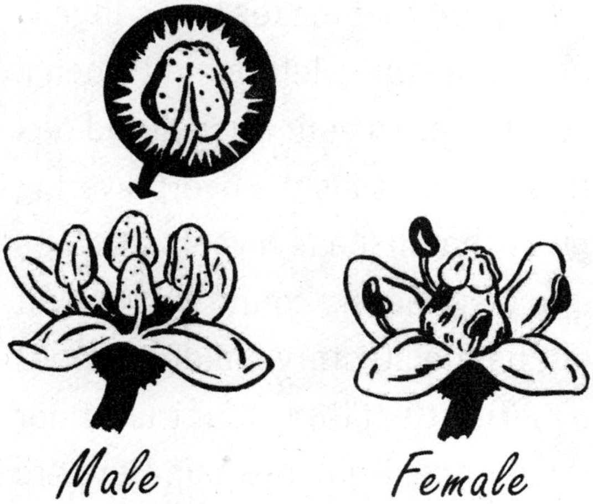


*YOU'LL NEED BOTH MALE AND FEMALE HOLLY BUSHES IF YOU WANT BERRIES. SO IF YOU AREN'T SURE OF THE SEX OF YOURS, TAKE A CLOSER LOOK: MALE HOLLY FLOWERS HAVE PRONOUNCED STAMEN COVERED WITH POLLEN; FEMALE FLOWERS HAVE A NUBBY STAMEN AND A DEVELOPED PISTIL.*

# Eyesores

Every garden has at least one. Maybe the sight that makes you cringe is the stump left behind when a nor'easter felled your 80-year-old oak tree. Perhaps it's the overpowering highway that just a few years ago was a meandering country lane. Or it might be the 20-story building across the street from your third-floor terrace. Don't despair. Here are four terrific techniques that will help banish visual clutter and reclaim your garden as a place of repose and contentment.

## Getting Off to a Good Start

If you take a look around your yard, you're sure to find *something* that needs concealing or enhancing. But before you rush off to the garden center to find a quick fix, heed the advice of Portland, Oregon, landscape architect Julia Lundy: "Think before you plant." Buy trees and shrubs that will be the height you're looking for when they reach maturity. That tidy little tree in its nursery pot might seem just the ticket for the front of your house now, but, Lundy warns, "a few years down the road it could be a monster and chances are it will have to go."

Never plant—or build—a taller screen than you need, Lundy says. "It may block necessary light and air circulation, and you'll have more problems than you started with."

Remember that plants grow out as well as up. Be especially aware of that horizontal dimension if you have a small garden or, says Paul Soniat, director of the New Orleans Botanical Garden, "You could sacrifice half your space to block a view." When space is limited, he says, vines on trellises can be your best friends. Or, try one of these plants for screening views:

- Leyland cyprus (*Cupressocyparis leylandii*). Hardy to Zone 6, leyland cyprus needs little or no water once it's established and thrives on the north side of a house.
- Holly-leaf osmanthus (*Osmanthus heterophyllus*). This plant takes heavy pruning so well that you can keep it skinny enough to suit the smallest yard.
- Mountain ash (*Sorbus aria*). This tree is slim, making it great for small gardens.

## Hide That Road!

Penny Grist's garden on Washington's Vashon Island overlooks the breathtaking blue waters of Puget Sound. Unfortunately, it also overlooks a two-lane highway that skirts the shoreline. Grist could have planted trees to hide the highway, but eventually they would have grown tall enough to hide the blue water, too. So Grist devised this simple method for figuring out how high a view blocker really needs to be, based on the fact that the eye is a trickster, seeing objects grow smaller as one moves away from them.

For example, let's say you want to block your neighbor's metal shed from view when you're on your patio. First, stand on your patio, looking at the shed. Have a friend stand at the edge of your property in front of the shed, holding against the ground a wooden strip marked at 1-foot increments. At the spot where you no longer see the structure above the strip, note the measurement. Then plant something that will reach that height at maturity. "In our case," Grist says, "a 4-foot hedge banished the road from sight but left the Sound in full view." Good hedges for hiding eyesores include forsythias (*Forsythia* spp.), hollies (*Ilex spp.),* northern bayberry (*Myrica pensylvanica*), azaleas (*Rhododendron* spp.), and yews (*Taxus* spp.).

## The Cold Shoulder Treatment

If the object of your discontent is a 10-story building right behind your house, don't try to block it from view. Instead, create a lovely scene that will draw your attention down and away from the monstrosity, says Master Gardener Caroline Wiejek of East Longmeadow, Massachusetts. A tall hedge will create an illusion of separation, says Wiejek, "but it won't begin to cover something that big, and it might even emphasize it." But add a pond, a garden seat, or a sculpture at the base of the hedge, and your eye will naturally gravitate toward it, rather than the building towering above.

## Flowery Makeovers

What do you do with eyesores that are hard to hide, yet important to your creature comfort—such as heating-oil tanks and air-conditioning units? Why not put your creative juices to work and have some fun with them?

Natasha Zahn Pristas of Juneau, Alaska, painted her heating-oil tank blue, perched flower-filled window boxes on its support frame, and erected a picket-fence gate in front for service access. Rosalia Kung, a gardener from Skillman, New Jersey, surrounded her air-conditioning unit with a four-sided lattice box decked with realistically painted vines. The lattice allows plenty of air movement and the painted vines keep their distance from the air vents without the constant clipping real ones demand.

*Have some fun turning an eyesore like an oil tank into an eye soother. Flower boxes and a picket fence disguise the bulky tank and its ugly metal frame.*

# Fencing Problems

Fences can be beautiful or functional, or—ideally—both. But if you're like many gardeners, you may have a fence that has seen better days. So whether your fence is falling down on the job or just not getting any easier on the eyes, we have the secrets to making your fence work for you! Read on for some innovative ways to enliven and secure the perimeter of your yard or garden.

## Liven Up That Ugly Fence

Whether you have an old split-rail fence with wire, a designer fence that's lost its pizazz, or plain chicken wire, you can bring your tired old fence to life. Literally.

Marzee Etheridge, who gardens in Ider, Alabama, did exactly that when she made a "living fence" around her nearly quarter-acre garden. "I was tired of getting wiped out by deer or rabbits, you name it. They'd eat a whole row of beans like nothing," she says. So she constructed a barrier fence with nothing more than twine, posts, and a little help from Mother Nature.

Here's Etheridge's method: Pound posts (she used steel, although anything durable and about 5 feet long will do) 1 foot into the ground about every 8 feet. ("They should be close enough so that the heavy-duty twine you'll put between them doesn't sag," she says.) Then she runs twine securely between the posts, starting about 1 foot above the ground and continuing upward, making three or four rows 1 to 1½ feet apart.

She completely plants the spaces between the posts (don't forget to leave an entrance for yourself) with plants that benefit from support—cucumbers, morning glories, melons, pole beans, sunflowers, and more. Then, she further enhances the barrier properties of her living fence by spraying the plants with hot pepper sauce. It has worked beautifully, she says. The 32 kinds of peppers and 15 to 20 tomato varieties, beans, and other veggies growing inside the living fence haven't been bothered since the fence went up, and the fruits and vegetables growing right on the fence do well, too.

"Deer don't like to get tangled in the twine. And the other animals don't like the twine or the hot sauce," she says.

If you already have "a big ugly" you'd like to make more attractive but you don't want to pull it out entirely and go with Etheridge's all-living fence, you can use your fence as a backdrop for flowering vines, clusters of flowers, or climbing roses. Or you could use Etheridge's planting plan of putting veggies and flowers along your fence (add a trellis or string some twine along the inside for those plants that need some climbing handholds)—and enjoy the beauty and the bounty that your former eyesore will bring to your landscape!

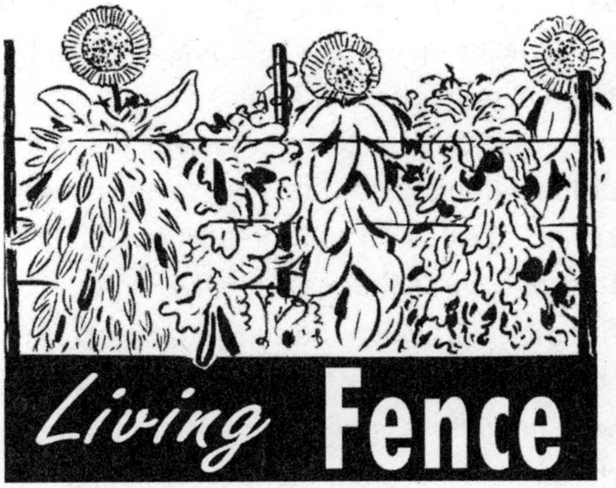


*BRING AN OLD, UGLY FENCE TO LIFE BY PLANTING FLOWERS AND VEGGIES THAT NEED SUPPORT BETWEEN THE POSTS.*

## WHAT WEEDS?

Fencing, particularly around a garden's edge, needs to be kept relatively free from weeds to keep its appearance neat and to keep the vole and harmful insect populations down. So here's a great idea that kills two birds with one stone: Build a fence that keeps out weeds as well as garden pests.

Before setting in the fence posts, cut out a 1-foot section of sod around your fence perimeter. You can partially backfill with soil after putting in the fence posts, lay weed barrier fabric on each side of the buried fencing, and then fill in the trench with crushed rock, chipped bark, or another permanent mulch. You may have an occasional stray weed that needs to be pulled, but they'll pull out easily and the perimeter will stay neat—saving you hours of labor!

## SAVE THAT BROKEN FENCE POST

You don't have to trash a perfectly good fence just because a post rots or breaks off at the soil line. Such problems can usually be fixed, rather than replaced, relatively easily. Just follow these four simple steps:

1. Get two 3-foot lengths of 1 × 4-inch lumber to brace each faulty post. (If the post is heavy and wide, you may need to go to 1 × 6-inch lumber to make sure the braces are strong enough.)
2. Sharpen one end of each 3-foot piece of lumber into a point and position one brace next to one side of the post, with the pointed end toward the ground.
3. Nail a piece of scrap wood atop the other end of the brace (so it doesn't split), and hammer the brace in for at least 1½ feet—tight against the post.
4. Fasten the top of the brace to the failing post with screws or nails. Then repeat with the other brace on the opposite side of the post in the same manner. Wrap a wire collar around both braces and the post to add more strength.

This system should hold your fence securely for years. If several post sections are broken in a row, however, you'll most likely need to remove the old posts entirely and install new ones.

# Flea Beetles

There's no way of knowing whether flea beetle feeding plagues plants in the same way that fleas pester people and pets. But it's clear that these tiny beetles that jump like fleas can do some serious damage in your garden if you let them. A large infestation of flea beetles can kill young plants with heavy feeding early in the growing season, and plants that withstand the injury to their leaves may fall prey to viruses spread by the beetles. Several flea beetle species are common in gardens, including potato flea beetles, striped flea beetles, spinach flea beetles, and a special species that feeds on corn. All of them chew small, circular gouges in leaves, and they multiply like mad. If you see lots of little holes in leaves and dark jumping beetles the size of sesame seeds, prepare for a flea beetle battle.

## Stick 'Em Up

In her organic market garden in southwestern Ohio, Lucy Goodman-Owsley captures thousands of flea beetles with sticky traps made from plastic dish-washing, soda, or water bottles (yellow bottles work best) covered with petroleum jelly or Tanglefoot. "We bought a gallon of Tanglefoot, which turns out to be enough to cover 5 to 6 acres if you spread it out thinly like they tell you to," Goodman-Owsley says. She fills the empty yellow bottles with water to keep them from blowing in the wind, coats each bottle with Tanglefoot, and sets the sticky bottles on the ground between mature eggplants. "Besides being attracted by the yellow color, flea beetles are attracted to the nighttime warmth given off by the water-filled bottles," Goodman-Owsley explains. "They jump right down onto the side closest to the plants. When that bottle gets black with beetles, it's time to put a new bottle in the garden.

(Goodman-Owsley also notes that these sticky traps work well for catching flea beetles under row covers, too.)

## Swing a Flea Swatter

Aiko Scales, a quick-thinking gardener in Woodinville, Washington, makes her flea beetles hop to a sticky death. "I paint a scrap piece of illustration board with yellow acrylic paint, coat it with Tanglefoot, and staple it onto a stake like a wooden row marker," Scales says. "I stick the traps in the ground around plants that have flea beetle problems. When I'm in the garden, I pull up a trap, hold it just above a leaf where flea beetles are feeding, and gently tap the leaf. They hop right up!" Scales reports.

*HOLD A STICKY TRAP OVER FEEDING FLEA BEETLES WHILE DISTURBING THE PLANTS TO MAKE THE BEETLES JUMP UP AND ONTO THE TRAP.*

### COVERED EGGPLANT CAGES

Eggplant are particularly vulnerable to flea beetle damage. But don't despair! You can shield your eggplants from this pest and encourage plant growth by surrounding your plants with tomato cages covered with floating row covers. Set up the cages as soon as you transplant your seedlings to the garden. Wrap the cages with row cover fabric, fold over the seams at the top and sides, then staple them closed. Remove the staples and open the tops for pollination when the plants begin to bloom. (Don't remove the cages because you might damage the plant. Plus, you'll find that your eggplants are so big and vigorous, they'll need the support!)

## Solutions at a Glance

**PROBLEM:** Your cabbage, eggplant, and potato foliage have lots of small holes in them.

**CULPRIT:** Flea beetles

**SOLVE IT!** Use row covers to keep these pesky critters out and to keep your plants intact.

### SEEDLING PROTECTION

Plant the crops most susceptible to flea beetles such as eggplant and cabbage as late as possible in the spring. Flea beetles are the most damaging in early spring when seedlings may be killed by a heavy infestation of overwintering adults. (Larger plants can usually survive the feeding damage.)

# Flower Garden Problems

If only they'd look like the pictures in the magazine. But flowers have minds of their own. They grow too small or too big, bloom only a little or not at all, fall prey to nasty pests, or even get stomped out by the kids. Take heart, however. You can indeed have flowers that are as gorgeous as those glossy photos. All it takes is a little know-how. Read on and you'll be a few steps closer to realizing the beautiful blooming garden of your dreams.

## Freshening Up

Ugh. It's late summer and your flowerbeds are looking the way you feel in all that heat and humidity. Perk up lackluster late-season beds and borders with reinforcements. Buy large pots or other lush containers of annuals—by late summer they're usually half-price—and plant them in your flowerbed right in their pots. Just pull a little mulch or soil over the rim. Trailing petunias and other hanging basket plants are ideal because they cover a large area.

## Divide and Conquer

No need to dig up the whole gigantic root ball when you're dividing perennials. As long as there's no dead spot in the center of the plant, simply slice off a piece or two—or three, or four—of the outside portion of the plant with a healthy chunk of roots attached.

*Divide perennials simply by digging up an outside portion of the plant.*

## Killing It Softly

What a quandary. You want to plant a wildflower meadow because it seems like such a wonderful, earth-friendly way to landscape an open area. Then you find out you have to kill the weeds first. Instead of resorting to chemicals, try this no-drug method. In just five steps you'll be well on your way to creating a beautiful, weed-free wildflower meadow.

1. Dig or till under existing weeds and turf.
2. Give the area a good soaking to encourage dormant weed seeds to germinate.
3. Cover the entire area with a tarp or spread it with newspapers, wetting them and weighting with rocks or bricks to prevent them from blowing away.
4. Allow to set at least a couple of weeks, then remove the cover.
5. Water again. Wait another week or two and then till, dig, or hoe up germinating seedlings.

## A Summer Place

Summering houseplants outdoors is great, but may take up precious deck and porch space. So instead, summer your houseplants outdoors—in your flowerbed. (And save a little money on not having to buy as many flowers, too.)

The lovely colors and textures of your favorite houseplants are wonderful combined with garden flowers. Simply set the houseplants in their pots right on the soil, or sink the pot and all into the soil, concealing the rim with soil. In the fall, lift the pot and give the plant and the pot a gentle rinse with the garden hose to wash away any pests or problems that might spread indoors.

*Give your houseplants a new summer home in your flowerbed.*

### Solutions at a Glance

**Problem:** You keep forgetting when you're supposed to fertilize or repeat a pest control application.

**Culprit:** Your memory

**Solve It!** Put those little white plastic labels to a new use. Write down what you're supposed to do and when you're supposed to do it. Then push the label into the soil by the plant.

## Flower Garden Understudies

The Heath, Massachusetts, acreage of gardener extraordinaire Elsa Bakalar is a mecca for visitors and tour groups, so she has to keep it looking tip-top all season long. She recommends filling in bare spots by first sowing seeds of annual "understudies" between rows in her vegetable garden in the spring. By early summer, when problems become apparent but there are few annuals to be found in local nurseries, Bakalar just digs up her understudies and plants them into troublesome areas, a pretty fill-in for the garden "star" or two that didn't come through. Bakalar uses only those understudies that are shallow-rooted and don't resent transplanting. Her recommendations include

**For the back of the border.** Cosmos (*Cosmos bipinnatus*) 'Purity' in white or 'Dazzler' in red and 'Italian White' sunflower (*Helianthus annuus* 'Italian White').

**For midborder.** 'Marine' heliotrope (*Heliotropium arborescens* 'Marine') and flowering tobacco (*Nicotiana alata*) in white or other colors.

## Solutions at a Glance

**PROBLEM:** Your flowerbeds are being squashed.

**CULPRIT:** Your kids

**SOLVE IT!** Visual clues can help keep kids in line. Edging, both flat and raised, clearly delineates which is a stay-off flowerbed and which is walk-on-me lawn. Paths of any sort also are a tremendous help, clearly identifying where kids may walk.

**FOR THE FRONT OF THE BORDER.** 'Red Plume' blanket flower *(Gaillardia pulchella* 'Red Plume') in deep red; annual candytuft (*Iberis umbellata*) in mixed colors; 'White Rocket' (*Iberis amara* 'White Rocket'); and a white variety of the low, groundcover-like Mexican zinnia (*Zinnia angustifolia*).

## LATE BLOOMERS

Late summer into fall tends to be garden downtime for many perennials. But it doesn't have to be, says gardener Elsa Bakalar of Heath, Massachusetts. Here are some of her favorite perennials that burst forth with color as the season starts to wind down.

- Azure monkshood (*Aconitum carmichaelii*)
- White baneberry (*Actaea alba*)
- Garlic chives (*Allium tuberosum*)
- Japanese anemones, particularly 'Honorine Jobert' (*Anemone* cultivars)
- Purple parsnip (*Angelica gigas*)
- White mugwort (*Artemisia lactiflora*)
- New England aster (*Aster novae-angliae*)
- New York aster (*A. novi-belgii*)
- Boltonia (*Boltonia asteroides*)
- Rose turtlehead (*Chelone obliqua*)
- Late-blooming Kamchatka bugbane (*Cimicifuga simplex*)
- Weyrich chrysanthemum (*Dendranthema weyrichii,* also called *Chrysanthemum weyrichii*)
- Joe-pye weed (*Eupatorium purpureum*)
- Bottle gentian (*Gentiana andrewsii*)
- Common sneezeweed (*Helenium autumnale*)
- Late cultivars of obedient plant, such as 'Vivid' (*Physostegia* cultivars)
- Blue sage (*Salvia azurea*)
- Late-blooming goldenrods (*Solidago sphacelata* 'Golden Fleece')

## SPEEDY DEADHEADING

Using bypass shears to deadhead long-blooming flowers with many small blooms, such as coreopsis or golden marguerite (*Anthemis tinctoria*) can take forever. To speed things up, get out those hedge clippers or the lawn shears that you use for tall grass along the fence. They'll make quick work of those offending blossoms, and you'll be done in no time.

*USE LAWN SHEARS TO MAKE QUICK WORK OF DEADHEADING PERENNIALS WITH MANY SMALL FLOWERS.*

## No-Brainer Flowers

Need a garden you can't kill and has something in bloom all season long? No, we aren't talking about silk flowers. We're talking about easy-to-grow perennials and bulbs. Plant our baker's dozen here and you'll have something going from early spring to late fall.

**Late winter:** Crocuses
**Very early spring:** Daffodils
**Early spring:** Columbines (*Aquilegia* spp.), fringed bleeding heart (*Dicentra eximia*)
**Late spring:** Peonies
**Early summer:** 'Moonbeam' threadleaf coreopsis (*Coreopsis verticillata* 'Moonbeam'), Siberian iris (*Iris sibirica*)
**Midsummer:** Daylilies, Shasta daisies (*Leucanthemum* × *superbum*, also called *Chrysanthemum* × *superbum*)
**Late summer:** Obedient plant (*Physostegia* spp.), 'Autumn Joy' sedum
**Early fall:** Chrysanthemums (*Dendranthema* × *grandiflorum,* also called *Chrysanthemum* × *morifolium*)
**Late fall:** Asters

## Dry Ideas

Just because you live where rainfall is scant doesn't mean you can't have beds full of lovely annuals and perennials—you just have to know what to look for when buying plants. Usually, if a plant has one or more of the following characteristics, it can go without water longer than most:

- Hairy leaves or stems
- Silver-gray foliage
- Stickers or thorns
- Thick, succulent-type leaves
- Waxy leaves

## More Flowers Longer

Do you have a fairly large stand of perennials that bloom in mid- to late summer and then peter out? Here's a way you can prolong the bloom.

Once the plants are several inches high in early or mid-spring, trim back a row in the center of the stand, about a third of its depth. Then, about 1 week later, trim the front third.

You'll create a stair-step effect of bloom. The back "row" will bloom first. Once those have faded, the second "row" will start; at that time, trim the back row to deadhead and to conceal unsightly foliage. Then, when the front row starts blooming—about the time the second row is fading—cut back the second and third rows to remove unsightly spent blooms and foliage.

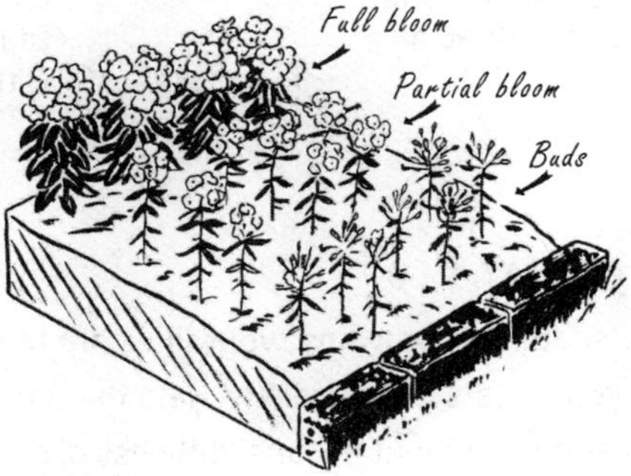


*TRIM YOUR PERENNIALS IN STAGES FOR CONTINUOUS WAVES OF BLOOM.*

## Standing Up for Shrubs

If your flowerbeds and borders look too flat or ragged early and late in the season, tuck in a few shrubs, advises Gloria Seborg of Seattle, Washington. "Shrubs can give a garden a sculptural quality," Seborg says.

Evergreens are especially good choices because they look great year-round. And during the height of the blooming season, evergreens provide a pleasantly neutral backdrop that sets off flowers nicely.

# Pest Detective

*Flowers are ailing, but you aren't sure why? Check out these three common pests that love annuals and perennials and see if they might be visiting your garden without an invitation.*

| Symptom | Cause | What to Do |
|---|---|---|
| Leaves are curled and yellow. May be coated with a sticky substance. | Aphids | Aphids do little damage in small numbers. For more extensive infestations, spray plant with a garden hose. Follow with an application of insecticidal soap, and reapply as the label directs. |
| Leaf tissue becoming lacey from insect damage. Flowers are being eaten, too. | Japanese beetles | Flick beetles off plants into a bucket of soapy water; apply milky spore disease to lawn to control grubs. |
| A small white cloud arises when you brush the plant. Plant may be mottled and yellow. | Whiteflies | If it's the end of the season and your region gets freezing temperatures you don't have to do anything. Whiteflies can't survive the winter. But earlier in the season, spray with an insecticidal soap, and reapply as the label directs. |

## Flip That Flop

Your sedum is sprawling, your lilies are lolling, and your asters are all askew. Help them regain their stature without the unsightliness of stakes. Simply take a length of clear monofilament fishing line and tie the plants up into a big, loose bundle. The great thing about using the fishing line is that it's nearly invisible, so it looks as if your plants never flopped in the first place.

## Rx for Wonderful Wildflowers

When the call of the wildflowers beckons, follow this advice from native-plant gardener Danielle Green of Chicago.

**WORK WITH YOUR SITE; DON'T STRUGGLE TO MAKE IT A HAVEN FOR WHATEVER STRIKES YOUR FANCY IN THE CATALOGS.** Discover what your geographic niche offers in the way of hospitality, including soil quality, light level, drainage, and hardiness. Then find plants that naturally flourish in those surroundings.

**START WITH PLANTS RATHER THAN SEEDS.** Many wildflower seeds take 2 to 3 years to germinate, and that's a long time to spend looking at bare ground and fending off weeds. The price tag will be much higher for plants than seeds (another reason to start small) but your success rate will increase dramatically.

**BUY YOUR PLANTS AS CLOSE TO HOME AS POSSIBLE.** They'll be better adapted to your microclimate. Buy only from reputable nurseries, and make sure the plants were propagated, not illegally taken from the wild.

**STEER CLEAR OF PREPACKAGED MIXES WHEN YOU DO BUY SEED.** Instead, look for individual species that are native to your area.

# Fruit Tree Problems

Biting into an apple, pear, peach—or any fruit that you've picked from your own tree—is simply divine, isn't it? After all, it's hard to beat the luscious flavor of fruit you've grown yourself. (And desserts taste oh so much better made with fresh-from-the-backyard fruit.) But fruit trees can have an intimidating side to them, too. Lost all your cherries to the birds? Not sure how much you should thin those apples? And how the heck do you know when fruit is ripe for the picking? Luckily, some gardeners out there do have the lowdown on fruit trees—and they were happy to share their wisdom with us.

## Rx for Healthy Fruit Trees

Tom Burford, a former Virginia orchardist and nurseryman who's now an orchard designer and fruit tree consultant, has put together five tips to help you keep your fruit trees healthy.

**KEEP THE GROUND UNDER YOUR FRUIT TREES CLEAN.** Remove grass from the base of the trees (so you can easily inspect the tree for damage from insects and rodents). Make sure any mulch is about 6 inches away from the trunk of the tree to discourage mice from nesting against the trunk and nibbling it. Also, pick all ripe fruit and any branches or leaves up off the ground, and remove all mummies (shriveled fruit) from the tree.

**WRAP THE TRUNK OF NEWLY PLANTED TREES IN LATE FALL WITH A SPIRAL VINYL WRAP.** Wide swings in temperature can cause fissures in young trees, and the fissures can be home to insects and diseases. Wrapping the trunk will help protect the tree (remove the wrap in spring when temperatures have stabilized; wrapping will also protect the tree from nibbling animals and mechanical damage).

**PLANT NEW FRUIT TREES AWAY FROM COMPETING MATURE TREES.** Also, never plant fruit trees near walnut trees; the juglone in the walnut trees is toxic to some members of the rose family.

**PRUNE FRUIT TREES ANNUALLY SO SUNLIGHT CAN PENETRATE AND AIR CAN CIRCULATE THROUGHOUT THE TREE.** Allowing sun to get in through the branches helps reduce the growth of fungus. "You want to keep a tree open enough so that ideally a robin could fly through without its wing tips touching any branches," says Burford.

**FEED YOUR TREES—ESPECIALLY YOUNG ONES.** Fish emulsion is a great fruit tree fertilizer, says Burford. Give your trees a good application in spring, and then follow that up with a monthly feeding. "As long as the leaves remain bright and green, your tree is getting enough nutrition," Burford notes. "If the leaves become dull and overall growth slows down, you should have a soil test done to determine which nutrients your soil needs."

*YOU'LL KNOW YOU'VE PRUNED JUST ENOUGH FROM YOUR FRUIT TREES IF A ROBIN CAN FLY THROUGH WITHOUT ITS WINGS TOUCHING THE BRANCHES.*

## Faster Fruit

If you can't wait years to taste your first apples or pears, add a little weight to the tree and you'll get your fruit faster, says Lee Reich, Ph.D., a garden writer from New Paltz, New York. Simply hang weights on the branches to bend the branches down to about a 60-degree angle. (You can fill plastic sandwich bags with sand and use them for the weights.) The bent branches slow down vegetative growth, so the tree has more energy to form fruit buds.

## The Skinny on Thinning

Thinning excess fruit from a tree is as important as pruning dormant wood because overbearing is damaging to trees and affects future production, says Tom Burford, a former Virginia orchardist and nurseryman who's now an orchard designer and fruit tree consultant. "If you thin you'll get larger, higher quality fruit," Burford notes, "and the tree will be very appreciative. If you don't thin, especially on a young tree, the fruit will be degraded and the tree will take a number of years to recover."

In an effort to avoid stressing your tree, Burford offers this thinning advice.

"Use your hand as a guide," he says. "Thin fruit so the spread is about the distance between your thumb and index finger—4 to 6 inches. And if you're thinning from a young tree, make sure to remove fruit from the main stem. If you don't, you'll end up with a great crook in the main stem the following year."

(Also keep in mind that you should thin fruit early in the growing season, when the fruit is no larger than a dime.)

*THIS HANDY GUIDE TO HELP YOU THIN FRUIT IS RIGHT AT YOUR FINGERTIPS.*

## Pear-Picking Pointer

Sam Benowitz, owner of Raintree Nursery in Morton, Washington, offers this tip for timely pear picking. "Put the palm of your hand underneath the pear and raise your palm," says Benowitz. "If the pear breaks off the stem then it's ready to be picked, even though it may still be hard. Then simply store it on a counter until it softens."

*Give a pear a hand to tell if it's ready to be picked.*

## A Touch of Lime

Here's a way to control fungus and insect problems from Frank Pollock, who runs an organic fruit and vegetable farm in the Pocono Mountains of Pennsylvania. "We follow an old practice of using lime to dust our fruit trees from time to time," says Pollock. "We generally do it in early to late spring. Using lime is cheap, and it's relatively effective."

## One-Two Punch

Looking for easy ways to thin out large fruit, like apples and peaches? Try hitting the fruit with a strong stream of water from a hose, advises Lee Reich, Ph.D., a garden writer from New Paltz, New York. You can also attach a rubber hose to the end of a stick and bat at the branches.

### Solutions at a Glance

**Problem:** Your apples are damaged.

**Culprit:** All kinds of pests

**Solve It!** Tie paper bags over the fruit as soon as the fruit has set and leave the bags on until 2 to 4 weeks before harvest.

## Wonder of Whitewash

The trunks of many young peach and cherry trees are susceptible to cracking, says Frank Pollock, who runs an organic fruit and vegetable farm in the Pocono Mountains in Pennsylvania. To prevent cracking, Pollock paints the first 3 to 4 feet of the trunk with a whitewash—but he *doesn't* use latex paint, as some people recommend. Instead, he mixes lime with water and an extender and paints the lower trunks in late spring. (Pollock says the lime whitewash also helps to repel insects.)

## Beating the Birds I

Lon Rombough, a horticulturist from Aurora, Oregon, offers two suggestions for winning the birds versus your cherries game.

"You can buy bush cherries (a cross of *Prunus japonica* and *P. jacquemontii*); at maturity they're around 6 feet tall, and they look and taste like a pie cherry. They ripen in late August, so the birds usually leave them alone, plus the bushes are small enough that you can easily throw a net over them."

### Beating the Birds II

Frank Pollock, who runs an organic fruit and vegetable farm in the Pocono Mountains in Pennsylvania, suggests putting up purple martin houses among your cherry trees. "Purple martins are very proprietary," says Pollock, "and they'll chase other birds away from your cherries. And because purple mar-

## Solutions at a Glance

**Problem:** You hate picking fruit.

**Culprit:** You

**Solve It!** Pick all the fruit you can easily reach and then shake the rest down and use it for canning and freezing; it's the lazy man's way of harvesting.

## Pest Detective

*A little brown spot here, a hole or crack there—something is turning all that sweet fruit on your trees into sour grapes. But once you know what the troublemaker is, you can fight back. Here are the tools you need to do just that.*

| Symptom | Cause | What to Do |
|---|---|---|
| Thin brown tunnels throughout the apple | Apple maggot larvae | Catch adult apple maggots on red ball traps coated with Tanglefoot. Hang the traps in June—one per dwarf tree and four per semidwarf tree. Hang the traps at eye level and 2 to 3 feet within the tree. Clear the leaves from right around the trap. Clean up dropped apples weekly to help prevent problems next year. |
| Curled cherry leaves with a sticky coating; small, shiny black insects on leaf undersides | Black cherry aphids | Cherry aphids leave the trees by midsummer, so you may not have to do anything. If the infestation is severe, remove the aphids with a strong spray of water or spray them with insecticidal soap or neem |
| Tunnels to the core of the apple with perhaps a plumb pink larvae still in the fruit | Codling moth | Pick up dropped fruit; wrap corrugated cardboard wraps around the tree trunk. The cardboard will attract the larvae looking for a protected spot to pupate. Destroy the old wraps and replace the cardboard weekly during the summer. |
| Tiny red and green insects on pear trees | Pear psylla | Limit fertilization; use thinning cuts when pruning so you don't encourage a lot of succulent new growth that will attract psylla. (Pear psylla are sucking insects that can spread fire blight, a deadly pear bacterial disease). If psylla are on the tree during the growing season, spray insecticidal soap or summer oil to control them. |

tins are in the swallow family, they primarily eat insects—meaning they'll leave your cherries alone."

## Ashes to Ashes

Are your peach or cherry trees plagued by borers? If so, do what organic fruit and vegetable farmer Frank Pollock does.

"Every year we put a scoop of wood ashes around the base of all of our peach and cherry trees," explains Pollock. "We put the ashes right up against the tree, and the ashes tend to repel the borers. The ashes also deter ants to some extent, which are often a problem in spring."

## Frosty Protection

Early-blooming fruit trees like apricots and peaches may pay the penalty for their early budding by being hit with frost. You can help prevent frost damage on early bloomers by planting them near the north side of a building, says Lee Reich, Ph.D., a garden writer from New Paltz, New York. That way, the trees won't warm up as quickly as they would in another location.

| Symptom | Cause | What to Do |
|---|---|---|
| Brown or olive green spots on apples, or knobby apples with corky, cracked areas | Apple scab | Avoid this problem entirely by planting disease-resistant apples like 'Liberty', 'Goldrush', 'Freedom', and 'Enterprise', which are resistant to scab. Spray scab-susceptible trees with sulfur beginning when the tree leafs out in the spring and repeat after a heavy rain or weekly until midsummer. (The scab fungus takes about 12 days to appear on leaves and fruit from when the infection occurs. Once you can see it, you have a problem on your hands.) You can eat the scabby apples. |
| Dark spots that fall out from plum leaves, leaving holes | Bacterial leaf spot | Prune for good air circulation; remove affected fruit and leaves; spray lime sulfur every 10 to 21 days. If bacterial spot is a serious problem in your growing area, plant disease-resistant cultivars such as 'Au-Amber', 'Au-Rosa', 'Red Heart', and 'Crimson'. |
| Olive green spots on immature peaches; peaches become distorted | Peach scab | Collect and destroy infected or dropped peaches and fallen leaves. Prune to increase air circulation. You can eat lightly damaged peaches. |
| Deformed flowers on your apple tree that don't open and whitish velvetlike patches on the flower stems in spring. | Powdery mildew | Prune for good air circulation within the tree—remember a robin should be able to fly through the tree (old-timers used to suggest throwing a cat through the tree but that seems to be a technique your kitty wouldn't care for). Cut off and destroy infected shoots when you see them. Spray the tree with sulfur when the weather is wet or humid and the temperature is above 59°F. Repeat after rain or every 7 to 10 days until midsummer. Plant disease-resistant apple varieties; many are also resistant to mildew. |

# Garden Design Problems

The pros make it look so easy. A few flowering shrubs here, some perennials there, a lovely brick pathway to tie it all together—the perfect garden. But those of us who have struggled to plan a wonderful garden know better: Good garden design takes practice. It's a lot easier, though, if you know a few tricks of the trade. Armed with a little knowledge, you'll soon find yourself building a beautiful work of art. And unlike the pros, you'll design the garden for yourself they never could—a garden that uniquely reflects your personality.

## Safety in Numbers

Prevent yourself from digging up or "weeding" newly emerging perennials in early spring by planting at least three—and preferably five—together. One tiny plant all by its lonesome can look very much like a weed. But five, evenly spaced, are less likely to be misidentified.

## Arbor Dos and Don'ts

Stumped on where to position one of those pretty walk-through arbors? Here are some rules of thumb to get you started:

***Do Place an Arbor***

At the beginning or end of a path

As a bridge between two flower borders

Where a gate would naturally go into a fence or hedge

At the entrance of a vegetable or cutting garden

At the end of a vista

***Don't Place an Arbor***

In the middle of a lawn

On a steep slope where it would be difficult to walk

Under a tree all by itself

By a pond all by itself

## Doggy Design

Take a cue from your pet when laying out your garden—let it go to the dogs. Millie Kiggins and Penny Vogel, owners of Kinzsy Faire Garden in Estacada, Oregon, have 50 acres to deal with, 2 of them flower gardens. When it came time to figure out how to landscape the wide-open spaces, they simply mulched over a network of paths that the dogs had beaten in their daily roamings. Then they started designing beds that fit with the paths.

## Repeat Yourself

To avoid ending up with a chaotic jumble of plants when designing flowerbeds, keep in mind that repetition is important, says Eve Davis, owner of the Hawk and Ivy Bed and Breakfast and its accompanying large garden in Barnardsville, North Carolina.

Choose a plant or two that looks terrific all season long and has a distinctive shape, such as an ornamental grass, Siberian iris (*Iris sibirica*), or peony. Then use it at regular intervals throughout the border or garden, to give order to your beds.

## Rookie Tryouts

How often have you given a new plant a whirl in an established bed, only to have its performance be less than stellar? Next time you're unsure how a plant might do in a bed or border, try it in a nursery bed first.

Karen Strohbeen and Bill Luchsinger of Macksburg, Iowa—artists, gardeners, and producers of the PBS television show *The Perennial Gardener with Karen Strohbeen*—use a series of raised beds to experiment with new plants before they add the little newcomers to their main borders.

Not only does this method keep their main garden at its prime, it also saves money. By the time Strohbeen and Luchsinger are ready to put a perennial into the main border, it's usually large enough to divide.

### Solutions at a Glance

**Problem:** Wasted outdoor space; people keep using the wrong door.

**Culprit:** A seldom-used side door

**Solve It!** Turn it into a container garden. Dennis Ahl of Minneapolis, Minnesota, filled his seldom-used steps and landing with pots large and small, making it clear that this wasn't a door to use. He also gained a little extra planting space and found an excellent staging area for his pots.

Although Strohbeen and Luchsinger have several of these 4 by 4-foot nursery beds in their sprawling country garden, urban gardeners with more limited space could set aside a corner or two of the vegetable garden.

## Cracking Up

When Lenore Chen's seldom-used driveway in Des Moines began to crumble, she turned a major problem into an asset. Here's how she did it.

Because the driveway connects with the entranceway to the house, she left the front portion of the driveway (which was fairly sound) intact and created a curving edge to help it gracefully flow into the front walk.

Then, a jackhammer crew broke up the remaining concrete into rough chunks. Chen salvaged the concrete, using it to create a retaining wall alongside the drive. She placed the rough edges out to give it the look of natural stone.

Over time, the concrete has become weathered, mossy, and the perfect spot for rock garden plants and others that demand excellent drainage.

*TURN BITS OF AN OLD DRIVEWAY INTO A USEFUL RETAINING WALL.*

## THE BIG PICTURE

Having trouble envisioning just where the new beds you want to plant should go? Follow the lead of Linda Corson, a landscape architect in Philadelphia.

Corson photographs gardens she's going to design by standing in one spot and snapping shots as she turns around 360 degrees. After the film is developed, she tapes the pictures together, end to end.

"A landscape is very different when you view it in a photograph, as opposed to when you look at it with the naked eye," Corson says. "Because you're looking at all the elements of the landscape on a much smaller scale in a photo, you tend to see aesthetic detractors such as phone lines."

And even if you don't know a lot about plants, a photo guides you to the right shapes and forms. "It helps you figure out the heights of plants, where the windows are—that sort of thing," Corson says.

Once the landscape is neatly spread out before her, Corson then likes to take tracing paper and lay it over the photos, drawing in her dream landscape and experimenting with different designs.

## TAKE YOUR GARDENING TO NEW HEIGHTS

Pete Black of Halstead, Kansas, likes raised beds, but he doesn't like the cost or hassle of building them. So he creates his raised beds with concrete blocks.

Black often finds the blocks for just pennies at garage sales or for free from neighbors. Also try your local landfill, which may be happy to give them away.

To build his concrete block raised beds, Black simply lays the blocks right on the soil surface, holes facing upward. He fills the holes with sand to further weight the blocks down and discourage weeds.

Black's raised beds are just one block high, but you can make them two blocks high without having to use any reinforcement.

*CREATE EASY, INEXPENSIVE RAISED BEDS WITH RECYCLED CONCRETE BLOCKS.*

## Grand Illusions

Herb Kessner of Fairfax, California, likes to create the illusion of space in his small Bay-area garden by putting smaller plants at the far end of the garden. Keeping smaller things off in the distance creates a sort of forced perspective, making the yard look longer than it really is. Old-hand gardeners have been doing a version of this for years—trimming hedges so that they're slightly shorter at the far end to make them look longer and more imposing.

*MAKE YOUR GARDEN LOOK BIGGER BY PUTTING SMALLER PLANTS AT THE FAR END, CREATING A FORCED PERSPECTIVE.*

## Mix & Match a Garden Path

Looking for something different in a garden path that isn't too expensive? One way to do it is to combine materials. Dianne Olivieri of Santa Cruz, California, has created wonderful paths doing just that.

She might combine flagstone, brick, and round pavers she has covered in a pottery mosaic, for example. And this mixing of materials makes sense. It lets you better use recycled items, which can be hard to find in large quantities, especially if you're using bits and pieces you have around the house. After all, mixing adds variety and personality to your garden in a way a plain old brick path never could. Here are some more mix-and-match ideas.

- Bark mulch
- Bricks from a landfill
- Plastic bucket lids painted a funky color or with designs
- Clay tiles purchased as remnants or on clearance
- Bits of broken concrete
- Old ceramic or plastic dinner plates and platters
- Flagstones painted with fun designs
- Pea or colored gravel, laid in a pattern divided with edging
- Old iron manhole covers or other flat scrap metal
- "Mini-decks"—lumber cut into 24-inch squares and joined together on the back with lengths of other lumber
- Concrete pavers painted with concrete paint or stained with a concrete stain
- Concrete pavers topped with pottery or tile mosaic
- Homemade concrete pavers, made from concrete mix and poured into a pizza box for a mold and inset with marble, tiles, stones, or anything else
- Wood pavers cut from horizontal lengths of an old tree and coated in deck sealer
- Crushed seashells
- Terra-cotta pot drainage trays, turned upside down
- Leftover bits of marble or slate tile from a demolition project

## Don't Get Strung Out

Whenever you're using stake and string to lay out a garden bed, be sure to use mason's line, which you can buy at any hardware store. Unlike regular string, it won't stretch, requiring you to position and reposition your stakes to accommodate sagging.

## Stop and Compare

When Gloria Seborg of Seattle, Washington, is mulling over how to move around her perennials and small shrubs so that they combine well, she uses an old trick first espoused by that famous English gardener Vita Sackville-West. She snips a clipping of one plant and takes it over to the other plant to see how well they go together.

## Patio Plant Pockets

Need a home for plants that like to grow in tight spots? If you're building a patio, leave a few planting holes here and there in the overall surface. Or how about setting your pavers, stone, or tile in sand instead of concrete to accommodate plants that love to grow in cracks, especially reseeders.

Ann Bauer of Palos Verdes Estates, California, has a tile patio that has a few tiles missing here and there—on purpose. She loves the little holes for planting creeping herbs and other plants that like it tight.

And sometimes, when a plant has reseeded itself in a crack, she pops out the tile to give it a little more room to sprawl. "And when the plant dies, if it looks bad, we just put the tile back in again," Bauer says.

*Pop a paver or two to create charming planting pockets in your patio.*

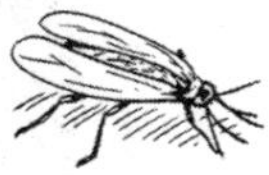

# Gnats

Gnats are, in a word, annoying. Not dangerous, not destructive, not particularly painful. (Although some varieties do bite, and if you've ever had a gnat in your eye, you know how uncomfortable that is!) If it weren't for gnats, summer evenings would be the perfect time to garden or relax outside. But a cloud of gnats—sometimes called midges or no-see-ums—can send you fleeing indoors in an effort to keep the tiny creatures out of your eyes, nose, mouth, and ears. But don't try to take out these tiny torturers with a chemical bug spray; we can help you reclaim the night the herbal way.

## Give Gnats a Pinch

If you grow herbs in your garden, a quick-and-easy gnat repellent may be right at your fingertips. Betzy Bancroft, an herbalist living in Port Murray, New Jersey, says she simply pinches off some peppermint or basil leaves and rubs them on her exposed skin to help repel insects. But be careful if you have sensitive skin, she warns. Test these herbs on a small area, wait at least 15 minutes, and watch for signs of irritation. If no such signs appear, pinch away!

*Rub freshly picked peppermint leaves on your skin and say good-bye to gnats.*

## Gno More Gnats!

According to Mindy Green, director of education at the Herb Research Foundation in Boulder, Colorado, and co-author of *Aromatherapy: A*

**Solutions at a Glance**

**PROBLEM:** When you're in your yard or maybe even your home, you spend most of your energy swatting tiny bugs away from your face and your ears.

**CULPRIT:** Gnats

**SOLVE IT!** Gnats like standing water and moist places and are attracted to lights, so reduce sources of standing water, and position outdoor lighting away from air-conditioner units or windows where gnats may be able to enter your home.

*Complete Guide to the Healing Art*, you can make your own natural bug repellent by using some common essential oils.

Combine 1 ounce of carrier oil (a vegetable oil like canola will do) with 4 drops of cedar, 2 drops of eucalyptus, 4 drops of lavender, 2 drops of orange, 1 drop of peppermint, and 2 drops of rosemary. (*Note:* Orange oil heightens sun sensitivity, so if you'll be using this repellent during the day, leave the orange out.) Smooth the mixture on the exposed skin of anyone age 5 or older.

Do a patch test before you apply this concoction (and don't attempt to use it if you have a known allergy to any of the ingredients). Rub a small amount on the inside of your forearm and watch it for 15 minutes to see if you have an allergic reaction.

## Fish Food

The larval stage of gnats is aquatic and is actually an important food item for fish. If you have a water garden in your home landscape, stock it with sturdy goldfish and these brightly colored beauties will get rid of gnat larvae for you. (A good rule of thumb is to plan for one fish for every 2 or 3 square feet of surface.)

# Groundcover Problems

Groundcovers are supposed to solve problems, not cause them, right? After all, a groundcover can turn a hard-to-mow slope into a beautiful flowering bank. It can replace the lawn you're tired of mowing every weekend. And it can cloak the soil under your shade trees where grass won't grow. But if you choose the *wrong* groundcover, you can end up with more problems than you started with. Whether you've already learned that the hard way, or you're about to choose and plant a groundcover and want to get it right the first time, expert help is close at hand.

### Natives to the Rescue

In the last big rainstorm, your hillside got an itch to travel and took the groundcover with it, much to your dismay. That's not uncommon, especially on sites where developers' bulldozers scraped the plate clean before the houses went up. The solution: Plant a groundcover that grabs the soil—a job at which native plants excel, says Danielle Green, who gardens with native species in Chicago. "Plants that grow on stream banks, on steep hillsides, or in wind-swept areas tend to have fine, dense, and often very deep root systems, and that's what it takes to control erosion." Her suggestion: Replant your slope with deep-rooted trees, shrubs, flowering perennials, or grasses native to your area and your terrain. (See page 344 for sources of native plants.)

*When you need to cover a hillside, choose plants with strong roots. Turf grass can't perform half as well as native grasses.*

## INVASION OF THE GROUND SNATCHERS

There's often a fine line between a plant that will neatly carpet that awkward spot by the mailbox and one that will turn into a force worthy of the D-Day invasion. Says Jack Poff, alpine plants curator at the Berry Botanic Garden in Portland, Oregon, "The very thing that makes a plant a good groundcover—its ability to spread quickly—can also make it a menace." So how do you get the curative qualities of a groundcover without the nasty side effects? Here are a few good prescriptions:

- Beware of plants that spread by underground stems called rhizomes, such as *Anemone nemerosa*, says Poff. Some very choice groundcovers do produce rhizomes, "but you have to be careful where you put them. They're much harder to control than plants that increase by above-ground means. Make sure you know what you have before you plant it."
- Master Gardener Judy Wong of Menlo Park, California, takes an aggressive approach to overly energetic groundcovers. "I put two kinds next to each other and let 'em duke it out," she says. "It seems to keep them both under control."
- For Marilyn Dube, owner of Natural Design Plants in Portland, Oregon, the key to curtailing a groundcover's wayward ways is simple: "Put it where it isn't happiest." For instance, she says, "Sweet woodruff will tolerate anything from dense shade to full sun, but its home of homes is a moist site in morning sun. If you put it there it will take over everything. If you plant it in dry shade it will still thrive, but it will be more likely to stay within bounds."

## BYE-BYE BACKACHE

If you have a big lawn, replacing some of it with groundcover will save a lot of hassle in the long run. But when you set out to remove turf by hand so you can plant groundcover, even a tiny area of grass looks as big as a golf course. Betsy Becker, horticulturist and propagator at the Berry Botanic Garden in Portland, Oregon, offers this easy alternative to cutting sod by hand:

1. In late summer, cover the grass with a layer of newspapers at least 1 inch thick. Water thoroughly and keep the papers moist enough so they don't blow away. (If winds are fierce where you live, add rocks at strategic spots.)
2. In the fall, spread 6 to 12 inches of leaves across the papers.
3. Let it all decompose through the winter. In the spring, add a foot or so of good soil (Becker uses a sandy loam, sold in many nurseries as three-way planting mix). Then just set in your plants.

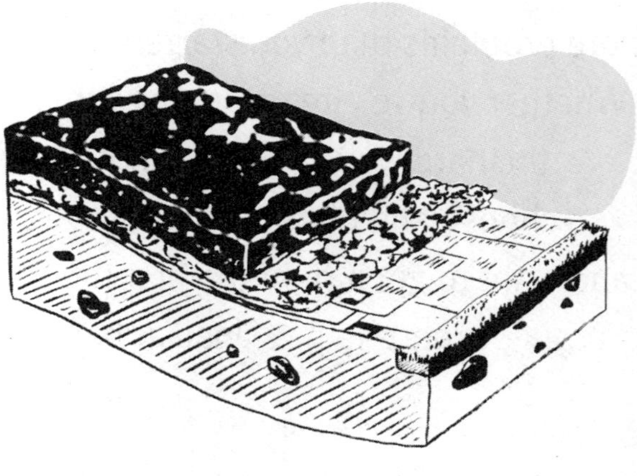

*GETTING RID OF LAWN TAKES ABOUT 6 MONTHS USING THE NEWSPAPER METHOD, BUT IT'S NOT NEARLY AS DIFFICULT AS CUTTING SOD AND DIGGING THE SOIL UNDERNEATH.*

## Cure for Baldness

If you're starting to see bare ground where there used to be a healthy planting of groundcovers, it's time to take action. Here are some possible causes and cures:

**TOO LITTLE LIGHT.** If you planted a sun-worshiping groundcover several years ago, and since then nearby trees have grown bigger, or a house has been built next door, chances are the shade they spread is your problem. The solution: Limb up the surrounding trees to let in more light, or dig up your site and plant a shade lover like bugleweed (*Ajuga* spp.) or sweet woodruff (*Galium odoratum*).

**TIME FOR A HAIRCUT.** Many groundcover plants—especially herbs—need shearing now and then. Give your blanket of greenery a pass with the lawn mower, and set the blade at about 2 inches. You'll encourage the groundcover to grow fuller and fill in those bare spots.

**TUCKERED OUT.** If your groundcover has been in place for several years and nothing in its environment has changed, the plants may be feeling the need for more nourishment. To get them off and running again, remove any dead plants and dig rotted manure or compost into the bare spots. They'll soon disappear under new growth.

## Proper Soil Prep

When you're trying to grow a good groundcover, thorough soil preparation is essential, especially in difficult sites. Plants will take off and grow faster if you give them a head start, and you'll have less competition from weeds. (If you haven't had your soil tested, consider it; you'll learn a lot about its condition.) Before you plant perennial groundcovers, spread 2 to 3 inches of compost over the area and dig it into the soil. The organic matter and nutrients the compost provides will give your planting a boost.

After planting, cover the soil between plants with a fine mulch like shredded leaves to protect the soil and also to suppress weeds while the groundcover plants establish themselves.

# Groundhog Problems

Woodchucks, whistle pigs, groundhogs—whatever you call them, these oversize rodents can do a number on your garden. Their dens are a menace to livestock and machinery (and people, as anyone who has inadvertently stepped in a hidden groundhog hole can attest). Groundhogs hibernate in the winter, but they wake up hungry. They also eat heavily in the fall to store up fat for their long snooze. In between, well, they eat more. Here are some ways to encourage them to do their dining elsewhere.

## Hound Groundhogs out of the Garden

One way to defeat groundhogs is to "Get a dog," says market gardener Tony Ricci from Three Springs, Pennsylvania. The dog doesn't have to be a Jack Russell terrier (renowned for its groundhog-hunting prowess). It doesn't even have to be a large dog. A minimutt, Lily, patrols Ricci's farm. She isn't big enough to kill a groundhog, but she chases the rodents and barks at them. "She worries them to death," Ricci says. "Either that or they get tired of hearing her and move on."

## Make 'Em Think You Have a Dog

If a canine companion isn't an option, borrow the essence of someone else's. Give an old rug, towel, or piece of carpet to a friend to use as bedding for his dog. Then transfer the dog-scented material to your garden. Loan bedding to several dog-owning friends, and rotate the scraps often to keep the scent fresh and varied. The groundhogs will think you have a kennel full of canines.

## Kitty Can Help, Too—Litter-ally

Got an indoor cat? Empty the litter box into the groundhog's entrance hole. The rodent will clear away the cat box contents for a while, but persistence pays off. Eventually, the scent of used kitty litter discourages even the toughest groundhog.

When the groundhog departs, fill up the entrance hole and all the exit holes with rocks or soil to keep other animals from moving in. If you aren't sure where all the exit holes are, toss a few Fourth of July smoke bombs into the entrance hole and seal it tightly with a clump of sod. Wait a few minutes, then look around to see where smoke is rising from the ground.

## En Garde! Fence Them Out

Although fences are effective against groundhogs, the best are partly buried below ground to foil the burrowing animals. For this, a permanent fence of welded wire works best because it won't rust out as quickly as chicken wire or woven-wire fencing. Here's how to install it:

1. Dig a trench all the way around your garden, about 24 inches deep.
2. Install metal T-stakes at each corner and at least every 8 feet on the sides.
3. Attach a 6-foot-high piece of welded-wire fence to the T-stakes. Bury 2 feet of the fence below ground in the trench you've dug, and bend the top foot over to form a baffle.
4. To disguise the fence in the spring, plant daffodils and Siberian squills (*Scilla siberica*) in the trench before you fill it in.

*Fence groundhogs out below ground, as well as above.*

## Keep Your Crops under Wraps

If other vegetation is around for groundhogs to eat, simply covering vulnerable garden crops can sometimes be enough to prevent damage. "I put floating row covers over the things they like, and usually they get discouraged," says market gardener Sylvia Ehrhardt, whose Knoxville, Maryland, farm is surrounded by woods.

*Discourage groundhogs from dining in your garden with over-the-top fencing.*

Floating row covers are available in rolls of 25 feet or more. Anchor one to the ground with boards, bricks, or sandbags, instead of burying the edges with soil. The row cover will last longer, and you'll be able to remove and replace it more easily.

Chicken-wire fence or plastic netting installed over wire hoops is also an effective groundhog deterrent. Use 6-inch pieces of heavy 9-mil wire, bent into U-shapes, to pin the fence or netting to the ground and prevent groundhogs from nosing underneath. For extra protection, use bloodmeal as a repellent. Put a tablespoon or so in a margarine container or yogurt cup, add a little water and a rock for weight, and place it among the vegetables to discourage the pests.

## No Place to Hide

If you want to control groundhogs on your property, thinking like a groundhog will help. They'd rather take a long detour through a meadow than cross a mowed lawn, and they dart for cover when discovered in the garden. "Animals don't like to be in the open," says market gardener Tony Ricci of Three Springs, Pennsylvania. "So don't put veggies in an area that backs up to the woods or is surrounded by tall weeds."

Groundhogs love to burrow under woodpiles, mulch piles, and hay stacks. If possible, move these piles around every year to keep them from becoming a permanent shelter for groundhogs or other animal pests. Even a slight dip in the ground provides a place for animals to lie low and escape notice. So if you have holes and dips near the garden, fill 'em up to discourage the pests.

## Easy Movable Fencing

If you just haven't had the time to install permanent fencing to keep out groundhogs, here's another alternative—a temporary, portable fence to protect individual beds or crops from those munching varmints. Here's what you'll need to do:

Cut several 4- or 5-foot lengths of 1-inch-mesh chicken wire.

Attach a metal or fiberglass post to each end of each chicken-wire panel. Allow an extra foot or so of the post to extend past the bottom of the fencing, so that the posts can be pushed into the ground.

Use the panels to surround susceptible crops such as young broccoli or lettuce plants. Just be sure to put the fence up before the groundhogs start nibbling on your tender plants. When you don't need the fence anymore, take the panels down, and store them flat.

# Herb Garden Problems

Herbs rank among the garden's most trouble-free plants. Still, growing them isn't without its challenges. If you've discovered that already—or if you've been seduced by the magic of herbs and want to start your garden on the right foot—read on as some long-time herbalists share their secrets for dealing with aphids, whiteflies, hardpan, powdery mildew, poor drainage, and more.

## Keeping Mint in Check

If you're singin' the "Mint Strangulation" blues because your herb garden is now nothing but mint, here's a workable solution to growing mint in harmony with other herbs, from Linda D. Harris of Fulton, Kentucky. "Use an old, deep, 5-gallon bucket with the handle removed. Drill 8 to 10 ¼-inch holes in the bottom (or punch them in using a large-bore screwdriver). Put a layer of gravel in the bottom of the bucket. Dig out your mint, then plant it in the bucket. Dig a large hole in your garden, set the bucket down in the hole, and fill in soil around it. Keep the lip of the bucket just a little bit above the soil surface," says Harris.

The bucket walls will prevent mint stolons from spreading. (For a while, mint will keep sprouting from any underground pieces you missed when you dug up the plant. Pull those up and toss them—or use them to make iced tea!) Every few years, it's a good idea to lift and divide the mint in the bucket to keep it healthy and full. Give some away (along with the bucket idea) to a friend. This method of taming invasive plants also works well for bee balm (*Monarda* spp.), catnip *(Nepeta cataria)*, and other plants that are too rampant for your garden taste.

## Hot Pepper Helper

You say something's devouring your herbs and there's nary a pest in sight? When Savannah, Georgia, gardener Ashby Angell found herself in that predicament recently, she gave her plants a spritz of a special hot sauce. Here's how she makes it:

Boil together a handful of hot peppers and a handful of southernwood in a half gallon of water. Let the mixture cool, then strain it through a piece of cheesecloth. After straining, add a few drops of dishwashing liquid, and then spray or pour the mixture on your herbs.

## Pest Detective

*The flavors and aromas that attract us to herbs seem repugnant to most insects. Indeed, some herbs are so abhorrent to multilegged creepers, crawlers, and fliers that you can use them as efficient insect repellents. So if your herb garden seems to be attracting pests, it's probably because conditions on the home front don't measure up to your plants' standards, such as too much or too little light or poor drainage. Whichever the reason, here are a few unwelcome visitors you might see and how you can cut their party time short.*

| Symptom | Cause | What to Do |
|---|---|---|
| Stunted or malformed leaves or stems coated with a clear, sticky substance | Aphids | Wash them off with a spray of water or rub them off between thumb and forefinger and squash them; spray with insectidical soap. |
| Chewed leaves or flowers (especially on members of the carrot family, such as angelica, chervil, and dill) | Caterpillars | Unless your whole crop is under attack, identify the critter before you do anything. It may be the larva of a butterfly whose presence will be well worth a little cosmetic damage. But if the invasion is too intense, pick the caterpillars off by hand and destroy them. |
| Stunted growth; leaves stippled yellow, curling or turning brown; sooty black substance on leaves or stems | Whiteflies | Use yellow sticky traps or insecticidal soap sprays, or spray plants with water, wiping them off if needed. If infestation is severe, dig up plants and destroy them. |

### What's the Problem?

If your herbs fall prey to a fungus disease—such as powdery mildew, rust, or root rot—you might be watering too much, says Menlo Park, California, herb gardener Judee Humburg. If you catch the problem when the plants are just turning yellow—a sure sign of overwatering—you can probably head off further trouble by simply easing up on the hose trigger. Most herbs, says Humburg, especially those of Mediterranean origin (such as thyme, lavender, rosemary, oregano, and marjoram) like their soil on the dry side. Her testing method: "Stick your finger in the ground 1 to 1½ inches. It should feel dry from the tip up."

### Raised Beds to the Rescue

Another way to help improve drainage for herbs is by planting them in raised beds. In Juneau, Alaska, where Natasha Zahn Pristas gardens, adding some height also helps the soil warm up more quickly in the spring. Here's how she builds her beds: "I dig down about a foot and a half to loosen the soil," she says. "Then I add edging about $1\frac{1}{2}$ feet high. Finally, I throw on commercial potting soil, peat moss, and either chicken or steer manure or mushroom compost and mix it all together." (*Note:* Remember to always use *rotted* manure on food crops.)

*RAISED BEDS HELP THE SOIL WARM UP FASTER IN SPRING, HELPING HERBS TO GET OFF TO A GOOD START AFTER A LONG, COLD WINTER.*

## Hardpan, Hit the Road

Hardpan equals poor drainage which equals poor herbs (and everything else you're trying to grow). Here's a simple method for getting better drainage and more oomph into the soil, from Jack Talerico, who gardens on Washington's Vashon Island. "What I do is essentially underground composting," he says. "I dig a hole as deep as I can reasonably go. Sometimes that's only a foot or so; sometimes it's 3 to 4 feet. Then I dump everything in and cover it up. I use the shallower holes for leaves and grass clippings, the deeper ones for substantial things like watermelon rind that take longer to decompose. I give it a couple of months to cook, then plant right on top."

## Too Darn Hot

Even heat-tolerant herbs give up the ghost in sweltering southern climes. Gardener Ashby Angell from Savannah, Georgia, has developed a handful of coping mechanisms that let her herbs take the humid heat almost in stride. Here are some of her secrets.

**GROW EVERYTHING IN RAISED BEDS.** "Raised beds improve not only drainage but also air circulation," she says. "That's crucial in preventing fungus diseases in a humid climate."

**ADD PLENTY OF MANURE AND COMPOST TO THE SOIL.** They help maintain a healthy nutrient balance and help prevent undue stress.

**PROVIDE SOME SHADE.** All herbs need shelter from 2 P.M. on, Angell says. Otherwise, "the late afternoon sun just wipes them out." Some plants need even more protection. Angell grows parsley and lemon balm (*Melissa officinalis*) in a bed permanently covered with shade cloth. And chives thrive under a lattice roof.

**ADJUST YOUR CALENDAR.** Some herbs won't survive a southern summer no matter how much you coddle them. "Chervil and coriander are winter plants here," Angell says.

*WHERE SUMMER HEAT IS INTENSE, LOTS OF HERBS PREFER LIFE IN THE SHADE, SUCH AS UNDER THIS LATTICE ROOF.*

## Getting a Good Start

One of the best ways to avoid trouble in the herb garden is to start out with healthy plants. Here are some points to keep in mind when shopping for herbs at a nursery.

**CHOOSE HERB PLANTS THAT LOOK HEALTHY AND VIGOROUS,** not stressed with brown, shriveled, or insect-damaged leaves. Check the undersides of leaves for any insect pests.

**TRY TO BUY YOUR HERBS FROM AN ORGANIC GROWER** so your herb seedlings will be free from pesticide residue.

**CHOOSE HERBS THAT HAVE WELL-DEVELOPED CROWNS AND ROOTS THAT FILL THE POT.** Gently dump the plant out into your hand so you can look at what's going on with its roots. If the roots go right to the bottom of the pot, it's a sign the plant has been growing for a year or so. If there's more soil than roots, it means the nursery has bought the plant as a "seed plug" in the early spring, potted it up, and is selling it a few months later. The top growth might be similar in size to the older plant but in 2 to 3 months the more mature plant will be much bigger and stronger.

*YOUR CLUE TO THE BEST PLANT CHOICE IS IN THE ROOTS, NOT THE FOLIAGE. FIND A LOCAL OR MAIL-ORDER NURSERY THAT GROWS ITS HERBS IN THE FIELD FOR A YEAR BEFORE SELLING THEM.*

## Keeping Flavor in the Bag

Bundles of drying herbs hanging from the rafters of a country kitchen might look picturesque, but they tend to lose color and flavor this way. If your herbs are lacking oomph, switch from that romantic but unsatisfactory technique to the practical paper bag system, says Patrick Rogers, a Master Gardener from Portland, Oregon.

*PROTECT HERBS WHILE THEY DRY BY SEALING THEM IN PAPER BAGS TO HELP THEM RETAIN COLOR AND FLAVOR.*

1. Cut the herbs early in the morning when their volatile oils are still fresh.
2. Gather them into bunches of 5 to 10 sprigs each. The bushier the herbs, the fewer sprigs you need per bundle.
3. Put each bundle stem-side up in a brown paper bag with the stems sticking out about 1 inch. Wrap a rubber band around bag and stems.
4. Tuck the bags away in any moisture-free space (a closet will do) and check them every week till they're dry.

# Houseplant Problems

One way to turn a house into more of a home is to add houseplants. After all, houseplants can give a room that extra oomph it needs to make it warm and inviting. And with tons of houseplants to choose from, you can even pick them to go with your decorating style. Maybe you have cactus for a Southwestern feel or African violets for a more Victorian look. No matter what kind of houseplants you have, though, they all may suffer from problems at one time or another, such as whiteflies, spider mites, lack of humidity, and pot-bound roots. So to keep your charges happy in their home, check out the following advice.

## Rx for Healthy Houseplants

How often have you had a houseplant start to head downhill, while you fight to keep it from dying? Instead of using energy to keep dying plants alive, head off problems *before* they start by focusing your energy on what you need to do to help healthy houseplants stay that way.

**BE CONSISTENT.** Once you figure out what a plant needs, deliver it consistently. But don't put all your plants on the same schedule. Each plant is unique. For example, some plants only need to be watered once a month (such as a cactus).

**CHECK FOR STRESS.** Although Penny Engel, a gardener from Jamaica Bay, New York, doesn't water all of her 100 houseplants every day, she examines each one daily for signs of stress, such as yellowed leaves. With so many plants, she can't allow a pest or disease to spread. If she sees a problem, she isolates the plant and treats it promptly, protecting the other plants.

**CUT THE CHLORINE.** Engel has municipal water, which is chlorinated and thus is harmful to plants. So she leaves uncovered old soda bottles full of water around the house. That way, the chlorine evaporates before she uses the water on her plants. Plus, the water is always room temperature (ice cold water can shock plant roots, and hot water can scald them), and as the water evaporates, it adds humidity to the air.

**GIVE THEM A SUMMER VACATION.** Every summer, Engel gives herself and her indoor

## Pest Detective

*Something's flitting around your houseplants or has made its home on the undersides of their leaves. Don't be so quick to pitch the plant; rather, match the symptoms to those in the following chart, and find out what's causing the problem and what you can do about it.*

| Symptom | Cause | What to Do |
|---|---|---|
| Honeydew on plant leaves; white, waxy insects on undersides of leaves | Mealybugs | Wash plant with soapy water (2 teaspoons of dishwashing soap, not detergent, to 1 gallon of water). A jet of clean water may knock insects off the plant, or remove them with tweezers or a toothpick. You can also use rubbing alcohol on a swab. Dip the swab into the alcohol, and gently touch the insect to remove it. Be careful not to spread alcohol on the plant tissue because you may injure the plant. |
| Very tiny waxy or hard shells on plants | Scale | Wash plant with soapy water (2 teaspoons of dishwashing soap, not detergent, to 1 gallon of water). A jet of clean water may knock insects off the plant, or remove scale with tweezers or a toothpick. You can also use rubbing alcohol on a swab. Dip the swab into the alcohol, and gently touch the insect to remove it. Be careful not to spread alcohol on the plant tissue because you may injure the plant. |
| Slow-moving dots on the undersides of leaves; you may be able to see webbing if you hold the plant up to light. | Spider mites | Wash with soapy water; a jet of water will knock mites off plant. |
| Tiny white flies flitting around your plants; plants may send up white "clouds" when disturbed | Whiteflies | Wash plants, including tops and undersides of leaves, with soapy water and a soft brush. Use 2 teaspoons of a dishwashing soap, not detergent, to 1 gallon of water. A strong jet of water may also knock insects off. |

garden a vacation by putting all her houseplants outside. She tries to mimic their natural habitat when she does, by putting some in the shade, some in the sun, and some in the screened porch. The rain and the warm, moist breezes off Jamaica Bay keep the plants watered and happy, and she gets a break to go to the beach. Plants thrive outside because the light conditions in the shadiest place outdoors are better than the brightest place in the house. If you give your houseplants a break outside during warm weather, by the end of the summer they'll have a postvacation glow, looking strong and healthy. (Engel suggests bringing the plants back indoors at least 3 weeks before you turn on the heat. This gives the plants a chance to get acclimated to the decreased light and dry air in the house before they're assaulted by central heat.)

**CLEAN OUT THE PESTS.** Many of you may fear your plants will be invaded by insects if you put them outside. Engel has a solution for this, too. Before you bring the plants in the house, add a squirt of liquid detergent to a full watering can. Water everything thoroughly. Engel has been doing this for 40 years and hasn't had an insect problem yet. You also might want to wash the leaves, including their undersides, with soap and water.

*IF YOUR WATER CONTAINS CHLORINE, FILL EMPTY CONTAINERS, SUCH AS SODA BOTTLES, LEAVE THE TOPS OFF, AND PLACE THEM AROUND YOUR HOME. THE CHLORINE WILL EVAPORATE, ALLOWING YOU TO GIVE YOUR HOUSEPLANTS A CHLORINE-FREE DRINK.*

## HOME ALONE

How do you keep your houseplants from drying out if you're going to be away from home for a while? Cross your fingers and hope they don't get overly thirsty? Ask a friend to come over for watering duty? Try to teach the dog to do it? Gardeners Harold and Penny Engel of Jamaica Bay, New York, found an easy solution to the problem.

*KEEP YOUR HOUSEPLANTS HYDRATED WHILE YOU'RE ON VACATION BY PUTTING THEM ALL IN A SUNNY ROOM, WATERING THOROUGHLY, AND THEN HANGING A HEAVY SHEET OF PLASTIC ACROSS THE DOORWAY TO SEAL IN HUMIDITY.*

They move all their plants into the sunroom, water everything thoroughly, and turn the heat down. Then they hang a heavy (3-mil) sheet of plastic across the entrance to the room (they attach the plastic to the doorway with duct tape). The plastic seals in the humidity. And, the Engels say the plants like being crowded together; they collectively add humidity to one another. The Engels always do this before they head off on vacation. They haven't lost a plant yet in all the years they've done this.

## Solutions at a Glance

**Problem:** Long and leggy plants
**Culprit:** Winter—specifically, its decreased light and lack of humidity
**Solve It!** Bring the plant closer to a natural light source. Raise the humidity by putting the pot in a tray of pebbles and water.

---

**Problem:** Roots are potbound.
**Culprit:** Pot too small for plant
**Solve It!** Take the plant out of the pot. Using a knife, score the roots so they're not circling the plant—then repot the plant in a bigger container. If you don't have a larger container, trim the roots (using a sharp pair of scissors) after scoring until the rootball will fit comfortably back into the pot. (You might also want to trim the foliage to keep the top and bottom of the plant in balance.) Wash the pot and add fresh soil before replanting.

### Feline-Digging Discouragement

If you have a cat and also have large houseplants, you know that the two don't always mix. That's because cats love to dig in the soil. Linda D. Harris of Fulton, Kentucky, thwarts her cats' effort to use houseplants as a litter box by filling the area between the soil surface and the top of the container with whatever assortment of rocks or shells she has collected. Rocks can be of any shape or color, and about 3 to 6 inches in size (larger is better). Cats can't move the rocks, the rocks make a great mulch, and the weight of the rocks lends stability to tall foliage plants. Good sources for rocks include your garden, a quarry, a landscaper, or a farmer's field.

# Japanese Beetles

At the worst possible time—just as roses approach perfection, raspberries ripen, and hollyhocks stand tall—hoards of ½-inch-long beetles appear out of nowhere and munch their way through your garden and landscape. Roses, raspberries, hollyhocks, and grapes are all on the list of favorite Japanese beetle foods, but these voracious pests will eat almost any plant they land on. The shiny copper beetles with green and white markings would be beautiful if they weren't so ravenous. Indeed, the only good thing about Japanese beetles is that they're rarely seen west of the Mississippi River.

In spite of their numbers and the damage they do, Japanese beetles are controllable. Here are a few ways to do it, ranging from engaging in grub warfare to protecting preferred plants.

## Engaging in Grub Warfare

Two biological weapons can turn Japanese beetle larvae to mush. If you have terrible problems with Japanese beetles, you can use both of these at the same time.

**MILKY SPORE DISEASE** is a blend of two naturally occurring bacteria that make the grubs get sick and die. Milky spore takes a couple of years to become established in the soil, but then it persists for many seasons. It's sold as a powder; you apply it by placing spoonfuls of the powder on the surface of your grass just before a rain. Any time that the ground isn't frozen is a good time to inoculate your lawn with milky spore.

**BENEFICIAL NEMATODES** are another natural enemy of beetle grubs, but you'll need to apply them at just the right time, which is in mid- to late spring when the soil is warm enough to be hospitable to beneficial nematodes *and* when the grubs are close to the soil's surface. You apply beneficial nematodes by first mixing them with water and then spraying the solution on your lawn. Be sure to reapply every year as needed, to control Japanese beetle grubs—as well as cutworms, June beetles, and other pests that spend their larval stage in the soil.

## Protecting Preferred Plants

Japanese beetles adore roses, and they're crazy for grapes and a dozen other plants, too. While the adults are feeding, take steps to protect the plants they like the most. If you can limit the damage they cause, your plants can usually recover and grow more leaves later in the season when the beetles' food orgy has ended.

So try this trick that Eileen Squitiro in New Milton, West Virginia, uses. "Hot pepper spray works great!" Squitiro says. "I simply boil up a handful of dried cayennes and jalapeños in a gallon of water (make sure you cover the pan because the steam can make your eyes tear) and then strain and spray. Pepper spray has kept Japanese beetles off my roses and grapevines better than anything else I've ever tried. After rain it has to be reapplied, and you should be careful not to breathe the spray—it will bring tears to your eyes."

*Boil up a pot of peppers to make your own Japanese beetle spray.*

## The Japanese Beetle Death Drop

Everybody who has 'em hand-picks Japanese beetles one way or another, but you'll get more beetles if you take advantage of their tendency to drop from leaves or blossoms when they're disturbed. Don't try to gather them in midday when they usually fly off instead of dropping down. Hunt them in the morning or evening instead.

*Japanese beetles can't swim—so get rid of them the easy way by shaking them into a bowl full of soapy water.*

"I use a broad bowl filled with water with some soap added to break the surface tension," says Jenny Estes, a Master Gardener in Guntersville, Alabama. "Early in the morning, I go around and hold the bowl under branches with beetles on them, shake gently, and they just drop right in and drown." In addition to roses, Estes battles the beetles on her crape myrtles—a favorite flowering shrub in the South. "I keep my crape myrtles pruned low to make it easier to get the beetles," she says.

# Lawn Problems

If you believed everything you saw on TV, you'd think you needed to resort to chemical fertilizers, insecticides, or herbicides to evoke the envy of your turf-crazy neighbors. True, fertilization, pest insects, and weeds are lawn challenges, but that doesn't mean you have to douse your yard with chemicals. Instead, try earth-safe solutions—such as feeding your lawn less—and you'll have terrific turf.

## Rx for a Weed-Free Lawn

Here are three easy, organic approaches that can help you win the fight against weeds.

**FEED YOUR GRASS WHEN IT STARTS TO GROW.** Apply a slow-release organic fertilizer to your lawn just as robust new growth begins—early spring for bluegrass, early summer for warm-season grasses, and fall for turf-type fescues.

**MOW YOUR GRASS HIGH.** Set the blade of your mower at its highest, and leave it there. Tall blades of grass have more surface area exposed to the sun, which will help them produce greater root growth. And that will leave you with healthier grass that's better able to outcompete weeds.

**USE HAND-TO-HAND COMBAT.** Just get out there with a fishtail weeder and dig those weeds out, roots and all.

## Bargain-Basement Lawn Food

If your lawn has champagne taste and a beer budget, here are some inexpensive and natural fertilizers that may satisfy it. Look for them in 50- to 100-pound bags at local farm supply stores.

| *Fertilizer Type* | *NPK Ratio* | *Usage Guidelines* |
|---|---|---|
| Alfalfa meal | 5-1-2 | 35 lb. per 1,000 sq. ft. |
| Cottonseed meal | 6-2-1 | 25 lb. per 1,000 sq. ft. |
| Fish meal | 5-3-3 | 20 lb. per 1,000 sq. ft. |
| Soybean meal | 7-0.5-2.3 | 25 lb. per 1,000 sq. ft. |

## Managing Moles

Moles can take out an otherwise-healthy lawn by cutting off grass roots while they tunnel around in search of earthworms, grubs, and other protein-rich tidbits. Here are some tips on keeping your yard looking mole-free.

## Solutions at a Glance

**Problem:** Your grass is growing faster than normal, meaning you have to mow a lot.

**Culprit:** Chemical fertilizers

**Solution:** A no-brainer—switch to organic fertilizers. Organic fertilizers release their nutrients slowly, giving your lawn a long, luscious feast, meaning it won't grow so fast that it's impossible to keep up with the mowing.

At the first sign of mole activity, go out and flatten their tunnels by walking over them. This might give them the message to build their trails in someone else's yard.

When you identify a tunnel route that's used over and over again, open a hole in the tunnel with a stick and pour in a castor oil–based mole repellent. You can buy MoleMed (made from castor oil, soap, and water) and mix according to label directions to either pour down the tunnels or spray on the grass. Or, you can make your own brew by mixing together 1 cup of water, 3 ounces of castor oil, and 4 tablespoons of dishwashing liquid. Mix 2 tablespoons of this concentrate with 1 gallon of water before sloshing it into your mole holes.

Minimize the evidence of mole damage by repairing damaged spots with fresh seed or patches of sod taken from the edges of your lawn.

*LET MOLES KNOW THEY'RE NOT WELCOME BY POURING A CASTOR OIL–BASED REPELLENT INTO THEIR TUNNELS.*

## Snubbing Grubs

Probably the worst (and certainly the ugliest) lawn pests that you'll encounter are insect larvae that dig a diet heavy on grass roots. The worst of these are beetle larvae—the white grubs usually found 1 to 2 inches below the surface of your lawn. And though you don't need to launch a full-scale war on just a few grubs, you may find that you have so many that they're eating the feet right off your grass. If that's the case, you can get them under control by using milky spore disease or beneficial nematodes. See page 97 for more information on these solutions.

## No Spots from Spot

If you have a dog, you already know that his urine can easily burn yellow spots into a lawn—especially if he uses the same place over and over again. But try this resourceful tip and you'll regain your lush lawn in about 3 weeks.

"Before I trained my golden retriever to go in his small patch of gravel, I used this simple solution," reports Mike Holman of Brantford, Ontario. "I mixed a small (8-ounce, or 227-gram) box of baking soda into a full watering can of water (about 1 gallon) and walked around the yard saturating the dog spots every few days. The solution looks like watery milk, and you have to pour it shortly after it's mixed or the baking soda will settle in the bottom. The baking soda takes the acidity out of the soil where the urine is and helps the turf green up again. It does take a little time, but at least it's nontoxic to you and Rover, and it's cheap."

*A MIXTURE OF BAKING SODA AND WATER IS A NONTOXIC WAY OF GETTING RID OF THE SPOTS FROM SPOT.*

## Hair Plugs for Lawns

To make postweeding repairs to her large lawn in Moreno Valley, California, Tamara Utens keeps up to five flats of homemade fescue sod growing at any given time.

"I take the plastic flats that many plants come packed in, and I line them with foil, leaving one side of the flat with a low lip of foil so excess water can drain away. I fill them with ordinary soil from the garden and then sprinkle grass seed on top." Utens says she started out using potting soil, then switched to garden soil after she ran out one day. "With regular soil, there's less transition stress when the sod gets planted," she says. "I keep the flats near my patio door so I can wet them down twice a day. A thick turf grows in a few weeks, which I can peel out and place whole or in pieces into bare spots."

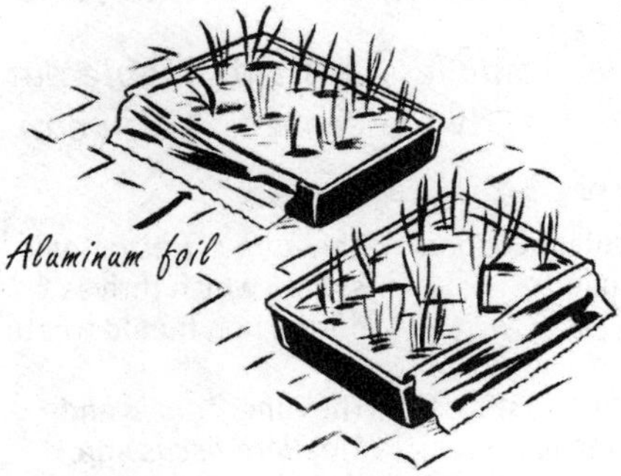


*GROWING YOUR OWN TURF IN PLASTIC FLATS MEANS YOU'LL ALWAYS HAVE SOME SOD TO REPLACE BARE PATCHES IN YOUR LAWN.*

## Repairing Rips and Ruts

Accidents happen everywhere, and lawns are no exception. Maybe a shrub or tree had to go, or perhaps you missed your driveway on a dark and muddy night and left a nice tire rut in your turf. Never fear, though—here are the secrets to seamless patching.

Repairs are easy if your lawn is bluegrass, improved tall fescue, or a cool-season blend that includes these two species along with a little perennial ryegrass. Simply fill in the spot with soil and rake it level, and plant seed that matches the rest of your yard. To allow for natural compaction, the freshly prepared soil should sit about $1/2$ inch higher than the surrounding soil before planting.

The fix isn't quite as easy with vegetatively propagated zoysiagrass or bermudagrass. Instead of patching with purchased sod that may be slightly different in terms of color, size, and vigor, take plugs from the edges of your

## Pest Detective

*Notice some less-than-desirable patches or spots turning up on your lawn? You might have a lawn disease that you can resolve by fine-tuning your fertilizer habits.*

| Symptom | Cause | What to Do |
|---|---|---|
| Large, circular sections of the lawn look scorched | The fungus *Rhizoctonia solani*, which thrives during hot, humid weather | Stop overwatering and overfertilizing, and rake out dead growth. |
| Brown circular patches just a few inches across | The fungi *Lanzia* and *Moellerodiscus* spp. (formerly *Sclerotinia homeocarpa*) | Dollar spot, as this disease is known, is most serious in lawns that need food. So give your lawn a moderate fertilizer followed by deep watering, done early in the day so the grass is dry by nightfall. Rake up infected grass clippings to reduce the spread of disease. |
| Lots of purple spots on grass blades that make patches look like they have melted | Melting out or leaf blotch (formerly *Helminthosporium* fungus, now thought to be several fungi, including *Drechslera, Bipolaris,* and *Exserohilum*) | Adding fertilizer that provides both nitrogen and potassium can help as can *not* watering your lawn after dark. (Just don't get carried away feeding your lawn because too much fertilizer can encourage the fungus that causes this disease in the first place. When using any type of lawn fertilizer, always use a drop spreader, and don't exceed the application rates given on the fertilizer label.) |

lawn and plant them close together where you need new grass. Cut out plugs with a sharp knife, making sure the roots are still attached. After transplanting, fill the crevices between the plugs with a mixture of sand and soil to help the plugs grow together quickly.

### Come Over to Clover

Beef up your lawn with Dutch white clover. It has a lot going for it—it fixes enough nitrogen from the air to share with grass, it produces loads of bee-pleasing flowers, and it even puts up with a fair amount of foot traffic.

*Add Dutch white clover to your lawn by sowing seeds in fall or scattering them in very early spring.*

# Lettuce Problems

Although lettuce is one of the most reliable spring garden crops, this leafy green loves the cool temperatures of fall, too. Growing the goods for great salads is trickier in summer (you have to fool the greens into thinking it's still spring), but it's doable. Lettuce is pretty easy to grow, but you do need to watch out for slugs so they don't make dinner of your lettuce before you do. Here are some "slug beaters" as well as other tips for growing great lettuce.

## Pace Yourself

To get the most lettuce from your plantings, don't plant it all at once. Mature lettuce only holds a week or two in the garden before bolting to seed or getting bitter, so plant small quantities every couple of weeks.

## Heat-Beating Helpers

A cooling shower in the middle of a hot summer day is just the ticket for people—and for lettuce, too. Market gardener Hui Newcomb uses micro-sprinklers to put out a fine mist on the summer lettuce growing on her Vienna, Virginia, farm. You can create the same effect with a sprinkler attached to a timer. Shower the lettuce from 12 noon until 2 P.M. when the sun is at its most intense.

A bit of shade helps, too. Greenhouse operators put shade cloth over their houses to cool them in the summer. You can apply the same principle to your lettuce patch with nylon netting or cast-off lace curtains stretched over wire hoops and fastened with clothespins. Or plant the summer crop under an overhang or next to a building or shrub that blocks the hot afternoon sun. Lettuce grows well with half-day sunshine.

*Summertime, but the lettuce living is easy—with a little shade.*

## Solutions at a Glance

**Problem:** Something's eating your lettuce.

**Culprit:** Slugs

**Solve It!** Make the slugs uncomfortable (and do a little recycling at the same time) by mulching with excelsior strips or the shredded computer paper commonly used as packing material. The slugs will detour to avoid dying of a thousand paper cuts. Got a sweet gum tree or know someone who does? Sweet gum seedpods look like prickly balls. Surround your lettuce with a layer of those and send the slugs elsewhere.

---

**Problem:** Your lettuce has yellows, a disease that makes lettuce leaves deformed and sickly looking.

**Culprit:** Leafhoppers

**Solve It!** Gum up their plans by coating disposable plastic picnic cups (preferably yellow ones) with Tangle-Trap or Vaseline and tacking them upside down to short stakes in the lettuce patch.

---

**Problem:** The lettuce looks great from the top, but the leaves are turning brown and slimy at the base.

**Culprit:** Bottom rot

**Solve It!** Bottom rot is caused by fungus, and it's most common in warm, humid conditions. If your summers are hot and humid, give lettuce extra space (at least 8 inches between plants), and grow romaine from late spring through summer. Lettuce that grows upright is less susceptible to bottom rot.

---

**Problem:** Less than half of the seed you planted germinated.

**Culprit:** Warm storage temperatures

**Solution:** Store leftover lettuce seed in the refrigerator during June, July, and August. Keeping the seed cool during these hot months will help improve its germination rate.

## Lettuce Varieties to Match the Season

*How do you keep the lettuce coming from the balmy days of spring until well past fall's first frosts? "Careful variety selection allows for a crop from spring through fall," says Melanie DeVault of Pheasant Hill Farm in Emmaus, Pennsylvania. Tender leaf and Bibb lettuces are the first to bolt when the weather gets hot, and romaines and summer Batavians, like 'Sierra' and 'Nevada', hang in there longer. Letttuce doesn't need long days of sunshine, so if you live where the winters aren't too severe—or are willing to provide some protection—some lettuces produce even while the snow flies.*

| Spring | Summer | Fall | Winter |
|---|---|---|---|
| 'Black-Seeded Simpson', 'Tango', and 'Royal Oak' (green leaf); | 'Summertime' and 'Ithaca' (iceberg); | 'Freckles' (romaine); | 'Rouge d'Hiver' (red romaine); |
| 'SuperPrize', 'Red Oak Leaf', 'Red Sails', and 'Lolla Rossa' (red leaf); | 'Nevada', 'Sierra', and 'Santa Fe' (Batavian); | 'Bronze', 'Green Mignonette', and 'Tom Thumb' (baby Bibb); | 'Winter Density' and 'Selma Wisa' (Bibb) |
| 'Pirat' (red Bibb) | 'Buttercrunch', 'Bronze Arrow', and 'Red Deer Tongue' (Bibb); | 'Salad Bowl' and 'Waldemann's Dark Green' (green leaf); | |
| | 'Cimmaron' and 'Green Towers' (romaine); | 'Brunia' (red leaf); | |
| | 'Red Fire' (red leaf); 'Slobolt' (green leaf) | 'Merville de Quatre Saisons' (Bibb) | |

### Leftover Salad Mix

It's easy to overbuy lettuce seed when you need only a pinch for each planting. But then what do you do with all the extra seed? Hui Newcomb, a market gardener from Fairfax County, Virginia, mixes the seed together and sows it in late summer as a cut-and-come-again salad mix. Or, you could save the seed and use it for next year's summer sowings. Fresh lettuce seed is usually reluctant to germinate in warm soil; older seed germinates more readily when the thermometer soars.

# Mexican Bean Beetles

The black sheep of the lady beetle family, Mexican bean beetles can turn a bean patch into a scene of devastation worthy of a science fiction movie. Preventive strategies include keeping a clean garden in winter and growing fast-maturing bush beans, which usually produce before the beetles cause serious damage. But pole beans seldom escape damage from this pest. So cover your plants with floating row covers to help keep the beetles out. And make a habit of checking under a few leaves in search of eggs and larvae. Pinch off egg-bearing leaves, and squash the larvae with your fingers. You might also want to try some of the following remedies, such as horticultural oil.

### Try an Oily Treatment

For small outbreaks, try spraying the leaf undersides with light horticultural oil, which smothers the larvae. Be sure to mix the oil at the rate recommended on the label for summer use. (That's because bean leaves are especially susceptible to damage from oil sprays during hot weather.)

### Win with Wasps

If you have problems with Mexican bean beetles year after year, enlist the help of beneficial *Pediobius foveolatus* wasps in your garden. Called *pedios* by gardeners, these tiny parasitic wasps are a plague on pesky bean beetles. Wait until you see Mexican beetle larvae actively feeding on your beans to release the wasps. In recent experiments in gardens in Wisconsin and Washington, the wasps wiped out nearly every last larvae. And don't worry that the pedios will turn into a pest. Native to India, this tiny wasp seldom survives winter north of Zone 8.

### Clean Up after Your Beans

To reduce future problems with Mexican bean beetles, be sure to clean up promptly after your beans finish producing. Remove the remains of your bean crop from the garden, or dig it into the soil along with any remaining beetles, eggs, and larvae.

## Plant a Decoy

Mexican bean beetles and their hungry yellow larvae are almost guaranteed to show up when you plant beans in your garden. So try planting a trap crop of soybeans away from your other beans to lure these pests into an early exit. When the beetles flock to the preferred soybeans, pull up the plants and remove them–pests and all–from your garden.

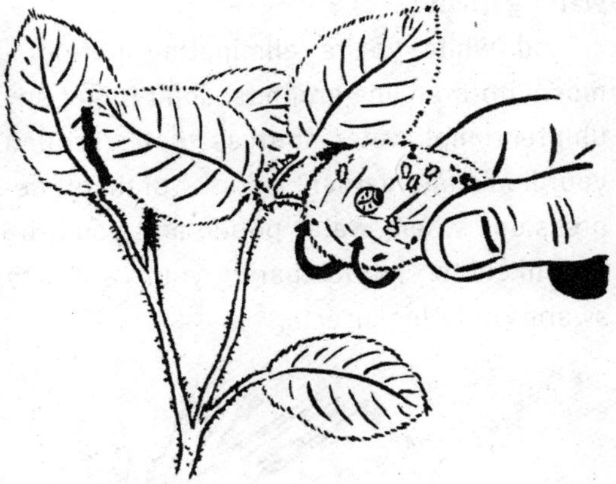

*Foil Mexican bean beetles by planting a trap crop of soybeans away from your other beans.*

## Know Thy Enemy

Knowing what Mexican bean beetles look like—as well as knowing their habits—can help you take the upper hand in keeping them under control.

The brownish beetles with eight black spots hide out in weeds and woods during the winter and flit about in spring until they find some beans. After feeding a bit, they lay clusters of orange-yellow eggs on the undersides of bean leaves. The eggs hatch in 1 to 2 weeks, and the slow-moving yellow larvae, shaped like blobs with soft points over their backs, quickly begin rasping away at the undersides of bean leaves. If left uncontrolled, the larvae will feed on the bean pods and stems after chewing away all but the veins from every bean leaf.

## Go for the Purple

Yellow wax beans seem to have been voted the bean of choice by this pest. If you have a bean beetle problem in your garden, you might want to try growing 'Royal Burgundy' or other purple-podded snap beans instead, which suffer less beetle damage than yellow wax beans.

# Mosquitoes

By the time you feel the bite and slap your arm, it's too late—you've been bitten by summer's perennial pest, the mosquito. The silent-but-deadly females need a bit of your blood so they can lay their eggs, but all you'll get out of the deal is an itchy red welt that could last for days. Take heart, though: We have some great tips to keep these thirsty flyers from bugging you all summer long!

## Get 'Em While They're Young

If you want to control mosquitoes, you've got to start at the beginning—their beginning, that is. Mosquito larvae need standing, undisturbed water to survive the first 2 weeks of their lives, so your mission is to make sure that the water in your yard isn't someplace that would make a great mosquito nursery.

You can keep your waters mosquito-unfriendly by doing something as simple as changing the water in your birdbaths often. Or, if you have a pond in your yard, you can add native fish or goldfish to its waters—the fish will enjoy snacking on the mosquitoes.

You might also try placing donut-shaped rings made out of BTI (*Bacillus thuringiensis* var. *israelensis*), which are available through garden-supply catalogs (see "Resources" on page 344), in your pond. These rings are also safe for use in water barrels, birdbaths, and water gardens.

And while you're eliminating potential mosquito-breeding grounds, don't forget any unintentional water sources that surround your home and garden. Fill in or drain off depressions where water pools, and you'll be less likely to end up sharing your yard with swarms of biting insects.

*Let mosquitoes know they're not welcome by placing BTI rings in your water gardens and ponds.*

## Lather Away Larvae

Banish mosquitoes from your rain barrels and buckets with a simple squirt of liquid dish soap. Use just enough soap to kill any larvae that hatch in your rain-collecting containers, but too little to do any harm to the plants that'll be soaking up that water. About 1 teaspoon of soap per gallon of water should be perfect for washing away your mosquito problems. (You might also want to consider keeping lids over your barrels and buckets to help prevent mosquitoes from laying larvae in the water in the first place.)

## Use Good "Scents" When Repelling Mosquitoes

Some scents will draw mosquitoes to you the same way fresh-baked cookies may draw you into a neighbor's home. So when you're outside in mosquito country, avoid smelling like perfumes, shampoos, soaps, and hair spray—to mosquitoes, they all have that "come hither" appeal. Instead, use aromatic herbs like lavender, geranium, lemon balm, and lemon thyme to repel these biting pests. Simply grow these herbs in containers or beds around your patio, and when you need a little mosquito protection, crush a few of their leaves to release their oils. Or you can apply the herbs directly to your skin, but be sure to patch test a small area first to make sure you aren't allergic. If your skin shows no signs of irritation 15 minutes after the test, go ahead and use that herb to chase away these bloodsuckers.

### Solutions at a Glance

**Problem:** Something is snacking on you.

**Culprit:** Mosquitoes

**Solve It!** Mosquitoes are attracted to the heat retained by dark colors, so stick with white, yellow, or beige clothing, and chances are good you'll fly in under the mosquito radar.

You can also try diffusing a scent mosquitoes hate—such as rosemary, spearmint, or geranium—into the air. Surround yourself in a mist of these mosquito repellents and the pests will give your yard a wide berth. To make these scents airborne, combine 10 to 20 drops of rosemary, spearmint, or geranium oil with 2 ounces of water in an atomizer, says Mindy Green, director of education at the Herb Research Foundation in Boulder, Colorado, and co-author of *Aromatherapy: A Complete Guide to the Healing Art*. Lightly spray the mixture on your skin or clothes no more than five times a day. You can also use these oils undiluted in an electric diffusor, she notes. Or, if you have a potpourri burner, simply add water to the receptacle, and 5 to 10 drops of oil to the water, and light the candle below. Then sit back, relax, and enjoy a mosquito-free evening by candlelight!

# Mulch Problems

Savvy gardeners have been using mulch for generations. The ideal mulch keeps weeds down, prevents water from evaporating, moderates soil temperature, provides nutrients to plants, adds organic matter to the soil, and improves soil texture. But despite all its positives, mulch does have some downsides. Depending on your mulch of choice, it may blow away, rob the soil of moisture or nitrogen, or form a hard crust that water can't penetrate. These problems are easily solved, however, with just a little effort on your part. Here's how.

### Terrific Twosome

Two mulches earn the distinction of not having any problems at all—compost and leaf mold—which makes them wise choices for your mulching needs.

Compost is a wonder mulch for several reasons. First of all, you can make it yourself without having to buy any special ingredients—it's free, and it's the ultimate in recycling. Compost does everything a mulch should, plus it contains disease-fighting microorganisms. It looks fine in the garden as is and doesn't blow around. Compost also really holds moisture without waterlogging the soil. Since Nancy Engel, a gardener from Cold Spring, New York, started adding compost to her window-box planting mix, she cut her watering down from three to four times a week to once a week—even for her boxes that get full sun.

*Leaves are a priceless source of mulch—and free for the taking. All you have to do is rake them up, shred them, and let them decompose.*

## Solutions at a Glance

**Problem:** A hard crust has formed on top of your soil.
**Culprit:** Sawdust
**Solve It!** Occasionally break it up with a cultivating fork.

---

**Problem:** Your plants aren't getting the nitrogen they need.
**Culprit:** Fresh bark chips
**Solve It!** Use shredded bark instead.

---

**Problem:** Corn cob mulch and newspaper mulch are blowing around.
**Culprit:** Wind
**Solve It!** Water the mulch as you lay it down, then anchor it with a covering of something more attractive, such as wood chips.

---

**Problem:** Nitrogen is being robbed from the soil.
**Culprit:** Wood chips, sawdust, and leaves
**Solve It!** Add bloodmeal or alfalfa meal to your soil.

---

**Problem:** Something's hanging out under your mulch.
**Culprit:** Slugs and voles
**Solve It!** Remove the mulch.

Leaf mold is wonderful, too, and if you have deciduous trees, then you have an inexhaustible source of leaf mold. All you need is a lawn mower to shred the leaves and a place to pile them while they decompose. Like compost, leaf mold puts valuable nutrients back into the soil, improves the texture of the soil, and is a great mulch for all types of plants.

### Free Chips

If buying bags of wood chips for mulch is putting a good dent in your budget, don't throw in the towel. Instead of paying for wood chips, check with a tree trimming company. They may be more than happy to supply you with free wood chips.

### Too Much of a Good Thing

Don't go overboard on the mulch. Too much mulch around a tree can smother its roots and cause bark rot on its trunk. So how much should you use? A good rule of thumb is to not put more than a 2- to 3-inch layer of mulch around a tree and keep mulch 4 inches away from the trunk.

# Poison Ivy

As gardeners, we all do our best to avoid the plant with three shiny green leaves. But occasionally we still manage to find ourselves covered in the red, itchy rash that tells the world we've tangled with a patch of poison ivy. If your yard is crawling with it, you may be at your wit's end trying to avoid the stuff. But don't give up—here are some great suggestions for a rashless year outdoors, plus some home remedies to help relieve the itch if poison ivy has already gotten to you this season.

## This Oil Really Gets Around

You may not know it, but the leaves of the poison ivy plant aren't the bad guys.

According to Susan Carol Hauser, author of *Nature's Revenge: The Secrets of Poison Ivy, Poison Oak, Poison Sumac, and Their Remedies*, it's the oil urushiol (you-ROO-she-ol), which is found in the plant's sap, that gives you the rash. And that oil can be carried around on animal fur, garden tools, or any other object that it touches. But that's not even the worst of it: The oil retains its rash-spreading, itch-starting properties for up to a year while it sits on those objects. That means that if your gardening gloves, tools, or boots come in contact with poison ivy at the end of this season and you put them away until next spring—surprise! You can get poison ivy again just by touching them.

*THE ITCH-CAUSING OIL IN POISON IVY CAN HANG AROUND FOR A LONG TIME, SO MAKE SURE TO THOROUGHLY WASH ANY GLOVES, TOOLS, OR BOOTS THAT COME IN CONTACT WITH IT.*

So what's your best strategy for avoiding this perennial irritation? Whether you already have the telltale rash or you just know you've had a brush with poison ivy, "make sure you clean everything you've been in contact with," Hauser says. "The rubber boots you were wearing, your clothing, tools, gloves." A thorough cleaning with water should do the trick, but your defensive strategy doesn't end there. Even after you've stripped and washed yourself, you could still expose yourself to the oil simply by coming in contact with your soiled clothing. So take care when handling your clothes, and wipe down the outside of the washing machine after tossing them in, Hauser says. And also hose down your garden tools.

## Treat the Skin You're In!

Prevention is your best bet when it comes to poison ivy, but even the most cautious gardener will find herself elbow deep in the stuff at least once in her life. If you do get ivy-oiled, here are a few things you can do to stop the itch before it starts.

**REMOVE YOUR CLOTHING AND TAKE A LONG SHOWER RIGHT AWAY AFTER YOU FINISH OUTDOOR ACTIVITIES.** Immediately flooding the skin with water is the best way to get rid of the urushiol oil, according to Susan Carol Hauser, author of *Nature's Revenge: The Secrets of Poison Ivy, Poison Oak, Poison Sumac, and Their Remedies.*

**HAVE A POISON IVY KIT HANDY.** Hauser uses a mason jar filled with rubbing alcohol and a washcloth. If you think you've come in contact with poison ivy, simply slosh the wet cloth over the area of skin you're worried about. Then wipe down your hands and the outside of the jar, and return the cloth to the jar for the next ivy emergency.

**TRY THE HERBAL RELIEF OFFERED BY JEWELWEED OR TOUCH-ME-NOT, HAUSER SAYS.** If you think you've brushed against some poison ivy, simply break off a stem of jewelweed and apply the juice as you would aloe. This pale green plant can grow to 5 feet tall, is a succulent, and prefers moist and partial shade locations. It has slipper-shaped

### Solutions at a Glance

**PROBLEM:** Your yard is overrun with a weed, and you're sure removing the plants is the only way to keep from getting a rash again and again.

**CULPRIT:** Poison ivy

**SOLVE IT!** Dig the plants out—carefully!—by the roots. Make sure you wear protective clothing, and wash with plenty of water afterward. Or, suffocate the plants by covering them with black plastic or cardboard. It takes some time, but eventually the plants will die. Be sure to seal down the edges of the cover, and keep a sharp lookout for runners that can sneak out and start new plants. (You can also keep mowing poison ivy off; the plant will weaken and eventually die.)

seedpods, and the healing juice is a watery orange that flows freely from broken stems or torn leaves.

## But Ma, It Itches!

We've all heard it: "Don't scratch—you'll only make it worse." But is it true?

"People tend to think scratching spreads the rash," explains Susan Carol Hauser, author of *Nature's Revenge: The Secrets of Poison Ivy, Poison Oak, Poison Sumac, and Their Remedies.* "Itching may feel good, and it won't spread the rash," Hauser assures us. But scratching can cause infection or nerve damage, so you should still listen to your mother—she really does know best.

Try these ideas for some quick relief while you're busy *not* scratching your rash.

- One garden remedy you can try is a peppermint tea compress. Add 1 cup of hot water to 1 tablespoon of fresh peppermint leaves. Steep for 10 to 15 minutes. "Keep the tea covered as it steeps," says Betzy Bancroft, an herbalist from Port Murray, New Jersey, because evaporation will make your tea less effective. Soak a cloth in the liquid, and apply it to the skin.
- You can use hot tap water to release the histamines (which cause the awful itching in the first place) in the skin and gain some relief, says Hauser. Use tap water that's as hot as you can stand, but not so hot that it will burn you. Immerse the part of your body that has the rash in a basin of hot water, or hold it under running water (where you can gradually increase the temperature). After several minutes, you'll feel the histamine release from your skin in little bursts. Keep the water hot until the bursts stop (change the basin water if needed)—usually in 10 minutes or so. Relief from itching lasts up to 8 hours, so using this treatment before going to bed should help you get a good night's sleep.
- Try applying a paste made with water, cornstarch, baking soda, oatmeal, or Epsom salts to relieve the itch. Use 1 teaspoon of water to 3 teaspoons of the dry ingredient, and apply to the skin as needed.

*Get much-needed itch relief by applying a paste made from cornstarch and water to your irritated skin.*

# Potato Problems

There's nothing like digging your hands into the earth and coming out with a bounty of delicious, homegrown potatoes. These subterranean veggies are universally loved (have you ever met someone who *didn't* like potatoes?) and are super easy to grow—especially if you know a few expert tips. Read on to discover the secrets to planting, growing, and harvesting picture-perfect potatoes year after year.

## Rx for Healthy Potatoes

There's a lot that can be said about how to grow healthy potatoes, but all potato experts agree on one thing: You should only plant seed potatoes that are certified to be disease-free. Follow these tips to have the healthiest taters in town.

**TRY TO AVOID SAVING YOUR OWN POTATOES TO PLANT FROM YEAR TO YEAR.** That's because various viruses can affect potatoes, and if you save your own seed potatoes, over time you'll probably see a decline in the size and quality of your spuds.

**DON'T TRY TO USE SUPERMARKET SPUDS.** Odds are good that they won't grow because they've been sprayed with chemicals to keep them from sprouting.

**BE TWICE AS SURE OF YOUR SEED POTATOES.** Use double-certified seed potatoes, if you can. They're becoming more readily available, and they're both free from disease and produced without any chemicals whatsoever.

## Spring Ahead with Green Sprouting

To help ensure a successful crop and to get a head start on the growing season, potato experts recommend a practice called "green sprouting." Here's how it works.

"About 30 days before you plant, put the potatoes in a dark, 70° to 75°F area," says Megan Gerritsen, co-owner of Wood Prairie Farm, an organic potato seed supplier in Bridgewater, Maine. "Then, as soon as you see sprouts, move the potatoes to cooler temperatures (50° to 55°F) in the light. You want the tubers and sprouts to turn green." Exceptionally vigorous seed potatoes (the sprouts get too long too fast) should be held at 42° to 45°F.

Keep the sprouted potatoes in the cool and light conditions for about 3 weeks. By then, sprouts will be about $\frac{1}{2}$ inch long and the tubers will be ready to plant.

Jim Gerritsen, the other co-owner of Wood Prairie Farm, gives green sprouting the credit for their successful crops in an area where the season is very short and the crops have a lot of late-season challenges. "If we can give those potatoes a good head start indoors, where there are no bugs and no blight, we gain 2 weeks on our season," Gerritsen says, adding that green sprouting is great for areas where cold or wet weather might rot seed potatoes. "If the potatoes are green sprouted, they're already in gear before they have a chance to rot." Even holding potatoes for 24 to 48 hours at 70°F is a huge benefit."

*If you're practicing "green sprouting," you'll need to move your potatoes out of the dark and into the light as soon as you see sprouts.*

## Save Time Spent Slicing

Don't bother cutting up small seed potatoes (those about half the size of a golf ball or hen's egg)—you can plant them whole. Cut larger seed potatoes so that each piece has at least two or three eyes and weighs an ounce or two. And be sure to allow cut seed spuds to dry in the sunshine for 24 hours before you plant them.

*When you cut larger potatoes for seed, make sure each piece has at least two eyes.*

## Stick It in the Fridge

Don't toss that old refrigerator that still works—it's a great place to store your potatoes after the harvest (as long as it's not self-defrosting—which would cause your potatoes to shrivel). The tubers should be stored in a completely dark place, at about 40°F, so if you were planning on just sticking them in the basement, you might want to rethink that strategy. (Make sure your fridge doesn't get too cool, though; potatoes convert their sugars to starch at temps below 36°F.)

# Powdery Mildew

If your plants look like someone just dusted them with baby powder, you know you have powdery mildew. Actually a fungus, powdery mildew thrives in summer when evenings are cool and days are warm and humid. But don't despair. Powdery mildew seldom kills or causes serious damage—it just looks ugly. And clever gardeners can avoid even that.

## Pestered by Powdery Mildew

Half the battle against powdery mildew is knowing which plants are most likely to be affected. If you know, then you can be more careful about taking steps to prevent powdery mildew in the first place. Here's a list of common victims.

***Trees and Shrubs***

Hackberries (*Celtis* spp.)
Euonymus (*Euonymus* spp.)
Crape myrtle (*Lagerstroemia indica*)
Privets (*Ligustrum* spp.)
Honeysuckles (*Lonicera* spp.)
Crabapples (*Malus* spp.)
English oak (*Quercus robur*)
Roses (*Rosa* spp.)
Lilacs (*Syringa* spp.)

***Flowers***

Dahlias (*Dahlia* hybrids)
Hybrid delphinium (*Delphinium* × *elatum*)
Bee balm (*Monarda didyma*)
Garden phlox (*Phlox paniculata*)
Common zinnias (*Zinnia elegans*)

***Fruits and Vegetables***

Apples
Cucumbers
Grapes
Melons
Peas
Pumpkins
Squash
Strawberries

## 5 Ways to Prevent Powdery Mildew

**PLANT DISEASE-RESISTANT VARIETIES.** As a rule of thumb, newer varieties tend to have more powdery mildew resistance. As much as possible, read the label or check the seed catalog description.

**GIVE 'EM ROOM.** Good air circulation keeps leaves drier and prevents fungi from getting a foothold. Plant at the recommended spacing to prevent crowding.

**GIVE 'EM LIGHT.** If a plant is prone to powdery mildew, plant it in (or move it to) to full sun. There, the leaves will dry faster and better.

**DESTROY DISEASED PLANT PARTS.** Even if the plant can't be saved, fast action may prevent the spread of the disease to another completely different plant. As much as is practical, trim or pick off diseased leaves or stems and destroy them. Rake or pick up diseased leaves that fall to the ground.

**WATER WITH CARE.** Don't water overhead, spraying leaves. Instead, water the soil directly. Not only does this prevent the leaves from staying wet, creating ideal fungi-spreading conditions, it also prevents powdery mildew spores that may be in the soil from splashing up onto leaves.

## Preventive Potion

You can help keep powdery mildew at bay with this home brew of baking soda, water, and Murphy Oil Soap. The baking soda alters the pH of the leaf, making it harder for fungi to get started. The oil soap serves as a sticker-spreader to help the spray spread and stay. Simply mix together 1 gallon water, 3 tablespoons baking soda, and 1 tablespoon Murphy Oil Soap.

Spray before powdery mildew strikes, in early spring—as soon as plants have leafed out. Start spraying those that have been plagued by powdery mildew in the past. Spray every 7 to 10 days, getting in at least four applications before temperatures hit the 70s.

You can also apply the spray at the very first sign of powdery mildew, repeating every 7 to 10 days until temperatures hit the 70s. (Spray it on when it's any warmer and you might burn the leaves.)

*Spray plants with a nontoxic "home brew" that prevents powdery mildew.*

# Propagation Problems

Propagating plants is kind of like raising animals, only better, because you don't need one of each sex to get new ones—you can propagate your own offspring from cuttings. Propagation is a great way to increase your plantings or to share a favorite plant with friends. And it's easy, as long as you avoid a few pitfalls.

## Rx for Healthy Propagating

As we said before, propagating is easy, if you avoid a few pitfalls. Because we want to help you do just that, we've put together a few tips for avoiding common mistakes.

**USE GENTLE BOTTOM HEAT.** Gentle bottom heat can hasten rooting, "but be careful not to fry them," says Tony Ricci of Three Springs, Pennsylvania. If you do a lot of propagating, it might be worthwhile to invest in an electric propagation mat because you'll be able to regulate the heat easily.

**WATCH THE MOISTURE LEVEL CAREFULLY** because heat also dries out the rooting medium. Regular misting helps keep cuttings from drying out, or you can cover the pots holding your cuttings with a clear plastic bag to create a miniature mist tent. It's fine for the plastic to fog up, but if it starts dripping moisture, the medium is too wet. Take the plastic off temporarily to prevent the cuttings from molding in the excess moisture.

**AVOID DIRECT SUNLIGHT.** Don't put your propagation flats in direct sunlight, either, because direct sun can cause leaves to scorch and wilt. In fact, cuttings need no sun at all until they have rooted and are starting to produce new leaves.

## A Nick Saves Time

If you want to get hardwood and softwood cuttings to root faster, try wounding the lower stem by nicking it with a sharp knife or the blade of your pruning shears. This is especially helpful if the cutting is from older wood, which roots more slowly than new wood.

## Smaller Equals More Success

Smaller cuttings tend to root better and faster—you'll root close to 100 percent of 1½-inch-long rosemary cuttings, for example, while only

## Solutions at a Glance

**Problem:** Your cuttings are infected.

**Culprit:** Fungal spores

**Solve It!** Add a few drops of hydrogen peroxide to the water when you water or mist the cutting flat to reduce the chance of infection.

about 10 percent of 4-inch cuttings will root. (The only drawback is that smaller cuttings are also more prone to wilt, so they need more immediate attention.)

### Flag That Plant

Few perennials should be divided when they're in bloom, but that's when you're likely to notice that one plant is superior to its neighbors. And, of course, that's the plant you want to propagate. Use a bamboo stake with a colorful strip of plastic stapled to the top to mark the special plant so you won't forget which one it is when the time is right to propagate.

## Timely Cuts

*One tricky aspect to propagation is knowing the right time to take cuttings. Soft-stemmed plants—like impatiens, geraniums, and many perennials—will root from cuttings anytime. Perennials are usually best divided in the early spring when they first show growth or propagated from cuttings in midsummer. Some woody plants—like berry bushes, shrubs, and trees—will root successfully only if the cuttings are taken at certain times of the year. Trial and error usually works best, but here are some guidelines to get you started.*

| Plant | When to Take Cuttings |
|---|---|
| Hydrangeas (*Hydrangea* spp.) | Softwood cuttings, spring and summer |
| Privets (*Ligustrum* spp.) | Anytime |
| Ornamental cherries (*Prunus* spp.) | Softwood cuttings in spring |
| Currants and gooseberries (*Ribes* spp.) | When dormant (late fall to early spring) |
| Azaleas (*Rhododendron* spp.) | During active growth in spring |
| Lilacs (*Syringa* spp.) | During active growth in spring |
| Deciduous trees and shrubs (hardwood) | When dormant (late fall to early spring) |
| Deciduous trees and shrubs (softwood) | Spring (when budded) to early summer |
| Evergreens | During a growth flush (there are several annually) |

## Solutions at a Glance

**Problem:** The impatiens (or coleus or geraniums), which were started from cuttings, are growing straight up and won't branch out.

**Culprit:** Cuttings from the wrong shoot

**Solve It!** The temptation is to root the leading shoot from annual bedding plants when you pinch them to encourage bushiness. That shoot is already programmed to grow upright. Take cuttings from side branches instead, and your plants will be bushier.

---

**Problem:** Your divisions of oriental poppy (*Papaver orientale*) die.

**Culprit:** Wrong form of propagation

**Solve It!** Oriental poppy is one perennial that's hard to divide successfully. Take root cuttings instead in July or August when the plant is dormant. Dig it up and cut the fleshy roots into 4- to 5-inch pieces. Be sure to insert them in your rooting medium the same way they were growing in the garden. Cutting the bottom at an angle and the top straight will help you remember which end was up.

---

**Problem:** Your cuttings wilt and die before they develop roots.

**Culprit:** Loss of moisture

**Solve It!** The cuttings are losing moisture too fast. Strip all but the topmost leaves from cuttings to prevent excess moisture loss, and never let the rooting medium dry out.

---

**Problem:** Your cuttings mold before they develop roots.

**Culprit:** Excess moisture

**Solve It!** If you're covering the propagation flat to increase humidity, remove it occasionally to vent excess moisture. Sprinkle milled sphagnum moss over the surface of the flat to wick moisture away from the cutting stems.

## Lots of Herbs

Cuttings are an easy way to grow lots of herb plants for yourself and for your friends. Basil, scented geraniums, lavender, rosemary, and sage are just a few of the herbs that grow well from cuttings. To take cuttings, use a sharp knife, then remove the leaves on the bottom half of the cutting and push it into the soil mix in your container. Cuttings need high humidity—put the pot with your cuttings inside a plastic produce bag that has slits for ventilation. Keep your new cuttings out of direct sunlight for a few days. Then be patient—your cuttings will need at least a month before they form new roots.

## Putting Down Roots

Although many plants root in nothing more than plain water, some harder-to-root species need a little help. Here are a couple of tricks of the trade.

**USE WILLOW BRANCHES.** "Willow trees (*Salix* spp.) have a natural rooting hormone (salicylic acid) in them," says Tony Ricci, an organic grower from Three Springs, Pennsylvania. "Take some twigs, soak them in water for a few days, and then either dip the cuttings in the water or water the flats with it."

**USE BORIC ACID.** Trying to root hollies (*Ilex* spp.)? Do the above, and add a pinch of boric acid to the willow water. Researchers have found that boron enhances holly rooting when used with rooting hormones.

*ADDING A PINCH OF BORIC ACID TO WILLOW WATER IS ONE TRICK TO HELP GET HOLLIES TO ROOT.*

## Humidity Helper

Give cuttings the humidity they need by placing your containers of cuttings on a tray of pebbles. Put just a small amount of water in the tray—enough to create humid conditions, but not enough to touch the bottom of the pots. (Also use fingernail-size pebbles.)

# Pruning Problems

Many plants and trees in your landscape can benefit from pruning now and then. But how often have you taken a little too much off? Or not enough? What about the hydrangea you pruned that subsequently failed to flower? Results like these can be enough to make you want to turn in your loppers. Pruning doesn't have to be an ordeal, however. Take the following tips for healthy pruning, including how to do it safely, to heart and we're sure you'll have better luck the next time that tree or bush needs a trim.

## Removing Large Limbs Safely

You've probably been there. In one fell swoop you hack a large branch off of a tree—and the wood splinters, tears away and leaves you with an injured tree. You can avoid such damage in the future, however, simply by knowing how to remove large limbs correctly. Here's what to do:

1. Make an undercut about one-third to one-half of the way through the branch.
2. Make a second cut into the top of the limb just outside of the first cut. (The weight of the limb should make most of the branch snap off at that spot.)
3. Make your third—and final—cut just outside of the branch collar.

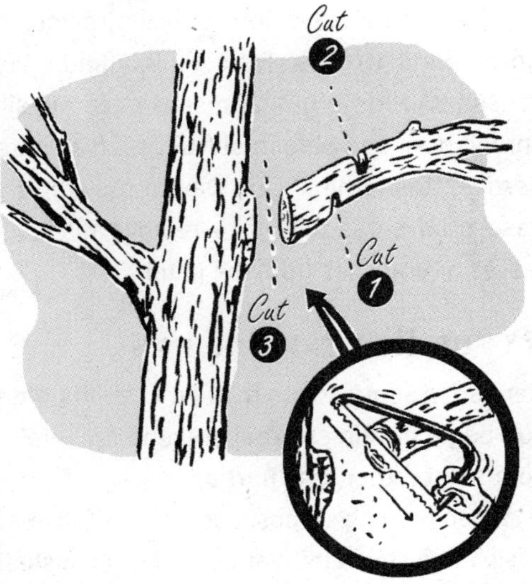


*Removing large limbs with three cuts instead of one can help protect your tree—and your head.*

## Disease Prevention and Control

Bill Adams, extension horticulturist for the Texas Agricultural Extension Service in Houston, recommends dipping pruning tools in a 10 percent bleach solution in between fruit trees with disease symptoms to prevent spreading the disease. "Dipping is particularly important when pruning peaches and nectarines, to avoid spreading bacterial canker," Adams says. Prune the diseased trees last and try to prune well below any disease cankers.

Patrick Curran, owner of Curran's Orchard in Rockford, Illinois, uses a simple rule to prevent disease in his apple orchard. "If two limbs are close together, or if they cross, or if they touch, one of them should come out," he says. "Two limbs rubbing together will eventually result in disease." Not only does this help to ensure a healthy orchard, it encourages superior fruit production. "Open trees allow more sunlight and air to enter the tree canopy—this helps fruit stay dry and reduces growth of fungus and bacteria."

"Cut it out!" says Tom Galazen, owner of North Wind Organic Farm in Bayfield, Wisconsin. "Airborne fungal diseases can easily spread from one perennial fruit, such as blueberries, to another." One way to prevent disease from spreading is to remove diseased leaves or branches from the plant.

## Rx for Healthy Pruning

Here are a some points to keep in mind before you begin pruning so that you end up helping your plant rather than hurting it.

When pruning shrubs, use loppers to cut off a few large stems right at ground level, instead of using hedge shears. Plants will then need fewer cuts and will maintain a better form, says Lee Reich, Ph.D., garden writer and author of *The Pruning Book*.

The best time to prune to promote quick healing and help prevent disease is just before growth begins in the spring, advises Reich. But hold off on pruning early bloomers such as forsythia until after they've finished blooming, or else you'll be removing some flower buds whose blossoms you could have otherwise enjoyed!

"Orange flagging tape is a great thing to use if you aren't an experienced pruner," says Carol Bradford, a Master Gardener and garden columnist from Syracuse, New York. "Use the tape to tie good-sized bows around the branches you want to cut off—then visualize the way the tree will look without the branches."

Make sure your loppers are sharp because sharp blades will make cleaner cuts and won't bruise the back sides of branches. Clean cuts and a lack of tree damage will also help to prevent disease.

*Avert a pruning disaster by using orange flagging tape to help you visualize how your finished masterpiece will look.*

## Keep on Bloomin'

Hate to say good-bye to those delphinium blooms? You can extend the plants' bloom time by pruning out all but three growing stems when the delphiniums reach 18 inches tall, says Jeff Cox, noted garden author from Kenwood, California. After pruning the plant, stake the three remaining stems. The plant's roots will compensate by sending up new stems that will produce a second bloom much later in the season, giving you more time with these gorgeous flowers.

## Pruning Patience

You can help your peach trees fend off the deadly cytospora canker by making sure not to prune them too early, says Frank Pollack, who runs an organic fruit and vegetable farm in Pennsylvania's Pocono Mountains. "Research has shown that cytospora will do more damage to peach trees if you prune them before the sap is moving again," he explains. "So wait to prune the trees until things have warmed up—that way, any pruning-related wounds will have a chance to heal quickly because the sap is moving," says Pollack.

## Whack Those Blueberries Back

David Martinson, an organic fruit farmer from northern Wisconsin, errs on the side of overpruning his blueberries in early spring. "You may think you're pruning too much," he explains. "But blueberries are resilient shrubs that thrive on pruning." In fact, when pruning individual canes, Martinson recommends pruning them back to ground level. "In the growing season following pruning, my blueberries increase in size." What better way to encourage vigorous shrub growth?

## Solutions at a Glance

**Problem:** Something's getting the better of your stone fruits (peaches, plums, and cherries).

**Culprit:** Frost

**Solve It!** Wait to prune until the flower buds are just beginning to swell. Pruning tends to spur the trees into growth and bloom, so waiting to prune delays the bloom and helps avoid frost damage.

## Lilac Time-Saver

Pruning, as you well know, can take a lot of time. When it comes to lilacs, save yourself some work later on by cutting lots of lilacs for your house when they're in bloom. Don't think of it as robbing the bush, but rather as saving work later, because you should also cut off all the old flower heads when pruning the bush.

## Increasing Apple Production

You can help your apple trees produce more fruit simply by fashioning them after a Christmas tree.

"Apple trees should resemble evergreen trees," says to Patrick Curran, who gardens in Rockford, Illinois. An apple tree should be wider at the bottom than it is at the top, so prune your trees so the upper limbs are shorter than the lower ones. This will allow enough sunlight to penetrate through the tree canopy to the lower limbs, will increase photosynthesis, and will increase the overall fruit production of your tree.

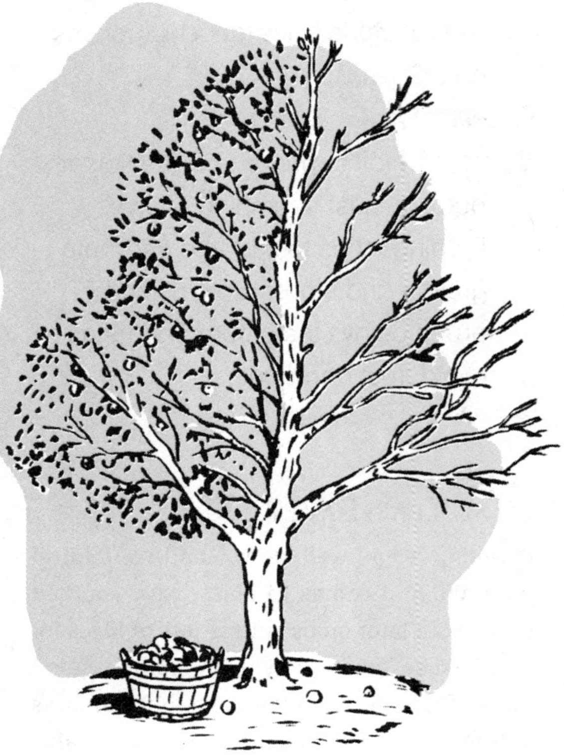

*LET THE SUN SHINE IN ON YOUR APPLE TREE BY PRUNING IT SO THAT IT'S WIDER AT THE BOTTOM THAN THE TOP.*

## Bushier Blooms

Want to have bushier fall-blooming asters? Simply cut them back to half their height when they're 12 to 15 inches tall. By cutting them back they'll bear more flowers on shorter stems that require less staking.

## Flush Cuts Are Out

Create a healthy cut when you prune by leaving 1/16 inch of branch on the tree, says Frank Pollack, an organic fruit and vegetable farmer from the Pocono Mountains in Pennsylvania. "You'd think an absolute flush cut with the tree is the way to do it," says Pollack, "but leaving just the barest piece of the branch permits the outer ring of the pruned cut to grow back and heal faster than a flush cut."

## Reigning in Strawberry Runners

You can control vigorous runner growth in strawberries by gently clipping them back so they aren't as long and are less dense, says Tom Galazen of North Wind Organic Farm in Bayfield, Wisconsin. "Ideal spacing for the new plantlets formed on the runners is 4 to 6 inches," says Galazen. "Keeping rows narrower—around 18 to 24 inches across—should result in greater production than wider rows."

# Rabbit Problems

Remember back before you were a gardener, back when you thought that rabbits were just so cute? Now that you have a garden, though, you're aware of the fact that Thumper could be the one taking out your bean, lettuce, or carrot seedlings or nibbling off your bulb foliage. Cutting it right down to the ground, in fact! And though you haven't caught the rabbits red-handed, you're pretty sure they're the culprits. So what can you do to save your crops and your sanity in the face of marauding bunnies? Plenty—including fencing them out or repelling them with the scent of rotten eggs.

## Positive I.D.

Before you initiate a full-scale war on Peter Cottontail, make sure that's actually who you're dealing with. There are a few surefire ways you can determine that rabbits are the ones destroying your garden.

First, rabbit tracks are unique. With two back thumper legs propelling them, the indentations of their prints are easy to spot. Second, you can tell rabbits have been around if you find small, hard, pea-size dark brown pellets, generally left in neat little piles. Third, rabbits use their sharp teeth to cleanly clip small branches from a stem or trunk, as opposed to deer, who bite twigs bluntly off and chew leaves, or plow through a vegetable patch willy-nilly, leaving a mess.

*Peter Rabbit's tracks are unique in that the indentations of their prints—especially their two back thumper legs—are easy to spot.*

## Solutions at a Glance

**Problem:** Your tender young seedlings are being eaten.

**Culprit:** Rabbits

**Solve It!** Sprinkle wood ash on and around vulnerable crops. (If you have a wood stove or fireplace, you can save the ash in a bucket all winter.) And remember to reapply wood ash after it rains.

### Play Chicken with Rabbits

If rabbits are the major pest in a small yard, a simple, sturdy chicken-wire fence (1-inch mesh or smaller) works like a charm. The important thing to remember when designing the rabbit-proof garden with rabbit-impenetrable fencing is to bury at least 6 inches of the wire fencing in your trench so that these furry fellows can't burrow underneath the fence.

### Barrier Protection

Maybe you don't mind sharing parts of your yard or garden with rabbits, but you have a few plants whose safety you want to ensure. In that case, you can make simple protective barriers from ¼-inch hardware cloth for specific plants and young trees (because rabbits also enjoy snacking on tree bark). Make hardware cloth cylinders that cover the bottom 2 feet of the tree, plus a few inches of trunk below the surface of the soil. Keep the cylinder loose enough to accommodate several years' growth of the tree or plant. (Overlap the hardware cloth and secure it by inserting a piece of wire through the mesh and twisting it like a twist-tie.)

You can also cut strips of chicken wire into cylinders to wrap around young trees. (Commercially made tree guards are also available.)

Early in the season, protect small plants from rabbits with plastic milk jugs. Cut the bottom out of a jug, place it over a plant, and pile dirt around its base to keep it from blowing away. Remember to remove the jugs once the weather gets warmer, or the plants will get too hot and shrivel up.

*Recycle plastic milk jugs and use them to protect young plants from hungry bunnies.*

### Smelly Resolution

Some gardeners swear by homemade rotten egg sprays, bloodmeal, and hot pepper sauce as rabbit repellents. But if you don't feel like whipping up a batch of something homemade and smelly, commercial sprays are also available from mail-order sources (see "Resources" on page 344). One such spray, N.I.M.B.Y., is an emulsion of natural oils, available in a 32-ounce trigger spray bottle, that's an environmentally safe way to help repel rabbits.

# Rose Problems

Who can imagine a world without roses? For song writers, poets, and lovers—not to mention those of us who find sheer delight in their fanciful names—it would be a pretty bleak place without them. Yet multitudes of gardeners are convinced roses are more trouble than they're worth. Sure, roses can hand you a challenge or two. (What living thing can't?) But once you've learned a few tricks of the trade for beating fungus and pests and for putting into practice some general growing guidelines, roses are as easy to live with as any other shrub.

## Rx for Healthy Roses

Your surest road to rose-garden bliss is preventing problems before they happen. That includes making sure you choose varieties that are hardy and are resistant to the diseases that occur in your growing area (if you're not sure which roses will do best where you live, call your local Cooperative Extension office for information). Also use the following techniques.

**PRACTICE GOOD HYGIENE.** Like you, roses want their bodies and their homes clean and tidy. It makes them better able to fend off pests and disease. Keeping them shipshape is easy, says Akron, Ohio, gardener Mary Frances Jarrold. "Pick up debris when you see it," she advises, especially from the bases of the plants, where fungal spores can thrive. Cut off anything that doesn't look right—spent flowers, odd-looking leaves or canes. Then burn the pickings and prunings or dispose of them in sealed containers with your household trash—never compost them, or else you'll end up with fungal woes throughout the rest of your garden.

**DON'T BE AFRAID TO PRUNE.** New, vigorous wood is far less susceptible to pests and disease. Every year in late winter or early spring, cut out all diseased or damaged canes and some of the older canes of hybrid tea roses and grandifloras so that new canes can develop. Prune once-blooming roses like old garden roses and ramblers right after they finish blooming because they bloom on 1-year-old wood. (If you prune during the dormant season, you'll cut off your blooms.)

**PROVIDE AIR CIRCULATION.** You tend to pick up germs when you're in a hot, stuffy, crowded space. So do roses. When you plant, make sure to give them elbow room. And prune them so air can circulate freely to all parts of the plant. Your aim is "a bowl shape of branches," says Jane Anders, a Master Gardener from Portland, Oregon. "Open up the structure so the air and sunlight can get to the bud union where new canes develop."

*HELP AVOID DISEASE BY PRUNING YOUR ROSES TO AN OPEN, BOWL-LIKE FORM THAT LETS IN AIR AND LIGHT TO ALL PARTS OF THE PLANT.*

**SUPPLY GOOD NUTRITION.** We all feel, look, and perform our best with a healthy diet. Roses are no different. Furthermore, where nutrition is concerned roses are bottomless pits. The food of choice for roses, of course, is manure. "Roses love manure and lots of it," says Anders. It scarcely matters what kind—cow, horse, llama—as long as it comes from an herbivore and it has had at least 6 months to cool down so it doesn't burn delicate roots. The exception to the waiting period: rabbit droppings. "They work like time-release capsules," Anders says. Sprinkle the rabbit pellets around the drip line, cover them lightly, and each time water hits them the nutrients will soak into the soil and to the hungry rose roots.

Feed roses heavily in spring, when the soil temperature reaches 50°F or so, and again in summer, just after the first big flowering. Then in late fall (around Thanksgiving in Portland) cover the whole root zone with compost, and mound it up over the bud union if you have a grafted rose plant.

In mid-March and mid-July, Anders gives her roses a dose of Epsom salts to stimulate new growth. "Sprinkle about a third of a cup around the drip line, where the feeder roots are, and water it in," she says.

## Recipe for Success

Do your roses traditionally get off to a slow start each year? Here's a way to give them a boost from Master Gardener Marilyn Dube of Portland, Oregon. (This recipe makes enough for one plant.)

Fill a large bucket with about 5 gallons of water. Then add

2 dried banana peels
1 cup Epsom salts
2 cups alfalfa meal or pellets
½ to 1 cup dolomitic lime

Stir the ingredients together and pour the mixture around the base of the plant. Then work the solids into the soil along with any remaining winter mulch such as compost. "Your roses will be off and running," Dube guarantees.

## Fend off Fungi

Most of the diseases that plague roses are caused by fungi. A few of the worst are black spot, powdery mildew, rust, and canker. Black spot, the best-known ill in all of rosedom, occurs mostly in rainy or humid climates. Small black spots show on leaves; later, yellow haloes appear. In advanced stages, leaves drop off. Powdery mildew appears as a white or gray powder on leaves and flowers—never on canes. It thrives where cool nights follow hot days. Rust first appears as orange pimples on the undersides of leaves; later leaves turn orange or yellow. Spores can lie dormant in leaves, stems, or plant debris until rain, overhead watering, or high humidity spur them to action. Canker shows as brown areas on canes and usually attacks plants that have been under stress.

To prevent these fungi, follow these practices.

- Choose resistant plant varieties.
- Water early in the day so foliage dries out before nightfall.
- Diligently practice the preventive techniques described in "Rx for Healthy Roses" (on page 129).
- If your favorite roses are susceptible to disease and you have humid, damp growing conditions, spray once a week with the following organic fungicide developed at Cornell University. In 1 gallon of water, mix 3 teaspoons of baking soda and 1 teaspoon of canola oil *or* 1 teaspoon of nondetergent dishwashing liquid like Ivory (not both).
- If your roses do succumb to a fungus, the best thing to do is remove and destroy infected leaves or canes. To avoid spreading the disease, dip your pruners in alcohol or other disinfectant after each cut.

**Black Spot**

*In the later stages of black spot, yellow haloes appear in rose leaves.*

**Powdery Mildew**

*You'll find the gray or white powder of this fungus on rose leaves and flowers.*

**Rust**

*The first sign that your roses have rust is orange pimples on the undersides of leaves.*

**Canker**

*Keep your roses stress-free to help them avoid falling victim to canker.*

*Note:* The pests and diseases most likely to bully your roses—and the critters most likely to charge to your rescue—vary from one part of the country to another. See page 344 for some comprehensive rose books and regional problem solvers.

# Pest Detective

*The bugs that chow down on roses aren't the arch-villains they're cracked up to be, Master Gardener Jane Anders from Portland, Oregon, says, and most of them have natural predators. Even if the bad guys seem to get the upper hand now and then, they rarely do permanent damage. Here are some to watch for, including leaf-cutting bees and borers.*

| Symptom | Cause | What to Do |
|---|---|---|
| Curled, distorted, and sticky foliage | Aphids | Knock aphids off with a strong spray of water, and use insecticidal soap. Also, keep in mind that lady beetles and other predators will eat them. |
| Clean circular, oval, or scalloped holes in leaves | Leaf-cutting bees | Nothing—these bees are important pollinators of many garden plants, and they don't do serious harm to roses. If the damaged leaves bother you, cut them off. |
| Skeletonized leaves and holes in buds and flowers in midsummer | Japanese beetle and other beetles | Apply milky spore disease to the lawn to control the grub stage of the beetles and hand-pick the adults. |
| Spirals at the ends of cut canes in the pithy part of the cane | Borers. There are many types, and none fatal to rose plants. The most common, and the least damaging, is the pith borer. | Prune off canes below the infested part, destroy the prunings, and put a dab of petroleum jelly or white glue on all pruning cuts. |
| Small holes in foliage and eventually skeletonized leaves | Bristly rose slug | Spray the underside of the leaves (where the slug is) with insecticidal soap. |
| Flower buds and shoots that turn black and die | Rose midges. Unchecked, a heavy midge infestation can eliminate all bloom from late spring through early fall. | As soon as you spot midge damage, remove and destroy infected growth. |

## Going to Towering Heights to Beat the Cold

When you run a nursery on Alaska's Glacier Highway, you develop some pretty inventive ways to coddle plants. Says Mike Barrett, co-owner of Auke Bay Gardens north of Juneau, "Many of the best roses in these cold parts are untidy in habit—meaning they need support—and bloom best when they aren't cut back much. We like to train them on towers rather than trellises, not only because we like the way they look but also because a tower makes a nice cage to wrap the canes in when drying winter winds come up." Here's how to wrap roses that are trained on towers. (*Note:* You *don't* want to take such extreme measures unless you live an area with severe winters.)

1. Bury the rose's crown with a mound of soil (about 6 inches or so).
2. Wrap the rose-covered tower in floating row cover, such as Reemay.
3. Drop enough wood chips in through the opening at the top of the tower to cover the soil at the bottom (the chips should be about 1 foot deep).
4. Fill the rest of the structure with straw.
5. Fit a heavy plastic bag over the top to keep the straw from rotting and matting.
6. Pile a 1-foot layer of wood chips around the outside base to further protect the plant's crown and help brace the whole setup against the wind.

If you're in a very windy spot, Barrett says, "you could anchor it even with guy lines and stakes, but so far we haven't had to do that." Don't be surprised if your garden draws startled looks from passers-by. Says Barrett, "The finished structure looks just like a mummy."

*TURN YOUR ROSES INTO MUMMIES AND HELP THEM BEAT WINTER WINDS AND FREEZING TEMPS.*

# Seed Problems

How hopeful we start out! A packet of seed, a flat of soil, and a leap of faith. Then the things don't germinate, or they do and then promptly die, or they lag behind their fancy greenhouse-bought counterparts. Are seeds really worth all that work and disappointment?

Yes! Just like riding a bike, starting plants from seeds takes a certain knack. But once you've acquired that knack, it's as easy (and fun) as coasting that bike down a gentle hill on a sunny day. And, of course, seeds save you money big time. A flat of established seedlings can cost you $25 or more at a greenhouse—but the cost would be just a dollar or two if you started them yourself. Also, variety selection is so much better from the seed racks and mail-order catalogs. A whole new world of plants are suddenly open to you for less than a cup of fancy coffee.

## Mix Your Own

Disappointed with the results of sowing a packet of mixed annual seed? Why not make your own and have a wonderful cottage garden effect? You'll save money and you'll get to include only the flowers you love in the colors you adore. To get you started, mix and match your choices of the following easy-to-grow annuals. (Many of these will even reseed next season if you let some of the flowers go to seed, providing a free garden!)

- Calendula (*Calendula officinalis*)
- Cleome (*Cleome hasslerana*)
- Larkspur (*Consolida ajacis*)
- Cosmos (*Cosmos bipinnatus*)
- Snow-on-the-montain (*Euphorbia marginata*)
- Sweet alyssum (*Lobularia maritima*)
- Nicotiana (*Nicotiana alata*)
- Nigella (*Nigella damascena*)
- Four o'clock (*Mirabilis jalapa*)
- Marigold (*Tagetes* spp.)
- Johnny-jump-up (*Viola tricolor*)

## Eggshell Tonic

If you have a history of ending up with spindly, leggy seedlings, you might want to try feeding the next batch eggshell water. You'll need

1 gallon container with a tight-fitting lid (a milk jug works fine)
1 scant gallon water
1 dozen or more eggshells

Simply fill the container nearly full with water. Then, as you use the eggshells over a week or two, crush them lightly and pitch them in the container (no need to rinse the shells). Keep the container on the porch or in the garage; you'll know the water is ready to use once it starts to smell like, well, rotten eggs. Before you pour it on your plants, dilute with an equal part water.

*MAKE A COMFORTING BREW OUT OF EGGSHELLS AND WATER TO HELP SEEDLINGS GET OFF TO A GOOD START.*

## READ THE LABEL

Not sure when those seeds are supposed to go into the ground? Confused over the planting depth? Next time you go to buy seeds, take a good look at the packets and make sure they have explicit planting directions on them. The best packets give detailed instructions, right down to optimum planting temperatures and ideal seed-starting mediums—and should provide guidance when you aren't sure what to do.

## LET THERE BE ABSOLUTELY NO LIGHT

When you're planting seeds indoors and the package says to cover the seeds with soil, use vermiculite instead. Its light color lets you see exactly where you've covered and where you haven't. And its special moisture-holding properties prevent damping-off.

## BLOW YOUR DAMPING-OFF TROUBLES AWAY

Dave and Delores Johnson of Golden Valley, Minnesota, seldom have problems with damping-off, even though they start thousands of plants from seed. They create good air circulation in their basement by turning on a fan or two. Don't put the fan right on the seeds—just a gentle breeze in the general vicinity will do fine.

*SAY GOOD-BYE TO DAMPING-OFF WITH THE GENTLE BREEZE FROM A FAN.*

## SWEET SEEDS

Here's an easy way to see just where you're planting those fine seeds, such as carrots or poppies. Mix them with sugar before planting.

Sugar's light color and sparkle helps you better see where seeds are scattered and the sugar feeds helpful soil organisms.

*Mix fine seeds with sugar to plant more precisely.*

## Easy Germinators

If starting seeds gives you gray hair, you might want to take a look at the seeds you're using before throwing in the towel. After all, some seeds are easier to germinate than others. As a rule, annuals are usually less tricky than perennials. And nearly all annual vegetables are easy to start from seed. So before you call it quits, try starting seed from some of the easy germinators listed on this page.

***Very Easy***
Hollyhock (*Alcea rosea*)
Snapdragons (*Antirrhinum* spp.)
Centaureas (*Centaurea* spp.)
Cosmos (*Cosmos* spp.)
Common sunflower (*Helianthus annuus*)
Sweet basil (*Ocimum basilicum*)
Marjorams (*Origanum* spp.)
Annual poppies (*Papaver* spp.)
Marigolds (*Tagetes* spp.)
Garden nasturtium (*Tropaeolum majus*)
Pansy (*Viola* × *wittrockiana*)
Zinnias (*Zinnia* spp.)
Most vegetables

***Moderately Easy***
Swan River daisy (*Brachycome iberidifolia*)
Sweet woodruff (*Galium odoratum*)
Globe amaranth (*Gomphrena globosa*)
Impatiens (*Impatiens walleriana*)
Parsley (*Petroselinum crispum*)
Petunias (*Petunia* cultivars)
Salvias (*Salvia* spp.)

***More Difficult***
Wax begonias (*Begonia Semperflorens-Cultorum* hybrids)
Heliotrope (*Heliotropium arborescens*)
Lantanas (*Lantana* spp.)
Geraniums (*Pelargonium* spp.)

## Baby Food for Plants

Regular potting soil and garden loam won't do any more for starting seedlings than raw steak would do for a baby. So give this special seed-pampering soil mix for seedlings a try:

1 part compost, purchased or sifted
1 part perlite
1 part vermiculite

## Some Like It Hot

Ever threw out a flat of ungerminated seeds and decided you must have a black thumb after all? The problem may not be your black thumb, but rather, that you aren't providing the proper soil temperature required for germination, says Roy Ann Moulton, a horticulturist at Thompson & Morgan in Jackson, New Jersey.

Different species require different temperatures to germinate. To ensure success, you need to provide a soil temperature that's at least in the same ball park as the one required for the seeds you're growing. "If the seed packet says to germinate the seeds at 75°F, that means the *soil* must be 75°F, not the air," says Moulton.

The most accurate way to measure soil temperature is to use a soil thermometer. However, keep in mind that warm air rises. If the room temperature is 70°F and you're aiming for a soil temperature of 75°F, place the seed container on top of the refrigerator or a high shelf to help raise the soil temperature.

## Money-Saving Mesclun

Want to grow your own mesclun but don't want to pay the extra money for a seed packet of prepared mesclun mix? Then create your own. Here's a recipe for budget gourmet mesclun to get you started.

1 seed packet 'Très Fine' curly endive
2 seed packets 'Salad Bowl' lettuce
1 seed packet 'Red Oak Leaf' lettuce
1 seed packet 'Rouge d'Hiver' lettuce
1 seed packet arugula

If you decide to deviate from the above recipe and come up with your own, keep these points in mind.

- Use annual greens that have about the same maturation date (check the seed packet).
- Go for a combination of colors—a little red lettuce helps.
- Try to include at least one bitter green and one mild green for a contrast of flavors.

## Solutions at a Glance

**Problem:** Something's eating your newly planted seedlings.

**Culprit:** Birds, particularly crows

**Solve It!** After planting the seeds and covering them with a little soil, cover the planting area with about 1 inch of dried grass clippings before watering, says Al Bridgers of Maryville, Tennessee. Besides discouraging birds, the clippings also prevent the seeds from washing away and keep them moist.

- For the most interesting mesclun, also go for a variety of shapes, such as a feathery endive with an aptly named oak leaf lettuce.

## Don't Forget to Remember

If you're a seed saver, keeping track of when you bought those old packages of seed can be a problem. A simple trick is to jot down the year purchased on the outside of the seed packet in permanent marker. No more guessing how old those seeds might be!

## Designer Seed Packets

Baby food jars and camera film canisters make fine containers for seeds you've saved from a package or collected in your own garden. But these seed storers tend to take up space.

You can make your own space-saving seed packet with wax paper and tape. Simply fold the paper over, tape both sides, and create a flap. Then tape the flap down, and lift and reseal it as needed. Label the packet with a marker or cut out and tape the seed catalog or seed packet photo and description on your new waxed paper packet.

*USE TAPE AND WAX PAPER TO CREATE A CONVENIENT SEED PACKET.*

## MOIST MIX

Before filling your seed-starting containers, you always need to wet the soil mix. But commercial soil mixes can be difficult to wet thoroughly. To make sure your mix is moist throughout, put it in a plastic bucket or basin, add a bit of warm water, and stir. Keep adding water until the mix is evenly moist. You'll know the mix is evenly moist if you squeeze a handful tightly and only a few drops of water ooze out. (If the mix is too wet, add more dry mix.)

## THE BIG CHILL

Make your spring plantings a success by following these tips when direct seeding in cold weather.

- Choose cold-resistant varieties whenever you can.
- Pre-sprout seeds. Layer the seeds in a damp paper towel until tiny sprouts emerge, then plant them.
- Plant on a south slope or in an area that collects warmth from a nearby brick or stone wall or light-colored building.
- Plant in well-drained humus-rich soil, which warms more quickly than heavier soils.
- Use tunnels and row covers to protect your plantings and to collect heat.
- Cover the seeds with compost. Research shows that having fertilizer immediately available during cold spring plantings boosts yields in the long run.

# Shade

Do most of your garden beds happen to fall where the sun doesn't shine? Or is your once sunny garden getting shadier and shadier with each passing day? If so, you aren't alone. Marilyn Dube, owner of Natural Design Plants in Portland, Oregon, says that in terms of her sales, "Shade plants represent a larger piece of the pie every year." Whether your sunlight is disappearing behind your own growing trees or new houses are rising around you, don't throw in the towel. You *can* have luscious beds—you just need to work with the shade. Here's the lowdown on analyzing shade, fighting shade pests, and brightening those shady spots.

## The Many Shades of Shade

Shade isn't an absolute like a pH number or a mark on the thermometer that you can measure quickly and easily. Before you set out to replace sun-loving plants that are languishing in shade, find out how much shade you have, when you have it, and where it's coming from. Knowing those shade factors is important because different plants thrive in different types of shade.

Vicki Webster, who has gardened for many years behind high brick walls in Boston, recommends making a drawing of your garden and its immediate surroundings. It needn't be a work of art—a rough sketch will do fine—but be sure to include the following items:

- All sources of shade (such as your neighbor's giant spruce tree, a lattice-topped fence, the walls of your house, and the roof of your garage).
- Circumstances that could alter the light level in the near future (for instance, young trees that will block more light as time goes on, a diseased street tree you know is destined for removal, a house under construction next door).
- Conditions you can change if you want to (such as trees or shrubs you could remove or prune, or a solid fence you could replace with lattice panels).
- For a full day (about every 30 minutes), track the sun's light as it travels across your garden from dawn until dark. It is important to note on your sketch the times the sun's

light enters and leaves each planting area and established bed.

- Repeat the above tip at each of the next three seasons.

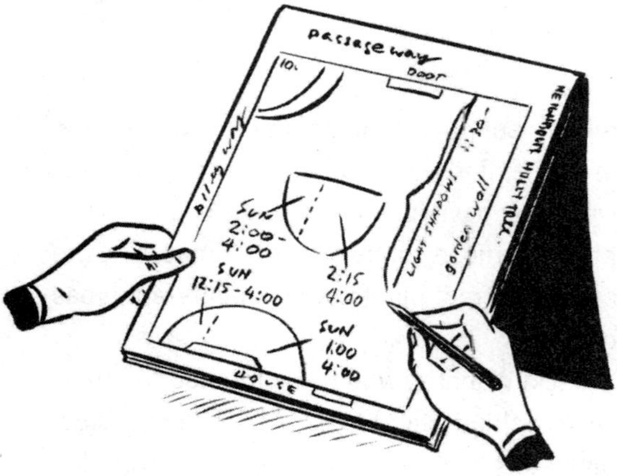

CAPTURE YOUR SHADE ON PAPER TO FIND OUT HOW MUCH, WHEN, AND WHERE YOU HAVE IT. KNOWING THESE THINGS WILL HELP YOU DECIDE WHICH TYPES OF SHADE-LOVING PLANTS WILL DO BEST IN YOUR SHADY SPOTS.

## Analyzing Your Shade

Armed with your raw data from your four seasonal sketches, you'll be able to tell which kind of shade you have in which places and at what times—you're bound to have at least a couple of types (unless your garden is entirely in the shadow of a neighboring building). Here are the basic types.

**DENSE SHADE** is cast by north-facing walls or fences, or by the low, dense branches of evergreen trees. Your plant choices here will be limited. Says Marilyn Dube, owner of Natural Design Plants in Portland, Oregon, "Depending on how much reflected light you get, you're probably better off with hardscaping—attractive pavers or bricks, with a shade-tolerant vine, such a climbing hydrangea, dutchman's pipe, or trumpet honeysuckle on a fence."

**DAPPLED SHADE** comes from large-leaved trees like maples (*Acer* spp.) or oaks (*Quercus* spp.). They block the sun but still allow light to enter the site. Your plant palate is a little broader here. Many ferns and hostas will grow well in dappled shade, as will early-blooming wildflowers and spring bulbs.

**BRIGHT LIGHT** in a garden sense means that no direct sun reaches the site, but nothing blocks the sky. It's a situation common in city gardens, or on the north sides of houses. Many plants, including rhododendrons, camellias, and other broad-leaved evergreens, thrive in bright light, as do ferns, lungwort (*Pulmonaria saccharata*), and violets.

**FILTERED LIGHT** drifts through the small leaves of trees such as birches (*Betula* spp.) or laburnums (*Laburnum* spp.) or through openings in a lath-covered arbor. This is what many plant catalogs *really* mean by shade. Plants such as hostas, bleeding hearts (*Dicentra spectabilis*), and goat's beards (*Aruncus dioicus*) do well in filtered light.

**PARTIAL SHADE,** also referred to as part shade or part sun, means a site gets direct sun for part of the day—as few as 2 hours or as many as 5. (Usually a site that gets direct sun for 6 or more hours a day is described as being in "full sun.") Partial shade is the trickiest kind to work with but it's also the most fun to experiment with because the effect of sunlight on plants depends not only on how long it lasts but also how intense it is—and that varies depending on the season, the time of day it arrives, and the part of the country you live in. Some plants that do well in partial shade include columbines (*Aquilegia spp.*), foxgloves (*Digitalis spp.*), and coral bells (*Heuchera sanguinea*).

*For plants that need filtered light, such as bleeding hearts, an arbor or pergola provides the right conditions.*

## Feathery Seedling Protection

Even up north, a freshly sown bed can benefit from some shade, and a few fern fronds snipped from your garden can be the perfect thing for creating instant shade. That's how Sunia Yang protects delicate seedlings in her Menlo Park, California, garden: "Cut a fresh fern frond and stick it in the ground so it shades the area you've just sown. As the seeds germinate, grow, and need more sun, the frond dies back and lets in more light." This method works best, she says, with something light and feathery, like brackens (*Pteridium* spp.) or wood ferns (*Dryopteris* spp.), rather than heavier sword ferns (*Nephrolepis* spp.).

## Getting the Shady Story

Just moved to a different part of the country and not sure what shade is really like on your new landscape? Take a tip from Rosalia Kung, who currently hails from Skillman, New Jersey, but who has planned gardens from scratch and has given new life to old ones in many a state: Start a newcomers' garden group, as she did when she first moved to Shaker Heights, Ohio. "The group was very informal," she says. "We'd gather every week or so in one of our gardens—bag lunches in hand—and talk about our problems and what we wanted to accomplish. We'd exchange plants. We'd walk through our neighborhoods, look at the gardens, study the light levels, and see what plants were doing best." Since then she's made a habit of rallying newly transplanted gardeners. "The group is a wonderful extension of friendship," she says, "and it's a great problem solver."

## Fabulous Foliage

If you can't adjust the light conditions in your garden (that is, you have to live with shade), the one thing you can do is adjust your vision for your garden. Instead of pining for ornamentals with lots of blooms, turn your thoughts to foliage.

A well-planned foliage garden can have a dramatic impact without the need for flowers. Make the best of leaves—they come in all colors, sizes, shapes, and textures. Use bold leaves as focal points, brightly colored leaves for dramatic effect, silver and variegated leaves to brighten a dull spot, and fine-textured leaves such as ferns for the background.

## Fighting the Slug Wars

Without a doubt the most dreaded denizen of moist shade is the slug, and its close cousin the snail. In the Pacific Northwest—which, to hear the locals tell it, ranks as the moist shade capital of the world—keeping the slimy pests at bay takes on all the attributes of trench warfare. Here's how some otherwise peaceful gardeners do battle with the arch villains.

- "I mulch with seaweed. Something about it—probably the salt content—keeps them away, though it isn't high enough to damage the plants," says Jack Talerico, from Vashon Island, Washington.
- "I went to a salvage yard and bought enough copper radiator strips to make a border around my whole shade garden. They don't climb over it," says Penny Grist, also from Vashon Island.
- Connie Kiener of Portland, Oregon, comments that slugs and snails "make me so mad I go out at night and chop them in half with a sharp scissors."
- Jane Anders of Portland, Oregon, picks slugs up and drops them into a bag of salt, and Susan LeMaster of Portland notes, "I feed them to my turtle, Mister Big. He considers them a great delicacy."
- "The slugs I whack with my Japanese knife," says Judy Davison of Seattle. "The snails—I have so many snails I could raise escargot—I pick up and throw over the back fence. They make a satisfying plunk when they hit the pavement in the alley, and I've developed a terrific hook shot."

## Public Enemy Number 2

Aside from slugs and snails, the critter that most plagues shade plants is the black vine weevil, also known as the taxus weevil because the choicest items on its menu are plants of the genus *Taxus* (known commonly as yews). The adult weevils chew the edges of leaves, which causes merely cosmetic damage, but their eggs hatch into grubs which in turn tunnel into the soil and eat the roots of whatever plants they encounter—in many cases with fatal results. Your treatment options are as follows:

- Trap adult weevils by wrapping double-faced tape around the base of the trunks of your yews or—if you aren't squeamish about scurrying bugs—wrap a piece of cloth loosely around the trunk. The weevils will duck under it for shelter during the day. At dusk, remove the cloth and shake it over a bucket of soapy water.
- Wipe out weevils by encouraging their natural predators: birds, beneficial nematodes, ground beetles, and spiders. (The best way to encourage natural predators is to avoid using pesticides. You can also attract birds by erecting bird houses for them; beneficial nematodes will automatically appear if you keep your soil well laced with compost.)
- Dig up any plants that are too far gone to save and destroy them.

Prevention is simple. Weevils and their grubby offspring thrive in dead plant debris, so *Taxus* devotee Rosalia Kung of Skillman, New Jersey, says, "Just keep everything clean." She has an easy, tidy-as-you-go approach: "I carry a plastic bin with me all the time, lined with a trash bag. That way I can set the bin on the ground and use both hands to toss in litter. It's faster than using a wheelbarrow," Kung says, "because you have to handle the stuff only once."

*KEEP BLACK VINE WEEVILS FROM HELPING THEMSELVES TO YOUR SHADE PLANTS BY ENCOURAGING PREDATORS SUCH AS GROUND BEETLES.*

## DRY SHADE

One of the most problematic conditions for gardeners is a dry, shady spot. But some plant will grow even in this difficult site. Here's a list of perennial plants that will at least tolerate dry shade:

Fairy bells (*Disporum* spp.)
Lenten rose (*Helleborus orientalis*)
Hostas (*Hosta* spp. )
Solomon's seal (*Polygonatum odoratum*)
Christmas fern (*Polystichum acrostichoides*)
Candy tuft (*Iberis saxatilis* (candytuft)
Crested iris (*Iris cristata*)
Canada columbine (*Aquilegia canadensis*)

## LETTING LIGHT IN

If the source of your problem shade is the tall building across the street or your neighbor's treasured fir trees, you have little choice but to plant shade-loving plants. Oftentimes, though, you *can* shed more light on the scene simply. Topping trees is tree abuse, says Marilyn Dube, owner of Natural Plant Designs in Portland, Oregon, so here are some other ways to lighten up.

- Increase reflected light by painting walls white or installing mirrors in strategic spots.
- Insert lattice panels into solid fences.
- Replace solid overhangs or porch roofs with lattice or panels of clear fiberglass.

*A PATIO WITH A LATTICE ROOF CAN HELP YOU LET IN MORE LIGHT TO A SHADY AREA THAN A PATIO WITH A SOLID ROOF CAN.*

# Slugs and Snails

Ugh—a slug. Or a snail. Slimy with a penchant for popping up every time you lift a stone or pot, slugs and snails also do real damage to many a broad-leaved plant. Telltale signs are small holes and tears throughout the leaf where these little critters have dined in style.

You *can* outsmart slugs and snails, though, without resorting to beds filled with plastic plants. All it takes is a little resourcefulness—such as changing the time of day you water your plants.

## Slug Motel

Here's how to create a "slug motel" where slugs and snails can check in but they can't check out, courtesy of Marianne Binetti, a garden columnist and writer in Enumclaw, Washington. Cut the top off an empty, clean, small (not 2-liter) plastic soda bottle right where it begins to taper inward. Put slug and snail bait (such as beer, or a solution of 1 teaspoon dry yeast dissolved in ¼ cup of water) in the bottle and firmly insert the cut-off portion upside down. Place the bottle on its side in your garden among your hostas and other slug-prone plantings. Change the bait every few days or as needed when you empty out the slugs and snails.

For a more elegant, Stone Age version of the slug motel—and one that naturally attracts snails and slugs—arrange four small rocks in a square and top with a larger, flat stone. Put the bait underneath in an empty, small cat food can; the moisture that collects under the stone will make the motel even more inviting for slugs and snails. (Again, remove the bait every few days and replace it with fresh bait.)

*Slugs can check in but they can't check out of this soda bottle slug motel.*

*Don't have a soda bottle? All you need is five stones to create a Stone Age version of the slug motel.*

## Avoiding Slugs and Snails

Need some easy solutions for minimizing the slug problem in your garden? Here are six to get you started.

**DON'T OVERWATER.** Slugs love moisture. The wetter the soil, the happier they'll be.

**MULCH SPARSELY.** Particularly in problem areas, use compost as your mulch or no mulch at all. Slugs and snails love to hide under thick layers of wood chips and such.

**MOVE SLUG-RIDDLED PLANTS INTO THE SUN WHEN PRACTICAL.** The more sun and less moisture, the less slugs are likely to bother a plant.

**PINCH OFF LOWER LEAVES WHEN PRACTICAL.** Leaves dragging on the soil are an invitation for slugs and snails to climb on. If the growth habit of your plant makes it feasible, allow as few leaves as possible to touch the ground.

**INSTALL COPPER STRIPS.** Available at most garden centers, you can put these strips around prized plants. Slugs dislike the copper and the strips' sharp edges. Follow installation instructions exactly.

**GET RID OF PLANTS THAT SLUGS DECIMATE EVERY YEAR.** Or seek out cultivars of those plants that are less prone to slug damage. Some hosta cultivars, for example, are less tempting to slugs and snails than others.

## Outsmart Slimy Slugs

"If you water in the morning instead of the evening, you can reduce your slug damage by up to 80 percent," says Cheryl Long, senior editor at *Organic Gardening* magazine. "One study found that with lettuce, morning watering reduced slug damage just as well as using slug baits. Morning watering lets the soil dry out during the day, so the moisture-loving slugs can't feed as much when they come out at night," she says.

## Handle with Care

Avoid touching those icky slugs and snails when you're picking them off plants by using a pair of long, scissor-handled tweezers—technically called hemostats. They give a firm grip without the gross-out. (You can buy hemostats at a drugstore or medical supply store.)

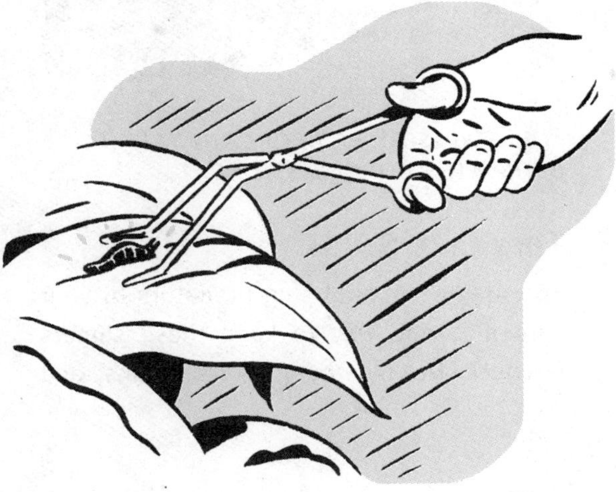

*USE LONG-HANDLED TWEEZERS TO GET A GRIP ON SLIMY SLUGS.*

## Copper Cut-Off

You've built raised beds, hoping the height factor will deter slugs, but yet they still find their way in to dine. Don't worry, all isn't lost. Deter them by rimming your beds with copper. Simply cut a sheet of copper into strips (or purchase strips at your local garden center) about 3 inches wide. Nail the strips to the inside of the raised bed, then make notches using metal (tin) snips about every 3/4 inch or so along the top of the strips. Fold the notches outward with pliers, and you'll have a slug-proof barrier.

*Foil slugs by reinforcing raised beds with copper strips.*

## They Like Slugs

Encouraging natural slug predators to your garden is one way to keep these slimers in check. Downy woodpeckers, robins, and other garden birds are happy to bite into a nice juicy slug. Other slug enemies include garter snakes, grass snakes, salamanders, shrews, toads, and turtles. To encourage predators to work in your favor, provide plenty of water sources and places for predators to hide in your garden. (And keep Kitty and Fido inside.)

## An Ounce of Prevention

Slugs and snails will arrive in your garden in early spring. Monitoring for the first arrivals is time well spent—eliminating the first slugs and snails of the season will prevent future generations. So set out your beer traps early and check them often whether or not you've actually seen any problems.

When falls arrives, take action to prevent slugs and snails from spending the cold months in your garden. Removing boards, rocks, clippings, and other debris will deny slugs and snails a ready shelter for the winter. And keep a sharp eye out for egg clusters.

# Soil Problems

Just as no one is ever happy with their weight, no one, it seems, is ever happy with their soil. It's either too full of clay or of sand, too acid or too sweet, too rocky or too riddled with hardpan. But, just like those extra pounds, bad soil can become a thing of the past. With some ingenuity and a few labor-saving tricks, you can have the black, loamy stuff all gardeners dream about.

## Create a Trudi Pit

Chicago-area gardener Trudi Temple has come up with an innovative method of getting rid of garden waste and enriching the soil without ever spending time turning a heap. Instead of building a compost pile, Temple digs a hole in an inconspicuous spot in her garden. The hole might be as small as 1 × 1 foot or as large as 5 × 5 feet. "It depends if I just do a little bit of weeding and how much space I have," Temple says. "Sometimes I do dig the hole right between two perennials and even take a little of their roots off. It doesn't hurt the plants at all."

Temple puts weeds, trimmed plant parts, cardboard boxes, and whatever organic matter she finds during her gardening chores into the hole. Then she puts 5 to 6 inches of soil on top of the hole to speed decomposition, and puts a stepping stone on top of the soil to mark the spot. After 6 months to a year, the site is ready to be planted.

*Create a no-turn compost pile by using a pit that does all the work for you.*

**Problem:** Lavender, rosemary, thyme, oregano, and other Mediterranean-type plants don't do well in your climate.

**Culprit:** Your soil is too rich. These are plants that like lean, rocky, soil and hot, dry conditions. Too much moisture and nutrients in the soil lead to fungal problems and poor flavor or fragrance.

**Solve It!** Create a "bad soil" bed. First, dig a pit, preferably next to a driveway or sidewalk that gets baked by the sun much of the day. Excellent drainage is a must, so a slight slope is ideal. Then fill the bottom of the pit with crushed rock or broken bricks. Next, fill the top foot or so with soil that is 4 parts garden loam, 1 part sand, 1 part perlite, and 1 part vermiculite. For good measure, arrange various stones or rocks on the soil surface to further re-create the warmth-drenched Mediterranean climate.

## Plow It Under

Building a new bed? Don't worry too much about getting rid of that sod, says Gloria Seborg of Seattle, Washington. She just tills hers under, figuring it adds important organic matter to the soil.

First, Seborg tills the area she wants to plant. Then she spreads any soil amendments and tills again, which chops the sod more finely. As she rakes the bed smooth with a ground rake, she tosses out any remaining chunks of sod she might find.

The first year after tilling the sod under she has to be diligent in weeding any grass that crops up. But weeding is much less work, Seborg says, than the traditional method of first cutting or digging off all that sod.

## Topsoil Tribulations

If you're thinking about buying some topsoil, take care not to get dumped on, warns Alvin Cruise, an avid gardener in Tulsa, Oklahoma. Too often, what is billed as topsoil might be of poor quality, laden with sand or clay, and filled with debris. Cruise recommends that you be present when the topsoil is delivered to your home so you can inspect it before a ton or two is dumped on the driveway. Another alternative is to inspect the soil beforehand. "You really need to check out the source because what would be one person's good soil isn't necessarily a gardener's good soil," Cruise says.

## Rain Drain

Living on Bainbridge Island near Seattle, Shelly Johansson knows that flowerbeds need good drainage. But as a garden designer, she often encounters the worst soil, laying on top of hardpan a foot or so down, which obviously isn't conducive to good drainage.

When she's presented a problem site like that, Johansson creates drainage from the flowerbed by digging a trench along the bed's lowest part, where water would naturally collect. She then lays a length of perforated drainage pipe into the trench, making sure the pipe taps off onto a driveway or other good drainage area. She covers the pipe with gravel or rock, and it provides excellent drainage even in the wettest weather.

*ENSURE GOOD DRAINAGE IN PROBLEM SITES BY INSTALLING A DRAINAGE PIPE.*

## A Forkful of Air

Try this fast, easy way to aerate small areas of soil—those places where you step down from a deck, the area along a driveway, or the place where kids cut across a lawn.

After a good rain, when the ground is moist but not wet, plunge a spading fork 3 to 6 inches into the soil. Rock the fork back and forth a couple of times to widen the holes and then repeat in other areas as needed.

## Leafy Soil Amendment

You don't have to spend time bagging all those fall leaves—or even raking them up and hauling them to your compost heap. Instead, just throw them right on top of your beds, where they'll add valuable humus and leaf mold to the soil, absolute candy for beneficial earthworms.

Rae Haws of Ames, Iowa, has incorporated fall leaves into her abundant vegetable garden for several years and says the most efficient way to do it is to first mow over the leaves with the lawn mower or chop them with a chipper/shredder. Then spread them over the vegetable garden and till them in. If you don't have a tiller, you could simply toss spadesful of soil on top of the leaves to keep them from blowing and to speed decomposition.

## Easy-on-the-Back Beds

Digging new beds takes time—and can take a toll on your back. So instead of digging, create new beds by simply layering materials in three easy steps. You can build a huge bed in less than an hour—and your back will feel great when you're done! Here's how.

1. As long as the soil is reasonably good and the area isn't badly infested with tall, highly invasive weeds, simply spread three or four layers of newspaper on top of the area where the new bed will be. Wet the newspapers down to prevent blowing and speed decomposition.

2. Spread on any soil amendments you wish to use, such as sand or sphagnum peat moss. Then add good-quality topsoil, compost, or better yet a mixture of the two. (It doesn't even matter if the compost is only half-rotted. Just be sure you mix it in thoroughly.) In all, the new bed should be 2 to 8 inches high (it will settle over time).
3. Plant! Waiting 4 to 6 weeks or over the winter is ideal, but you can also plant immediately if you need to.

*SAVE TIME AND BACK PAIN WITH THIS BED THAT TAKES JUST LESS THAN AN HOUR TO CREATE.*

## SEASONAL SOIL IMPROVER

Improving bad soil isn't as difficult as you might think. You just need to have patience. Here's a season-by-season approach to turning your soil into stuff beds are made of.

**FALL.** Dig the bed. Plant a cover crop, such as annual rye (*Lolium multiflorum*). The roots help break up the soil, as does the freezing and thawing of winter and early spring.

**SPRING.** Till in the rye, which adds important organic matter. Then plant annuals only. Go for plants with well-developed root systems, such as tall marigolds and sunflowers; their roots further break up the soil.

**SUMMER.** Mulch the annuals with compost about 3 inches thick. By the end of the season, you'll have vastly improved soil in which you can plant just about anything you want.

### Solutions at a Glance

**PROBLEM:** You're missing out on valuable planting space.

**CULPRIT:** A stump right in the middle of your flowerbed or garden. You've tried to dig it up but can't.

**SOLVE IT!** Plunk a bird bath basin on the stump and suddenly you have a rustic focal point to plant around.

# Squash and Melon Problems

Squash and melons, being members of the same family, have similar growing habits. And if you've ever grown zucchini, you know they can be really easy to grow and grow and grow. . . . But a surprising number of home gardeners don't grow beyond zukes. Too many problems, they say. Too many squash bugs on the summer squash. Too many wilted vines! Too hard to grow melons, and even harder to know when they're ripe. But these great tips and problem solvers will squash your fears in no time!

## Rx for Healthy Squash

Squash expert Dr. Richard Robinson, vegetable breeder at the New York State Agricultural Experiment Station, Cornell University, in Geneva, New York, recommends the following tips. Remember: An ounce of prevention and preparation may, indeed, bring you a pound of great little patty pan squash.

**USE PLENTY OF ORGANIC MATTER.** Squash don't like a starvation diet, so make sure there's plenty of humus in your garden bed.

**HEAT THINGS UP.** Use black plastic to warm the soil. Remember to prepare your ground with the organic matter and lay the plastic before you plant out seeds or transplants.

**GIVE 'EM SHELTER.** Plastic tunnels with wire hoops covered with row cover can get squash off to a bit of an earlier start, plus the cover keeps pest bugs at bay.

**CHOOSE DISEASE-RESISTANT VARIETIES.** These are some of your best defenses against perennial squash pests. (See "Holy Disease Resistance!" on page 152.)

**MAKE 'EM FEEL AT HOME.** Start seeds indoors, 2 to 3 weeks before the last predicted frost. (Squash seeds are so large that they'll quickly grow out of their pots, so bear that in mind when you sprout seeds.) Or direct seed them outdoors when the ground is warm (at least 70°F).

**KEEP THEIR FEET DRY.** Whether you use a row system or a "hill" system (a grouping of five or six seeds together in a raised section of garden soil), make sure you have good drainage. "Drip irrigation is a help," Robinson says, adding that with raised beds or hill systems it's especially important to watch moisture during dry days because the hills dry out quickly. "I personally like to have the seeds evenly spaced, rather than grouping several in one spot," he adds. (And if crows are a problem in your garden, hills are usually too convenient a stop, so make marauding harder on the black birds and plant seeds individually.)

**PICK 'EM SMALL.** It'll send the plant a signal to keep producing fruit. And that means more squash for you!

*IF YOU DECIDE TO GROW YOUR SQUASH USING THE HILL SYSTEM, MAKE SURE TO WATER REGULARLY BECAUSE THE HILLS DRY OUT QUICKLY.*

**STARVE OUT THE ENEMY.** If squash bugs seem to be everywhere at the end of the growing season, your best strategy may be to deny them their favorite food the following year. Substitute another crop for squash—potatoes, for example. In the third year, skip the potatoes, but plant the squash. You should find that the squash bug population has decreased.

## Holy Disease Resistance!

If you're looking for a disease-resistant squash, 'Whitaker' is a godsend for the organic gardener. It's the only squash variety resistant to four of the most devastating diseases faced by the home gardener, especially in the Northeast: powdery mildew, zucchini yellow mosaic virus, cucumber mosaic virus, and papaya ring spot virus.

"This disease resistance, especially to powdery mildew, makes 'Whitaker' very useful to the organic grower," says Dr. Richard Robinson, vegetable breeder at the New York State Agricultural Experiment Station, Cornell University, in Geneva, New York, who developed the squash variety with research support specialist Joseph Shail and virologist Rosario Provvidenti. Robinson notes that the variety is open-pollinated and will set fruit even if it isn't pollinated. That makes it a natural for growing in low plastic row tunnels or hoop houses.

'Whitaker' resembles an Italian Cocozelle-type squash in character and taste. It has medium green fruit that's straight, with blocky ends and dark green stripes. The white flesh is firm, and the compact bush plants are erect and tend to hold the fruit up off the ground.

*When it comes to squash, 'Whitaker' wins the prize for disease resistance—especially against powdery mildew.*

## Rx for Healthy Melons

Dave Wolverton grows killer melons, even though he lives in Arlee, Montana—a beautiful valley surrounded by high mountains that cause tremendous variation in temperatures, even in August, the crucial month for melon maturity. Wolverton also has to work around a short growing season. So how *does* he do it? Here are his tips for raising incredible melons, against all odds.

**Don't rush to start your seeds.** Wolverton starts his indoors May 1 because melons don't need a lot of lead time. But, especially for a short season, starting seeds indoors is an absolute must, he says.

**Heat is critical for a healthy start.** "I place seeds on the surface of moist vermiculite inside a covered plastic tray, then place the tray where the temperature stays in the 80s," Wolverton says. The living room of his parents' home next door works great for him. Heat mats will also work.

**Let seedlings lie.** As the seeds sprout, Wolverton transfers them to Paperpots (30-pot size for melons, available through mail-order suppliers) with two or three sprouted seeds to a pot. (The paper stretches out to form a honeycomb design, which he fills with planting mix.) At planting time, the paper separates into individual pots that can be carefully removed, which is important because melons don't like their roots to be disturbed.

**Prepare the planting area.** Wolverton incorporates compost and fish meal (about 3 pounds per 100 square feet) into the area that will become home to his melons. He spaces rows 9 feet apart, mounds rows about 6 inches higher than the surface of the bed, and positions drip irrigation. Then he lays black plastic over the mounded rows.

**Get 'em in the ground.** Wolverton plants one Paperpot of two or three seedlings every 5 feet. Smaller varieties can be spaced 2½ feet apart in rows 6 feet apart. He covers his seedlings with row covers to create a warmer microclimate. (In other parts of the country, he notes, the covers may be more important for helping fight insect pests.) He pulls the covers back around July 1, but leaves them near the melon plants in case quick cover is needed on a cold night.

**Spray, spray, spray—naturally.** Of course we aren't talking harmful chemicals here! Wolverton says the plants respond very well to fish fertilizer sprays, seaweed sprays, and a twice-a-season baking soda and water spray, which keeps mildew at bay. "Spray the leaves with 1 tablespoon of baking soda mixed with a

# Pest Detective

*Having a problem with your squash or melons? Here are some of the most common pests and ailments—and the best organic solutions for dealing with them.*

| Symptom | Cause | What to Do |
|---|---|---|
| Holes chewed in leaves | Cucumber beetles | Use row covers until flowers open. Try planting later in the season to avoid this spring pest, and set out yellow pans with soapy water to trap beetles once they arrive. |
| Leaves and fruit with mottled spots, and stunted growth | Mosaic viruses | Use resistant cultivars and don't touch wet plants, to avoid spreading the disease. Control sucking insects such as aphids by knocking them off plants with a strong spray of water. Use floating row covers to protect the plants, and remove and destroy virus-infected plants immediately. |
| Wilted leaves with pale blotches, blackened shoots | Squash bugs | Hand-pick these gray-brown, oval bugs. You can lay boards on the soil near the plant at night, lift the boards up in the morning, and pick and destroy bugs off the board daily. Religiously clearing plant waste at the end of the season can prevent recurrence. |
| Vines that suddenly wilt and die, and orange sawdustlike droppings at base of the plant | Vine borers | Plant resistant cultivars, such as 'Butternut' winter squash. Use floating row covers until blossom. Then use preventive methods, such as wrapping the base of the vine in aluminum foil, spraying with garlic or hot pepper solution, or wiping the vine base often. If you spot a borer in a vine, slit the vine, remove the borer, and mound soil over the cut portion of the vine. Or you can inject BT (*Bacillus thuringiensis*) into the vine with a syringe if you notice borer symptoms. |
| White powdery coating on leaves, and plant dies | Powdery mildew | Choose resistant cultivars such as the melons 'Sweet' and 'Edisto 47', allow good air circulation, and remove and destroy affected vines. To control the disease and prevent recurrence, spray weekly with 1 tablespoon of baking soda and 2½ teaspoons of summer oil mixed with 1 gallon of water. Plant squash and melon varieties (such as 'Redlands Trailblazer' winter squash) that are resistant to cucumber mosaic virus and other viral diseases that cucumber beetles transmit. |

gallon of water around July 25 and again around August 15. This is all the more important in my marginal climate, where leaf disorders are likely to occur," he says. One caution, though: "The fish fertilizer spray needs to be timed so as not to offend visitors; it smells horrible," he says.

**VARIETY SELECTION IS IMPORTANT.** His favorite watermelon is 'Lucky Sweet'; 'Earlidew', his favorite melon. He's also experimenting with long-keepers, with hopes of extending the growing season.

**FOLLOW THE WASP RULE.** "For the muskmelon types that slip easily from the stem when they're ripe, the 'wasp rule' is useful: One wasp sipping nectar where the stem meets the fruit means leave it another day or two. Two wasps sipping nectar means you may pick it now. Three wasps on the stem means pick it immediately—but watch out for the wasps!" he explains.

**FOLLOW THE WATERMELON RULE.** Wolverton's watermelon rule is that when the underside touching the ground turns a rich, golden yellow, it's ready. Also, the tendril closest to the melon dries up fully. (Wolverton prefers these tests to the traditional thumping test—where you thunk a melon with your finger and listen for a hollow "ripe" sound—because that takes a lot of skill and different varieties thump differently.)

*WHEN THE UNDERSIDE OF YOUR WATERMELON TURNS A RICH YELLOW, THE MELON IS READY TO MEET YOUR TASTE BUDS.*

**PROP 'EM UP.** Melon fruits can rot in the field even before they ripen. To prevent this from happening, raise them up on overturned cans or plastic containers to keep them dry and intact.

# Squirrel Problems

Squirrels are fun to watch when they're harmlessly gathering acorns in fall. But as anyone with a bird feeder and garden can attest, squirrels can be stubborn and downright gluttonous. They've also been known to dig up bulbs, corms, and newly sown seed—as well as dine on tomatoes and other soft fruit. And 9 times out of 10, they'll find a way to your birdfeeder—in spite of any high-tech squirrel-thwarting contraption you've installed! But you can keep peace in the garden. Read on for some tips to help you outsmart these persistent pests.

## Fence Tactics for Squirrels

Squirrels are good climbers, and that means that nice, sturdy wire fences that deter rabbits or groundhogs may not faze the them. They may just skip the fence entirely, climb a post, and hop right over. But one way to deter climbing squirrels is to use chicken wire fencing, leaving a floppy roll of wire (about a foot) at the top, to act as a baffle. That way, as a squirrel climbs the fence, the fence flops backward and Mr. Squirrel won't be able to make the hop over: humans, 1; squirrels, 0!

## Squirrel-Be-Gone

If it seems like nothing in your yard can be kept safe from squirrels, you might want to try one of the chemical-free commercial products available to help keep squirrels away. In fact, Squirrel Away can be found at most major discount stores and garden centers. It's an all-natural formula that uses powdered capsicum pepper, which is distasteful and harmlessly irritating to squirrels, and which provides birds with a good source of Vitamin A—talk about a win-win situation! You can sprinkle Squirrel Away in bird food, over rows of bulbs, or around tender seedlings.

Also available is N.I.M.B.Y., an emulsion of natural oils designed to help keep squirrels, chipmunks, rabbits, and deer away from precious plants and other areas (see "Resources" on page 344). You can also find organic pepper spray deterrents at garden-supply companies and nursery centers, or you can even try whipping up a batch at home (see "Cabbage Problems" on page 23).

## Have a Drink on Me

A Springfield, Virginia, gardener had a problem with squirrels chewing her tomatoes. But this observant gardener also noticed that this usually happened when there wasn't much water around. So she positioned several birdbaths around the garden and yard, and lo and behold, the squirrels left her tomatoes alone. (But alas, they still ate the bird feed.)

*Provide plenty of water sources around your garden so that squirrels will be able to quench their thirst without having to nibble on your tomatoes.*

## Solutions at a Glance

**Problem:** Something's eating your just-planted bulbs and seeds.

**Culprit:** Squirrels

**Solve It!** Put wire screening or hardware cloth over the soil where you've planted bulbs and seeds to deter squirrels from digging.

## The Feline Factor

It doesn't take a rocket scientist to figure out that squirrels and cats don't get along. To trick squirrels into thinking a hungry cat is lurking near your flowerbeds, apply a light sprinkling of used cat litter around the base of your tulip bulbs (don't use the litter in your vegetable or herb gardens, though).

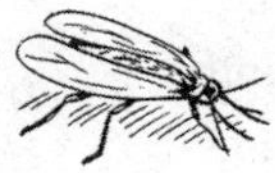

# Ticks

After a day of working in your yard or garden, you might come in to find one of these unwelcome guests—ticks—attached to your skin or clothes. Besides being nasty (they're blood suckers) and just plain ugly, some ticks can carry blood-borne diseases (such as Lyme disease and Rocky Mountain spotted fever, both serious threats to your health). But before you start thinking about hiding indoors all summer, read on for ways to prevent ticks from getting the better of you.

## Ticks Are Such a Drag

According to Stan G. Green, Ph.D., an urban entomologist with the Pennsylvania State Extension Service, based in Philadelphia, dragging tall vegetation growing on the edge of your property is a great way to check on tick populations. It won't help you wipe out ticks if your property is teeming with them, but it will give you a good idea of whether you're dealing with a small army of ticks or just a handful.

You can create a drag from a piece of smooth cotton cloth or an old sheet—use a piece as large as you can comfortably handle. Staple the edge of the cloth or sheet to a piece of wood that's about 1 inch wide (and the length of the sheet). Then tie a piece of string to the wood. Hold on to the string, and pull the drag around the edge of your property. As you pull the drag over your turf, any ticks hanging out in the tall grass or weeds will attach themselves to the sheet. (Just make sure you wear long sleeves and pants while dragging, or you may end up with a few ticks on yourself.)

When you're finished, dispose of any ticks on the drag, or put them in glass jars with tight-fitting lids so they can be analyzed, especially if you live in an area with a high incidence of Lyme disease. (If you find a lot of ticks covering the drag, you should drag daily until you end up with fewer ticks. To keep tick numbers low, drag every 2 weeks throughout spring and summer.)

*Check on the tick population on your property by turning an old sheet into a tick drag.*

## Don't Hold an Open House for Ticks

Has your yard become a haven for ticks? Here are a couple of easy tricks that take in the welcome mat on these blood-thirsty critters.

Start by keeping your yard neat. By eliminating brush and leaf piles, you'll eliminate some prime hiding spots for ticks. Woodpiles should be kept off the ground, too, so that mice—another favorite tick host—don't set up housing there.

You could also consider giving your lawn a crew cut, advises Stan G. Green, Ph.D., an urban entomologist with the Pennsylvania State Extension Service, based in Philadelphia. Tick larvae, which usually aren't carriers of the disease, need moisture to survive. By cropping your lawn shorter than 6 inches, the sun can dry out the larvae and kill them off. And while this won't cure a tick problem, it will definitely cut down on tick populations, Green says.

Keep one thing in mind, though: Short lawns aren't happy, healthy lawns, so if you're going to try this tactic, target spring and early summer to best get at the larval cycle, and then let your lawn grow longer for the rest of the season. (There's no point trying this later in the season, anyway; once tick youngsters grow up, they're able to take the heat.)

### Solutions at a Glance

**Problem:** Something's infesting your backyard.

**Culprit:** Ticks

**Solve It!** Keep a flock of guinea hens. These hungry gobblers of deer ticks are the perfect solution if you have the space and ability to keep them.

Fortunately, lawns aren't the favored habitat of most tick species. You're more likely to pick up ticks from hiking through brushy, wooded areas and meadows of tall grass. If you're out in natural areas, wear a light-colored, long-sleeve shirt and tuck your pants into your socks. When you get back, be sure to check yourself carefully for ticks. (Ticks need to feed for several hours before transmitting any diseases.) If you do find an attached tick, use a narrow tweezer to slowly and carefully remove the tick, then drop it into a jar of alcohol. Observe the bite area for the next several weeks to make sure you don't exhibit any symptoms of disease, such as a rash that looks like a bull's eye.

# Tomato Problems

Chances are, tomatoes are your favorite vegetable. After all, who doesn't enjoy sinking their teeth into a freshly picked love apple? Even small space gardeners grow tomatoes in tubs or patio containers. But for all their goodness, tomatoes aren't problem-free. Diseases are the most common headache, but sometimes critters or insects go after them. Too much fertilizer can reduce yield; too much or too little water can spoil the fruit. To err is human, and tomatoes are forgiving. But heeding a few rules will make for happier plants and lots of luscious fruit.

## Harvest Hints

Pick fruit when it's still firm and a bit underripe and let it finish ripening indoors in a dark, cool place (but not the refrigerator). By picking fruit while it's a bit underripe, you'll lose far fewer tomatoes to ravenous critters and molds, and you won't lose much flavor, either. When picking, be sure to remove the stem to keep the tomatoes from piercing each other in the harvest basket. Ripen them by laying them out stem-end down, on their shoulders, and don't let them touch each other. Fully ripe tomatoes will stay in good condition for a week with care, but even gentle pressure on the flesh will cause a ripe tomato to soften and rot.

*Ripen tomatoes stem end down to prevent bruising and rot.*

## To Pinch or Not To Pinch?

Should you allow a tomato seedling to blossom before you plant it? Most market gardeners say it depends on the size of the plant. If the seedling is small, maybe in a six-pack with its siblings, it's better to pinch off any blossoms before setting the plant into the garden. If it's in a quart-sized or even larger pot, it's likely to have a large enough root ball to set that early fruit and ripen it. The moral? Move your seedlings into the largest pot you can manage if you want robust plants and early fruit.

## PRUNING: ONCE AND DONE

You want early fruit but don't want to decrease overall yield? Do what market gardener Sylvia Ehrhardt does. "We want fruit as early as we can have it, so we prune to two stems early in the season," says Ehrhardt. "But then we don't prune them anymore." In Ehrhardt's Knoxville, Maryland, garden, early tomato varieties start ripening their fruit in May.

## A STAKE IN TIME

Staking tomatoes is a must to help prevent fruit from being attacked by insects or rotting on the ground. Cone-shaped or collapsible wire cages are convenient if you only have a few tomato plants in your garden, but off-season storage of these monstrosities is a problem if your tomato plants number in the dozens. A solution? Stake-and-weave trellises. Here's how to create one.

1. Drive a metal T-stake into the end of the tomato bed, and another after every third tomato plant. Heavy-duty stakes are best if you grow indeterminate tomatoes; lighter-weight stakes are fine for more compact determinates.
2. When the tomatoes are about 1 foot tall, attach a strand of plastic baling twine to the first stake. Draw the twine to the second stake, loop it around the stake, and pull it tight. Continue to the next stake, and the next, until you reach the end of the tomato row.
3. Do the same on the other side of the tomato row. This creates a twine "cage" on either side of the tomato plants.
4. Once a week or so, as the tomatoes grow, add another level of twine. Four or five levels should be enough to corral the tomatoes.

*STAKE-AND-WEAVE TRELLISES ARE QUICK TO PUT UP AND EASY TO PULL DOWN IF YOU GROW LOTS OF TOMATOES.*

**PROBLEM:** It's the end of the season, and you have lots of green tomatoes out there.

**CULPRIT:** Frost

**SOLVE IT!** About 6 weeks before the first expected frost, give your tomato plants a haircut. Doing this prevents new fruit from forming and hastens the ripening of the fruit already set. You can still have vine-ripened fruit if you pull the entire plant before frost, lay it on top of some straw in a frost-free area (such as a barn), and put another layer of straw on top of the plant.

# Pest Detective

*Gardeners aren't the only ones who love tomatoes—so do all kinds of pests and diseases. But that doesn't have to mean you'll end up with a measly couple of love apples at harvest time. Solutions to tomato problems are at hand; in fact, here are five common bugaboos and what to do about them.*

| Symptom | Problem | What to Do |
|---|---|---|
| Holes in leaves and stems of plants—maybe even severe defoliation | Colorado potato beetles | Use beetle-busting straw mulch. Young potato beetles come up from the ground and can't fly for a week. So if you mulch early, they end up dying while crawling through the mulch. |
| Little sunken black spots on the tomatoes, which sometimes don't show up until the fruit is fully ripe | Anthracnose | As soon as you see the first evidence of anthracnose, spray the tomatoes with a solution of 1 cup of hydrogen peroxide to 1 gallon of water, and repeat every 7 to 10 days. |
| The tomatoes bloom like gangbusters but set no fruit | Blossom drop | Tomatoes won't set fruit at very low (below 40°F) or very high (above 85°F) temperatures. Cover early tomatoes to help keep them warm. When it's sweltering outside, throw a shade cloth over the plants (an old lace curtain or tablecloth works well) or give them a cold shower with a sprinkler in midday to keep the blossoms cool. |
| Black, sunken spots on the bottoms of tomatoes | Blossom end rot | Blossom end rot means the tomato isn't getting enough calcium. Even if the soil has plenty of calcium, too much or too little moisture will prevent the tomato plant from taking it up. Keep the tomatoes steadily watered by poking pinholes in the bottoms of plastic milk jugs and half-burying them next to the plants. Fill the jugs once a week or so from the garden hose. |
| Leaves curl up, turn yellow, and drop off | Verticillium and fusarium wilt | Pull up and destroy infected plants. Choose tomato varieties that are resistant to these diseases. |

# Transplant Problems

You have to plant some crops as seedlings, not seeds, or they won't have time to do their thing before the season ends. But young plants are tender, making them easy victims of weather and pests. So no matter whether you grow your own or buy seedlings from a garden center, you'll want to be sure they get off to a good start.

## Halfway House for Hardening Off

You know that you have to harden-off those transplants before setting them in the garden, by gradually introducing them to outdoor conditions. Instead of having to constantly be moving garden-bound seedlings from indoors to out and back again, you can make a simple coldframe as a halfway house for them. Just nail together a plywood frame, then staple Velcro strips to heavy plastic and to the top outside edge of the plywood to hold the plastic in place at night and on windy days.

*This easy-to-build coldframe serves as a halfway house for garden-bound seedlings.*

## Rx for Healthy Transplants

If your green thumb turns to black when trying to start transplants, don't despair. You might just need to tweak your technique a bit. Here are four tips to help you back on the road toward starting seedlings successfully.

**SOW DRY, SET WET.** This old-time advice still holds true. Transplanting works best when the soil is damp. And if it isn't? "I carry buckets of water into the garden and fill the holes with water before I put in the transplants," says Jerry Worrell of Ferry Landing Farm in Dunkirk, Maryland. "I do that with tomatoes, peppers, eggplants, and all my perennials." The water settles soil around the roots of the plant, preventing potential air pockets that could dry out the roots.

**PLANT TOMATOES DEEP.** Bury tomato seedlings all the way up to their top leaves and they'll sprout roots along the buried stem. (A long-handled bulb planter makes it easy to dig a deep hole).

**BE GENTLE WITH SQUASH, FOR PEAT'S SAKE.** Squash, cucumbers, and melons have tender roots that are easily broken, which can send the plant into transplant shock. Start these seedlings in individual peat pots and plant them pot and all before the roots start to penetrate the sides of the pot. Too many plants in a peat pot? Pinch off, don't pull, the excess plants, to avoid disturbing the roots of the ones that remain.

**FOIL CUTWORMS.** Cutworms can mean death to transplants. To protect seedlings, wrap plant stems loosely with small strips of aluminum foil. (The shiny foil helps repel aphids, too!) You can also keep cutworms at bay by placing tuna or cat food cans with the tops and bottoms cut out over your seedlings.

## A Little TLC

Transplants need extra care when you put them out into your garden. To avoid shocking them with bright sunlight, try to transplant on a cloudy or drizzly day or in the evening to spare transplants. You'll also need to protect them from extremes of drought, heat, cold, and wind for the first week after transplanting. Overturned baskets, milk jugs, or fabric row covers work well to keep them from the elements.

## Tough or Tender?

You'll have better luck hardening-off seedlings outdoors if you know whether or not the plants can take a visit from Jack Frost. That's because seedlings of hardy vegetables can withstand some frost; half-hardy vegetables benefit from some frost protection; and tender vegetables can't take any frost at all. (If frost is predicted while you're hardening-off seedlings, protect half-hardy transplants by covering them at night. To protect tender seedlings, bring them indoors overnight.)

Here's a list of how tough or tender your crops are.

**Hardy:** broccoli, brussels sprouts, cabbage, collard, kale, kohlrabi, leek, onion, spinach

**Half-hardy:** cauliflower, celery, chard, chicory, Chinese cabbage, endive, lettuce

**Tender:** cucumber, eggplant, muskmelon, okra, pepper, pumpkin, squash, tomato, watermelon

# Tree and Shrub Problems

Trees and shrubs truly are the backbone of any landscape. We count on them to bring a sense of grandeur and timelessness to our plantings and to provide form in our yards when the last annuals or perennials have said goodbye for the season. But even trees and shrubs aren't immune to problems such as poor drainage, nitrogen deficiency, or scale. That's why this section covers ways to head off problems before they start, along with troubleshooting tips.

## Avoiding Trouble

Avoiding trouble is always easier than coping with it after it strikes—especially when you're dealing with something as big as a tree. Says Matt Vehr, manager of horticulture at Cincinnati's Spring Grove Cemetery and Arboretum, "Most problems with trees and shrubs occur because you have the wrong plant for your site." It's fairly easy to alter growing conditions enough to please a few perennials; it's often impossible when you're dealing with trees and big shrubs. If your woody plants are constantly plagued by pests and diseases, if their growth is sickly and stunted, or if those cute little saplings have grown into monsters you hadn't bargained for, says Vehr, "You're probably better off getting rid of them and starting over again."

Before you even start perusing catalogs, spend some time analyzing your site, advises Vehr, along with Ray McNeilan, retired extension agent for Multnomah County, Oregon. Here's how to do that in four easy steps.

1. Analyze your site for prevailing winds, temperature ranges, humidity levels, and the amount of sunlight your tree or shrub will get. Look at nearby trees and shrubs. Are branches missing on one side that would indicate damage from strong winds on that side? You can gauge temperature ranges by finding out which USDA Hardiness Zone you're in (see the map on page 374). To determine humidity levels, look at the weeds that are growing at the site. Are they weeds like common purslane (*Portulaca oleracea*), which can survive under dry conditions, or are they weeds like pigweeds (*Amaranthus*

## Cultural Culprits

*If your formerly happy trees and shrubs are looking haggard, the source of the trouble may not be pests or disease; it could be cultural problems. Here are some common things to look for and what to do if you find them.*

| Symptom | Possible Cause | What to Do |
|---|---|---|
| Dropping, scorched or wilted leaves | Not enough water is reaching the roots | Soak the ground slowly and thoroughly from the trunk to the drip line, then mulch with compost or well-rotted manure. |
| General decline in appearance and vigor | Compaction of the soil from foot or vehicle traffic | Re-route traffic (erect a barrier around the root zone if you have to). Dig organic matter such as compost into the soil as far as you can without disturbing the roots, and then add mulch. |
| Leaves mottled, speckled tan or white, or turning silvery in color; branches dying | Air or ground pollution, or damage from road salt | Avoid using salt to melt snow. Instead, use cinders, sand, or clay cat litter to provide traction on ice and snow, or check in your local hardware store for an environmentally friendly ice melter. Feed and water the tree thoroughly or remove it and plant a more resistant variety. |
| Older, lower leaves turn yellow and may drop; plant growth is slow and spindly | Nitrogen deficiency | Dig in compost, supplemented with a high-nitrogen additive such as bloodmeal or fish meal. Avoid low-nitrogen mulches such as wood bark. |
| Leaves wilted or turning brown; top branches dying; general decline in appearance and vigor | Poor drainage | If the plant is small enough, move it to a better site. Otherwise, improve the drainage (you may need help from a professional landscaper). |

spp.) and common lamb's-quarters (*Chenopodium album*), which grow best in areas where humidity is higher? To determine how much sunlight your tree or shrub will get, see "Shade" on page 139.

2. Test your soil for pH, fertility, and drainage.
3. Think about what you want the trees or shrubs to accomplish. Do you want a background for your perennial border? A leafy canopy to shade your hammock on hot summer days? A soldier in the war against winter gales and high heating bills? Also, consider how big the tree needs to be to do its job and how long it will take to grow to maturity.
4. Get help. Trees and shrubs can be big investments in terms of money. If you aren't sure what will feel most at home on your range, ask the advice of a knowledgeable friend or a professional arborist.

## Rx for Healthy Trees and Shrubs

For healthy, problem-free trees and shrubs, follow this three-part formula, says Akron, Ohio, gardener Mary Frances Jarrold.

**RELY ON NATIVE PLANTS.** "They look better, and they're much less susceptible to pests and diseases," she says.

**ENCOURAGE PREDATORS THAT PREY ON PEST INSECTS.** Jarrold's favorites: toads and bats. "I used to spray," she admits. "Almost immediately after I quit, a family of toads showed up. Soon after that my husband put bat houses in all the trees, and that was the end of the pest problems."

**KEEP IT CLEAN.** "Never go into the garden without a bag and a pair of pruners," she advises. "Pick up debris as soon as you see it, and clip off any leaves or twigs that don't look right. Diseases thrive in litter and weakened tissue."

## Get a Good Start

If you've inherited a tree or shrub that has never performed up to snuff, the trouble might well stem from improper planting. Trees and large shrubs need to be treated differently from perennials if they're going to grow up strong, healthy, and able to fend off pests and disease. If you're fond of the plant and it's small enough for you to manage, move it to a new site and give it a fresh start. Here's how to transplant a tree or shrub, from Ray McNeilan, retired extension agent for Multnomah County, Oregon.

1. Dig a planting hole wide enough to accommodate the roots without circling or kinking, but only deep enough to set the plant at the same depth as it was planted before. (Don't add soil amendments. If you do, the roots will confine themselves to the beefed-up area, rather than spreading out as they need to do. The plant's growth will be stunted, maybe severely.)
2. If a tree can't stand on its own, you'll need to stake it. (Young trees develop stronger root systems and sturdier, more resilient trunks when they're allowed to move with the wind.) When the rootball is in its planting hole and before you replace the soil, drive in two posts, one on each side of the hole and well clear of the roots.
3. Fasten the tree to the posts with soft, broad straps; never use wire or wire-filled hose, which can girdle the bark.
4. Allow enough slack so the trunk can move 2 inches in every direction.
5. Remove the stakes and ties within 6 months to 1 year after planting.

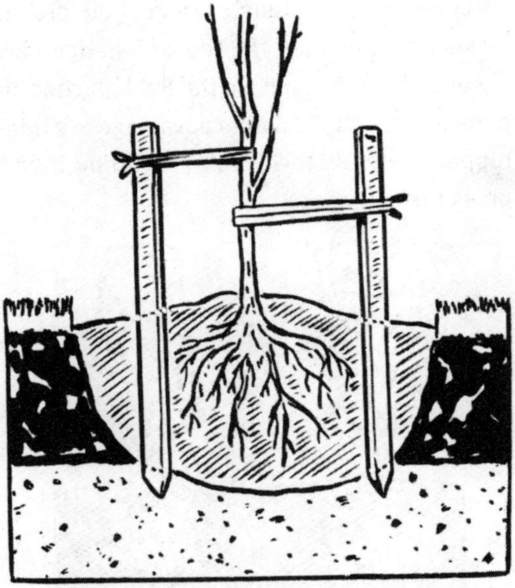

*STAKE YOUR TREE PROPERLY TO AVOID INJURING—OR EVEN KILLING—IT.*

## Solutions at a Glance

**Problem:** Your trees are losing their bark.

**Culprit:** Deer (They're using your trees as scratching posts to get the velvet off their new antlers.)

**Solve It!** Loosely wrap green plastic construction fence around the trees to a height of about 4 feet. The bucks will get their head rubs elsewhere.

### Balding from the Bottom

Got a hedge that's looking sparse and scraggly toward the bottom? That's probably because it's suffering from the shade brought on by the leaves above it. Advises Skillman, New Jersey, gardener Rosalia Kung, "When you prune, make sure you keep the top of a hedge narrower than the bottom, so the light reaches all parts of it equally." Another advantage to a thin-topped hedge: Snow won't pile up on it and break the branches.

*Your hedge will stay healthier if the sun can reach the bottom foliage as well as the top.*

### Home Sweet Pot

Itching to plant a certain tree or shrub but know it will be a struggle to make it survive on your home ground? Give up the fight before you begin—the results are sure to be marginal at best. Instead, advises Linda Waller, container-plant specialist and owner of Doolittle Gardens in Seattle, pot it up. Here's how.

- For best results, plant dwarf varieties with limited growth potential. For example, a sugar maple (*Acer saccharum*) won't find happiness in a pot, but plenty of its little cousins will, such as Japanese maples (*A. palmatum*).
- Choose a container that's big and sturdy enough to handle the rootball and that has good drainage. High-fired terra cotta (not the thin, mass-produced kind), fiberglass, or wood will all work fine—but if you opt for wood, use a plastic liner or the roots will grow into the container.
- Raise the pot an inch or two above the ground to allow air circulation. A wheeled plant caddie the size of the container will do the job nicely, and will allow you to move the plant easily for maintenance, winter protection, or simply to change the scene in the garden.
- Whatever you do, Waller warns, don't line the bottom of the pot with clay shards, stones or foam peanuts. "Roots confined to a pot need all the room they can get. If you use well-amended soil your drainage will be plenty good enough without adding material that deprives roots of soil in an already limited space."

After that, says Waller, "The two crucial factors are water—never let the container dry out completely—and placement." In particular, she says, be aware of reflected sun from glass doors or light-colored walls. It can work for you or against you. On the plus side, the added warmth can extend the season and let you grow more tender plants than you could otherwise. On the flip side, intense light will give them a thirst that won't quit—and if it's too brutal, it could cook them. If your sunbathing tree starts looking stressed, move it to a cooler spot.

*SMALL AND DWARF VARIETIES OF TREES AND SHRUBS CAN LIVE HAPPILY EVER AFTER IN POTS. JUST GIVE THEM ROOT ROOM, GOOD AIR CIRCULATION, AND SOIL AMENDED TO SUIT THEIR TASTE.*

## Solutions at a Glance

**PROBLEM:** Crust white or brown patches are all over your shrub's branches.

**CULPRIT:** Scale

**SOLVE IT!** Put rings of double-faced tape around several branches, says Judy Wong, a Master Gardener from Menlo Park, California. As the tiny scale hatchlings scamper about, some of them will be trapped on the sticky stuff (they'll look like grayish dust). Be sure to leave a little tab at the end of the tape so you can get it off the plant easily.

### DOING THE ROOTBALL ROCK

When planting a tree, getting the top of the rootball even with the soil surface can be tricky. So what do you do if you slide the tree into the hole you just dug, only to find the tree is at the wrong height?

Simply pull on the trunk a little to rock the still-intact rootball onto an angle. If the tree is set too low, add some soil under the rootball. If it's too high, remove some soil. Then rock the tree back in the other direction, and add or remove soil under the other side of the rootball.

# Vegetable Garden Problems

Working in a vegetable garden on a beautiful summer day can be terrifically relaxing, and it can also bring tremendous rewards to the dinner table. But as you know, to reap a garden's rewards you have to battle weeds, weather, and pest bugs. The following hints will give you some insight on the best bug beaters, how to use compost for a healthy garden, and more, so you'll be well on your way to vegetable riches.

## Rx for a Healthy Garden

Veteran gardener Paul Doscher follows six basic tenets to ensure a healthy vegetable garden. Here are this Weare, New Hampshire, expert's resourceful tips to help you plan a picture-perfect vegetable garden and stop problems before they start.

**SITE IT RIGHT.** It's important to site your garden rows or plants so that they get optimum sun during the day, says Doscher. "Running rows or beds from north to south ensures that as the sun tracks across the sky in summer (in an arc from northeast to southwest) every plant that needs full sun will get some," he explains. And remember to plant taller plants at the north end of a bed so they won't shade smaller plants early and late in the season, when the sun is lower in the sky.

If, however, your land is on a slope, the sun orientation rule doesn't apply—stopping erosion is more vital. In that case, Doscher notes, you should run your rows parallel with the slope so that heavy rains won't create erosion gullies.

*If you have to plant your garden on a hill, run the rows parallel with the slope so you don't end up with heavy erosion.*

## Solutions at a Glance

**PROBLEM:** You tilled your veggie garden midseason, and now it has more weeds than veggies in it.

**CULPRIT:** Weeds

**SOLVE IT!** Tilling in summer brings weed seeds to the surface, where they can germinate, causing a weed-farm effect. Till only twice a year: once in spring, to turn over the soil and mix in organic matter, and once again in fall, to turn in waste organic matter, such as spent plants and spoiled veggies.

**RAISE YOUR GARDEN'S POTENTIAL.** "I've used raised intensive beds for more than 20 years now. They're the most efficient way to produce high yields with less work," Doscher says. In the North, the beds don't take a lot of work to make. You don't need to double-dig, because the freezing and thawing of soil in winter breaks it up, aerates it, and lets plant roots grow down deep.

Doscher uses his rotary tiller to build beds easily. First, he tills an area, then he uses the furrower device on the rear of his tiller to push up soil from the paths into the beds. This ensures deeper soil in the beds (where you *don't* walk) and less soil in the paths (where you do).

**MAKE COMPOST.** One of the most important keys to a successful organic garden is compost, and making it doesn't have to be a chore, says Doscher. "We make lots of compost, but not with fanaticism. You'll find no compost starters or special biological injections here," he says. "Compost makes itself," along with the natural organisms that are found in soil, he says. And by having several compost piles in various stages of development, you'll always have some ready to nourish your garden with. See "Whip Up a Batch of Homemade Compost" on page 172 for Doscher's compost-making tactics.

**REMEMBER TO MULCH.** Keeping moisture in the garden is another key to success. Doscher accomplishes this by mulching the entire garden, especially the paths between the beds, early in the season. (He uses spoiled hay, but grass clippings or other organic covers will work, too.) But don't put the mulch down too early, he warns, or slugs and cold soil will stop your plants before they get started. Put the mulch down after the soil has warmed (the exact timing will depend on your location and a particular year's weather). Doscher then waters with soaker hoses, giving each bed a good soak about twice a week.

**CONTROL GARDEN PESTS.** There's more than one way to fool a bug, but the best way to keep them guessing, says Doscher, is to faithfully rotate your crops from year to year. Don't plant tomatoes or cabbage or beans in the same spot 2 years in a row. And a 3-year or longer rotation is most effective.

Another antipest tactic is to choose resistant varieties that are less susceptible to pests. "We have a standard collection of varieties we use because, in our experience, they suffer from fewer pests in our location," he says. Check with your neighbors or the Cooperative Extension Service for variety recommendations in your area.

Finally, when these tactics don't control a pest problem, Doscher's weapon of choice is Sunspray oil for dormant perennials and occasional use on the garden in summer. Floating row covers also will help keep bugs off the small plants, he says.

**KEEP FEATHERED PESTS AT BAY.** Doscher uses bird scare or flash tape (available from a number of seed catalogs and nursery centers) to keep birds out of his strawberries and crows away from his young corn seedlings. He attaches the shiny red-and-silver tape to stakes and runs it the length of the garden rows, about 12 inches off the ground. The wind makes the tape flash in the sun, scaring birds away. "It really works," Doscher says.

## Keep 'Em from Bolting

Having your lettuce or other leafy greens bolt before you get the chance to even enjoy a couple of salads can be a frustrating experience. But you can't blame the plants—when their biological clock tells them it's time to make a flower stalk, they just can't refuse. But there are some tips that can ensure a few salads before the inevitable occurs.

Your first option is to move your timetable. Many plants that bolt when grown in spring show great staying power if grown in the fall, when days are getting shorter. Your second option is to choose varieties that are less likely to bolt (such as 'Green Ice', 'Red Sails', 'Sierra', and 'Matchless'). Bolt resistance also has been bred into many vegetables, so start looking for it when you shop for seeds.

## Whip Up a Batch of Homemade Compost

Veteran gardener Paul Doscher of Weare, New Hampshire, makes a quick-and-easy compost to supply his garden with all the nutrients it needs. Here's his surefire method:

1. Shred or chop all the waste to put in the pile for the fastest results. (You'll still get compost if you don't shred—it will just take longer.)
2. Add a layer of fresh manure (chicken works well, but any animal manure will do), soil, or finished compost every 6 inches or so as you build the pile.
3. Keep your pile moist, but not soggy, and open up air holes in the pile with your pitch fork.
4. Use garden waste that's fresh or green so you capture the nitrogen in it for feeding the organisms that are so important to making compost.
5. Once you've finished the compost—brown, crumbly material with a lot of the waste so decomposed you don't recognize it—cover the pile with a sheet of black plastic. This will protect it from rain and keep it from losing important nutrients through leaching.

*SHREDDING FALL LEAVES BEFORE ADDING THEM TO YOUR COMPOST PILE WILL HELP THEM DECOMPOSE FASTER.*

## Beat Back Bugs

There's no reason to let the bugs take over your garden. With the great expert tips on page 174, you can keep everything from aphids to Mex-

# Pest Detective

*Not all garden pests have four (or six) legs and a healthy appetite. Some of your foes are microscopic organisms that sneak in and leave your plants diseased and ailing. But don't fret if your garden gets sick—resourceful organic cures exist for most garden diseases. The main thing is to act fast, so keep a close eye on your vegetable garden and identify diseases before they take a firm hold. Then try these solutions when you spot a problem.*

| Symptom | Cause | What to Do |
|---|---|---|
| Flesh-tone spore masses that ooze out of lesions; dark brown spots on bean plants, melon leaves, and cucumbers; or tomatoes with dark, sunken lesions | Anthracnose caused by fungus | Remove infected plants, and don't work in the garden when leaves are wet. Rotate crops and keep plant leaves off the soil surface to help prevent the disease. |
| Young, just-emerging seedlings rot at soil level and die, or fail to emerge at all | Damping-off caused by parasitic fungi | Indoors: Remove dying seedlings if the problem isn't too severe; for a severe problem, discard the whole flat. Provide good air circulation (a fan works well), and be careful not to overwater. Also, use a commercial soilless growing mix and bottom heat at 70° to 75°F. Outdoors: Wait until temps warm up to plant, or put black plastic over the soil to warm it up. Thin seedlings for good air circulation. |
| Nightshade crops, especially tomatoes, potatoes, and eggplant, develop circular leaf spots; their leaves yellow and the plants die | Early blight caused by fungus | Pick bottom leaves as they brown, and remove and destroy badly infected plants. To prevent early blight, avoid subjecting plants to stress and overhead irrigation, use mulch, plant crops in full sun, space them for good air circulation, clean up garden debris in the fall, and rotate crops. |
| Small, pale green spots develop on tomato, potato, and eggplant leaves; spots grow into large brown areas, leaves shrivel, and plant dies; fruit is infected with brown spots that look greasy | Late blight caused by fungus | Promptly remove infected leaves or, if necessary, destroy infected plants. To reduce late blight in your garden, plant certified disease-free potato varieties with late blight resistance (such as 'Elba'), avoid overhead irrigation, space plants for good air circulation, and rotate crops. |
| Whitish gray powder coating on leaves and buds | Powdery mildew caused by spores of fungi spread by wind | Plant resistant varieties and water them with a strong stream of water during dry conditions, when powdery mildew thrives. Spray affected plants once a week with 1 tablespoon each of vegetable oil and baking soda, plus a drop of dishwashing soap in a gallon of water. Prune and destroy infected parts that don't improve after spraying. |

ican bean beetles under control and away from your tender eggplant seedlings or thriving filet beans. (See individual entries for tips on controlling pests specific to certain veggies.)

**USE FLOATING ROW COVERS AS BARRIERS** to keep insects (and those pesty moths that start many problems) off crops. Row covers work well on cabbage, Asian greens, eggplant, squash, melons, and more. Just remember to remove the covers when your plants blossom (for pollination purposes). Row covers are available from most seed companies and nurseries in various widths and weights.

**HAND-PICK THOSE BAD BUGS.** If your garden is small, it's easy to find pests with the help of a good insect guide. Check leaves often for egg masses and young and adult pests (or the damage they leave in their wake), and you'll soon become an expert at identifying them. Just watch out that you don't remove beneficial insects. Early removal of pests goes a long way toward improving the health—and the production—of your crops.

*HAND-PICKING PESTS IS A GREAT WAY TO KEEP GARDEN BAD GUYS UNDER CONTROL.*

**EXPERIMENT WITH HOMEMADE, NATURAL SPRAYS.** Auburn University entomologist Geoff Zehnder says that sprays made with ground red pepper and garlic work well on cabbage. (See "Cabbage Problems" on page 23 for details.) Commercial hot pepper and garlic pest repellents are also widely available. Animal pests can be chased off with these sprays, too.

**ENCOURAGE BENEFICIAL INSECTS.** This can be done by planting a border of companion plants, such as dill and yarrow, which are rich in nectar and pollen, to attract many beneficials. Add stones to containers of water or birdbaths around the garden so little beneficials can drink without drowning. Beneficial insects include the aphid midge, braconid wasp, lady beetles, lacewings, dragonflies, minute pirate bugs, scale predator beetles, and spined soldier bugs.

**USE BIOLOGICAL INSECTICIDES WHEN NECESSARY.** Products with BT (*Bacillus thuringiensis*) can control both moth and butterfly larvae, cabbageworms, loopers, hornworms, and crop-damaging caterpillars.

**DO SOME CLEAN UP IN FALL.** Remove diseased plants and any crops where you've had pest problems—or where you know the pest overwinters in the debris. (Leave flower borders for spring to provide overwintering sites for beneficial insects.)

## Make Veggies Wait on You

Nothing feels worse than watching your veggies spoil before you have a chance to harvest or enjoy them. So seek out veggies that keep, and you'll be able to feast on them over a long period. Some of those "keepers" will wait in the ground until you have a chance to gather them. Others will store well into winter with the right conditions. Here are a few friends to the harried gardener who just doesn't have the time to deal with her veggies right now:

- Cabbage can be a real trooper, but there are two tricks to keeping it—pick it young and store it cold (but not so cold it freezes). Ideal conditions are between 32° and 40°F and 90 percent humidity.

- Carrots, beets, and parsnips all store well in the ground through fall. In fact, carrots and parsnips sweeten as the temperature turns colder. Before the ground freezes, mulch the plants with 8 to 12 inches of straw. Or, harvest them, brush off the soil, cut off the tops of the leaves (leaving an inch of greens), and store the veggies in sand in a cool place.
- Long-keeper tomatoes will last you well into winter. Just pick them when they turn a pale white-green, wrap them in newspaper, and store them in a cool (around 60°F), dark place to ripen slowly.
- Onions, leeks, shallots, and garlic are all good long keepers.
- Potatoes, especially 'Yukon Gold' and 'Butte', are also good keepers. Just remember to store them where it's cool (about 40°F) and dark because light produces green potatoes with poisonous alkaloids that will make for bitter potatoes and sick potato eaters.
- Winter, butternut, and spaghetti squash are all great keepers. Store at 45° to 50°F and 65 to 70 percent humidity.

*STORE LONG-KEEPER TOMATOES IN NEWSPAPER AND YOU CAN ENJOY BLT SANDWICHES IN JANUARY.*

## BABY VEGGIES ARE IN!

You can get vegetables to do double-duty by harvesting some when they're "babies" rather than waiting until they're mature. Lettuce is a great example of a natural baby veggie, taking only about 5 weeks to be ready for harvest (from transplant). Some romaines and Batavian varieties are fine for baby lettuce, but the best varieties are those bred to be compact, such as Bibbs. Other great baby veggies include:

- Beans, particularly haricot vert or filet beans
- Beets, which are flavorful when young
- Broccoli, which can be spaced closely (8 inches apart) so heads will stay small
- Carrots, such as 'Kinko' and 'Thumbelina', which can be planted closely and are ready about 55 days after seeding

*YOU CAN ENJOY SOME VEGETABLES EARLY IN THE SEASON, SUCH AS CARROTS AND BEETS, BY HARVESTING THEM WHEN THEY'RE YOUNG.*

- Corn (an early-maturing variety), which can be planted 6 inches apart and picked when there is a bulge inside the husk
- Eggplant, which is delicious when young
- Squash, including patty pan, zucchini, and all summer squash

# Vole Problems

Voles (also called meadow mice or field mice) are so small that you might be tempted to look at them and think "How much damage can that little thing do?" But these 1- to 2½-ounce critters eat almost their own weight in vegetable matter every day. And because they can have 5 to 10 litters of four to seven young at a time, an awful lot of your garden can get eaten up by voles in just one season. Read on for great ways to spare your plants from these voracious vegetarians.

## Build a Better Vole Barrier

Master Gardener Joan Reese-Gorecki decided that enough was enough after watching—and hearing—a gladiolus keel over one morning in her suburban Memphis garden. That's when she came up with a plan to take care of her vole problem once and for all.

"My husband built a wooden frame the size of a raised bed. Before I put the frame in place, I turned the frame on its side and stapled a piece of hardware cloth across the bottom," she explains. (Hardware cloth is wire welded into mesh that comes in rolls from the hardware store. To protect against voles, use mesh that's ¼ inch or smaller in size.)

"I set the frame into my bed, filled it with a mixture of soil and compost, and then planted my vegetables and flowers right into the frame, where they remained all season," says Reese-Gorecki.

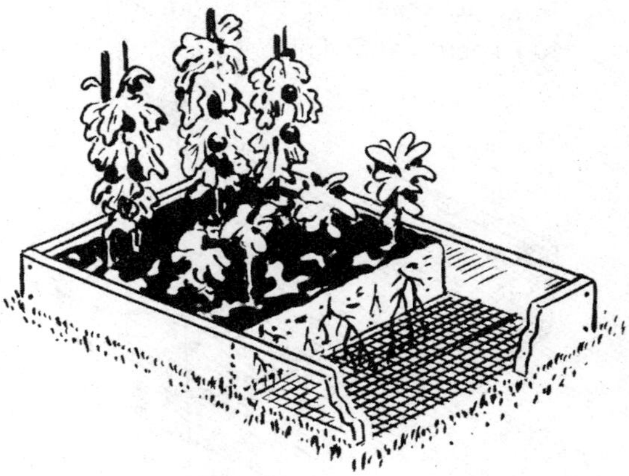

*Hardware cloth stapled to the bottom of a frame keeps voles out but lets roots reach the soil.*

"It worked out spectacularly well!" she says. Plant roots easily grow down into the soil through the ¼-inch openings in the hardware cloth, but voles can't reach the bulbs and tender plant shoots.

"I plant asparagus the same way. The asparagus beds need to be 8 inches high, though, so we use a double width of lumber," Reese-Gorecki says. (And remember: Avoid using pressure-treated lumber to build raised beds.)

## Winter Warfare

The worst vole damage comes during winter, when they feast on the trunks and root systems of your trees and shrubs. You can put an end to their snacking, though, by removing any wood chips or mulch from the base of young trees and shrubs in fall. (Without the wood chips or mulch, voles won't have any protective cover.) You can also wrap hardware cloth around the tree trunks (keep the cloth about 6 inches away from the trunks so the trees will have room to grow), then push the cloth about 6 inches into the ground.

## Fight for Your Tulips

Voles can be the guilty party if your prize tulip bulbs fail to appear in the spring. Try planting tulips in plastic pots with drainage holes, and then sinking the containers into the ground, keeping the pot rim at the soil surface. You can also put a handful of sharp crushed gravel around bulbs when you plant them to deter voles from digging down to your bulbs. For the most fool-proof technique—plant daffodils. They're poisonous to voles, so the voles won't bother them.

## Solutions at a Glance

**Problem:** Critters are eating their way through most of your precious plants.

**Culprit:** Voles

**Solve It!** Reduce their presence in your yard and garden by making them feel unwelcome. Remove weeds and brush piles and keep tunneled areas mowed regularly. Pull mulch away from trees and shrubs in the fall so voles won't move in and eat roots and bark through the winter.

# Water Garden Problems

Who doesn't love a water garden? They're beautiful, restful, cooling, and calming, no matter if they're big or small. But they can also be green, algae-ridden messes, fraught with a host of problems: predators that eat fish, plants that become invasive, and slippery surfaces that pose a hazard for children.

Forethought and resourcefulness, however, can put the fun back into water gardening. Plan and manage your water garden (instead of just building one willy-nilly and letting it care for itself), and you'll have the delight of water for years to come.

## Keeping Fish Safe

No matter if you have $200 koi or $2 goldfish in your water pond, you'll want to help protect them from predators. Shelly Johansson, a gardener and garden designer from Bainbridge Island, Washington, recommends creating a pond 4 to 5 feet deep. A deep pond lets fish dive away from predators. If you can't build a deep pond, put a pot turned on its side on the bottom of the pond, so the fish can dive in and hide there.

*Don't let your fish become a tasty snack; protect them from critters by giving them a pot to hide in.*

## How Low Will It Go?

That low-lying spot on your property may look like the perfect place to build a water garden, but it isn't, says Jamie Beyer, a water garden writer and consultant in Ames, Iowa. In fact, a low-lying area is among the *worst* places to locate a water garden because runoff from the surrounding landscape may contain contaminants such as pet feces and lawn chemicals, which will collect in the spot. So what to do? You can either burm up the edges of the pond to divert runoff or convert the area into a bog garden, which can take excess runoff, says Beyer.

## Savvy Substitutes

Don't panic if you can't afford to shell out top dollar for special water-gardening supplies. Here are some ways to keep your hard-earned money in your pocket and still have what you need to create a great water garden, from Jamie Beyer, a water garden writer and consultant in Ames, Iowa.

**RECYCLE BLACK PLASTIC POTS.** Avoid buying those expensive water garden planting containers. Instead, use ordinary black plastic pots left over from other plant purchases. Just rinse them off and cover the holes in the bottom with plastic window screen or landscape fabric to prevent the soil from washing out.

**USE ROOF LINER.** Roof liner is an economical substitute for regular pond liner. Although some pond experts recommend pond liner because it's guaranteed fish safe, Beyer says he has never known a fish to have gotten lost because of roof liner. One of the best pond liners is 45 mil EPDM, and Beyer says you can buy roof liner made out of the same material. (If you still aren't sure the roof liner is fish safe, ask the supplier about using their product in a pond.) The savings, especially for large gardens, are substantial because roofing liner costs about one-third less than pond liner.

**LOOK AROUND THE HOUSE FOR CUSHIONING MATERIAL.** Although you can buy special cushioning liners to lay between the soil and liner to prevent rips and tears, you can save big by cushioning with either old carpet scraps or several layers of newspaper.

*SAVE MONEY BY USING LEFTOVER PLASTIC POTS FOR WATER GARDEN PLANTS.*

## Square Foot Fish

You're all ready to add some fish to your water garden. But will they have enough room? Fish require a surprising amount of space—and your water garden isn't any goldfish bowl. As a rule of thumb, each inch of fish should have about 6 square inches to 1 square foot of water surface. Koi are the exception, needing about 25 square feet for each fish. But for other fish, here's the space you need—at a minimum.

- One 2-inch fish: 1 square foot of water surface
- Two 8-inch fish: 8 square feet
- Six 6-inch fish: 18 square feet
- Twelve 4-inch fish: 24 square feet

# Pest Detective

*Hmmm. Something suspicious is happening in your water garden, and it isn't pretty. Here are some symptoms, causes, and cures.*

| Symptom | Cause | What to Do |
|---|---|---|
| Chewed holes in foliage, often skeletonized | Aphids | Keep aging, yellowing, and dying foliage trimmed from plants; apply an oil spray of two parts vegetable oil to eight parts water and a teaspoon dishwashing detergent; then remove oil film from water surface by skimming or carefully absorbing it with paper towels. |
| Foliage is yellowing and dying; traces of tiny webs | Red spider mites | Spray plants with garden hose. If that doesn't work, apply an insecticidal soap, removing the plant from the pond for spraying if possible. |
| Holes chewed around the edges and throughout floating vegetation; tiny brown stippling as well | Water lily beetles | Prune damaged vegetation; wipe any eggs from bottom of plants, especially water lilies (*Nymphaea* spp.). If problem is severe, remove plants and isolate them in a special tub. |
| Large oval chunks eaten out of water lily leaf margins | China moth larvae | Remove caterpillar cases from the underside of leaves, spray with *Bacillus thuringiensis* (BT). |

## Rx for an Algae-Free Pond

Algae—yucky, thick, mucky algae—is the bane of many a water garden. You can control algae, however, by doing the following:

**GET SNAILS.** Black Japanese snails are voracious algae eaters, and they won't feed on your water plants.

**PLANT FLOATERS.** These plants, such as water lilies (*Nymphaea* spp.), grow in colonies on the surface of the water and shade it, thereby keeping it cool (algae loves warm water). Floaters also block out light algae need to thrive.

**HAVE A FEW FISH.** They also eat algae.

**CONSIDER A BIOLOGICAL FILTER OR UV CLARIFIER.** Both of these defend your pond or pool from algae, as well as destroy many types of bacteria, viruses, and fungi that can harm fish. (You can purchase filters or clarifiers from water-gardening supply stores.)

**RAKE IT UP.** You can remove smaller amounts of filamentous algae, which looks like floating seaweed, by hand or with a leaf rake.

**SCRUB IT.** If algae forms on rocks, waterfall, or other hard surfaces, turn off the pump and let the algae dry. Then scrape or brush it off with a stiff brush. If that doesn't work, rewet the algae and sprinkle it with noniodized table salt. Leave it for several hours and then scrub again.

*USE A LEAF RAKE TO KEEP YOUR WATER GARDEN CLEAR OF SEAWEEDLIKE FILAMENTOUS ALGAE.*

## ROCK SOLID ADVICE

If you want your water garden to have a natural look—as if it just happened to crop up in your backyard—then using stone is the way to go. For the most natural effect, follow these tips for using stone in a water feature.

**USE WHAT'S LOCAL.** Not only is local stone usually less expensive than stone that has been hauled in, it also tends to fit in better with your region's trees and landscape.

### Solutions at a Glance

**PROBLEM:** Water garden plants and fish are sick.

**CULPRIT:** Too much chlorine

**SOLVE IT!** When filling the pond for the first time, or after a draining, let the water stand for about 5 days, enough time for the chlorine to dissipate. Then you can add plants and fish with confidence.

**PLACE STONE RANDOMLY.** Study naturally occurring creeks and ponds and follow their lead. Nature plunks stones down right along the edges and in the middle of streams

**FIND A PLACE FOR STONE ELSEWHERE IN YOUR LANDSCAPE.** If you have a flagstone path and a low flagstone retaining wall, the flagstone edging around your pond is going to look more at home.

**VARY STONE SIZES.** Again, nature includes very large, some medium, and very small stones (in the form of gravel) in her landscape. Mix it up in your landscape, too.

# Water Problems

Garden plants are pretty resilient, and they'll put up with a lot of neglect and laziness on our parts. But there's one thing they can't survive over the long haul: a lack of water. Unless, of course, you set them up to be camels from the get-go. Prepare their beds the right way and employ a few expert tricks, and they'll pull through any dry spell without so much as a wilted leaf, and without inviting in any moisture-loving pests and diseases. Read on for the hows, whens, and whys of watering so every drop counts.

### Have an Organic Defense

Protect your garden by making sure your soil is high in organic matter, and your plants will come through a drought like champs. Even if dry times don't come, your plants will still thank you for the nice meal!

Your best bet is to enrich your soil with plenty of compost, animal manure, or leguminous green manures, such as clover or alfalfa. For a drought-hardy green manure, try a perennial clover, or cowpeas (*Vigna unguiculata* subsp. *Unguiculata*). (See "Resources" on page 344.) This enrichment helps the soil act like a sponge, hanging on to moisture long after less-rich soils have completely dried out and turned to cement. This cooling moisture can mean the difference between life and death for your plants, especially if your area imposes watering restrictions during a drought.

*Enriching your soil with a green manure helps ensure your plants will make it through a drought.*

## Solutions at a Glance

**PROBLEM:** Your plants are left high and dry during drought.
**CULPRIT:** Sandy soil
**SOLVE IT!** Sandy soil is no day at the beach for your garden plants, so you'll need to add plenty of organic materials and a heavy organic mulch to it if you want your plants to come through looking green and happy.

---

**PROBLEM:** Blossoms are dropping, tomatoes are cracking while ripening, and blossom end rot is taking over your tomato plants.
**CULPRIT:** You haven't watered enough, or you've watered unevenly.
**SOLVE IT!** Run soaker hoses through the beds a few inches below the mulch, and you'll be able to provide even watering when and where your plants need it most.

## CHOOSE WISELY

If year after year you find yourself wishing for rain during the summer months, try following these words of wisdom from gardeners around the country; they'll help you deal easily with a lack of the wet stuff.

**MAKE IT QUICK.** Grow short-season varieties that are ready for harvest more quickly and therefore require less water than long-season varieties, recommends D. Keith Crotz, an avid organic gardener and college biology instructor in Chillicothe, Illinois.

**IMPORT SOME REINFORCEMENTS.** Plant southern varieties in the North, and you'll generally get better results during extended hot, dry spells, says Jim Gerritsen, co-owner of Wood Prairie Farm in Bridgewater, Maine. (This also works in the reverse: Northern varieties of many vegetables will show increased vigor and yield in longer, more hospitable southern climes.)

## MAKE SOAKER HOSES DO DOUBLE-DUTY

Paul Doscher of Weare, New Hampshire, has an ingenious way to get the most use out of the fewest number of soaker hoses.

"We don't have enough soaker hoses to put them out in each and every bed, so I've made most of our beds the same length and cut hoses to that length," explains Doscher. "I move them around the garden so each bed gets a soaking about twice a week." To make moving the hoses easier, Doscher uses quick-connect, snap-type couplings, available at garden or home centers.

## Solutions at a Glance

**Problem:** Plants in some parts of your yard are being wiped out, while others are spared.

**Culprit:** Drought

**Solve It!** Take a good look at the places where plants seem to be persisting—is the soil there wetter, of a slightly different type, or slightly more shaded from the sun? Design your garden to take greatest advantage of these microclimates, and you'll bolster your defenses against drought.

For extra insurance, Doscher uses soaker hoses and mulches the entire garden (especially the paths between the beds) with spoiled hay early in the season.

### Set It and Forget It

Sometimes we see our plants wilting and know Mother Nature isn't doing her part, but we just can't find the time to get out there and give our gardens a nice, long drink. When this is the case, Cheryl Long, senior editor at *Organic Gardening* magazine, recommends that you get an automatic shut-off attachment, like an oven timer, for your watering system (see "Resources" on page 344). Then, before you head to work in the morning, "you can set it to run for whatever length of time you want, and it will turn off automatically," says Long. (When you water in the morning, you ensure that your plants will be dry by the end of the day, making them less susceptible to diseases that prey on wet foliage and waterlogged roots.)

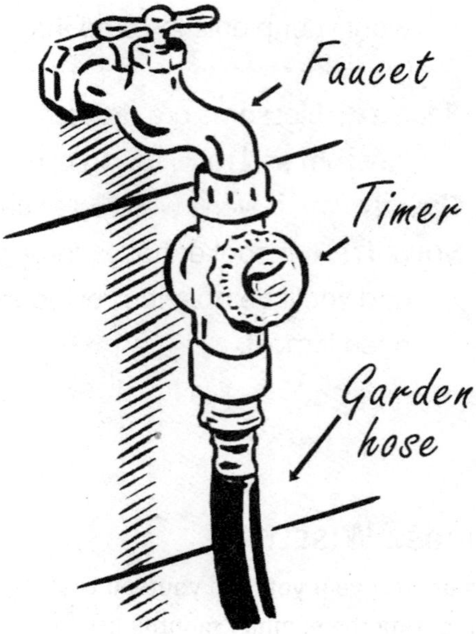


*A TIMER ATTACHED TO YOUR WATERING SYSTEM IS A CONVENIENT WAY OF WATERING YOUR PLANTS IN ABSENTIA.*

### Harvest the Little Ones

If it starts to get dry and you can see your crops becoming parched, don't try waiting it out to let vegetables grow to full maturity. Instead, harvest your crops early as so-called baby vegetables. Besides saving water that you'd otherwise spend nursing these veggies to maturity, you'll also enjoy better-tasting, more tender vegetables with shorter preparation and cooking times, says Pennsylvania market gardener Cass Peterson.

# Weeds

Gardeners who truly love to weed are rare. But it's a fact of life that soil made rich and hospitable by loving care is bound to sprout some uninvited guests. Not all weeds are a scourge, and the wise gardener learns to appreciate—or at least tolerate—the helpful ones. The rest can be kept under control with some savvy, timely action, and the right tools. Worry about weeds? Nah. Take a few tips from market gardeners, who have *acres* of vegetables to keep clean. What works for them will work for you, too.

## Rx for Healthy Mulching

Most gardeners have a single-word answer for weed problems: mulch. Straw, hay, newspaper, chopped-up leaves—almost any kind of mulch will do. The "best" mulch is whatever you happen to have on hand. But there are ways to mulch and "whens" to mulch, which make the practice easier and more effective. Here are a few tips.

**GROW THE MULCH IN PLACE.** "Broadcast oats over the strawberry beds in the fall and let it winter-kill," says Tony Ricci of Three Springs, Pennsylvania. "Your mulch will already be in place in the spring." Other gardeners grow living mulches such as perennial rye (*Lolium perenne*) between their garden beds and mow the mulch periodically, using the side-delivery chute of their lawn mower to blow the clippings onto the beds.

**WAIT UNTIL THE WEATHER WARMS UP TO MULCH HEAT-LOVING PLANTS.** Mulch cools the soil, which is good when summer heat sets in but is an early-season disadvantage to tomatoes, peppers, and eggplant. Conversely, cool-weather plants like broccoli and kale will produce longer if you mulch them while the soil is still cool.

**PUT DOWN A FEW LAYERS OF NEWSPAPER BEFORE MULCHING.** Newspaper is an added barrier to weeds, and it will keep some mulches, like sawdust or wood chips, from robbing nitrogen from your soil as they break down. "You can even use fresh sawdust if you want," says Sylvia Ehrhardt of Knoxville, Maryland. "By season's end, you can till it into the ground because it will be rotted enough by then."

**RECYCLE YOUR NEIGHBOR'S MULCH.** Ask your neighbors if you can have their unwanted bags of leaves and grass clippings (just make sure their leftovers haven't been sprayed with herbicides or pesticides).

*GROW MULCH RIGHT WHERE YOU WANT IT INSTEAD OF HAVING TO LUG IT AROUND.*

## Perennial Mulch for Asparagus

Some crops are just plain hard to keep weed-free. Asparagus is one of them. It's difficult to hoe because spears pop up all over the place. It's tedious to hand-weed. Here's a labor-saving alternative that's *good* for the asparagus: Grow it in a bed of clover, which will feed the asparagus while it crowds out weeds. Just follow these steps.

1. In the fall before you plant the asparagus, seed the patch with white Dutch clover (*Trifolium repens*), a low-growing variety.
2. Early the following spring, till or spade a narrow, 8-inch-deep trench for the asparagus crowns (get year-old crowns, which will be fairly small). Plant them as usual, filling the trench halfway with soil.
3. When the asparagus sprouts appear above the soil level in the trench, finish filling it in, and then seed more white Dutch clover over the top.
4. Once or twice in the first season, pull any weeds that come through the clover (if the clover was planted thickly enough, there won't be many).
5. Each fall, reseed any spots where the clover looks thin.

The technique works well with rhubarb, fruit trees, perennial berries, shrubs, and many perennial flowers such as bleeding heart (*Dicentra* spp.) and peonies. But don't use it with strawberries—the spring growth of the clover traps too much moisture, setting the strawberries up for fungal disease.

## Lazy Way to Weed

One of the easiest ways to prevent weeds is to grow plants that have allelopathic properties, meaning the plants secrete substances that prevent other plants from growing around them. Both common sunflower (*Helianthus annuus*) and annual rye (*Lolium multiflorum*) are allelopathic. If you decide to plant annual rye, plant it as a winter cover crop. It will inhibit weed growth for several weeks after you till it in the spring.

## A Fresh Idea: "Stale Beds"

You know the drill: Every time you stir the soil, another batch of weed seeds sees the sun and sprouts. But you can use a technique called "stale beds" to avoid tilling up new weed seeds before planting crops. Here's how to do it.

1. Prepare the seed bed by tilling or spading and raking.
2. Water the bed well to encourage weeds to sprout.
3. When the weeds have sprouted but are still very small (½ inch or so tall), rake or hoe very shallowly (don't spade or till again, or you'll bring up even more weed seeds!).
4. Water once more and let the weeds sprout in the beds again.
5. Rake or hoe again, and then plant your crops. You'll have done in most of the weeds in the top inch or so of soil—enough to give you a great head start on a season's worth of weeds!

## No, No, No. Don't Hoe, Hoe, Hoe

Some plants have fragile, shallow root systems and can actually be damaged by overzealous hoeing. What to do? Cultivate shallowly or mulch around squash, cucumbers, and melons. If the weeds get away from you in a planted row, it's better to cut them off than to pull them out—especially when they're in peas and beans.

## Read Your Weeds

Before you yank them all out, take a look at what weeds are growing where in your garden because they can tell you useful things about your soil. Where docks (*Rumex* spp.) and lady's thumb (*Polygonum persicaria*) grow, the soil is strongly acid. A good place for blueberries, perhaps, but not for lavender. Hawkweeds (*Hieracium* spp.) and knapweeds (*Centaureas* spp.) grow in slightly acid soil.

Where the soil is compacted, plantains (*Plantago* spp.), dandelion (*Taxacum officinale*), and smartweed (*Polygonum hydropiper*) grow. Toadflax (*Kickxia elatine*) and goldenrods (*Solidago* spp.) like sandy soil. Field pepperweed (*Lepidium campestre*) indicates limestone soils; sagebrush (*Artemisia tridentata*) and woody asters (*Aster* spp.) thrive in alkaline soils. Sedges (*Cyperus* spp.) suggest a drainage problem (they favor wet soils).

Lots of pigweeds (*Amaranthus* spp.), lamb's-quarters (*Chenopodium album*), galinsogas (*Galinsoga* spp.), and mallows (*Malva* spp.)? Well, at least you can take heart in the knowledge that your soil is rich, well drained, and mellow. A good garden grows great weeds.

## Can't Uproot 'Em? Smother 'Em

You've tilled, hoed, and got down on your hands and knees to pull weeds out—but you still have that tenacious quackgrass (*Agropyron repens*) hanging around. One way to get rid of a patch of established weeds is to cover-crop it repeatedly. Even tough quackgrass will succumb to a year of buckwheat as a cover crop. Sow the buckwheat in early summer (it likes warm weather). Each time it flowers, till it under and sow it again. You should get three stands of buckwheat during the season, and you can follow that with a winter cover crop of clover or annual rye.

## Solutions at a Glance

**Problem:** These weeds stay green almost all winter and are ready to flower and set seed at the first hint of warm weather.

**Culprit:** Cool season perennials, like common chickweed (*Stellaria media*), henbit (*Lamium amplexicaule*), and sheep sorrel (*Rumex acetosella*)

**Solve It!** Get a jump on spring cleaning by taking advantage of pleasant winter days to get those weeds out of the garden. Many are shallow-rooted, so you can pull or hoe them out with ease as long as the top inch or so of the soil isn't frozen.

---

**Problem:** This mulch looks nice, but it can add too much acidity to the soil for some ornamentals.

**Culprit:** Wood chip or shredded bark mulch

**Solve It!** A double layer of newspaper under the mulch will keep it from decomposing too quickly and adding too much acid to the soil at once.

---

For good measure, follow the clover the next year with a crop of pumpkins or winter squash. The large leaves will shade out any quackgrass that might remain.

### Easy, Weed-Free Carrots I

Carrots are slow to germinate, especially in the cool soil of early spring, which means that weeds may get a jump on the crop. Here's how to make the weeds' eager-beaver tendencies work for you.

1. Prepare a seed bed and plant the carrots as usual. Water the seeds well, if the soil isn't already moist.
2. Lay a sheet of black plastic over the entire bed, weighting it down with boards or bricks.
3. After 2 weeks, start peeking under the plastic every day. You'll see lots of pale, sun-starved weeds. What you're looking for, though, are the sprouting carrots.
4. When you see the carrots start to emerge, remove the plastic. Most of the weed seeds in the soil's surface will have sprouted and died for lack of light. The carrots have the bed to themselves. Works great for parsnips, too!

## Easy, Weed-Free Carrots II

Cass Peterson's gardening neighbors in Warfordsburg, Pennsylvania, use this method to save weeding work when planting carrots, parsnips, beets, or spinach.

1. Prepare a seed bed and furrow out a shallow row for the seeds of choice with the tip of a hoe (or use a push seeder with the chain that covers the seeds lifted out of the way).
2. Sprinkle the seeds in the furrow (or put them in with the push seeder, again with the chain attachment lifted out of the way). Don't cover the seeds.
3. Water the seeded furrow well.
4. Sprinkle ½ inch of dry peat moss down the furrow to cover the seeds.

Peat moss doesn't absorb moisture, so it will act as a mulch, helping to keep the seeds moist until they germinate. It's also free from weed seeds, so no weeds will sprout in the row with the carrots. And it's easy to see the planted row, so you can hoe on either side!

*Covering carrot seeds with peat moss helps the seeds sprout in a tidy row, free from weeds—saving you weeding woes.*

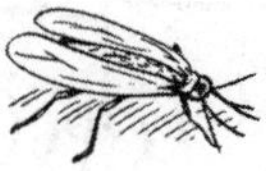

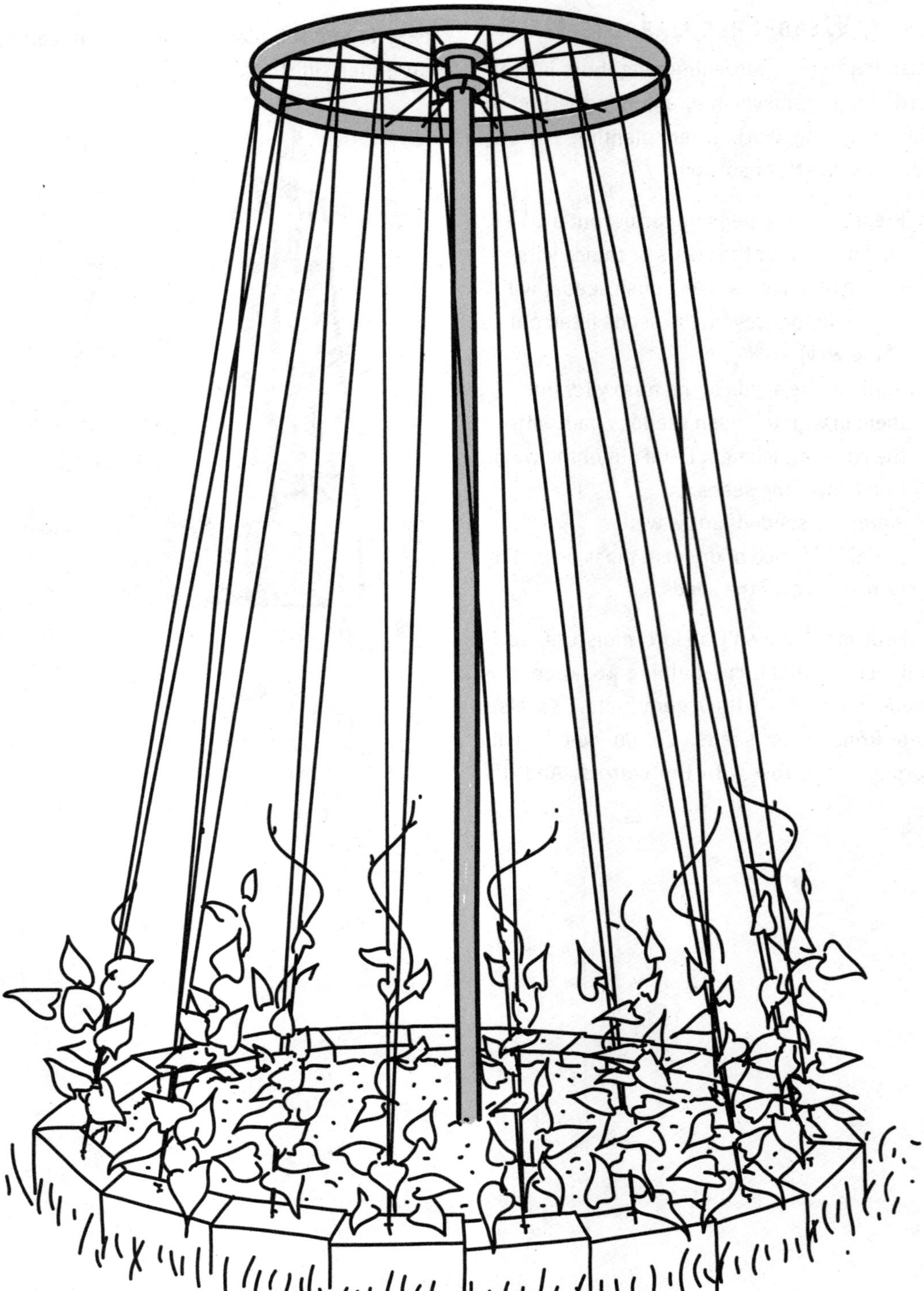

Part II

# GREAT GARDEN GADGETS

You can never have too many gardening gadgets. Gadgets save time and energy, especially when they make a difficult task easier. And they make gardening a lot more fun. Of course, mail-order catalogs, garden centers, and home stores all try to entice you with their fair share of gardening widgets and thingamabobs. But why spend your hard-earned money on something that you can make for virtually pennies—or maybe even for free?

Just take a look around your house and garage. Chances are, you have lots of items that you can recycle into plant markers, tool organizers, watering helpers, hand tools, and so on. All you need is the right combination of doodads and inspiration (which you'll find on the following pages) to help you turn your cast-offs into practical gardening gizmos that will make your gardening tasks go more smoothly—or just be more fun.

# Bird-Feeding Gadgets

Want to attract more birds to your yard? Try to create prime habitat in your backyard by making a plastic netting suet bag, gourd birdhouse, or an instant birdbath. Tired of starlings taking over your purple martin house? Duct tape may be the answer to your problem. Read on to learn how a few simple gadgets can help bring the right birds to your yard.

## Net Bags for Suet and Supplies

Use plastic netting bags from onions or citrus fruit to offer suet to birds in winter, suggests Linda Harris of Fulton, Kentucky. Here's how she does it: Place suet in the bag and tie a knot at the top. Cut the hook section off a wire clothes hanger, and bend it open into a single straight length of wire. Run the wire through the bag just under the knot. Bend the wire into a U-shape, twist the ends together, and then hang the bag on a tree branch near your house windows so you can watch birds feed.

In early spring, fill another bag with pet hair, longish human hair, 6-inch lengths of string, straw, or small clippings of plant material from your garden, and hang it up in the same way. Birds will help themselves to these nest-building materials and will thank you by nesting nearby.

## Duct Tape Says "No Vacancy"

Purple martins are wonderful residents of any backyard, both for their beauty and song as well as for their assistance in insect control. But these flying bug catchers face stiff competition from house sparrows, which often usurp their apartment houses before the martins return from migration.

Birdhouse suppliers market various guards to close off apartment entrances, but martin fancier Connie Wilson of Mt. Vernon, Indiana, found a simpler solution to keep out the unwanteds. "I just stick a piece of duct tape over the holes until I see the first martin scout arrive. Then I remove the tape so the martins can move in."

## Instant Birdbath

Every garden should have a birdbath, but store-bought birdbaths can cost a pretty penny. Rather than buying a birdbath, Janet

Carter, outreach coordinator at the Pennsylvania Horticultural Society's Philadelphia Green, recommends that gardeners take a round drainage tray for a potted plant (10 to 12 inches in diameter is best) and place it onto the top of a sturdy tomato cage (a four-legged cage is stronger than a three-legged one). The birdbath will hold about 2 inches of water without wobbling and you can easily move it around the garden, so you can find the places the birds like best. Smaller, shorter, and shallower models work great in butterfly and rock gardens.

*A DRAINAGE TRAY FILLED WITH 2 INCHES OF WATER AND PLACED ON TOP OF A TAPERED THREE- OR FOUR-LEGGED TOMATO CAGE WILL PROVIDE THE BIRDS THAT FREQUENT YOUR GARDEN WITH A SOURCE OF WATER.*

**Recycle It!**

***ON HAND:*** Old cracked concrete birdbath without its base

***TURN IT INTO:*** Ground-level bird feeder and sanctuary

***HOW TO DO IT:*** Dig a slight depression in a flowerbed and set in the birdbath saucer. Place a little bowl of water or fruit in the middle and pour seed around it.

**Recycle It!**

***ON HAND:*** Old door mat

***TURN IT INTO:*** Birdseed catcher

***HOW TO DO IT:*** Put a scrap of door mat under the bird feeder and on top of fresh snow so seed falls on it and not into the snow where the birds can't get to them.

# Build It!

## Gourd Birdhouse

If you like interesting and appealing birdhouses to adorn your garden and welcome your feathered friends, here's a way to grow and make your own. Grow large bottle-type gourds (sometimes called birdhouse gourds) and harvest them when they're fully mature (or just before frost hits, whichever comes first). Plan to grow them on a trellis, which helps keep the fruits rounded and at their best. When you harvest, leave several inches of stem on each fruit.

"I've seen these gourd birdhouses painted white and hung in colonies for martins," says Linda Harris of Fulton, Kentucky, "but I think it's best to leave the gourds untreated and unpainted, to avoid any possible toxic effect on the birds who'll be nesting in the gourd."

### Materials

- 1 dried large gourd
- 1/4-inch-diameter wooden dowel, 3 inches long
- Permanent glue
- 12 to 18 inches of sturdy twine or cord
- Narrow-bladed saw or sharp X-Acto knife
- Electric drill with 1/4-inch bit

### Directions

**1.** Harvest the gourd and hang it to dry, or place it on chicken wire or hardware cloth in a warm, airy, sheltered spot. When a gourd has thoroughly dried (which may take several months), it will be tan, and you can shake it and hear the dried flesh and seeds rattle.

**2.** Using a pencil, draw a 1-inch-diameter circle for the door about one-third of the way up from the bottom of the gourd. Carefully saw or cut through the gourd shell, following the pencil line, then remove the circle of shell. Shake out the flesh and seeds. Save the seeds to grow more gourds.

**3.** Drill a 1/4-inch-diameter hole about 1 inch below the door. Insert the dowel in the hole so about 1 inch is inside the gourd. Apply glue to the circle where the dowel and gourd meet, and then let the glue dry thoroughly.

**4.** Drill a 1/4-inch hole on both sides of the gourd about 2 inches from the top of the gourd. Insert twine through both holes, and tie the ends together in a knot.

**5.** Hang your birdhouse in a tree before spring nesting begins, and watch for visitors.

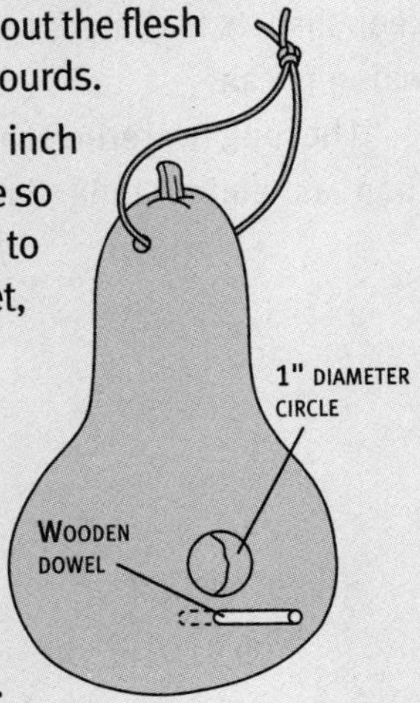

### Recycle It!

***On hand:*** Ceramic cup with a broken handle

***Turn it into:*** A miniature bird and butterfly bath

***How to do it:*** Sink the cup to its rim in the soil of a flowerbed or border, and fill the cup with water.

## $H_2O$ for Beneficials

The beneficial insects in your garden need water just as much as birds, but birdbaths don't serve the needs of ants, spiders, and beetles. Jeff Ball, a garden writer from West Chester, Pennsylvania, came up with a way to keep insects hydrated, too. He created a bug watering can.

"The bug watering can is nothing more than an empty tuna fish or cat food can stuffed with a plastic pot scrubber (netting bunched up into a ball)," says Ball. "The plastic scrubber lets the insects get down to the water without worrying about falling in. I have at least six of these bug watering cans situated in out-of-the-way places around my garden. The rain will usually keep them filled, but when the drought comes, the bug cans get filled with water right along with the birdbath."

## Cat Litter Is for the Birds

Heavy bags of birdseed are economical to buy, but hard to handle. And, once they're opened, mice or squirrels can make a feast on birdseed you store in a shed or garage. Today, some cat litter brands are available in handy plastic buckets with lids. So if you have a cat or two, switch to the economy-size bucket of litter. Once the litter pail is empty, rinse it out, dry it thoroughly, and use it as a secure storage bucket for birdseed. Says Karen Soltys of Sellersville, Pennsylvania, "Toss in a scoop, and you can carry the bucket of seed to any of your feeders and scoop out what you need. It's much easier than lugging a 20-pound bag of sunflower seed and hoisting it up to the feeder. The snap-on lid helps keep the seed fresh, too."

# Compost-Making Equipment

Every great garden starts with good soil. One of the ways to create good soil is by amending your beds with lots of compost. But there's no reason to shed sweat and tears while producing that black gold. Read on to find out what gadgets your fellow gardeners use to make composting a snap.

## Solve the Riddle Problem

Compost sieves, sometimes called riddles, tend to be small and expensive, but you can easily build one of your own that fits on top of your wheelbarrow—for just a few dollars. This sieve and wheelbarrow setup is perfect for resting next to the compost pile where you can scoop compost on top and work it through the screen with a trowel or spade. The resulting fine-textured compost is ideal for adding to indoor plants, starting seedlings, and doing other container gardening.

To make the sieve, nail four pieces of lumber, such as 1 × 2s, into a large square or rectangle big enough to rest across the wheelbarrow with a few inches to spare. Then use snips to cut a piece of galvanized hardware cloth to fit the wood frame. Attach the hardware cloth to the bottom of the frame with galvanized brads.

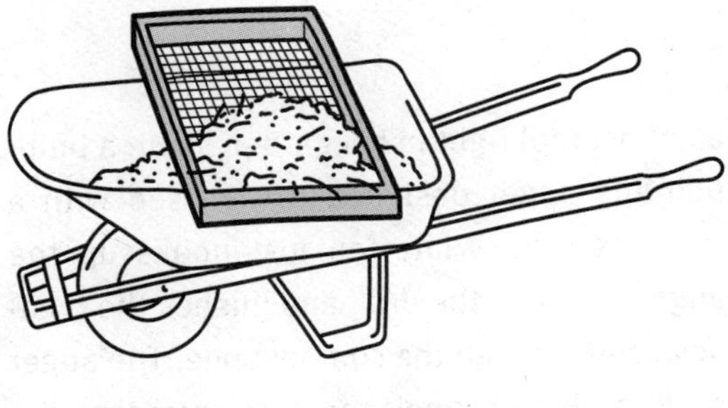

*Make your own fine-textured compost with an inexpensive, build-it-yourself sieve.*

## Easy Compost Aerator

Tired of spending hours turning your compost pile to keep it well aerated? Kelly Winterton of Mountain Green, Utah, discovered the perfect

**Recycle It!**

***On hand:*** Net onion bag

***Turn it into:*** Compost tea bag

***How to do it:*** When opening your next bag of onions, untie the string gathered at the top rather than ripping through the netting. Fill the bag with compost, retie it, and place it in a bucket of water. Allow it to steep for a week or more, then use the liquid to water plants and give them a fertilizer boost.

compost tool right in his garden shed: a bulb-planting auger designed to be used with a cordless drill. Winterton just hooks up the auger, turns on the drill, and pushes the business end through the compost pile. The auger easily makes channels for air to enter the pile. As a bonus, the auger mixes and chops the materials as it works, speeding up the composting process.

## Shimmying Compost Sieve

Martha Black and her husband, Les, of Anchorage, Alaska, came up with a vibrating compost sieve to make quick work of screening the compost. Les made the compost sieve out of $\frac{1}{2}$-inch rabbit mesh and four $2 \times 2$s. "I placed the sieve across the top of my wheelbarrow and shoveled on the compost," says Martha, "but getting the compost to go through the screen was quite a job. So Les found an old handheld vibrating sander and used some wire to attach the sander to the rabbit mesh. We turned on the sander, started shoveling, and the compost went through quickly and easily." (*Note:* For safety's sake, make sure you plug the sander into a grounded GFCI outlet.)

*A handheld vibrating sander adds just enough shake, rattle, and roll to get compost through a sieve easily.*

## Composting Tomato Cages

Tomatoes and peppers love rich soil. Help them thrive by providing them with their own supply of compost! Make a cylinder from a 6-foot length of wire fencing (chicken wire or varying grades of turkey wire are fine; just be

# Build It!

## Bus Tub Worm Bin

A worm bin is a great way to make rich, odorless compost indoors. You can spend $100 or more to buy a commercial worm bin kit, or you can do what Kelly Houston of San Francisco, California, did and make your own bin. Houston started with two "bus tubs" (containers used to gather up dirty dishes) from the restaurant where she works. Chances are you can buy them from a local restaurant supply company, or you can buy similar-size utility bins from a discount store.

### Materials

- 2 plastic tubs (each about 18 × 14 × 12 inches deep)
- Chicken wire
- 1 tub lid
- Black paint
- About 1,000 red worms
- Kitchen scraps (no citrus, potato peels, fat, bones, or eggshells)
- Damp, shredded newspaper
- Sturdy box or milk crate
- Large jar or 2-liter soda bottle with top cut off
- Electric drill with ¼-inch bit
- Utility knife
- Staple gun

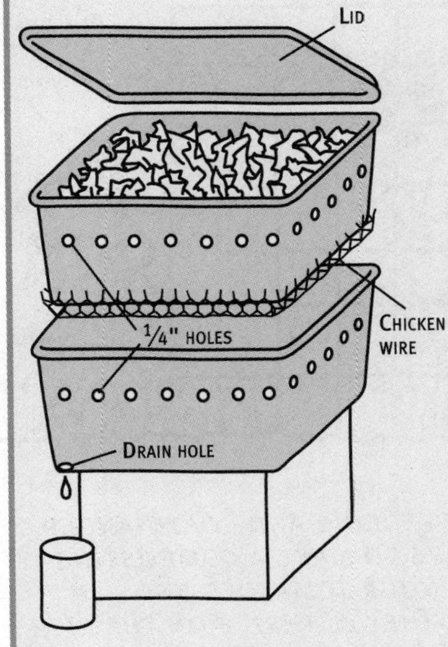


### Directions

**1.** Drill ¼-inch-diameter ventilation holes in a line parallel to and 4 inches below the top of each tub.

**2.** Cut the bottom from one of the tubs with the utility knife, and staple chicken wire over the bottom. This will be the worm tub.

**3.** Paint the tub lid black to keep light out.

**4.** Place red worms and kitchen scraps in worm tub, and cover completely with damp, shredded newspaper.

**5.** With the utility knife, cut a 1-inch-wide drain hole at a low point on one side of the bottom of the other tub. This will be the drain tub.

**6.** Cover the worm tub with the black lid, and place it inside the drain tub.

**7.** Set the assembled setup on top of a sturdy box or old milk crate, and place the large jar or 2-liter soda bottle under the drain hole.

"When there's a noticeable amount of worm castings in the worm tub, I lift it out and dump everything into the drain tub," Houston says. "Then I place the empty tub back into the bottom tub, right on top of the compost, and start over with new scraps in the empty tub, covering them well with damp newspaper strips. I empty the jar once in a while and water my houseplants with it." The worms will gradually move up through the wire mesh to where the "fresh" food scraps are; then you can harvest the compost in the lower tub without losing too many worms. After harvesting the lower tub, she places the worm tub back in the empty drain tub and begins again.

### Recycle It!

***On hand:*** 5-gallon or larger bucket with lid

***Turn it into:*** Direct composter

***How to do it:*** Cut out the bucket's bottom with a pair of heavy-duty shears or a utility knife. Push the bucket into one of your garden beds so the bottom of the bucket is 12 inches below the soil surface. Add compost, weeds without seeds, and plant wastes every day (no meat or processed food, please!). Keep the lid on to avoid attracting flies and other critters. When it's nearly full, pull the bucket up and cover the pile with soil. It will quickly settle as the compost rots and the earthworms do their work—and, as the compost breaks down, it will provide the bed with nutrients. Tomatoes and squash-family crops, both heavy feeders, will benefit greatly when planted close by.

sure it can stand without support). You can cut 5-foot-wide fencing in half to make a pair of 2½-foot-high cages—this height is visually unobtrusive but is still high enough to stake tomatoes. Cut the vertical wires in an alternating pattern to provide tinelike feet that will stick into the dirt. Clamp the cages closed with small pieces of wire coat hanger or extra pieces of fencing. Place the cage in a garden bed and use it to hold garden wastes, especially weeds.

As plant scraps break down, they'll directly feed plants growing near them, so plant tomatoes, peppers, or vine crops around the outside of the cylinder, and train them to grow up the sides of the fencing. At the end of the season, pull up the wire cylinder, shake off the dead vines, and move it to another section of the garden. Begin filling it again as you do your fall cleanup.

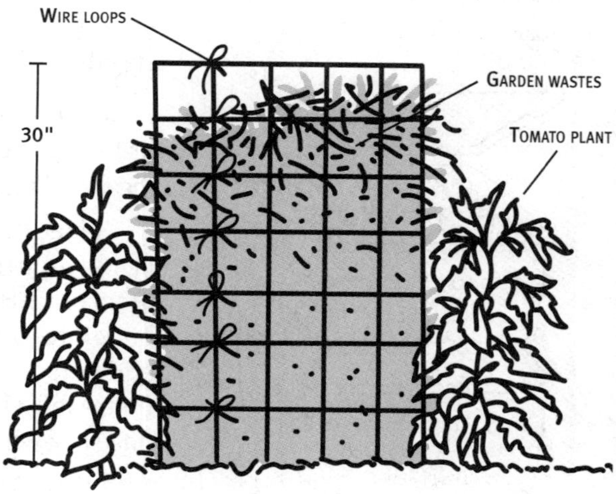


*Use wire fencing and coat-hanger wire loops to make a composting cage for your tomatoes and peppers. They'll thrive on the rich soil that the compost provides.*

# Build It!

## Lattice Compost Bin

Wooden lattice is a nice choice for screening around the base of a deck, and if you have some leftover sheets of lattice from a deck renovation project, use them around your compost. You can build a handsome two-bin compost structure from three sheets of lattice and a few scrap 2 × 4s. And it will only take about 3 hours from start to finish.

### Materials

Three 4 × 8-foot sheets of lattice

Six 5-foot 2 × 4s

6-penny galvanized nails or 1-inch galvanized screws

Four 4-foot wooden slats

Level

Hammer or screwdriver

### Directions

**1.** Cut two 4 × 8-foot sheets of lattice in half to make four panels, each 4 × 4 foot. (Only three panels are needed.)

**2.** Sink four 2 × 4s 1 foot deep in the ground to form the corners of a 4 × 8-foot rectangle. Use a level to set them straight.

**3.** Sink one 2 × 4 at the midpoint of each of the long sides of the rectangle.

**4.** Nail or screw the remaining 4 × 8-foot lattice panel to the 2 × 4s on one long side to form the back wall of the bin.

**5.** Make side walls by nailing one 4 × 4-foot panel between the 2 × 4s on each end.

**6.** Create a slot on the inside of each center 2 × 4 by nailing two slats parallel to each other onto the 2 × 4. Allow enough room in between for lattice to fit between them. (See detail.)

**7.** Slide a 4 × 4-foot panel into the slots to create a center wall.

**8.** When it's time to turn or move the compost, simply slide the center lattice out and go at it!

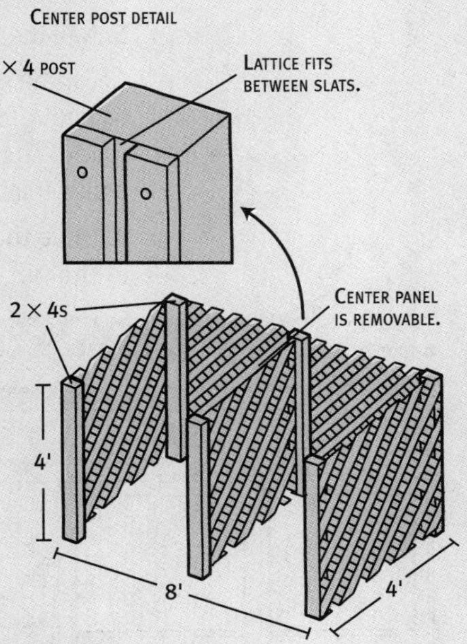

# Build It!

## A Simple Double Compost Bin

Ed Preneta of Unionville, Connecticut, put together a simple two-bin compost "corral" that has held up for almost 15 years. Though it's decidedly low-tech, it has proven secure enough to keep out deer, fox, coyotes, and even black bear. A removable front gate allows him to stack the bins full of compost material, yet it gives him access when it's time to turn or harvest the compost.

### Materials

Twenty-six 4-foot 2 × 4s

6-penny galvanized nails

Dog wire

Two 8-foot 2 × 4s

Chicken wire

Two 5-foot-tall metal stakes

Bird netting

Hammer

Staple gun

### Directions

**1.** Nail twelve 4-foot 2 × 4s together to form a simple 4 × 4 × 4-foot frame (as shown).

**2.** Repeat to construct a second frame.

**3.** Wrap dog wire around three sides of each frame, and staple in place.

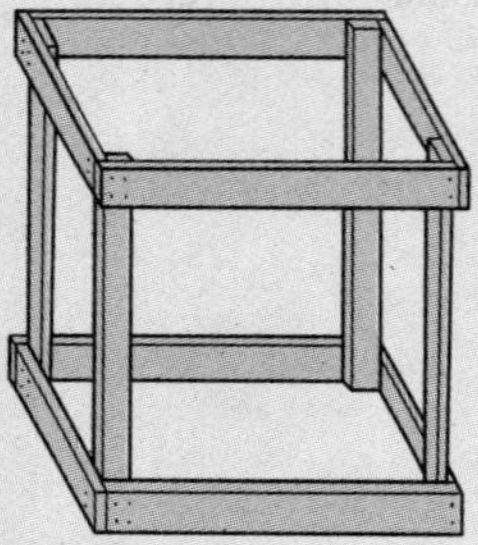

**4.** On a level surface, place the frames next to each other so the open ends are side by side, forming one 8-foot, open-sided double bin.

**5.** Nail the two frames together.

**6.** For the gate, nail the two 8-foot 2 × 4s to two 4-foot 2 × 4s to form a 4 × 8-foot frame. Then, cover it with chicken wire, and staple it in place.

**7.** Drive the 5-foot stakes into the ground at the front corners of the bin, leaving about 2 inches of clearance between the stakes and the bin.

**8.** Slide the gate between a stake and the corner of the bin, until both ends are held in place by the stakes.

The stakes hold the gate firmly in place, but when it's time to turn the compost, Preneta simply slides the gate away from the front of the bin. He also drapes bird netting over top of the bin to keep the birds from robbing his precious compost.

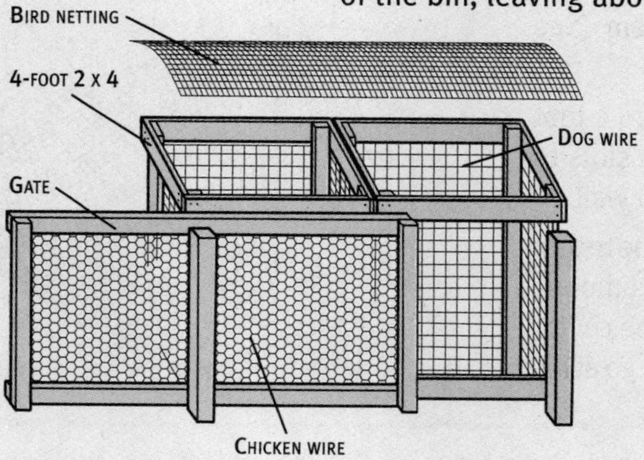

# Homemade Hand Tools

Hoes, shovels, trowels, rakes. So many tools to choose from — so little time. Even though gardening tools don't last forever, you can revamp and refurbish your tools to make them last twice as long. The following tips will help you keep your favorite tools (and your hands) usable in the years to come.

## A Better Ax

Tired of swinging a heavy, clumsy mattock to remove sod, chop roots and stumps, or break up hard soil? "Try a Pulaski," advises 74-year-old Don DeVault of Delaware, Ohio. "It's a lightweight ax that firefighters use in forest fires and brush fires. It's about half the weight of a normal mattock." The Pulaski has an ax blade on one side and a scaled-down mattock on the other. "It's great for edging, lifting sod, and chopping roots. My firefighter son gave me one for Christmas," DeVault says. "I can use it all day in the garden and woods." (See "Resources" on page 344 for ordering information.)

## Shear Gladness

Like many great inventions, Frederick Theilig's favorite garden gadget came from a misguided attempt to solve a problem. The problem? A large Christmas tree that had to be removed from a small room in their Cranston, Rhode Island, apartment. Rather than dragging the tree intact through the door and scattering pine needles everywhere, Theilig decided that the best way to get it out of the apartment after the holiday would be to cut the branches from the trunk. So, he grabbed the nearest cutting tool—a pair of scissors. Too bad they were his wife Sona's best kitchen shears.

It worked. In no time at all, those sturdy 8-inch-long shears had reduced the tree to a trunk and a pile of boughs. As proud as he was of his creative thinking, he found that Sona wasn't pleased, so Fred bought her a belated Christmas present: a new pair of shears. That meant that he could take full possession of the old ones.

Several years later, the shears remain among his favorite tools. "I still use them to harvest tomatoes, peas, beans, and similar small-stemmed fruit," he says "They're strong, conveniently sized, and relatively cheap, and you can find them at any kitchen store. They even have a notch for cutting bones, which is perfect for pruning the smaller growth on shrubs and trees. I also use them for deadheading and killing tough weedy vines and have even used them to trim plastic mulch."

Nothing seems to dull or harm the stainless-steel shears. "They've survived three intense seasons in the garden without significantly dulling," Fred says.

## The Cutting Edge

Tired of trying to pry apart tough perennial clumps when dividing them? Gayle Jamison of Woodstock, New York, keeps a long-bladed, stainless steel, serrated kitchen knife handy for dividing perennials. "It works great for all sorts of divisions," she says, "such as for grasses, daylilies, hostas, and even more delicate root structures that don't pull apart easily." She sometimes even leaves the plant in the ground and just saws off a section of it, to minimize trauma to the parent plant.

A serrated bread knife also can be extremely useful and versatile in the garden. It's great for separating plants in a flat, and particularly for cutting heavy plastic pots to release potbound plants. You can also use it to trim the roots of potted plants and to divide water lilies.

***On hand:*** Net bags, such as those that onions, potatoes, and citrus come in

***Turn them into:*** "Pot scrubbers" for cleaning tools

***How to do it:*** "Just cut off a chunk of the bag," says Lon Rombough of Aurora, Oregon, "or for larger tools, such as a shovel, use the whole bag." Rombough wads up the mesh bag and goes to town. "When you're finished cleaning, just unwad and shake out the bag."

## New Life for Old Tools

When the handle of a favorite long-handled tool breaks, don't throw the tool out. "Turn it into a short-handled tool that you might like even better," say Sandy and Dennis "Bones" Evers of Bayfield, Colorado.

If the handle broke in the middle, the tool transformation is super simple. Just saw it off and sand the rough edges. A tool that breaks at the business end is a little more difficult to modify, but it can be done.

1. Remove the wood from the metal part of the tool. You can either drill it out with a power drill or toss it in a fire, Bones says. (If you toss it in a fire and burn the remnant out, the metal may lose some of its temper but may still be good for years.)
2. Cut the remaining handle to the desired length. Taper it so it will fit into the metal part either by whittling it with a knife or sanding it.
3. Attach the two parts by standing the handle on a hard surface and placing the metal portion atop that. Holding onto the tool

end, give it a good rap against the floor several times to force the parts together.

4. If there's a hole in the tool's shank, work a screw or nail into it to further secure the new handle.

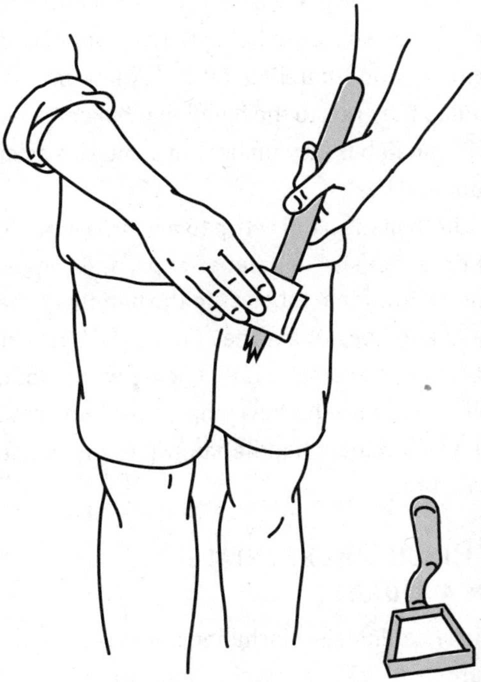

*If a tool handle breaks, remove the wooden stub from the metal part of the tool. Sand down the handle and fit it back into the tool head.*

## Two Tools from One

How many of us have snapped a hoe handle in half, either through overaggressive hoeing or in a fit of pique at an exceptionally recalcitrant weed? When that happens, we normally toss it in the trash and head to the hardware store to buy a new hoe. But Jo Meller and Jim Sluyter of Five Springs Farm in Bear Lake, Michigan, don't like to waste anything, so they decided to make the most of their broken tool. In fact, they turned one broken tool into two usable ones.

First, Jo and Jim took the bladed end of the hoe, which had about 18 inches of the handle left, and cut off the broken edges of the handle with a saw. Then they filed the end smooth, which left them with a short-handled hoe. To make it even easier to use the hoe in tight spots, Sluyter filed the blade down with a grinder so that it's 3 inches wide.

Then they turned their attention to the remaining piece of the broken handle. Again, using a saw, Jim cut the handle down to a 12-inch length. Using a rasp, he filed the end to a point and, voilà, "a pretty good dibble, big enough for large bulbs and suitable for the large plantings of garlic that we make every year," Sluyter says. "I made a better dibble, some years later, when the D-grip handle of a shovel broke—the D-grip handle makes it much more pleasant to work with."

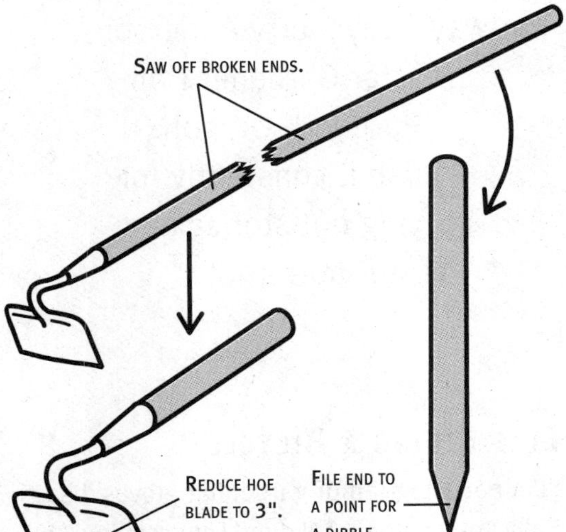


*Find new life for a broken hoe by turning the pieces into a short-handled hoe and a dibble.*

**Recycle It!**

***ON HAND:*** An old hoe

***TURN IT INTO:*** A useful hand tool

***HOW TO DO IT:*** Cut the end off so the remaining handle is about 18 inches long, and sand the end smooth. "This shorter tool is great for close-up jobs when you want good leverage and a broad surface without a long handle to get in the way," says Jerry Anderson, Master Gardener from Portland, Oregon. "I use it constantly for prying out stones and stubborn roots."

## LIKE RIDING A BICYCLE

"I'm not a big fan of gardening gloves," says Sally Roth, author of *Natural Landscaping*, "because I'm always playing with plants even while I'm raking or digging, and gloves make me fumble-fingered. But I'm prone to blisters when I do intensive garden work with a rake or hoe, so I was forever putting gloves on and taking them off."

After moving her son's bike out of the way so she could rake the fall leaves, inspiration struck. "Those fat, cushy, foam handlebar grips were so nice to hold after an hour of work with a wood-handled rake. I knew my son added the grips to the handlebar himself—and the handlebar was almost the same size as my tool handle."

Roth made a quick trip to a nearby store for the inexpensive handlebar grips, and wiggled the hollow foam tubes onto the handles of her rake and hoe, where they fit snugly. "Now my tools are so comfortable, I never worry about blisters, no matter how long I work," she says. "I even added a handlebar grip to my household broom."

## "PINCH" PERENNIALS IN A HURRY

Many perennials—including fall asters, mums, garden phlox, agastache, and others—push out vigorous side branches when the tip of the growing stem is nipped off, and that means more flowers from each plant plus a denser form. But nipping off the tips of dozens or hundreds of stems can be a tedious task.

"Pinching the tips of perennials gives me at least double the amount of flowers," says gardener Sally Roth of New Harmony, Indiana, "but my gardens get bigger every year, and it's harder to keep up when I pinch each stem by hand. I switched to hedge clippers a few years ago, and they're perfect. I can clip off the tips of an entire clump of phlox with just one or two swipes of the clippers."

Try this technique when your perennials are 6 to 12 inches tall, with at least four sets of leaves on the stem. You'll find it's easy to slice through the stems while they're still green.

## Electrical Tape Recharges an Old Tool

"I abuse my shovels regularly," says Sally Roth, who has been gardening since she was 2 years old. "They aren't made to be crowbars, I know, but I just can't restrain myself from using them to lever out heavy shrubs or trees. Even the most expensive ones crack a handle now and then."

When she hears that telltale sound of splitting wood, Roth reaches for a roll of black electrical tape and performs emergency surgery on the spot. "The tape fits nice and snug to the handle and isn't irritating to my hand when I'm using the tool," she says, noting that patched shovels get retired to the light-duty section of the tool shed. "They still have years of good use in them. I save them for easier jobs, like moving perennials or loosening the vegetable garden soil." If you don't have electrical tape on hand, turn to that old standby, duct tape. It's wider, stickier, and less slippery than electrical tape.

## Come-Clean Hands

Nonstick cooking spray is a gadget designed for the kitchen. But Linda Harris of Fulton, Kentucky, has turned it into a gardener's aid. "Squirt your hands with nonstick cooking spray before you go out to garden. It will make your hands easier to wash up, and even helps keep them cleaner inside garden gloves," says Harris.

### Recycle It!

***On hand:*** 5-gallon plastic buckets, an old garden hose, and duct tape

***Turn them into:*** Hand-friendly handles

***How to do it:*** Save your hands from the wrath of old bucket handles. When a bucket handle cracks and falls off, replace it with short sections of old garden hose, wrapped with duct tape. The hose gives your hands a bit of extra cushion, and the duct tape prevents the hose handles from sliding.

## All Soaped Up

Tired of having to traipse into the house to scrub off gardening grime? Well, traipse no more. Bea Kline of Fort Washington, Pennsylvania, created an outdoor soap station using a cake of soap and an old panty-hose leg—a low-tech soap on a rope! Simply drop the soap to the toe, tie off the end, and hang it near the hose. Now you can wash up right. The soap stays put and air-dries easily.

## "Bubby's" Gloves

How many times have you worked in the garden with gloves on and then pulled them off momentarily because you needed to work with bare hands? Of course, you forget to put them back on, and later lose them in the wheelbarrow or bury them in compost. For you, there are "Bubby," or "old country," gloves. These gloves either have no index finger (or no fingers at all) or a slit at the base of the thumb and index finger so you can have easy access to two digits without needing to remove (and lose) your gloves.

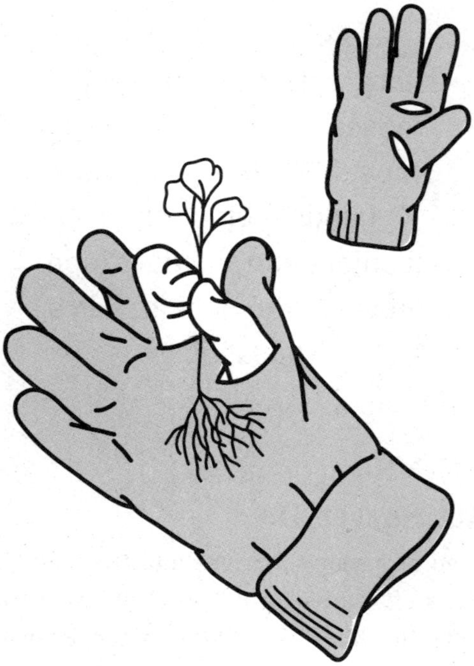

*Handy slits at the base of a glove's thumb and index finger make it easier for you to do more detailed work in your garden.*

## Hammer Out the Best of Black Walnuts

Black walnut nutmeats are delicious, but the nuts are notoriously hard to crack, and the force needed to break the shell often pulverizes the nut meat as well, leading to painstaking work to remove bits of shell from the goodies. Walnut lover Marie Bedics of Whitehall, Pennsylvania, who grew up smashing black walnuts between two rocks, learned a trick years ago that she still uses today, with a little more finesse.

Positioning the nut is what counts most, says Bedics. "Black walnuts are easiest to crack if you hold them pointy end down and whack them on the flatter stem end of the nut," she asserts. "The shell splits open that way to expose the biggest possible pieces of nut meat, so you don't end up with a handful of crumbs."

Bedics still uses a sturdy rock to support the nut for cracking, but nowadays she hits them with a hammer to break the shell. "I've tried nutcrackers," she says, "but with a little practice to get the amount of force just right, a hammer works much better."

## Beverage Bowl

Felder Rushing of Jackson, Mississippi, is never without a cold drink while gardening, thanks to the beverage spear he created. Rushing welded a shallow bowl to the top of a 4-foot-long metal rod. He sticks the rod in the ground wherever he's working in the garden and puts a glass or can with his drink of choice in the bowl, where it's in no danger of being knocked over. "Because I welded a metal flower to the bowl, I always think, 'Hey, this bud's for *me!*'" says Rushing.

## SAVE YOUR BACK WITH A DUSTPAN "SHOVEL"

When you have a big pile of soil to move, try this dustpan trick. "I've found that a dustpan is a lot easier to use than a shovel," confesses garden writer Tina James of Reisterstown, Maryland. "I kneel on a kneeling pad, dig in with the dustpan, and fill my wheelbarrow or buckets from that position. It may look a little silly, but who cares when you can get out of bed without groaning the next day!"

## TURN YOUR HOE INTO A RULER

For accurate measurements without carrying a yardstick, use an indelible marker to transfer the markings from a ruler onto the wooden handle of your favorite hoe, rake, or trowel. For a longer-lasting guide, carve the markings into the handle with a whittling knife.

### Recycle It!

***ON HAND:*** An old coal shovel (with a flat, not rounded, blade)

***TURN IT INTO:*** A heavy container mover

***HOW TO DO IT:*** Simply stick the shovel's blade under the container, and then pull the container like a sled.

# Irrigation and Feeding Devices

A plant is a plant is a plant. Right? Well, not quite. How much water a plant is given can make all the difference in the world. You can use soda bottles, PVC, milk jugs, old T-shirts, and much more to keep your house and garden plants healthy and hydrated. In the next few pages, you'll find out *how*.

## Low-Tech Irrigation

Deliver water right to the spot it's needed with a low-tech individual watering system made from a milk jug. To get started, wash out a 1-gallon plastic milk jug and make a pin prick or two in the bottom. You want a small enough hole to have a drip, not a steady stream.

Then bury the milk jug up to its neck next to the plant it will irrigate. This works especially well with tomatoes, which like generous, steady amounts of water deep down. You can also use it to deliver liquid fertilizer or compost tea. Be sure to strain the tea well first.

*Give tomatoes the deep watering they love with a low-tech milk-jug irrigation system.*

## Quick Fix with Wicks

If you live in a rainy climate, you know excess moisture can be a problem, particularly if you enjoy growing plants in containers. Heavy rains are certainly nothing new to Andres Mejides—his certified organic farm in Homestead, Florida, receives periodic drenchings throughout the season—but he found that his collection of unusual plants growing in unusual containers often became waterlogged. Some of his containers drained slowly, while others, such as an old tea kettle, didn't drain at all. Mejides solved this problem using kerosene lamp wicking, which you can find in most hardware stores. He placed one end in a pot that needed draining and let the other end trail down to the ground or into a larger potted plant that drained well. Now he doesn't have to constantly tip the dozens of pots after a big rain. "Plus," he says, "the mosquitoes have fewer places to breed."

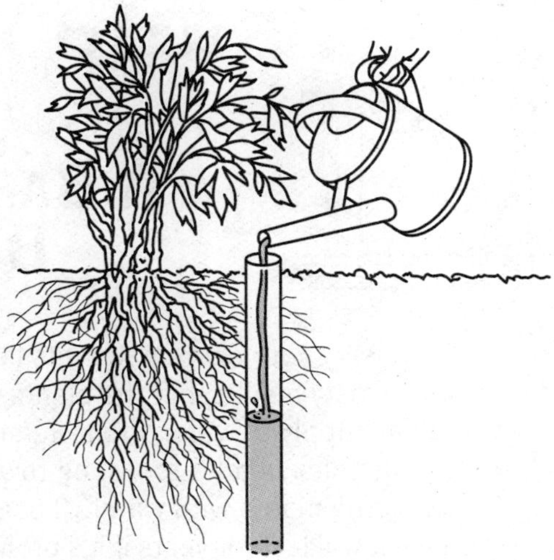

*WATER DIRECTLY TO PLANT ROOTS (AND CONSERVE WATER IN THE PROCESS) USING A PIECE OF PVC PIPE.*

## WATER NOT WASTED

Many plants thrive when given thorough waterings that encourage deep, strong roots. But that takes time and lots of water. Sally Cummings of Albany, New York, has come up with a simple solution. When planting, she buries one end of a PVC pipe next to the plant. She uses slender pipe for perennials and buries 6 to 12 inches of the pipe below ground. For shrubs she uses wider pipe and sinks them deeper into the ground—a foot or more. Just an inch or two needs to remain above ground to ensure it doesn't get covered or clogged with mulch.

"Every time I water I place the hose (or watering can) in the tube and give the plant a good drink. Water goes directly to the roots and isn't wasted by evaporation from the surface of the ground," Cummings says. "This system is especially useful during a drought when you aren't allowed to use hoses or sprinklers," she adds.

## GARDEN NURSE

You can tend to tender annuals or forlorn perennials that need some TLC without sacrificing a lot of your time or attention. Donna Armstrong of Harleysville, Pennsylvania, shares her simple plant-nursing secret. "I use a 3-inch-wide strip of cotton fabric for a wick to create a slow drip watering system. T-shirt strips work great."

Here's how Armstrong's system works. Fill a plastic jug with water, then roll the cotton into a wick and place one end in the jug. Tamp the other end of the fabric into the soil at the base of the plant that needs special attention. The water siphons through the wick, providing a gentle water supply.

## EASY AUTOMATIC WATERER

This literally cool idea comes from Geraldine Braswell who gardens in Fulton, Kentucky. One spring she planted two rather large new trees.

*(continued on page 214)*

# Build It!

## A Basic Bramble Drip Line

Growing your own small fruits like raspberries and blackberries can offer tremendously tasty results, but the plants won't produce big, juicy berries unless they get a regular supply of water. In the Tennessee Valley, gardener Barbara Pleasant planted her brambles in a 50-foot-long row and devised a permanent drip irrigation line to supply the plants with water. "I used plain old PVC pipe because it's cheap, and because it will last for years if it's protected from sun." To take care of the sun problem, Pleasant mulches her berries and the drip line with 3 inches of wheat straw. You can adapt Pleasant's technique for any length row.

**Materials**

- ½-inch-diameter PVC, the length of your crop row (sold in 10- and 20-foot lengths)
- ½-inch PVC coupling fittings (as needed to connect lengths of plastic pipe)
- PVC pipe cement and primer
- ½-inch-diameter PVC end cap
- ⅝-inch clamp-type female hose connector
- 12-inch piece of ⅝-inch garden hose
- Adjustable metal hose clamp
- Wheat straw or other coarse organic mulch
- Dark-colored marking pen
- Drill with ⅛-inch bit (A brad-point bit works best because it has a self-starting tip.)

### Directions

**1.** If you already have an existing patch of berries, rake back the mulch (and weed while you're at it). If you've just planted a new row of plants, don't spread mulch until you lay out your piping.

**2.** Lay the PVC pipe down the row, and cement the straight lengths together with coupling fittings to get the full length of the row. Also, cement the end cap in place. Cementing PVC pipe is a two-step procedure: First wet the mating surfaces with a primer, then immediately apply the glue to both parts and press them together. The pipe, couplings, and end cap must be dry for the cement to set properly.

**3.** Use the marking pen to mark the locations of drip holes. Mark holes at regular 6-inch intervals to water a continuous row of plants. Or, you can plan for holes only at the intervals that will work best to deliver water right at the bases of your plants.

4. Drill the holes. If the bit you're using slides off the pipe before it bites in, poke small indentations at each marked spot with an awl or nail to give the bit a starting point.

5. Install the female hose connector to one end of the garden hose, and attach the other end to the PVC pipe with the hose clamp.

6. Connect the system to a garden hose and turn on the water at very low pressure—less than one-quarter turn of the faucet. Wait a few minutes and check to see that water is dripping out all of the holes.

7. Once you're satisfied that the system is working properly, spread mulch over the hose and around the base of the plants.

8. To water your bramble patch, let the water run for 1 hour, and then check the moisture level in the soil. Brambles are fairly shallow-rooted, but it's a good idea to soak at least the top 6 inches of the soil. If necessary, turn the water back on for more time to complete the job. How often you'll need to water will depend on temperature, humidity, rainfall, and the amount of mulch you use. Rather than watering according to a rigid schedule, check soil moisture every few days, and water whenever the soil is dry from 2 to 6 inches below the surface.

9. At the end of the season, check the line to make sure the holes are facing downward so all the water will drain out because water left inside can crack the pipe if it freezes. You can also disconnect the pipe from the hose section and raise the capped end to fully drain the pipe.

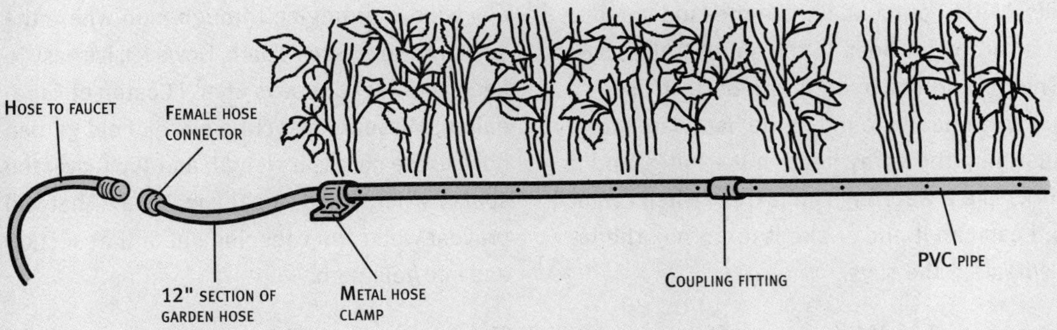

When a drought hit during the summer, she was able to keep her trees well watered throughout the blazingly dry year with minimum fuss—no heavy lifting or toting required! She turned two 5-gallon plastic buckets into a slow-but-sure drip system—one for each tree. Braswell punched a few small holes in the bottom of each bucket with an ice pick. (You could also use an awl.). She then placed the buckets near the tree trunks and over the rootball area. Braswell kept the bucket waterers filled with the help of a garden hose—no hauling of heavy watering cans. The slow-drip watering enabled her newly planted trees to establish well and quickly in their new landscape. You can also use a bucket waterer to slow-feed flowering trees and shrubs during the spring and summer. Just mix an organic fertilizer into the water of the 5-gallon bucket, and let it slowly soak into the ground around the plants.

## Not Your Mother's Watering Can

Milk jugs make the best watering cans for applying manure teas and herbal remedies to plants, says Lisa Ann Haynes of Mahomet, Illinois. "First I put a bung, like the kind you use on a carboy for beer, in the spout," she says. "The hole in the bung is the perfect fit for a tiny spray head I found in the hardware store. I just plug the spray head in the bung, and it works like a watering can, except when I want to, I can cap it and shake it up to mix the ingredients," she says.

## Custom-Fit Watering System

You can keep those difficult-to-water areas (such as under the eaves or out of the sprinkler's reach) nicely moist with this customized sprinkler system developed by Gary Prochaska, a professional gardener in Ames, Iowa.

Prochaska cuts a piece of ½-inch PVC pipe to the length needed. He caps one end of the pipe with a plug and the other with an adapter designed to fit a garden hose. He then drills holes in the PVC with a ¹⁄₁₆-inch drill bit in a straight line, 2 inches apart. Prochaska attaches a hose and places the PVC wherever he needs to water.

The advantage to this device, Prochaska says, is that he can adjust the flow slightly either by burying the pipe for a slow root soak or putting it on the surface of the soil for a gentle spraying effect.

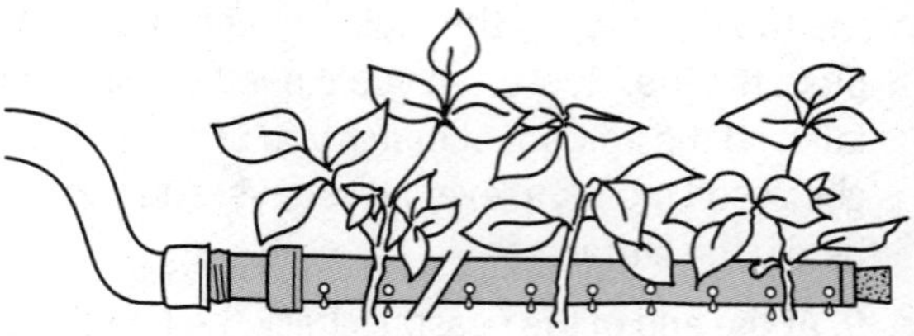

*Keep those hard-to-water areas from drying out with your own custom watering system.*

## Don't Get Soaked!

If you use soaker hoses in the garden, you usually wind up trudging through mud where the soaker hose crosses a path. However, it's easy to keep your feet dry, says Cheryl Coston of Fairdealing, Missouri. Just cut a piece of old garden hose to the necessary length and slip it over the soaker where it crosses the walkway. That will prevent water from seeping out of that section and into your path.

## Transplants Drink It Up

"After a full day of moving plants around in my garden or setting out new ones, I don't have the energy or the patience to stand

# Build It!

## Deep-Reach Irrigation Bottles

Dry-climate gardeners need to be resourceful to get water to their thirsty crops. Just wetting the surface isn't enough, though; you need to get the water down deep, where the roots are. An organic gardener from Senegal devised this clever way to convert recycled plastic bottles into deep-reaching irrigation bottles that are perfect for squash, melons, tomatoes, or any vegetable planted in hills.

### Materials

- Narrow-mouthed plastic soda or water bottles (1 or 2 liter)
- 1 foot length of ¾-inch PVC pipe for each bottle
- Durabond PVC adhesive
- Utility knife or sturdy scissors
- Hacksaw

### Directions

**1.** Cut away the bottom of each bottle using a utility knife or scissors.

**2.** Cut one end of each pipe at a steep angle with a hacksaw, or ask your hardware store clerk to cut it for you.

**3.** Insert the mouth of the soda bottle into the flat end of a PVC pipe section, or slip the pipe into the mouth of the bottle (whichever works with the bottle you've chosen).

**4.** Fasten the two parts together with nontoxic Durabond PVC adhesive and let dry.

To use the irrigation bottle, stick the pointed end of the PVC into the soil about 6 inches deep, several inches from the plant. Fill the bottle with water once a day or as often as needed to give plants a deep drink.

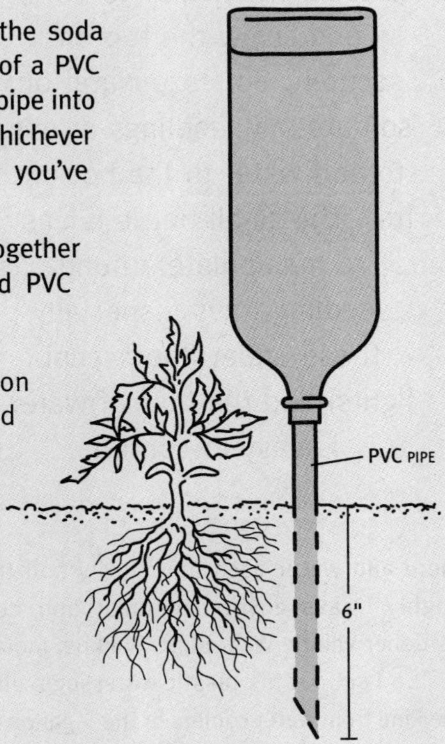

**Recycle It!**

***On hand:*** Plastic mustard squeeze bottle

***Turn it into:*** A watering device for fragile seedlings

***How to do it:*** Clean the mustard bottle in hot soapy water. Fill it with lukewarm to tepid water (70° to 90°F), and screw the top on securely. Squeeze water on soil around seedlings or use to add water to the bottom tray. The small bottle is easy to manipulate around seedling trays (especially those under fluorescent lights) and the flow of water is easy to control.

there and water each one slowly and thoroughly," says environmentalist and home gardener Valerie West of St. Phillips, Indiana.

"So I set out big plastic water jugs, either the kind from water coolers or the 3-gallon size from the supermarket, in my beds or at the base of new trees and shrubs. I punch a few holes near the bottom of the sides of the jug. I can fill the jug in minutes with the hose, and water dribbles out for hours at a slow rate so none is wasted." For the heavy-duty, 5-gallon, water cooler–size jugs, you may need to hammer a nail through the hard plastic to create the holes.

It's easy to delegate the refilling of the water jugs to your kids. They'll welcome a chance to play with the hose, and the task will make them feel like they're a part of making the garden grow.

## Watering the Greenhouse

Susan Cooker of Malvern, Pennsylvania, has an unheated greenhouse, but she makes the most of it, extending her indoor growing season from very early spring through late fall with the help of plastic soda bottles. Susan says the bottles are great for adding both heat and humidity to the air. "It isn't pretty, but it works," she remarks about the many bottles filled two-thirds full with water. Cooker lines the perimeter of her greenhouse with them.

For a handy supply of water, Cooker had gutters installed on the greenhouse roof to funnel rain water into a rain barrel. She then retrofitted an old hose into the draining valve of the barrel so she can easily fill watering cans or buckets from her clean water reserve.

## No-Bleed Feed

"After opening a 5-pound bag of organic fertilizer, I slip it into a plastic grocery bag so the fertilizer won't leak through to the floor or shelf where I store it," says Caroline Whitenack of Doylestown, Pennsylvania.

Although a plastic bag can prevent moisture from getting into the fertilizer bag, you can use a plastic bucket with a lid for even more security. Small critters like mice can chew through a plastic bag and then nibble on your fertilizer. If mice are a potential problem, recycle a food-grade plastic bucket (usually available from restaurants, bakeries, and grocery stores for free or a nominal charge).

## Easy Rain Gauge

Make your own rain gauge from a straight-sided clear plastic drinking cup (the disposable type is fine) with about 12- to 16-ounce capacity. Using a ruler and measuring from the bottom, mark with a permanent marker at ½-inch increments all the way up the outside of the glass. In a sunny area in the garden (where there are no overhanging trees or branches), set the glass down into the soil (sinking 2 to 3 inches). "After a rain, pull the cup out to read, or insert a ruler down into the cup to measure rainfall," says Linda Harris from Fulton, Kentucky. "This rain gauge will last one or two seasons."

## Fertilizer Fast

If you're tired of lugging watering cans and buckets filled with liquid fertilizer or compost tea to your plants, try this fast watering/fertilizing system developed by Tonya Halberstadt of Ben Wheeler, Texas.

Halberstadt puts a 55-gallon, food-safe drum (she finds hers at flea markets or salvage yards) in her vegetable garden. She punches a hole near the bottom and inserts a piece of PVC fitting, caulking well around the edge of the hole to prevent leakage. Then she attaches a soaker hose to the PVC and lays it around the vegetable garden. She fills the drum with water from the garden hose and mixes in the fertilizer.

"I've had a real time with fertilizers," Halberstadt says. "I'd do one row but not the next. This way everything gets fertilized at once."

In her large garden Halberstadt also likes to hook up more than one drum to the other to create an even bigger reservoir. To do this, she again punches a hole near the bottom in the side of the original drum as well as in a new drum. She attaches them with a short length of PVC and then caulks again.

*Make fertilizing as easy as turning a spigot with a system using low-cost, recycled metal drums.*

## Easy Indoor Watering

Nancy Engel, who gardens in Cold Spring, New York, has an extensive array of houseplants that used to be a bear to water. But not anymore since her husband devised an indoor-watering system. He screwed a quick-release

Build It!

# 55-Gallon Drum Watering System

Industrial 55-gallon drums are inexpensive and easy to find and hold almost as much water as a 100-square-foot garden needs in a week. Making a watering reservoir out of one of these drums isn't hard, and can sure save on time and muscle power devoted to hauling water. When buying or recycling drums for your garden, use only those that have held fruit juices or other nontoxic substances.

To make garden irrigation easier, use a "passive" 55-gallon drum watering system, recommended by Charles Young of Philadelphia's Pennsylvania State Urban Gardening Program. The system uses gravity to move the water instead of a pump. Two barrels are required for this system, with one barrel sunk slightly into the ground. The lower barrel provides a base for the second barrel giving needed height for effective, gravity-fed irrigation. Installing a faucet in the upper barrel is an easy way to control the flow of water to your garden.

**Materials**

- Two 55-gallon drums
- Hose bib (exterior faucet)
- Old garden hose
- Spade
- Electric drill with specialty bit or metal-cutting hole saw
- Welding kit

**Directions**

**1.** Using a spade, dig a hole 18 to 24 inches deep, and wide enough to receive a drum. Level the bottom of the hole.

**2.** Put one drum in the hole, then backfill around the edge of the drum, and tamp the soil.

male coupler onto each of the upstairs and downstairs faucets. Then he screwed together two 10-foot lengths of ½-inch-diameter plastic hose, screwed a female coupler onto one end of the hose, and snapped that end onto the male coupler on the downstairs faucet. He made the same setup for the upstairs faucet.

Engel can use her hoses as is by simply attaching a quick-connect system that has an on-off switch, or she can customize her watering by using either of two other attach-

**3.** Using a metal-cutting hole saw or a drill with a specialty bit, make a 1-inch hole in the side of the other drum, 1 to 3 inches from its bottom edge.

**4.** Push the long threaded end of the exterior faucet (plumbing suppliers call it a hose bib) into the hole. Use your welding kit to weld the faucet threads to the inside of the drum.

**5.** Position the drum on top of the sunken drum, making sure they nestle together securely.

**6.** Fill top drum with water.

**7.** Once you attach a hose to the drum's faucet, you're ready to have a well-watered garden.

One variation on this watering system involves connecting raised drums with spigots to drip irrigation hoses to create a gravity-powered irrigation drip system. Or, instead of irrigating your plants directly from a drum, you can feed water from a raised drum to a water reservoir and then connect gravity-fed, drip-irrigation garden hoses to the reservoir. Whatever technique you decide to use, your garden will benefit from a continuous and reliable source of water.

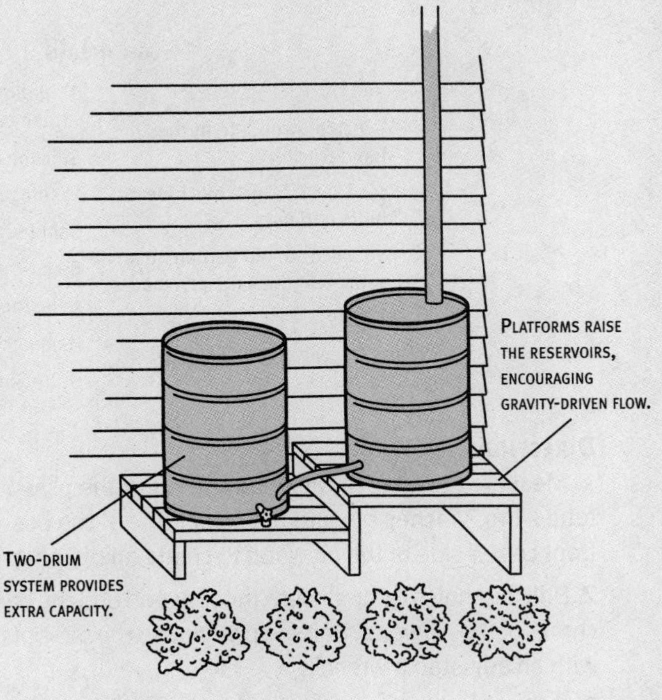


ments—a plastic hose nozzle with twist shut-off or a watering wand for window boxes.

"From the upstairs sink, I can reach plants in two bedrooms and all of my second-story window boxes," Engel says. "The downstairs connection allows me to get from the front to the back of my house as well as from one end to the other to water plants in every room. And the on-off switch allows me to keep the faucet turned on, but without dripping water on the floor as I move from plant to plant."

# Build It!

## Clark Park "Water on Wheels"

Lewis Mellman, a tree tender from Clark Park in west Philadelphia, built this contraption for watering trees when he had little or no access to a hose. He strapped a 35-gallon rectangular trash can to a hand truck and then mounted a beer tap at the bottom.

### Materials

- Hand truck
- ¾-inch plywood, to fit the hand truck
- Four ¼ × 1½-inch machine bolts and nuts
- Two pieces of old garden hose, same length as the plywood
- 12 nails
- PVC faucet and flange bolt
- 35-gallon rectangular plastic trash can
- Silicone caulk
- Lashing straps or rope
- Saber saw
- Electric drill with 5⁄16-inch bit
- Adjustable wrench
- Hammer
- Utility knife

### Directions

**1.** Measure the base of the hand truck. Cut the plywood to size with a saber saw so it extends 2 to 3 inches beyond the front edge of the base. Also, cut a U-shaped notch in the front center side of the plywood to create an opening for a faucet.

**2.** Drill four holes through both the plywood and the base of the hand truck—one near each corner of the plywood. Bolt the plywood to the base of the hand truck, and tighten the bolts with an adjustable wrench.

**3.** Split the two pieces of garden hose lengthwise, and nail the pieces to the front of the plywood to create bumpers on either side of the U-shaped notch.

**4.** Install the PVC faucet in the front bottom of the trash can so that when the can is placed on the base of the hand truck and liquid runs from the faucet, the liquid will flow through the plywood's U-shaped notch. To do this, cut a round hole in the trash can with a utility knife and insert the threaded end of the faucet into the hole from the outside of the can.

Apply a generous bead of silicone caulk to the base of the threads, and then connect and tighten the flange bolt to the faucet threads. Allow the silicone to dry overnight before filling the can with water.

**5.** Strap or tie the trash can to the hand truck so that the faucet hangs over the plywood's U-shaped notch.

**6.** Fill the trash can half-full with water. To use your super-size watering can on wheels, guide it up to the base of each tree, open the faucet, and water generously.

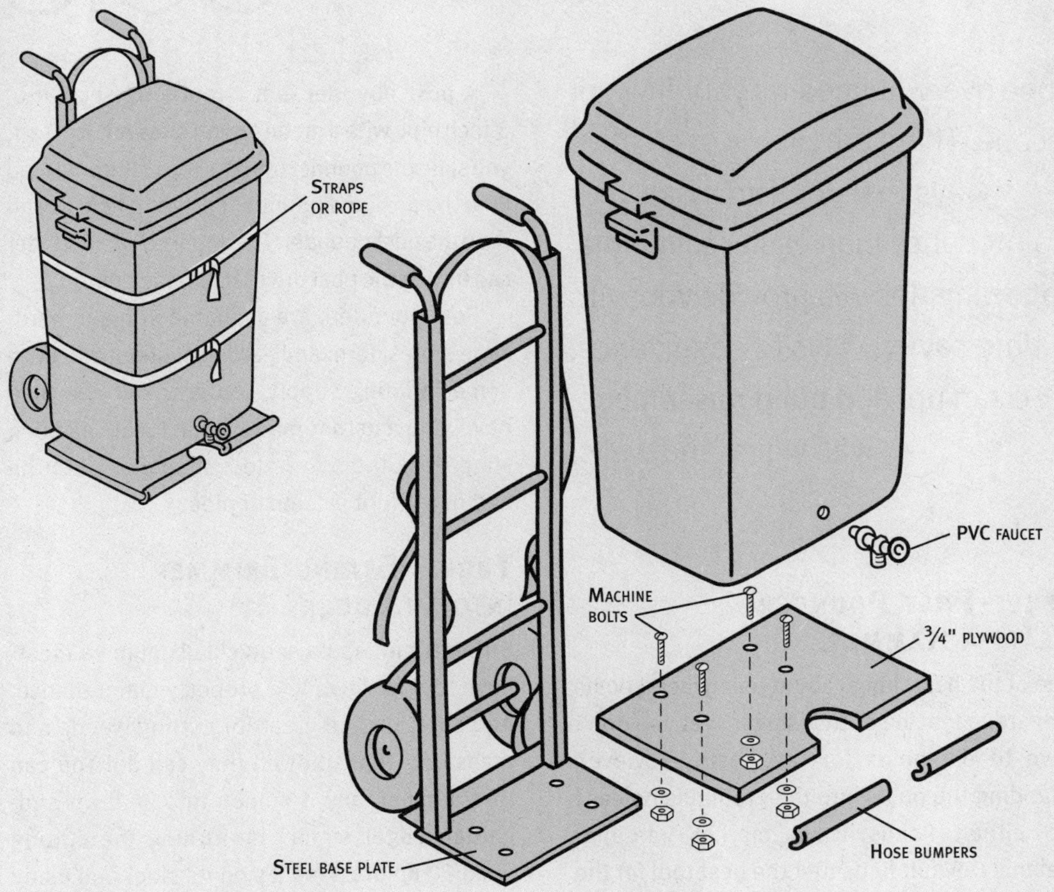

# Lawn and Landscape Tools

Don't be overwhelmed by your lawn or landscape. There are plenty of creative ways that you can make your maintenance plan easier to handle. The following tips will provide you with time-saving ways to edge, fence, clean up, and build raised beds, walkways, and walls.

## Fence-Post Pounder Beats a Hammer

One of the best things about using metal posts for garden fencing or trellising is that you don't have to dig holes for the posts. However, pounding the posts into the ground is no easy job either. Pennsylvania market gardener Melanie DeVault finds that the best tool for the job is a post pounder or driver. "I'm 5 foot, 2 inches tall, and I just don't have the reach or strength to drive a post into the ground with any kind of hammer," DeVault explains.

A post pounder is a 2-foot-long section of 3-inch pipe with a metal cap on one end. To use it, you slide the pounder over the top of the post, and lean the post and pounder upright. Then lift and drop the post pounder. The impact of the pounder cap hitting the post drives it into the ground.

Post pounders are available at many hardware stores, farm and garden centers, and even some building-supply centers. You can also have one custom-made at a local machine shop—ask them to weld a steel disk onto the end of a 2-foot section of pipe.

## Turn a String Trimmer into an Edger

String trimmers have quickly become a must-have tool for lawn and property maintenance. And sure, they're great for cutting weeds and grass, but that's not all they can do! You can turn almost any trimmer into a lawn-and-garden edger simply by turning the cutting head 90 degrees (so it's on its side) and using a steady hand to guide the rotating string head slightly above the ground.

"Gas-powered edgers work best," says Mike Ferrara, a gardener from the Minneapolis area, "because they can handle thicker line in their spools." Ferrara says a cord called "star line" (it's actually molded into the shape of a star) works great for this purpose because it cuts through thick vegetation and lasts a long time. It's also a good idea to use a trimmer that has a standard tap-and-feed head, which means that when the nylon line wears away, you simply tap the head on the ground to feed out a predetermined length of line.

When used as an edger, the star line will leave a nice, thick trench—ideal for tidying up around your raised beds and your sidewalks. When using your string trimmer/edger, it's important to wear safety goggles and leather gloves at all times and to make sure the stone guard is correctly attached to your trimmer.

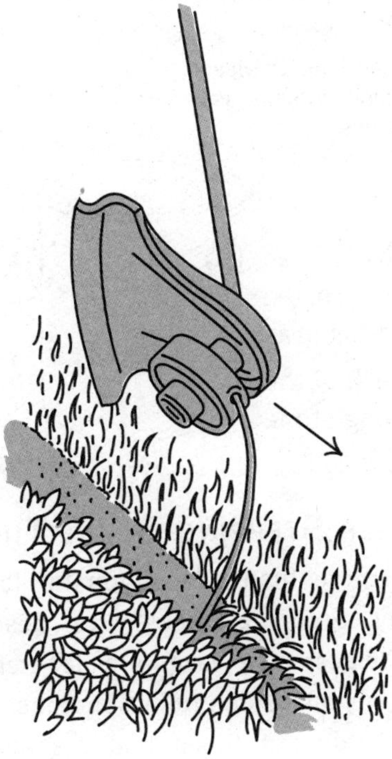

*TURNING THE CUTTING HEAD ON YOUR STRING TRIMMER GIVES YOU AN INSTANT EDGER.*

***ON HAND:*** An old vinyl rug runner

***TURN IT INTO:*** Sunken edging strips

***HOW TO DO IT:*** Using a utility knife, cut the runner into strips about 6 inches wide and sink them into the ground around a garden bed. They'll keep roots from moving into the lawn or path and will also help deter underground burrowers such as moles. (You can also use the vinyl strips around individual plants to deter cutworms.) If the ground is soft, simply sink the strips into the ground. If the soil is hard packed, dig a slim trench, place the strips in the trench, and then refill the trench with soil.

## RHODODENDRON FENCING

Rhododendrons tend to get big in Oregon, and sometimes they need a hearty pruning. A landscape architect by training, Rodney Wojtanik

# Build It!

## Snappy Stepping-Stones

Stepping-stones are a must for large garden beds so you can maneuver your way around the plants without tamping down the soil. But they can be expensive to buy. "Make your own and make them as pretty as you like," says Linda Harris of Fulton, Kentucky. "Press shells, pretty pebbles, or large leaves into the concrete after pouring. Or scratch in your own choice of names, dates, words, handprints, footprints, paw-prints, or drawings after pouring." Ask for a bucket at your grocery store, bakery, or local restaurant. They're usually willing to give them away for free. This idea came from a lady in Martin, Tennessee, that I met at a garden open house," says Harris. "It was such a neat idea that I want to pass it along."

**Materials**

- 5-gallon plastic bucket with straight sides
- 60-pound bag of concrete mix
- Wooden stirring paddle
- Tape measure or ruler
- Band saw or sharp X-Acto knife
- Plastic drop cloth
- Old pencil for drawing, or decorative shells, leaves, or pebbles

**Directions**

**1.** Measure the height of the bucket and divide by 5. Then mark that measurement (about 3 inches) down the side of the bucket. Repeat, making three more marks at the same interval.

**2.** Saw or cut through the bucket crosswise at each of the marked intervals to make five bands or stepping-stone

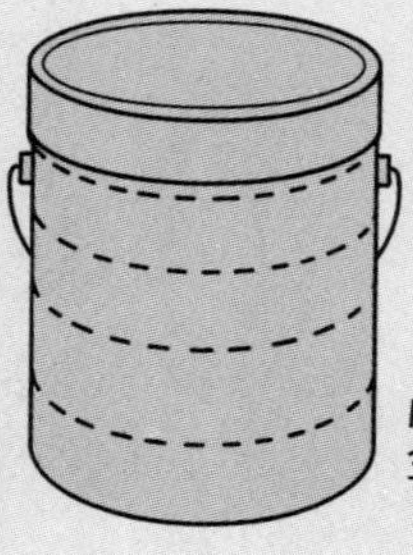

Measure at 3" intervals.

knows how to cut them back, and he also knows how to use all those prunings in a productive way. Wojtanik fenced in his wife's herb bed with his rhododendron trimmings. He pushed sturdier straight pieces into the ground to serve as uprights and then used longer, thinner branches as the "rails." He ties the pieces together with steel wire, which quickly rusts and becomes nearly invisible.

### Another Stepping-Stone Tip

There's more than one option for forming "Snappy Stepping-Stones" as described above. You can also make forms for stepping-stones in your garden from Sonotube, those sturdy cardboard tubes that are sold for pouring concrete footings; they're available at most home centers. Using a hacksaw, cut the Sonotube into sections as thick as you want molds. The top of the bucket with the handle attached is one mold. The bucket bottom is also a mold; you can keep the bottom intact or remove it.

**3.** Lay the bucket circles on a flat surface covered with a plastic drop cloth.

**4.** Mix concrete as directed on the package, and pour it into your circle molds. A 60-pound bag will yield enough concrete to pour five stepping-stones that are each a little more than 1 inch thick.

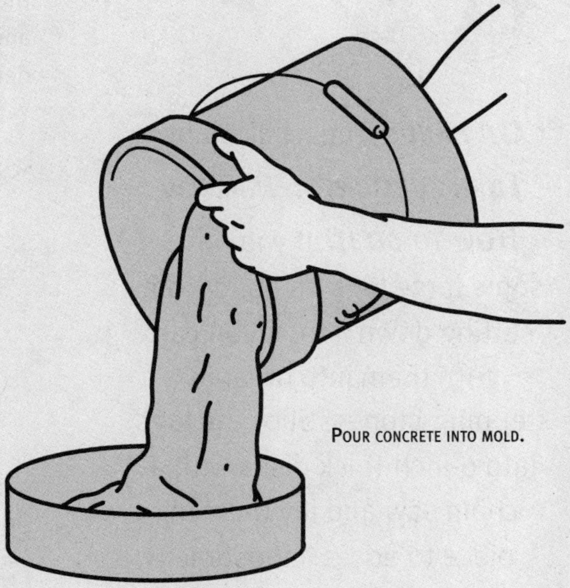

Pour concrete into mold.

Decorate as desired.

**5.** Level the surfaces, and decorate as desired, using an old pencil or decorative stones to make a pattern or design.

**6.** When the concrete is set, push your new stepping-stones out of the molds. Save your molds for the next pouring.

your stepping-stones to be. Lay the circular forms on the ground where you want the stones. Mix concrete according to the instructions on the bag, and fill the forms. Allow the concrete to set until nearly dry, then cut and peel off the cardboard Sonotube.

If you plan to decorate the stones with a design or imprint, be sure to do so before the concrete is thoroughly dry.

## Reused Concrete

Wherever concrete pavements are being replaced, you'll see dump trucks full of the old broken-up concrete headed to a landfill. Fred Conrad, the community garden coordinator for the Atlanta Food Bank, "saw gold in them-there trucks" and started salvaging the common refuse for garden walls and raised beds. Calling his material "recrete," Conrad collects old

***On hand:*** Tree trunk slabs

***Turn them into:*** Walkway

***How to do it:*** If you have some large logs on hand from cutting down a tree, you can turn them into organic stepping-stones. Slice the logs into 6-inch-thick disks with a chain saw and lay them in place to add a handsome rustic touch to your landscape!

broken slabs from areas where sidewalk, driveway, or road work is being done. The pieces are usually fairly uniform in thickness and flat on two or three surfaces, making them easy to dry-stack into a garden wall. You can also set them on one side to create a vertical wall for a raised bed. Conrad finds recrete ideal for many reasons. "It's considerably lighter than stone, it doesn't leach anything toxic like treated wood does, and its rough edges lend a natural look to your garden—especially in wet climates where the recrete gets nice and mossy."

## Break a Rake

When Jim Bray cleans out the six perennial beds on his 1-acre lot, he prefers to use a broken rake. It isn't because he can't afford a new one; it's just that he likes it that way! Bray found that by removing the bent or damaged side tines from his old leaf rake, he can create the perfect recycled tool for removing leaves and other debris that gets caught between the densely planted hostas and daylilies at his Yardley, Pennsylvania, home.

*To make your own mini rake, simply use tin snips or heavy shears to cut off all but four or five of the center tines from an old leaf rake.*

## Pretty Branch Spreaders

If Darlene White invites you to take a look at her pot plant, don't get nervous. This British Columbia garden writer has simply devised an elegant way to spread the branches of her pear tree using hanging terra-cotta pots!

Many shade and fruit trees—pears in particular—tend to hold their branches too tightly together as they grow, and gardeners have traditionally hung lead weights on the branches to force them to grow out and not up. White, however, wanted something a little prettier to gaze at during the growing months.

In the spring, she gathered about 2 dozen old terra-cotta pots all the same general size (usually about 6 to 7 inches wide). She tied one end of a 15-inch piece of fishing line around a long nail and threaded the other end through the drainage hole. The pot hung upside down like a bell, making it easy to attach it to a branch she wanted to spread. To adjust how much the branch will spread, simply move the weight in or out from the tree trunk. Add more pots until all the limbs that you want to spread have a pot attached.

White keeps the amount of line between the pot bottom and branch to about 5 inches, to keep the pots from smacking each other in the breeze. The limbs should be settled into their new growth pattern by the end of the growing season, so remove the pots before any unexpected early snowfall adds too much weight and snaps the branches.

*TURN UNUSED CLAY POTS INTO ATTRACTIVE BRANCH SPREADERS FOR FRUIT OR SHADE TREES. THEY MAKE AN INTERESTING GARDEN ACCENT, TOO!*

**Recycle It!**

***ON HAND:*** Scrap piece of ¼-inch wire mesh

***TURN IT INTO:*** A stepping "stone" near a water spigot

***HOW TO DO IT:*** Place a square of recycled ¼-inch wire mesh on the soil or mulch surface under a water spigot. The mesh prevents puddling, allowing water to pass through it and giving you a firm, clean place to step.

## PIPE DREAMS

It's fun to decorate your garden with lanterns and other ornaments, but it isn't much fun to keep straightening them up when soggy soil allows their stakes to keel over. Living in rainy Seattle, garden writer and consultant Madeleine Wilde knows that all too well! She solved her problem by installing a short section of galvanized or PVC pipe into the ground as a permanent mounting hole for each ornament. To use this great idea in your own garden, simply choose the appropriate diameter of pipe and, with a heavy hammer, pound it in flush or slightly lower than the ground level to facili-

**Recycle It!**

***On hand:*** 2-liter soda bottle

***Turn it into:*** Funnel

***How to do it:*** Tired of spilling gas on your driveway when refueling your lawn mower? Just take a 2-liter soda bottle, cut it in half with a hacksaw or utility knife, and you have an instant funnel!

tate mowing. Madeleine also finds a set of these pipe supports useful for positioning her spiked sprinkler during those rare dry spells.

## A Quicker Picker Upper

There's no question that sweet gum (*Liquidambar styraciflua*) trees are gorgeous, especially in autumn. But if you've ever had them in your landscape, you know that they have a down side: Their hard, spiky fruits are a nuisance when they fall to the lawn or sidewalk. Picking them up is a difficult, time-consuming, and sometimes even painful job. But Wendy Goldberg of Wilmington, Delaware, invented an ingenious sweet-gum-ball picker upper. "I took a stick (actually a hollow, dried Jerusalem artichoke stem because it's lighter than wood) and tied polyester batting (the kind used in pillows) to the end," she explains. Goldberg walks around the yard with her picker upper and just touches the end to the fallen fruit. The sweet gum balls stick to the batting, enabling her to pick them up without bending over. From there, it's a simple matter to pick off the sweet gum balls and drop them in a bucket for disposal later.

## Litter Grabber

Tired of jumping off your lawn tractor to pick up debris that blocks your path? Try this ingenious trash grabber devised by Carolyn Roof, Master Gardener and garden columnist for the *Paducah Sun* newspaper, Paducah, Kentucky. Take an old wooden handle from a broom, rake, or other tool, and saw it off to a comfortable length for you. Hammer three finishing nails into one end, and then take it with you when you mow by tractor. "Using this trash grabber is a lot simpler than getting off the tractor, picking up litter, and having to restart the tractor," says Roof. "There's some litter I don't want to pick up by hand. And this tool works for almost everything except glass. The nails will even puncture and pick up aluminum cans."

## Mowing Meter

What's the worst thing you can do to your lawn? Cut off too much at once. The golden rule of mowing says you should never remove more than one-third of a grass blade at any one time. But most of us don't mow according to the needs of the grass. That's why Warren Schultz of Essex Junction, Vermont, made a simple mowing meter that tells him when he should crank up the mower.

His lawn is made of tall fescue, which shouldn't be cut shorter than 3 inches. To make a measuring stick, he started with an 8-inch-long, 1 by 1-inch stake with a point at one end. He painted the bottom 2 inches brown, the next 3 inches green, the next 1½ inches yellow, and the rest red. Then he sank the brown section into the ground to one side of his lawn. When the height of the grass reaches the top of the green band, he knows it has reached its ideal height. As it grows into the yellow area, he knows it's time to mow it back down to the top of the green band. If the blades ever reach into the red area, he knows that he has let the grass grow too tall and that he needs to make a series of cuts to gradually trim it back down to the ideal height.

## Put Horsepower to Work

"I loved the big old forsythia bush that we inherited when we bought our farmhouse," says home gardener Linda Howard of Evansville, Indiana. "But it was in the wrong place—it blocked my view from the kitchen window so I couldn't see the garden beyond it."

Linda and her husband, Rick, decided to move the large shrub to a new site, but after 2 days of digging, it was still anchored like a buried boulder and gave no signs of budging. That's when she decided to turn to a mechanical aid—their small pickup truck. "I wrapped the bottom of the stems in burlap and fastened a strong rope around them. We tied the rope to the truck, and I stayed with the bush while Rick began to gently pull with the truck. I couldn't believe how easily the truck pulled it out—those big roots I had tried to dig and then tried to cut through came loose right away."

Rick and Linda dragged the forsythia to its new home and then settled it in place. It recovered quickly and blooms cheerfully each spring near the corner of the driveway. Linda reports she's planning to use pickup power to pull out a volunteer mulberry tree that she wants to move to a better spot and maybe a few other overgrown heirloom shrubs.

### Recycle It!

***On hand:*** Popsicle stick

***Turn it into:*** Engine maintenance tool

***How to do it:*** Keep your air-cooled engines running cool by making sure the fins around the cylinder are free from dirt and debris. A Popsicle stick works great for this job: Simply sharpen one end into a point to get stubborn bits of grass out of the fins.

## Quick Mower Cleanup

Environmentalist Valerie West of St. Phillips, Indiana, counts on her trusty, heavy-duty screwdriver "whenever anything needs prying, poking, digging," or for any other small-scale jobs where leverage counts. But her favorite use of this perfect, simple tool is for cleaning her lawn mower. "You can slide the screwdriver under the caked-on grass and lift off big chunks," she says. For safety's sake, always securely disconnect the spark plug wire and be sure the gas tank is empty before you do this.

A plain-tip screwdriver with a long, stout shaft also comes in handy for separating and lifting seedlings, particularly those of deep-rooted plants such as young trees or Oriental poppies and other tap-rooted perennials. And if you misplace your dandelion digger, use a trusty screwdriver to lift out tough weeds from the lawn and walks.

## Make a Fence More Friendly

"A high wood fence was a necessity around my yard because of my unruly dogs and my need for privacy," says Sally Roth, author of *Attracting Birds to Your Backyard*, "but once the fence was up, it really looked forbidding. I like my neighbors, and I like a yard that looks welcoming from the street, so I decided to make the outside walls of the fence just as appealing as the inside.

"Sweet autumn clematis (*Clematis terniflora*) and virgin's bower (*C. virginiana*) pop up everywhere in my yard, thanks to the birds who drop the seeds, so I transplanted every seedling I could find, spacing them about 2 feet apart along the outside of the fence. The problem is, clematis clings by winding the stems of its leaves around a support, but the solid wood face of my fence didn't give them any place to get a grip. So I bought 100 feet of green vinyl-coated 3-foot-high wire fencing and stapled it the long way to the outside of the fence, starting about 2 feet above the bottom of the fence.

"These vines grow like lightning, and within 2 weeks they had reached the wire. They swarmed over it, covering it so thickly I now have a living wall of greenery instead of bare boards. Soon the vines will be draping themselves along the top of the fence, and when summer arrives, they'll be crowning it with soft white flowers that will make my yard smell terrific. When the flowers ripen into fluffy seed heads in fall, my birds will have a banquet right through winter."

*A SOLID WOOD FENCE IS MUCH MORE NEIGHBORLY WHEN YOU COVER IT WITH PRETTY CLIMBING VINES.*

## Consider All the Angles

"If it weren't for my camera," says Gretel Hartman of the Boston area, "my garden wouldn't look half as good as I like to think it does!" Designing a garden before planting it can be an acquired skill, so Hartman depends on her camera to show her what works and what doesn't.

"When I'm in my garden, I get so involved looking at my plants," she says, "that I can't even tell whether the overall design works. So

I make it a point to snap a roll of film at least once a month, from all angles.

"It's amazing how much difference it makes looking at a picture, rather than looking at the real thing. I can tell right away when a tree or shrub is in the wrong spot, and I can see where the perennial garden looks bare of color."

Hartman files away the photos, month by month, for a record of her garden year. "I like to pull them out in the dead of winter," she says, "first, so I don't lose hope of spring, and second, so I can start thinking about any changes I want to make in the coming year. It's a good way to remind myself of what I need to shop for, too—more of those pink iris, or maybe a weeping cherry for the corner of the garden. . . . "

## Rock Hound to the Rescue

A rocky garden led garden photographer Rick Mark of Vancouver, Washington, to find a better tool for prying out rocks. It was a Pennsylvania garden where Mark discovered how well a rock hammer works for loosening rocks.

"My family are rock hounds," he says, "and we had a few strong rock hammers lying around. They're made for heavier work than a carpenter's hammer, and they have a head that's designed for levering out rocks." The long, curved piece on the back of the head slides easily under rocks to get a grip, and the strong handle stands up to mini-crowbar work much better than any other tool. The handle slides into the hammer loop on carpenter jeans, keeping the tool handy while gardening.

Mark bought his rock hammer at a lapidary supply shop. Most hardware stores will carry a similar tool, though they may call it a brick mason's hammer.

## Light Up Your Path

Another easy, inexpensive way to add evening light involves large glass containers, explains Melinda Rizzo, who gardens in Quakertown, Pennsylvania. Mayonnaise jars as well as industrial-strength pickle and hot pepper jars work great. "The bigger the better!" says Rizzo. Soak off the labels and rinse the jars clean. Pour 2 to 3 inches of sand in the jar, then insert a white pillar candle. Use these inexpensive garden lights in the garden at night, to line a brick path, or simply grouped by your favorite garden resting place.

***On hand:*** Old swingset

***Turn it into:*** Hammock frame

***How to do it:*** Strip all the play equipment off of the A-frame. Spray paint it a subtle color like brown or dark green, and use it to support a hammock in your garden. Recycle the poles from the teeter-totter feature to use as a bean teepee. Wrap them with wire mesh for the vines to twine around.

# Build It!

## The Shrub "Club"

"Each time we bought new shrubs and planted them in our whiskey barrels, they'd be stolen overnight," says Anna Maria Vona, who lives and gardens in south Philadelphia. She and her neighbors came up with some effective ways to protect their plants. This "shrub cable," devised by Joe Procaccini to foil the "jerk-and-run thief," is like the antitheft club device you lock onto your steering wheel to foil a car thief.

### Materials

- Half whiskey barrel or planter
- 1-inch-diameter threaded eyebolt and nut
- 2 large flat washers to fit bolt
- 4-foot length of ¼-inch or ⅜-inch braided cable
- Potted shrub or tree
- Soil mix
- Lightweight fill (optional)
- Electric drill and ½-inch bit

### Directions

**1.** Drill a ½-inch hole in the bottom of the whiskey barrel, and insert a threaded eyebolt with a washer on both sides of the bottom. Screw on the nut. (If the bottom of the planter rests too close to the ground, mount the eyebolt through the side, just above the bottom.)

**2.** Fasten one end of the braided cable onto the eyebolt by twisting the end of the cable around itself like a piece of picture frame wire.

**3.** If desired, put a layer of lightweight fill material in the bottom of the barrel.

**4.** Remove the shrub or tree from the nursery pot and position it in the planter so it will grow at the same level that it was growing in the nursery pot. Add soil mix to the planter as needed until the plant is at the right height.

**5.** Wrap the loose end of the braided cable around the trunk of the shrub or tree just above the rootball. Make a loop with enough slack for future growth, and fasten the cable by again twisting it around itself.

**6.** Finish filling the planter with soil mix. Be sure to bury the braided cable as much as possible in the soil mix so it isn't easy to see.

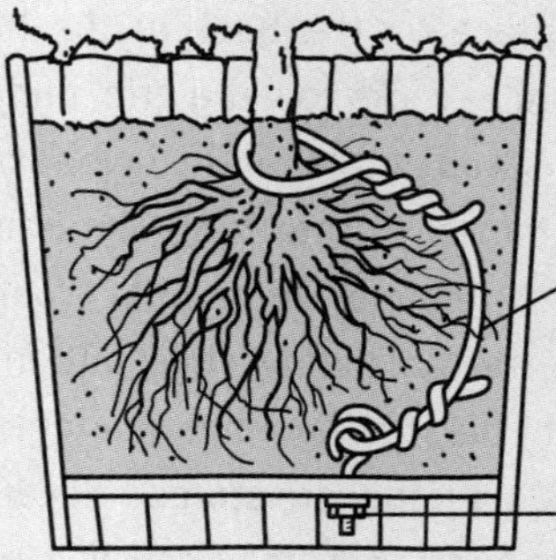

# Build It!

## Custom-Made Pond Cleaner

Ed Bender of Carlsbad, California, has discovered several garden uses for restaurant bus tubs. "They're very handy for carrying things—such as mulch—from one part of the yard to another and they're pretty sturdy," says Bender. However, the best use of all for these tubs may be for cleaning a garden pond. Bender needed a cleaning contraption that would eliminate the problem of ending up with a soaking wet mess. So he made a self-draining container that allows him to easily empty the contents into his compost pile. The water drains off into the bottom of the bus tub, leaving material in the basket, which he then throws in his compost.

**Materials**

1-inch-mesh chicken wire cut into pieces:

- 15 inches × 21 inches
- 11 inches × 7 inches
- 11 inches × 7 inches

One restaurant bus tub, 13 × 17 × 6 inches deep

**Directions**

**1.** Make a 90-degree bend 5 inches from each end of the large piece of chicken wire to form a U-shape.

**2.** Make a wire basket by attaching the smaller pieces to the open ends of the U, twisting the wires together and leaving a 2-inch overhang at the base of each end.

**3.** On each 2-inch overhang, bend the bottom 1 inch upward to form a 1-inch-deep foot on each end of the basket.

**4.** Place the basket inside the bus tub. You should have 1 inch of free space surrounding the basket.

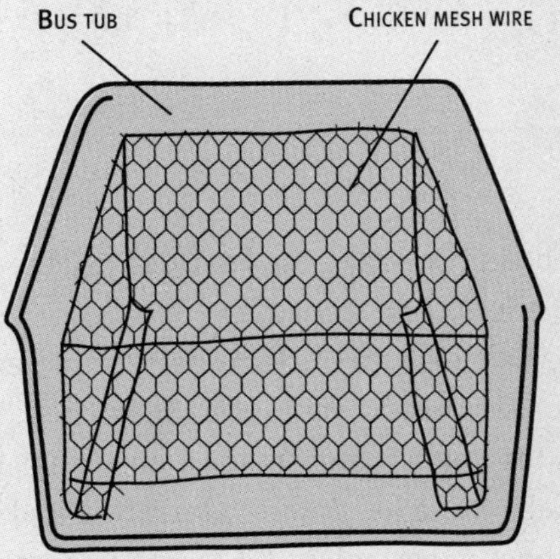


"Fastening doesn't need to be neat," adds Bender. "Just make sure there aren't loose wire ends to jab you." To use, scoop up pond debris and plop it in the tray, allowing the water to drain through the colander into the bus tub. Lift out colander and empty debris into your compost pile.

"In pond maintenance, I have to remove dead water lily leaves and blossoms, and I can't reach them all from the shore," Bender says. "So I take the bus tub arrangement in the water with me. Because the tub floats, I can pull it around as I walk in the pond."

# Build-It!

## Lantern Delights

Buying outdoor lighting from catalogs or garden shops can be expensive. To make her own, Melinda Rizzo, a home gardener in Quakertown, Pennsylvania, uses clean 4- and 6-ounce baby food jars. Once you soak off the labels, fine gauge wire and a small votive candle are all you need to create sparkling evening lights. You can hang these lights on hooks, nails driven into porch beams, or as lanterns on garden poles. Using a citronella votive gives extra bug-off advantages.

**Materials**

6 to 12 clean baby food jars

Spool of fine-gauge wire (not plastic coated)

6 to 12 votive candles

**Directions**

**1.** For each jar, cut a piece of wire 40 to 50 inches long. Vary the lengths so your finished lights can hang at different heights.

**2.** Bend a wire in half to form a V-shaped handle for the jar. Hold the bent wire over a jar so 6 to 10 inches of the V extends above the jar for hanging. Wrap the rest of the wire around the threads of the jar mouth.

**3.** Twist each end of the wire around the V-shaped handle to fasten the wire securely. Pull tight.

**4.** Place a votive candle in the jar, light, and hang.

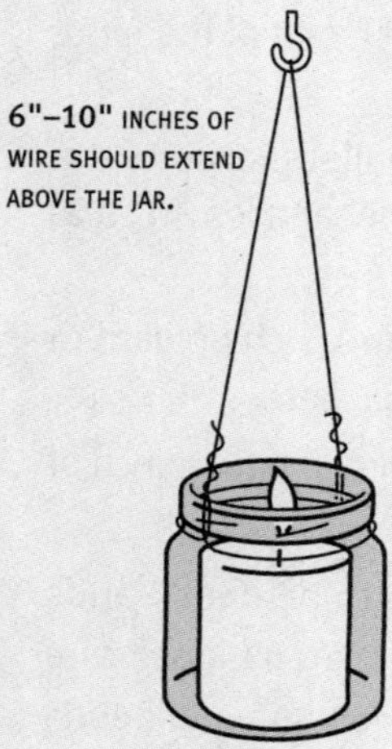


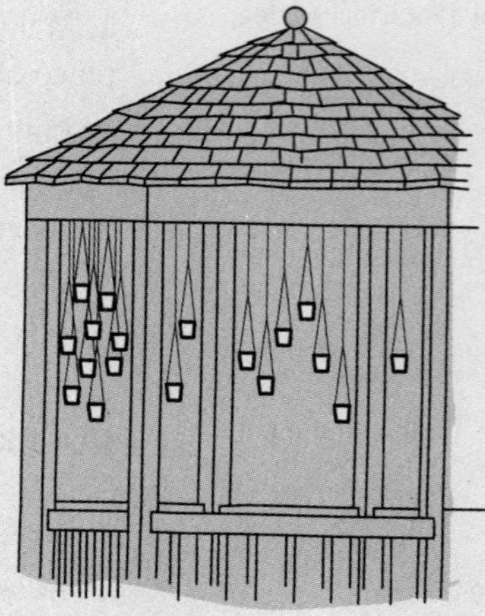

## Homemade Hose Guides

An unguided hose can quickly decapitate flowers, but the antique-reproduction hose guides that Pat Hoskins of Evansville, Indiana, had seen in stores and catalogues cost more than she wanted to invest.

"I could see there definitely was value in putting some kind of hose guide at the corners of my beds," she says, "so I decided to use salvaged bricks I had around."

Hoskins used 10 bricks at each corner and each outward bend of the bed. She paired the bricks for stability, and set them on a diagonal "to make them look more interesting and to give them some height." She made sure to use enough bricks so that she could create a curved corner that the hose would run smoothly around.

"My low hose guides work just fine," she reports. "Not once did I whip the head off a tulip or an iris this spring. And the bricks work in another way I hadn't expected: the basket-of-gold and alyssum in the beds spill over that extra little wall like a waterfall."

*A DOUBLE CURVED ROW OF BRICKS AT THE CORNERS OF YOUR GARDEN BEDS WILL PREVENT YOUR HOSE FROM STRAYING INTO YOUR PLANTS AND DAMAGING THEM.*

**Recycle It!**

***ON HAND:*** Old hose

***TURN IT INTO:*** Blade protectors

***HOW TO DO IT:*** Cut a piece of old rubber or plastic hose the length of your saw blade, garden hoe, or machete, then make a lengthwise slit in the hose. Slip it over the sharp edge of the blade or hoe to save the blade and protect your hand from cuts and scrapes, says Irv Breber of Bensalem, Pennsylvania.

## Keep Creeping Plants under Control

Have you ever planted mint or some other fast-creeping plant directly in your garden? If so, you know why traditional wisdom suggests planting them first in a pot, and then sinking the whole pot into the soil to help contain the spreading roots. Sometimes, though, the roots still manage to creep out the pot's drainage holes and romp through the garden. Fortunately, Cheryl Coston of Fairdealing, Missouri, has figured out a way to keep even the most determined roots in place within the pot. "I cut the bottom off the pot and then used a hot glue gun to fasten a scrap of fiberglass screen to the bottom and about 1 inch up the side of the pot before sinking the pot in the soil. The roots will have less of a chance to escape," she advises.

## Don't Say Good Night!

Want to extend your gardening time? Can't get outside until it's almost dark? Try camping or fishing head lamps! Steve Frowine, avid gardener and director of horticulture at Etera Corporation, says these lamps are great for working in the evening. "It's the most romantic time in the garden," he declares. You can easily extend your garden time by working with these lamps after dark. Small lamps are secured around your head with an elastic band. Your neighbors might think you're nuts, but when time is at a premium, this gadget offers you daylight in the dark.

## Garden Rain Drum

"I saw an incredible Tibetan rain drum in a catalog, but it cost more than $200, and I just couldn't justify it in my budget," says Linda Harris of Fulton, Kentucky. "So I made my own—really simply. Although it doesn't have the exotic appearance, it does amplify the sound of rain, and that's very soothing," adds Harris. To make yours, take a 1-gallon or 10-gallon galvanized metal bucket (or even a galvanized washtub) and set it upside down. Press outward any indentations which may be in the bottom. Hammer one of the edges or lips down (1 to 2 inches long) to make an escape route for the excess water to run out. Set your rain drum on a deck (for best acoustic effect) where there are no branches overhanging, and enjoy the sound of raindrops while it rains. When it's sunny, use the bucket for other purposes!

# Multipurpose Gadgets

In a garden, the possibilities for innovation are endless. Silverware can function as weeding tools, ironing boards as potting benches, shower curtains as planting totes. Below, read about "Versatile Wire Arches" or learn how to "Slide It in a Saucer"—you'll soon be eager to find new ways to use old things.

## Garden Tableware

"Odd pieces of tableware from garage sales are great garden tools," says Alabama gardener Barbara Pleasant. She uses a table fork for weeding, keeps a butter knife on her potting table for gently prying plants out of containers with roots intact, and wields a grapefruit spoon to tease apart matted roots when repotting houseplants. "A big serving spoon is also great for moving volunteer seedlings to better locations," Pleasant says.

## Roll Out the Barrel

"At Pheasant Hill Farm, we use old plastic barrels, cut in half, as huge vegetable trugs and even weed sleds," says market gardener Melanie DeVault. The barrels—which originally held pickles, apple juice concentrate, or vinegar—cost just $10 each. Husband George cuts them in half lengthwise with a saber saw. They're used for soaking carrots and radishes in icy well water to clean and freshen them and as storage containers. For hauling spent crops when it's time to clean out the garden, the DeVaults attach a rope handle through holes at either end of the half-barrels and easily slide the garden waste along the rows. "The barrels are easier to use than wheelbarrows," says DeVault. "Be creative—any rounded-bottom plastic item can work."

## Versatile Wire Arches

"The most indispensable items in my garden are sections of 5-foot-tall wire mesh fencing," reports Barbara Pleasant, who grows vegetables year-round in her Alabama garden. Many varieties of fence will work, including the mesh used for reinforcing concrete. Pleasant finds that sections about 7 feet long work best. "In winter I use them as support arches for plastic-covered grow tunnels because they stand up well to wind and occasional ice. In spring, the arches by themselves keep dogs and deer out of newly planted beds, and I also set up one of them covered with well-ventilated plastic to form my version of a coldframe," Pleasant says. In the summer, she bends the arches into cylinders, clasping the hooked ends of the wire together, and uses them as tomato cages. Pleasant notes that it's important to anchor the cages well with stakes because they can blow over when they're top-heavy with tomatoes. When summer ends and it's time to clean up the garden, Pleasant puts the tomato cages to work as temporary compost bins.

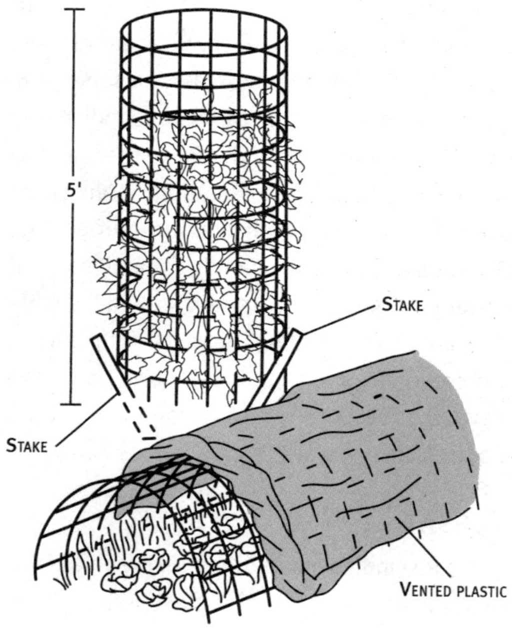


*ARCHES MADE FROM WIRE MESH FENCING OR CONCRETE REINFORCING WIRE CAN STAND ERECT TO MAKE A TOMATO CAGE OR ARCH LONGWAYS TO SUPPORT CLEAR PLASTIC AS A FAST-AND-EASY COLDFRAME.*

## KITCHEN GADGETS IN THE GARDEN

When you're looking around for great garden gadgets, don't forget to check your kitchen! Paring knives are great tools for weeding flower gardens. If there's a weed close to a plant, just slip the knife close to the stem and flick it away from the plant. These narrow-bladed knives are also great for weeding between bricks or in cracks in concrete and asphalt walkways. It's easy to lose these handy little knives among your plants. To avoid wasting time searching for them, dab their handles with a bit of bright paint so you can spot them easily in the garden.

Marianne Kaufman, a volunteer at the Minnesota Landscape Arboretum, has found a new use for another kitchen utensil: She keeps a pair of stainless steel salad tongs in her gardening toolbox. "They're ideal for pulling weeds around rose bushes," explains Kaufman. Like magic, this ordinary kitchen utensil extends your reach while keeping thorns at a safe distance from your hands.

## SLIDE IT IN A SAUCER

When her son outgrew his plastic snow-sliding saucer, Sally Roth of New Harmony, Indiana, commandeered it for her garden. "When my clay soil gets wet, it turns into mud that easily sucks in a loaded wheelbarrow so deep that it's hard to budge. But the plastic sled slides right over the top, no matter how heavy I have it piled."

Roth uses the plastic saucer to haul weeds, sticks, compost, manure, transplants, and "just about everything." She notes that it doesn't require much muscle to move the sled around, either, because she can take advantage of body strength rather than arm strength. "I loop the pull rope behind my head across the back of my neck and then under my arms," she describes, "so that it's the chest and shoulders that lean into it, not my already overworked arms or back."

Roth modified the sled by poking a pair of holes near the rim to hold the rope. The plastic handle that came with it was too flimsy to hold up to heavy work.

*A LONG-FORGOTTEN CHILD'S SNOW SAUCER IS PERFECT FOR SLIDING LOADS OF GARDEN MATERIALS OVER SLIPPERY CLAY SOIL OR WET GRASS.*

**Recycle It!**

***ON HAND:*** Plastic soda bottle

***TURN IT INTO:*** Flower vase giveaway

***HOW TO DO IT:*** Remove the label from the bottle, using hot water or a sticky substance remover (such as Goo Gone) to get rid of the adhesive, then carefully cut off the top one- to two-thirds of the bottle. Cut some flowers from your garden and take them to a friend!

## Not Just for Clothes

An old-fashioned laundry aid is just the gadget for drying herbs, says Deborah Burdick of Mt. Vernon, Indiana, who grows a selection of culinary flavorings.

"Most of my herbs dry fast, in a week or less," she says, "which is a good thing because my space is limited. I use a wooden fold-out clothes drying rack to hang the herbs. The air circulates well around them, just as it would for clothes, and they're dry in days. I can even use it outside in the shade for herbs that dry really fast, like parsley. And the rack folds flat, which makes it easy to slip in a storage space."

Burdick notes that wooden fold-out clothes drying racks, although well made and durable, are surprisingly inexpensive. "You can find them in just about any discount store for about $10," she says.

## Night Light

Do you ever find yourself gardening after dark? An organic farmer from Homestead, Florida, Andres Mejides does. He often works all day caring for zoo animals, then heads out to teach a class on organic gardening to local gardeners. It's dark by the time he arrives home, but his crops still need tending, so a good work light is a necessity. "At first, I tried a coal miner's-style headlamp, but too many bugs flew into my face. And, living in tropical Florida, those bugs were *big*." His solution? Portable fluorescent light fixtures fastened to old lamp stands or tripods. Simply attach these battery-operated lights to a stand with wire, clamps, or straps. If your ground is soft enough, you can also just strap a light onto a length of rebar (concrete reinforcing bar) and poke it into the soil where you need to work.

## No-Slip Knee Pads

Most gardeners approach knee pads like warriors putting on armor for battle. They pull the straps as tight as possible and vow, "This time, they're going to stay in place." But after just a few deep knee bends and a little crawling through the cannas, knee pads usually wind up halfway down to the ankles.

"Knee pads just don't fasten right. They don't stay in place," fumes Leota Cornett of Roanoke, Virginia. "I looked at my dirty knees one day and said, 'I wish I could attach those knee pads right to my pants.' " And that's exactly what she did. Cornett cut large pieces of fabric out of some old blue jeans and used them to sew a big "pocket" on each knee of another pair of pants. Then she slipped a piece of foam rubber padding into each pocket. "Now my knee pads are always in place," Cornett says. When her gardening pants need to be washed, Cornett just slides the foam pads out of the pockets.

***On hand:*** Old carving fork

***Turn it into:*** A soil cultivator

***How to do it:*** A stainless-steel carving fork makes a handy tool for scratching fertilizer into garden beds, says Don Engebretson of Minneapolis, Minnesota. He adds that using the fork with a plunge-and-twist motion quickly loosens compacted soil, and it's great for weeding in tight places, too.

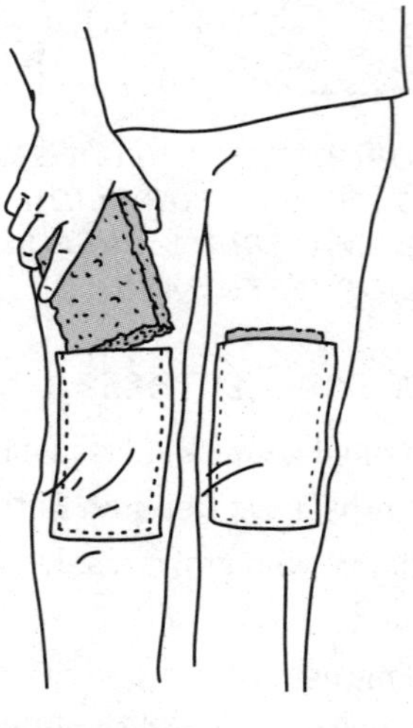

*Having trouble with slippery knee pads? Sew knee pad "pockets" on the knees of your garden pants.*

## Dressed to Till

If you spot Barbara Ashmun, the author of *The Garden Design Primer*, you might mistake her for a surgeon, a fisherman, or a welder. That's because she shops for her gardening togs at industrial stores, not gardening boutiques!

First stop is the sporting goods store where she finds her favorite rubber boots and a fishing vest (those small, zippered pockets and pouches are ideal for holding garden tags, notebooks, markers, twine, tissues, and any other small items). When she needs gloves, she visits a local medical supply store to pick up a box of disposable surgical gloves. Ashmun says these are great for keeping hands clean and dry while still allowing your fingers to move freely. These inexpensive gloves only cost about 6 cents a pair, but they'll last for a few hours of weeding or a whole day of potting up before they tear or get too clammy. If heavier chores are in store, Ashmun suggests picking up a well-priced pair of tough gloves at a welding-supply shop.

**Recycle It!**

***On hand:*** Old ironing board

***Turn it into:*** Portable potting bench

***How to do it:*** Simply remove the padded cover and set it up wherever you want to work. Barbara Ashmun, the author of *Garden Retreats*, loves the fact that the surface is smooth, and the whole thing can be folded and stored just about anywhere.

## Helping Handles

After a day of wielding tools in the garden, even strong hands can get tired, but it's especially difficult if you have arthritis. Cheryl Coston of Fairdealing, Missouri, has found a way to ease the pain by softening the handles of hand tools such as rakes, hoes, trowels, and even pruners. All it takes is a package or two of inexpensive foam pipe insulation, available at discount and hardware stores for about $4 for a pack of four or five pieces. She uses the long, large-diameter pieces of this cylindrical insulation to cover longer-handled tools like rakes and hoes. "Just slip it on, press the sticky edges together, and the grip is now larger and cushioned," she says. For hand tools, she cuts the smaller-diameter lengths of insulation to fit and slips them on the same way.

Sometimes Coston takes her handling just a step further. If the insulation is a bit loose on the handle, she wraps red tape a few times around the foam in a spiral. That also makes the tools easier to spot in the garden and the shed. "The original foam has been on my long-handled tools for years," she says. "Harder-working trowels get new foam every 2 years. This has really helped the arthritis in my hands. I no longer need gloves just to use a tool, and with all the red handles, I rarely lose a tool anymore!"

## Versatile Plant Flats

Plastic mesh plant flats have myriad uses aside from transporting plants. Position them over flats of seedlings that you're taking outside to harden off. Or set flats of plants on top of an upturned mesh flat to provide better air circulation and drainage. In the garden, use flats to cover

## Build It!

# Rustic Log Bench

Leave no stone (or in this case—log) unturned! This handmade log bench can double as a side table or coffee table. Native red cedar (*Juniperus virginiana*) and white birch (*Betula pendula*) are great woods for this project, but others would work equally well. Linda Harris, of Fulton, Kentucky, suggests looking for logs with holes, branch stubs, and intact bark because these features make the bench more interesting. Dry your selected log for several months in a covered place before you start the project.

**Materials**

- A large log or tree trunk, about 12 inches across and 36 to 48 inches long
- 4 smaller logs, about 2 to 3 inches across and 12 to 18 inches long
- 12 nails (about 3 inches long and 1/8 inch in diameter)
- Strong wood glue
- Saw, wood-chopping hatchet, or log splitter
- Hammer
- Wood planer, sander, or rasp (optional)

**Directions**

**1.** Using a saw, hatchet, or splitter, divide the large log in half lengthwise, keeping the cut fairly smooth and flat (it doesn't have to be perfect). Select one log half for the bench. Leave the bark, the branch stubs, and the saw marks for a rustic look. If you prefer a smoother surface, sand or plane the flat top surface or smooth it with a rasp.

young seedlings to protect them from wind, light frost, and nibbling critters. Mesh strawberry baskets make good individual plant cover-ups as well.

### Lavender Instead of Laundry

Another clothes-drying apparatus is favored by paper artist Pat Hoskins, who grows herbs and flowers to use in her artwork. "My clothesline is the easiest spot I know to dry herbs and flowers," says Hoskins, who loosely bundles the fresh material with cotton string, then clips the string to her clothesline with spring-type clothespins.

Hoskins keeps a ball of string and a child's pair of scissors in her clothespin bag for easy access when the mood strikes her. "I can clip geranium flowers, yarrow, lavender, whatever I

**2.** The finished height of the bench equals the leg length plus the thickness of the top log. To make the bench legs, cut the smaller logs to equal lengths. Choose the most attractive side of each smaller log to be the outer-facing side, then mark the opposite side with a pencil.

**3.** Saw the top and bottom ends of each of the smaller logs at about a 20-degree angle, putting the small angle on the outer side of each leg to create a slanted leg.

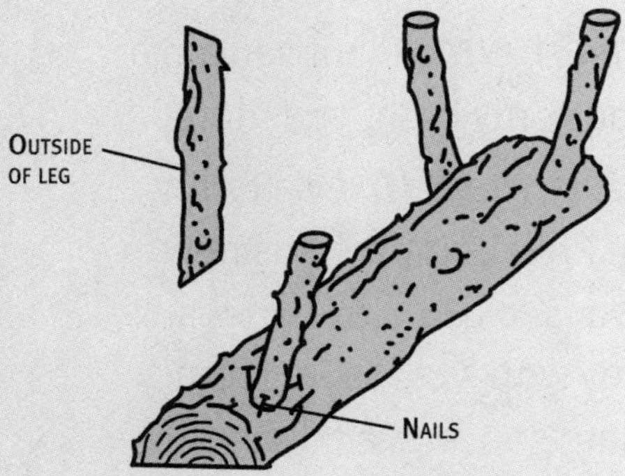


**4.** Turn the large log flat side down. Mark the positions for the four legs (the bench will be sturdier if the legs are close to the log end).

**5.** Using a helper to hold each log leg in place, place the leg's angled cut against the rounded part of the log and hammer three nails into each leg from different angles, driving the nails through the leg and into the bench.

**6.** Turn the bench right side up. Plane, sand, or rasp a little wood off the bottoms of the legs to get rid of any wobbling.

**7.** Turn the bench upside down again and apply glue at each of the four leg joins. Allow the glue to dry thoroughly. Apply clear finish, if you wish, and allow it to dry thoroughly before using.

have blooming, and hang it from the clothesline in just a minute or two, so I have a constant supply of new dried flowers for my projects." She uses the shadier end of the clothesline to dry her plant materials, so the sun doesn't fade blossoms. "They turn out so nice, I've started using them to make little wreaths and dried bouquets for friends and to decorate gift packages, too."

## Bucket Seat

Gardeners with stiff knees or a long job appreciate a place to sit while working. Pat Hoskins of Evansville, Indiana, found that a plastic 5-gallon bucket makes a perfect perch for tending her raised beds.

"It's strong, sturdy, and stable," she says. "Plus it's easy to pick up and move with me from place to place."

**Recycle It!**

***On hand:*** Old Frisbee

***Turn it into:*** Plant saucer, a butterfly bath, and more

***How to do it:*** Elsa Efran of Philadelphia finds new ways to use old Frisbees. They work well as temporary plant saucers, as dishes to hold cut melon halves in the refrigerator, as wind- and sun-breaks for new transplants, and as seed soakers. She fills them with water to create an instant bird or butterfly bath. She even pours beer into them and then sets them in her garden to trap marauding slugs.

Hoskins got her garden seats from a nearby restaurant, where they're free for the asking. She says she often uses two buckets at once: one to sit on and one to carry compost or hold trimmings and weeds.

## Detergent-Bottle Conversions

It seems as though those heavy-duty plastic, squarish detergent containers should have some use, other than taking up space in the recycling bin. They do: Just ask Cheryl Coston of Fairdealing, Missouri. In fact, for her, they serve more than one garden purpose. First, she cuts off the top of the container just above the handle to make a sturdy scoop for organic fertilizers or other materials. "I marked measurements on the outside so I could scoop the right amount to shake directly into my beds," she says. With the top cut off, the bottles also become handy garden carryalls. You can use them to tote trowels, other small tools, seeds, and necessities to and from the garden. Or put a little water in the bottom and use it when collecting flowers from the garden. "It's not as pretty as a basket," she says, "but your flowers will last longer when you put them into water right after you cut them."

## No Mud in the House

"You could always tell when I'd been out in the garden," says herbalist and gardener Valerie West of St. Phillips, Indiana. "No matter how thoroughly I thought I'd cleaned my shoes on the boot scraper or the doormat, I would drop packed mud from between my shoe treads as I walked around the house. And if I'm just coming in to get a drink or to check my phone messages, I don't want to waste time taking them off and putting them back on. Now I keep a sturdy, flat-tip screwdriver beside the front door. It takes just a minute to pry out the caked mud from the tread of my boots."

## Tomato Cage Holiday Tree

When removing the tomato cages from the garden at the end of the season, save one to use as a holiday centerpiece. To decorate, wrap grapevine around the cage, securing it with wire. Turn the cage upside down, string white lights on it, and plug it in! The cone-shaped "tree" looks beautiful indoors or out. When the New Year arrives, "untrim" the tree—or store it as is. When the holidays roll around again, you can put up the tree in minutes!

### From Sweaters to Sundried Tomatoes

If you have a mesh sweater drying rack on hand, you have an instant tomato dryer, too! Deborah Burdick of Mt. Vernon, Indiana, sometimes makes her drying rack do double-duty as a fruit and vegetable dryer in the sun. "When I harvest extra tomatoes, I slice them and spread them on sweater drying screens that I lay across the dowels of a wooden drying rack. In our hot Indiana summers, I can have sundried tomatoes by the end of the day." She drapes an old nylon window curtain over the rack to keep bugs away from the drying food.

**Recycle It!**

***On hand:*** An old plastic shower curtain

***Turn it into:*** Leaf catcher and planting tote

***How to do it:*** Place flats and small tools on the curtain, and drag it to the spot where you're working, says Linda Harris of Fulton, Kentucky. Or fill it with leaves you need to haul away. (Just make sure to keep your hauls at less than 20 pounds, or else the curtain might tear.)

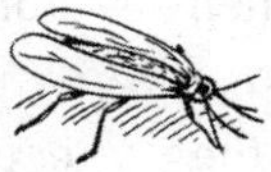

# Pest Control

Garden pests come in all shapes and sizes. And, unfortunately, there is no universal pest control technique. In this chapter, though, we've compiled a plethora of pest-deterrent tips and recipes. Find out how "Foil Collars Deter Cutworms and Slugs" and how to build a "Portable Porcupine Excluder." We've even provided a fantastic recipe for deer repellent.

## Foil Collars Deter Cutworms and Slugs

Foil hungry cutworms with aluminum foil, says gardener Anita Nielsen of Saugatuck, Michigan. Nielson had no luck keeping cutworms and slugs away from tender young cabbage, pepper, and tomato seedlings until she tried making plant collars out of aluminum foil. "It's just so easy. I have *no* cutworm problem at all," Nielsen says. To make a collar, she cuts a piece of aluminum foil about 6 inches square and then crumples it slightly. "Just until it feels rough to the touch," she explains. Then Nielsen tears the foil from the middle of one side to the center of the square. She slips the plant stem through that opening and pinches the foil closed around the stem, forming something like a mini-tree guard. "You just have to be sure that the foil covers the stem and reaches down into the soil just a little bit," Neilsen cautions.

## Slug Discouragement

Discourage slugs in the garden by sprinkling red cedar shavings (the kind used for hamster litter) around your plants. According to Carole Carpenter Russell, teacher and gardener, of Union City, Tennessee, "They hate crawling over the cedar."

## Slugs Say Ouch

"I've found a successful and inexpensive way to discourage slugs," says Caroline Whitenack of Doylestown, Pennsylvania. "I take a bucket of builder's sand to the garden with me when I'm transplanting. When I set each plant in the ground, I use an old laundry scoop to distribute sand around the base of each small plant. Slugs won't crawl over the sharp sand."

## Cup o' Deer Repellent

After having too many antlered visitors at his orchard, Jerald Deal of Deal's Orchard in Jefferson, Iowa, concocted this deterrent made from simple materials.

He asked his local barber to save him a bag or two of human hair. Then he wrapped a fistful of human hair into a square of nylon netting and tied it into a bundle with a string.

To protect the hair from rain—which can wash away the human smell and make the deterrent ineffective—he poked a hole in the bottom of a 12-ounce plastic foam cup. He placed the bundle in the cup, pulled the string through the hole, and tied it into a loop.

Deal hangs one cup per tree and replaces the cup each year. He says this tricks deer for about 3 years before they catch on and he has to find another clever way of keeping them out of his orchard.

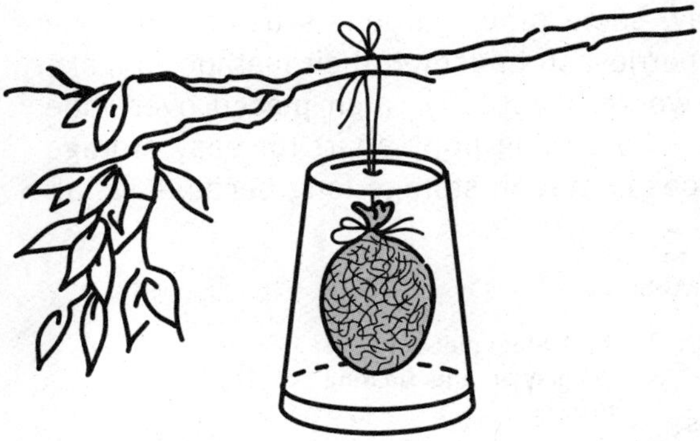

*THE DEER-REPELLING SCENT OF HUMAN HAIR LASTS LONGER WHEN SHELTERED FROM WEATHER BY A CUP.*

**Recycle It!**

***ON HAND:*** Empty 5½-ounce cat food cans

***TURN THEM INTO:*** Cutworm collars

***HOW TO DO IT:*** Wash the cans thoroughly, cut the bottoms off, and remove the labels. Place them over transplants and press them into the ground to prevent cutworms from chewing off tender plants.

## Catch More Flies with Honey

When Cleveland garden writer Thea Steinmetz found flies and gnats buzzing around her greenhouse, she remembered watching her mother make homemade honey flypaper back in Germany. Thea's adaptation of her mom's technique starts with cutting smallish pieces of yellow construction paper and smearing them with warmed honey. She then props them up in the greenhouse beds with a recycled card holder from a florist shop or simply in the tines of an old kitchen fork. The flying nasties are attracted to the color and the sweetness, only to become stuck in the honey. When the sticky paper is coated with bugs, she simply discards it and makes a new piece.

## Apple Trap Anyone?

Don't let your next wild tennis serve end up in George Weigel's yard: He may paint it red and hang it from his apple tree! No, this garden writer for the Harrisburg, Pennsylvania, *Patriot-News* hasn't gone mad—he has just found an inexpensive solution to apple pests. Weigel takes old tennis balls, spray paints them bright red, and then sticks a stiff piece of coat hanger wire through each one. He bends one end of the wire into a simple hook and curves the other end up so the ball won't

# Build It!

## A Pop-Apart Row-Cover Frame

"I'd rather spend 15 minutes installing a row cover than waste hours chasing after flighty cucumber beetles day after day," says Alabama gardener Barbara Pleasant. "Plus, row covers frustrate rabbits hungry for a taste of lettuce and keep deer from rummaging after my bush beans."

Row covers work best when they rest on a frame over the plants so that the fabric can't rub against tender new leaves. Pleasant came up with this pop-apart row-cover frame to do the job. "I saw some other gardeners using PVC pipe arches to hold bird netting over their berries, so I adapted their method to make this row-cover frame," she says. "It works beautifully when placed over wide rows. And when I'm not using it, the whole thing pops apart for easy storage against a wall of the garage. But it doesn't stay in storage long because it's always in use!"

**Materials**

- Six 3-foot lengths of $\frac{1}{2}$-inch-diameter PVC pipe
- Two $\frac{1}{2}$-inch PVC T-connectors
- Two 24-inch pieces of $\frac{1}{2}$-inch-diameter PVC pipe
- $\frac{1}{2}$-inch PVC cross connector
- $10 \times 10$-foot piece of Reemay or other floating row cover
- Hand saw or utility knife
- Sawhorse

slip off. He then wraps each one with a sandwich bag (secured by a rubber band at the top) and coats each bag with Tangle-Trap (a sticky material available at garden centers) or even petroleum jelly. By hanging three or four of the gooey look-alike apples in each tree before the real fruit turns red, he attracts and traps apple pests and limits their damage to his apples.

### Fly Sucker

Whiteflies getting in your face? Try busting them away with your battery-operated vacuum cleaner, suggests Thea Steinmetz, a scented-geranium lover in Cleveland, Ohio. Whiteflies love geraniums, she explains, so when they get to be a bother, she simply shakes the stem of each plant with one hand to stir up the flies and sucks them up with her handheld vacuum

**DIRECTIONS**

**1.** Cut PVC pipe into pieces with a hand saw or utility knife. Use a sawhorse to support the pipe as you cut it.

**2.** Fit two 3-foot pieces into one of the T-connectors to form a section of pipe that's about 6 feet long. Do the same with two more 3-foot pieces and the second connector. (These sections will form the ends of the frame). Fit the remaining 3-foot pieces into the cross connector to form the middle support of the frame.

**3.** Gently bend one end piece into a semicircle and push the ends 10 inches or more into the ground on either side of the row or bed, about 6 inches from where you want the end of the tunnel to be. Place one of the 24-inch long pieces into the T-connector at the top of the frame.

**4.** Bend the middle piece of the frame into an arch, and push the ends into the ground about 24 inches from the end piece so that the free end of the 24-inch piece of pipe fits firmly into the cross-connector.

**5.** Place the remaining 24-inch piece of pipe into the other side of the cross-connector. Bend the remaining long piece of pipe and push the ends into the ground 24 inches from the middle arch. Pop the end of the 24-inch piece of pipe into the T-connector.

**6.** Cover the frame with row cover, and secure the edges with boards or bricks. When you disassemble the frame to move or store it, the arched pieces of pipe will retain their shape.

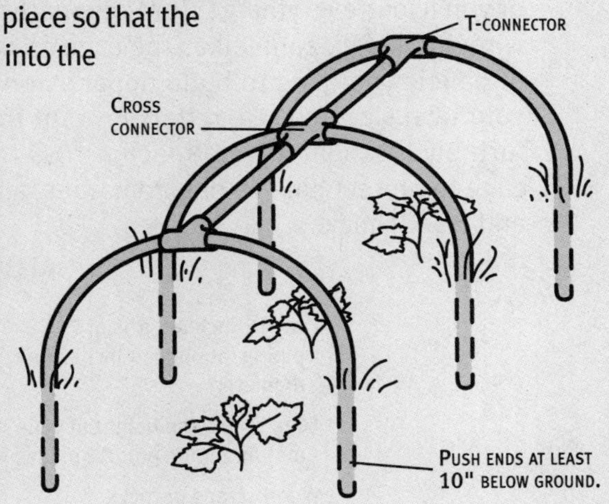


cleaner. Within 3 or 4 days, the fly population plummets and the plants go outside for a good hosing down. The result? No more whiteflies!

## VINEGAR DUNK STILLS THE JAPANESE BEETLE BRIGADE

Japanese beetles can be a real menace to roses, corn, raspberries, and many ornamentals. For short-term control, hand-picking is the safest and most effective measure. To make the job easier, place cans of vinegar solution (equal parts apple cider vinegar and water) next to vulnerable plants. Early and late in the day when beetles are sluggish, hold the can under the beetles and knock them into the vinegar solution. Vinegar kills them quickly but isn't harmful to kids or pets. Leave the can in place until it's full, and then empty dead bugs into

*(continued on page 253)*

# Build It!

## Portable Porcupine Excluder

For 20 years Mary Zahn's raspberry patch in Juneau, Alaska, was a salad bar for the neighborhood porcupines. "Finally," she says, "I decided I had to be smart enough to outwit these guys, so I designed a cage"—for the berries, that is. Zahn's clever cage is made of screen-wire panels that hook together; you remove them one at a time to pick the berries. (Don't let the canes grow through the wire or you won't be able to get the panels off!) Zahn puts up the cage the minute she spies the first buds in spring—"Porkies love the first new leaves," she says, "Don't procrastinate or you'll lose everything." Throughout the growing season the greenery conceals the wire; in the fall, Zahn takes the cage apart and stashes it in the garage. The number of panels you need to build depends on the size of your raspberry patch—and on your own size and strength. You want the panels small enough that you can comfortably lift them off and reach across to pick the berries. You could also use this cage to protect blueberries, tomatoes, and other crops and to help keep out rabbits and woodchucks.

**Materials**

- Four 12-inch lengths of PVC piping, about $4\frac{1}{4}$ inches in diameter
- Four 2 × 4s, the height of your mature plants plus 12 inches
- Wood scraps or rocks
- Twenty 2 × 2s of a height and width to make frames that you can handle comfortably
- Wood screws or nails, as needed
- Chicken wire
- 1 × 2s, short sections, as needed
- 16 sets of hooks and eyes
- Four 10-inch bungie cords
- Staple gun and staples
- Screwdriver

**Directions**

**1.** Measure out the area you want for your raspberry patch, and sink one length of PVC piping 12 inches into the ground at each corner of your plot.

**2.** Insert a 2 × 4 into each pipe, wedging it with scrap wood or rocks if necessary to hold it steady.

**3.** Build the frames for the side panels and the top panel using the 2 × 2s and nails. Cut sections of chicken wire large enough to cover each frame, and staple the chicken wire in place. To strengthen the sides of the cage, screw short sections of 1 × 2s for corner brackets to the frame.

**4.** Screw a hook into the outside corner of each chicken-wire panel so that the hook points downward.

**5.** Screw two eyes at the top and bottom of each 2 × 4 (on adjacent corners as shown below), measuring to make sure the eyes will line up with the hooks you've placed on the panels so the panels will hang straight.

**6.** Fit the side panels into place.

**7.** If birds or deer are a problem, fasten a top panel onto the frame with the bungie cords. Loop a cord through the chicken wire at each corner and fasten the hooks to the frame or the wire on the side panels.

**8.** Use rocks to fill any gaps between frame and ground.

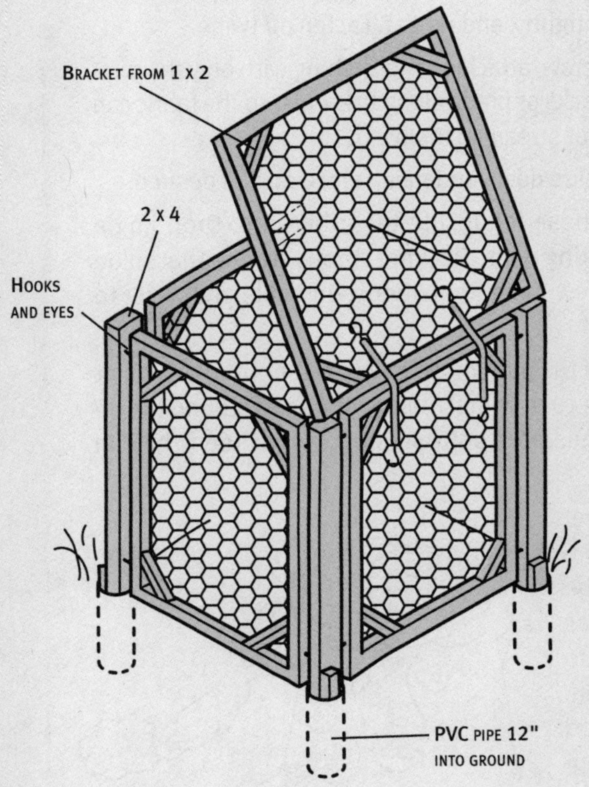


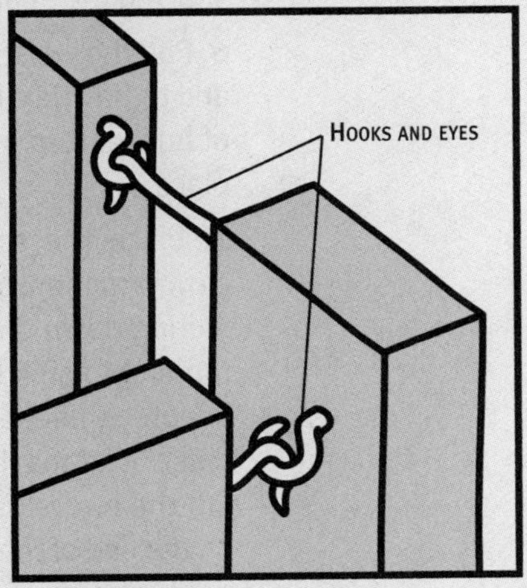

# Build It!

## Fun Scarecrow

"I like my scarecrows to look good. If they also help scare the crows away, that's good too," says Linda Harris of Fulton, Kentucky. "The head I've used here helps make some noise. Move the scarecrow around the garden to keep the birds guessing and the neighbors amused."

### Materials

- One 3- to 4-foot 1 × 2, for arms
- One 6- to 8-foot 1 × 2, for upright
- Heavy twine
- Old shirt, pants, or skirt and shirt
- Tacks or brads
- Galvanized 1-gallon bucket
- Waterproof paint or permanent markers (optional)
- Old pantyhose
- 10 to 12 metal jingle bells
- Twine, ribbon, or a scarf

### Directions

**1.** Position the shorter piece of lumber perpendicular to and about 12 inches below one end of the longer piece.

**2.** Lash pieces together by wrapping twine around the join, making an X. Wrap 3 or 4 times one way, then wrap the other way, pulling twine tightly, and repeat. Fasten off twine.

**3.** Dress the scarecrow, attaching the clothing with only the minimum number of tacks or brads along the arms, so the fabric can float free and flap or stream in the wind.

**4.** Turn bucket upside down and paint a face on it, if desired.

**5.** Put one pantyhose leg inside the other one. Drop jingle bells inside stocking foot, tie knot about where the ankle would be. Add a few more knots between ankle and waist to shorten the "hat."

**6.** Pull the waist of the pantyhose down over bottom of bucket and tightly tie a piece of twine, ribbon, or a scarf around the lip of bucket (top of head but bottom of bucket) to keep "hat" in place.

**7.** Place the scarecrow in garden, hammering down on the top end to sink it as deeply as needed to make it stand firm. Put the bucket head on the end of the upright, and give your creation a name!

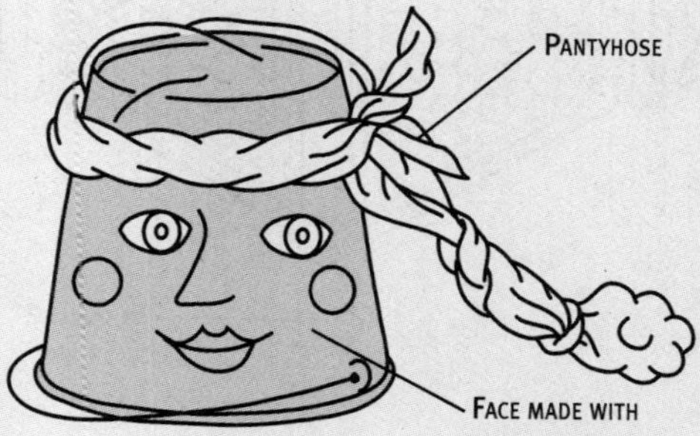

the compost pile and refill the cans. This is a great job for youngsters eager to earn vacation money! Over time, hand-picking can reduce beetle problems significantly.

## Boards Foil Birds

"Grackles and other blackbirds love to snatch up my pea seeds as soon as I plant them," says gardener and author Sally Roth of New Harmony, Indiana. "I like the blackbirds, but I also wanted peas. So I turned to an old trick my mother used in her big family garden when I was a child. After I plant and water the rows, I lay 2 × 4s or any other scrap boards I have around over the peas. I lift the boards after a few days to check whether the seeds are sprouting. When I see they've broken ground, I take off the boards. The seedlings green up in just a day or two. Once the peas sprout, the birds aren't as interested in them."

Sally says hiding peas under a board has another advantage: "The board keeps the soil nice and moist around the seeds, so my crop sprouts days faster than uncovered rows. And I don't have to water in the meantime."

## Red-Hot Squirrels

Did you know that you could use an old spice jar with a perforated lid to sprinkle cayenne pepper around your young transplants to repel squirrels? It not only works to keep squirrels out of your beds, but it also keeps squirrels off the bird feeder. And best of all, the cayenne pepper doesn't seem to bother the birds.

### Recycle It!

***On hand:*** Clear plastic 12- to 16-ounce water or soda bottles

***Turn them into:*** Cutworm barriers

***How to do it:*** Slice plastic bottles into 3-inch-high rings, then press into soil about 1 inch over newly planted seedlings. They make a very effective cutworm barrier, according to Irv Breber of Bensalem, Pennsylvania, and they don't show from a distance.

# Planters

Believe it or not, just about anything can be a planter. In this section, find out how you can use gourds, drawers, bushel baskets, buckets, plastic-foam coolers, tires, or plungers as containers for both outdoor and indoor plantings.

## Gourd Planters

Birdhouse gourds are good for more than just birdhouses. These gracefully shaped gourds also make beautifully shaped planters for all types of annuals, herbs, and even strawberries.

To grow a self-supporting gourd pot, position developing gourds on pieces of wood in your garden so the bottoms become flat. When the gourds have matured, harvest, dry thoroughly, and scrape off the flaky skin. Cut off the top of each gourd and drill a few holes in the bottom for drainage. Decorate with paint (if you feel creative) or shellac to help preserve them. If you have a gourd without a flat base, prepare it as above but drill three extra holes in the rim; add rope to enjoy it as a hanging basket.

## Souvenir Mulch

Rob Cardillo and his wife, Sue, of Ambler, Pennsylvania, love houseplants, but their dog Stella loves them even more! Too many times, they found her munching away at the potting soil of the bigger plants that sat on the floor. Unable to persuade Stella to eat a more sensible diet, they resolved to put a stone mulch over the potting soil to discourage her late-night raids.

As they began to look for suitable pebbles, they realized they already had dozens of beautiful stones and shells brought home as souvenirs from their many travels throughout the world. By artfully placing them around each plant, they not only solved the dog problem, they also found the perfect way to display their exotic rocks. "Plus," Sue adds, "they glisten and shine every time we water."

## Gardens-to-Go

Bushel baskets make ideal container gardens and the price is right. "I buy used baskets from the crab house for $2 a piece. A good hosing takes care of the fishy smell," says Tina James, a resourceful Maryland gardener, with a laugh. James lines the baskets with plastic bags, being sure to slash a few holes for drainage, and fills them with potting soil. She also adds a shovelful of compost to these basket containers. "Compost inoculates that sterilized potting soil with the microorganisms that support soil life, which in turns supports plant growth." Besides being cheap, James says the baskets are large enough to accommodate a mini salad-and-herb garden. "I plant lettuce, radishes, parsley, violas, and onion sets in the spring and then replant for the summer with bush beans, basil, and calendulas. If you position the basket near a railing or outfit it with a trellis, you can add vines like morning glories or cucumbers."

As a bonus, the baskets are portable—they even have handles! James likes to present them as gifts to shut-in gardening friends. "I've carried the baskets filled with dry potting soil up to the 11th floor of an apartment building with no trouble. Add the plants and water after the basket reaches its destination.

For best results, put something under the basket so it's not in direct contact with the ground or the deck—bricks, slates, or wood blocks work fine. The basket drains better and the increased air circulation retards rot." James says her gardens-to-go last for two seasons. Not bad for $2.

**Recycle It!**

***On hand:*** An old drawer from a kitchen or bathroom remodeling project or from old furniture

***Turn it into:*** A portable raised bed

***How to do it:*** Just drill several holes in the bottom of the drawer for drainage, fill with soil, and plant.

## Bubble Window Greenhouses

A plastic bubble window well protector makes a simple and inexpensive greenhouse—and you can pick one up at a home-supply store for less than $5. To use, place the bubble window against the wall of a shed or garage. Simply lift it up to move tender plants and seedlings in and out. Remember—you have to vent the bubble window just as you would any coldframe or greenhouse, or the space will quickly overheat when the sun is out. In early spring, use a brick to prop the window ajar a few inches. Once the weather is warmer, stand the brick on one end to hold the window higher off the ground. Eventually, you can remove the window during the day and replace it in the late afternoon to shelter plants from nighttime chills. If temperatures threaten to plummet below freezing, drape a wool blanket over the bubble for added protection because plastic retains only a few degrees of extra heat once the sun goes down.

## Plumber's and Florist's Helper

A plumber's helper can be a creative part of a topiary arrangement, says Philadelphia florist Bill Franklin, who often gives demonstrations at the Philadelphia Flower Show. Franklin paints a plumber's helper (or plunger) green, and sticks it handle-end down into floral foam in an

**Recycle It!**

***On hand:*** New or used coffee filters

***Turn them into:*** Large pot liners

***How to do it:*** Place coffee filters in the bottoms of larger pots before adding growing medium to keep soil from sifting out. Andrea Ray Chandler, a Master Gardener who hails from Olathe, Kansas, also suggests using shredded pieces of old spun-polyester row covers or old pantyhose in this manner.

arranging container. He then does matching arrangements in the plunger cup and in the container, making it look like a plant that has been grown as a standard.

### Designer Containers for a Fraction of the Price

Container gardening is all the rage, but buying lots of interesting-looking containers can get expensive. Linda Harris of Fulton, Kentucky, shares her clever idea for making her own—at a much lower cost than retail! Harris uses the bowl of an old round charcoal grill for casting containers. She mixes and pours concrete into the bowl, spreads it out to edges, and shapes the inner surface of the bowl as desired. "Shallow containers cast like this make nice planters for sedums, cacti, and ground covers.

For decorative containers, I like to put pebbles or shells in first, like you put the pineapple in first for an upside-down cake, then pour the concrete," says Harris. She adds that this type of container makes an equally nice birdbath. In that case, you might want to press pebbles, shells or pieces of colored glass into the inside surface for a designer look.

### Potatoes above the Ground

Another way to use a stacked bin composter for growing crops is to turn it into an above-ground potatoes planter. Simply unstack the sections in an open, sunny area with good drainage. Fill the first section with compost mixed with garden soil, and plant your potato tubers just deep enough to cover the tuber. As the plants grows, add the second and third sections of the composter. (Fill them with the compost/soil mixture, too.) When it's harvest time, says Susan LeMaster, who grows her spuds in Portland, Oregon, take the sections apart and the taters fall out—no muss, no fuss, no digging.

### Easy Raised Herb Bed

Those "tire gardens" many people make fun of still work very well, especially for herbs which tend to spread out and sprawl over the edge of the tire. Use a big old tire from a car, truck, or tractor. "What's especially nice about gardening in a raised bed like this is you get both moisture retention and excellent drainage, which is preferred by herbs such as lavender, oregano, sage, and thyme," advises Linda Harris of Fulton, Kentucky. "And kids get a kick out of gardening in a tire, which could help them develop a lifetime hobby of gardening."

Harris says you can set the tire down in an existing garden or on lawn grass; you don't need to dig the sod layer up. Then fill the tire with a mixture of garden soil and packaged soilless potting mixture. "This raised area in the garden works nicely to accent the plants, such as purple basil or variegated thyme. And plants around the tire can cover it up if you don't like its looks."

## Chilly Chest Planter

Sometimes a gardener has too many plants for one place or one planting effort. One way to heel them in (keep plants for a short time before you actually get them planted) is to pot up in temporary containers the way Lois Stringer of Bellefonte, Pennsylvania, does. "I've found that plastic-foam ice chests do the trick for up to about 2 weeks. The chests also make inexpensive patio planters for colorful summer plantings. They really hold the soil moisture well, which is great in dry climates."

## Trays of Light

Wash out and save those throwaway aluminum baking pans; they make excellent water trays for plants and seedlings because the aluminum reflects light back on to the plants.

Using aluminum trays can result in a noticeable growth spurt in plants. They're especially good for houseplants in a shady place.

## Creative Containers

Want to give your plants interesting homes without spending a lot of money on containers? Then make your own using recycled items from around your house the way Linda Harris of Fulton, Kentucky, does. Sometimes an unusual container can bring a smile, so use your imagi-

### Recycle It!

***On hand:*** An old stacked-bin composter

***Turn it into:*** Mini-raised beds

***How to do it:*** First, loosen the ground where you want the beds to go. Unstack the sections, fill them with a mix of half compost and half soil, and plant. Says Master Gardener Judy Wong of Menlo Park, California, "I use the sections for lettuce, which likes good drainage and good air circulation."

# Build It!

## Mini Plant Nursery and Tool Shed

A nursery bed is a handy place to grow seedlings until they are ready for the garden, but what if all your space is already filled with plants? George Weigel, garden writer for Harrisburg, Pennsylvania's *Patriot-News,* designed and built this waist-high seedling bed out of scrap lumber. He uses it as an outdoor nursery for vegetable seedlings to replace plants that he yanks out of the garden during the growing season. Because it's on legs, you don't have to bend over to use it—a bonus for gardeners with bad backs or trick knees. "The real kicker is that I mounted an old mailbox on the bottom to store my row markers, pruners, string, trowel, and all those other little things that I always used to forget back in the garage."

**Materials**

- Four 24-inch 2 × 6s
- 3-inch galvanized nails or screws
- Two 24 × 27-inch pieces of ½- or ¾-inch plywood
- ¼-inch galvanized nails or screws
- Four 36-inch 2 × 4s
- Two 27-inch 2 × 4s
- Primer and paint, or polyurethane
- Hammer or screwdriver
- Drill with ⅜-inch bit

**Directions**

**1.** Fasten together the 2 × 6s to form the seedling box, using 3-inch nails or screws.

**2.** Fasten one piece of plywood to the bottom of the assembled box with 1¼-inch nails or screws. Drill ⅜-inch drainage holes spaced 6 inches apart in the plywood.

nation before you throw something away—it might make an interesting planter. Choose plants that are in scale to the container. If there's no drainage, add a layer of gravel in the bottom before planting. Here are a few ideas: Hens and chicks look great in a beat-up boot or old running shoe. Try herbs in your old saucepan with a ripped-up nonstick coating. A chipped soup tureen is another fine container for herbs. A fern in a fishbowl or geraniums in a bucket are two more fun and fitting ideas.

### Cinder Blocks for Sedum

Cinder blocks (the ones with holes that go all the way through) make nice containers for sedums and succulents. "I think of cinder blocks

3. Attach the 36-inch 2 × 4 legs to the outer sides of the box with 3-inch nails or screws.

4. Fasten the 27-inch 2 × 4 leg supports to the legs, a couple of inches up from the bottom of the legs, with 3-inch nails or screws.

5. Attach the plywood shelf to the supports with 1¼-inch nails or screws.

6. Add a coat of paint (prime the wood first!) or polyurethane over the entire piece to help protect it from the elements.

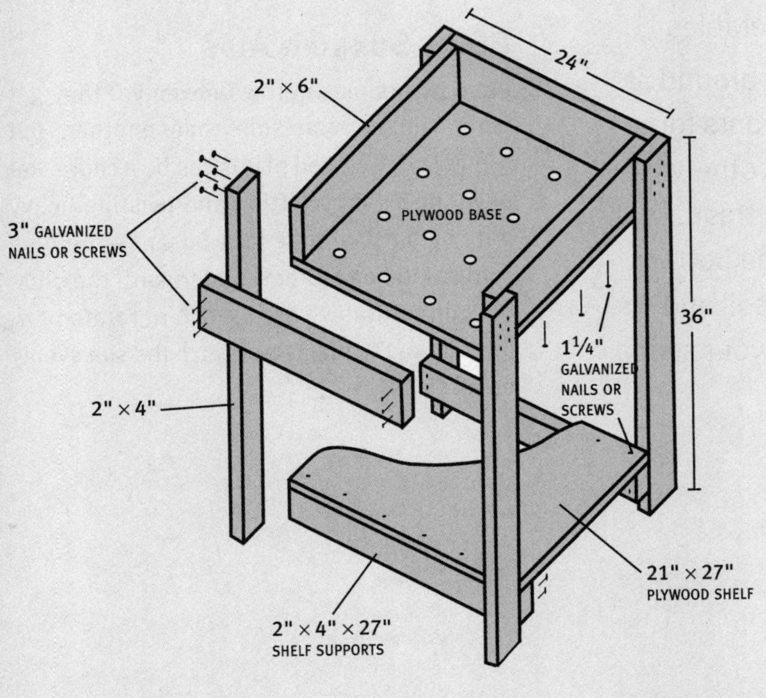


as the economy-conscious strawberry jar," says Linda Harris of Fulton, Kentucky. Set a block on its side so the holes are on top and fill the holes with a mixture of garden soil and packaged soilless potting mixture. Blocks can also be stacked in various ways and then planted with hens and chicks or low-growing sedums. In a very short time, the plants will cover the block.

"Set one of these near the front door for an attractive accent and conversation piece. It's fun to watch the plants grow and bloom."

## Plant Taxi

Moving container plants can be a chore, especially when you have a lot of them to move, or you have containers that are heavy. But

**Recycle It!**

***On hand:*** Used 5-gallon pickle or mayonnaise buckets

***Turn them into:*** Container gardens for vegetables

***How to do it:*** Ask around at fast-food restaurants for buckets that would otherwise find their way to the trash. Drill drainage holes in the bottom, fill with a mix of soil and compost, then plant your seeds.

with a plant taxi, moving containers is a breeze. All you need is a wooden packing-crate lid, four casters, and four screws. Just screw a caster to each corner of the lid's base—and, presto, easy transit for container plants. To make moving even easier, screw a large eye hook into the middle of one edge of the lid. When it's travel time, snap a rope—or your dog's leash—onto the eye hook and you're ready to ramble.

## Plant Sunning Aids

Patio plants make grow unevenly if they get more sun on one side than another, but turning large potted plants can be a chore. Relieve the strain of lifting and twisting heavy pots by putting large lazy Susans—the type sold in kitchen stores—underneath the pots. Pots on turntables are a cinch to rotate periodically so the plants can catch the sun evenly on all sides.

# Planting Helpers

One of the joys of being a gardener is at planting time. With every drop of a seed, the promise of a bountiful harvest later in the season hovers in the air. But planting is not always easy. In the following section, you'll read about how you can make this critical, early-season duty less of a chore—and more joyful.

## Perfect Mesclun Planting Frames

"My problems with mesclun and baby lettuce were caused partly by spring fever and partly by foraging cutworms," says Alabama gardener Barbara Pleasant. "I tended to plant way too much at one time instead of sowing a few pinches of seed at a time." To solve her problem, Pleasant came up with special planting frames that double as cutworm barriers.

Pleasant makes the frames by using a utility knife to cut the bottom 2 inches off of inexpensive plastic washbasins. "I stick the bottomless frame in the ground with the upper lip about 1 inch above the surface and the sides 2 inches deep in the soil," she explains. With the basin frame as the boundary, scatter seed over the soil inside. This produces a perfect small planting of lettuce, and you'll find that wandering cutworms rarely figure out how to worm their way under the plastic barriers. For a continuous supply of greens, every 2 to 3 weeks, fashion another frame and plant inside it.

*Cutworms can't mow down mesclun or baby lettuce planted in the protective frame of a bottomless plastic washbasin that's pushed firmly into the soil.*

## Penny-Pinching Planter

Do you like to plant a few new bulbs in your garden each year? Leota Cornett of Roanoke, Virginia, does, and she has devised a simple way to keep track of the spots where she wants to add those new bulbs. Each spring, Cornett al-

**Recycle It!**

***On hand:*** 15-inch-long metal pipe, at least 1 inch in diameter

***Turn it into:*** Bulb planter

***How to do it:*** Pound the pipe into wet ground, pull it out, and drop a small bulb in the hole. Use a stick or dowel to poke out the plug of soil stuck in the pipe, and crumble it over the bulb.

ways notices a few spots where more bulbs would look good. To help her locate those bare spots in fall when it's time to plant, she uses the plastic caps from spray cans, or even empty tuna cans, as planting markers. "You just tramp the caps down in the grass where you want the new bulbs," Cornett explains. "In fall, you scratch around that area until you find the cap. That's exactly where to plant the bulb. I even have a color-coding system," Cornett adds. "If I need to fill in with a blue hyacinth, I find a blue cap to mark the spot."

## Homemade Spacing Strips

A yardstick can be a great planting aid when you're setting out transplants in the garden, at least until you accidentally kneel on it and—"crack!"—snap it in half. Frustrated by a growing pile of broken yardsticks, George DeVault, who gardens near Emmaus, Pennsylvania, found the solution in a stack of scrap lumber in his basement.

DeVault found that furring strips—1 × 3-inch boards used to mount wall paneling and ceiling tile—are much sturdier than most yardsticks. To turn furring strips into spacing guides, saw them to length to fit along your garden beds. Then, using a permanent marker, draw lines across both sides of each strip at the desired spacing. DeVault has one customized furring strip each for 8-, 10-, 12-, and 18-inch spacings.

"When I use the guides in a bed with a straight border, it's easy to keep the rows parallel simply by measuring the distance between rows with a shorter piece of furring strip," DeVault explains. The furring strips are thick enough that you can lean or even step lightly on them when working in wide beds. So far, DeVault's homemade spacing strips have lasted 5 years without mishap.

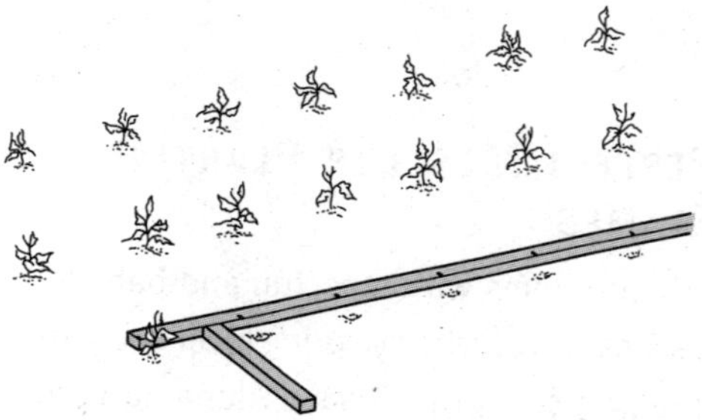

*Furring strips are much more durable than yardsticks as plant spacing guides.*

## Coffee Can to the Rescue

Tamping the soil firmly around the roots is an important step in planting new trees and shrubs, but it can be an awkward job. You can save yourself some strain by putting together a homemade soil tamper from an empty coffee can, concrete, and a sturdy shovel handle. Drive some nails through the bottom of the handle, as shown in the illustration, and set that end in the can. Mix up the concrete and pour it into the can until it's nearly full. Prop the handle upright until the concrete sets. This tamper is heavy and has a flat bottom, so it's the perfect tool for compressing soil in a planting hole to get rid of air pockets.

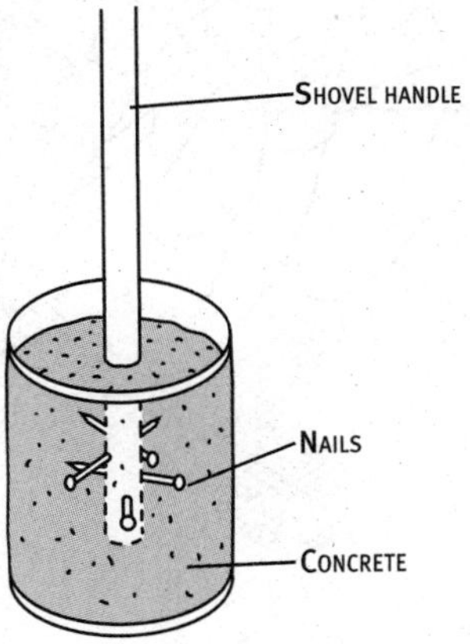


*YOU CAN EASILY MAKE THIS SOIL TAMPER WITH JUST A COFFEE CAN, CONCRETE, NAILS, AND A SHOVEL HANDLE.*

## POST-HOLE DIGGERS: NOT JUST FOR FENCES

Do you own a post-hole digger? If you're planning to install a large planting of perennials or shrubs, you should! Instead of a shovel, use this traditional fencing tool in a new way: to make planting holes for gallon-sized potted plants. It's especially good for planting in tight quarters where you don't have a lot of room to pile the soil next to the hole. To make using this tool less of a "knuckle-buster" when you squeeze the handles together, slip some foam pipe insulation around the handles and secure it with some electrical tape.

## NO-BEND PLANTING

Pat Porter of Big River, Saskatchewan, hates bending over when she plants. So she simply cuts a length of slender pipe (metal or smooth PVC would do) about 4 feet long. "Then I just drop the seeds through the pipe and down they go into their place in the ground," Porter says.

This method works better for larger seeds than small ones, but you can use small seeds as long as you mix them with an extender, such as fine, dry sand.

Pennsylvania market gardener Cass Peterson also plants seeds standing up, using a homemade seeder fashioned from a 1-gallon plastic milk jug and a 3-foot piece of plastic pipe. "A 2-liter soda pop bottle will work, too," Peterson says. "Just cut the bottom out of whatever container you're going to use. Solidly attach the plastic pipe to the spout with glue, a hose clamp, or duct tape—whichever works best. Then, just walk down the row, plunking little seeds into the hopper and watching them drop into the furrow—without ever bending over."

*SOW SEEDS WITHOUT A LOT OF BACK-BREAKING WORK WITH THE HELP OF A HANDY PIPE PLANTER.*

## Stand-Up Sowing

Don't throw out that broken umbrella! You can turn it into a great planting gadget! Direct-sowing seed in his quarter-acre garden always left Robert Southam of Nazareth, Pennsylvania, with a pain in the back. The constant bending and stooping made him sore, but if he tried dropping the seeds from a full upright position, they scattered and didn't land where he wanted them to. One day, when Southam was throwing out the trash, he spotted something that would make his task easier: the aluminum stem of a broken umbrella. At about 3 feet long, the lightweight, hollow tube was just what he needed.

Now Southam uses his found seed-sower to plant beans, peas, corn, and most other seed. After making a furrow of the proper depth with a hoe, he puts the seeds he wants to sow in a carpenter's apron he's wearing, and then walks along the furrow with his umbrella handle. As he walks, he places the bottom end in the furrow, and drops the seed through the top, one by one. There's no bending, and every seed falls in its proper place!

## Can't Beat It with a Stick

Direct seeding doesn't have to take all day, at least not if you have a custom-made planting stick. Marianne Binetti, a garden columnist from Enumclaw, Washington, says you can make a simple version from just about any piece of long, slender lumber, such as a length of stop-gap molding or a 1 × 2. Make notches or use a permanent marker to mark off every inch the entire length of the lumber. Now you'll have an extra-long yardstick to measure distance between seed plantings.

For a more elaborate version of the planting stick, cut notches into the lumber to create a form that looks like a giant comb. Simply press the planting stick notch-side down into the soil and you'll have a series of perfectly spaced planting holes for seedlings or seeds.

*Get perfect spacing every time with this custom-made planting stick.*

## Easy Planting Line and Anchor

Using a long string and two stakes to mark straight rows when you plant seeds works just fine—until the string becomes hopelessly tangled. That's why market gardener George DeVault of Emmaus, Pennsylvania, now uses a 100-foot plastic tape measure as a trouble-free planting line. "The tape is bright yellow. It doesn't get dirty and blend with the soil. And when I'm done planting, it takes only a minute to wind it up," DeVault says.

DeVault suggests making special anchors for the tape by sawing a 36-inch, ¼-inch-diameter metal rod in half with a hacksaw.

Bend the top 4 inches of each piece of rod to form a handle. It's easy to push these anchors into the ground by hand. Insert one anchor into your garden bed, and put the metal grip at the beginning of the tape over the handle of the anchor. Stretch out the tape, insert the other anchor through the handle of the measuring tape's carrying case, and push it into the soil to keep the tape taut and straight while you work.

## Homemade Dibble

Sometimes it's the simplest tools that give the best results. Every summer, Frank Conte's tiny front yard garden in Ambler, Pennsylvania, grows sky high with pole beans and tomatoes on an elaborate trellising system that often hides him completely from passersby. And although this 84-year-old Italian immigrant swears that this year's garden will be his last, you'll likely find him next spring planting his beans with a handmade dibble known in the old country as a *pizzucu*. Carved from a piece of bent tree limb, this useful tool fits his hand just as well as his old leather gloves.

To make your own pizzucu, first find a section of bent wood with an angle and girth that fit your hand nicely. Then with your favorite whittling knife, sharpen one end. If you want to get fancy, you can drill a hole in the handle end and loop some rope through so you can hang it up for storage.

## Heavy-Duty Bulb Planting

We asked Judy Glattstein "What's the best way to plant flowering bulbs?" and her answer was unequivocal: "With an 8-pound mattock!" She should know. This author of *Flowering Bulbs for Dummies* and instructor of a bulb course for professionals at the New York Botanical Gardens has planted more than 22,000 bulbs in the last 4 years at her 9-acre, New Jersey home.

Glattstein knew that planting bulbs with auger drill bits and those tin can-shaped bulb planters would be difficult given her tough rocky-clay soil. Her solution was to loosen entire patches of ground with the mattock, add compost and other soil amendments, and churn everything together. It's easy to plant bulbs in the prepared soil with nothing more than your favorite hand trowel!

**Recycle It!**

***On hand:*** Old rolling pin

***Turn it into:*** A dibble for making planting holes

***How to do it:*** Turn your old wooden pastry roller into a dibble for setting out vegetable and flower transplants. Just turn the roller on its end and press it into the soil to make a perfect planting hole.

# Build It!

## Dibbler Frame for Mass Plantings

Need to get lots of small plants into the ground quickly? Follow the lead of Ray McNeilan, a Master Gardener and retired extension agent for Multnomah County, Oregon. He devised this planting tool called a dibbler or dibble when he was propagating azaleas and wanted to get lots of small plants into the ground quickly. It works just as well for groundcover plants or any time you're setting out lots of seedlings.

Adjust the sizes of the 2 × 4s and the number of dibblers to suit your height, the size of your planting area, and the depth and spacing your plants require.

**Materials**

- Galvanized wood screws
- Four 3-foot 2 × 4s
- Four L-shaped corner braces
- 1½-inch-diameter wooden dowel, 18 inches long
- Screwdriver
- Handsaw

**Directions**

1. Screw the 2 × 4s together to make a frame.
2. Screw the four corner braces into place for added support.
3. Saw the dowel into four or six 3-inch pieces, depending on how far apart you want your dibbles spaced.
4. Cut the end of each piece of dowel into a point.

## A Bulb Hammer

The idea of a flowering lawn appealed to Rob Cardillo, a garden writer and photographer from Ambler, Pennsylvania. "Wouldn't the front yard look great with scores of early-blooming crocuses and snowdrops pushing up through the grass beneath the old maple trees?" he mused. That fall, he ordered the bulbs and began to plant them under the trees using a standard garden trowel to stab the ground, pull back the earth, and drop in the bulb. He found out quickly that even with a pointed trowel his hand and arm were cramping as a result of having to stab the ground forcefully to penetrate the root-filled soil. "I knew there had to be a better tool for this job, and I found it in my basement: a standard brick hammer." Used for breaking and setting bricks, this special hammer has a typical hammer face on one side and a long

**5.** Use screws to attach the dowel pieces to one side of the frame at 8-inch intervals. To do this, predrill holes at 8-inch intervals, then screw each dowel in place.

To use the dibbler, till or spade your garden area. Then mark a series of holes along one outside edge, pressing downward on the dibble to evenly mark off the rows. Then, starting at hole number one, match the outside dibble with the first hole. Hold the dibbler so the individual dibbles will mark a row of planting holes that are perpendicular to the first row you marked. Repeat to mark planting holes across each row, then place transplants in the holes.

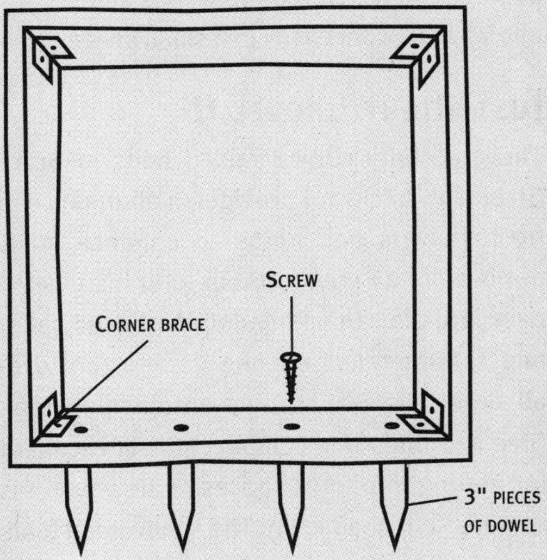

tapering chisel on the other. The chisel side was perfect for piercing the ground, and the weight and grip of the hammer helped immensely as Cardillo methodically planted his bunches of bulbs.

## Better Bulb Planter

She may not be the first gardener to find out that a bulb planter works great for planting seedlings, too, but Cheryl Coston of Fairdealing, Missouri, has a few tips of her own to make it work even better. First, she says, it's worthwhile to buy the kind of bulb planter that extracts the soil when you squeeze the handle; that way, you don't have to bend. If you're planting into plastic mulch, file the edge of the bulb planter to make it sharper; then you can cut through the plastic and dig the hole with one twisting stroke. And if you've ever used a bulb planter in clay soil,

**Recycle It!**

***On hand:*** Chopsticks

***Turn them into:*** Dibble for small seedlings

***How to do it:*** Use a single chopstick to poke seed holes when sowing seeds or to prick out seedlings when transplanting. Alison Kenny, a backyard gardener who also makes luscious skin creams and lotions in her Maryland kitchen, adds that chopsticks are great disposable "spoons" for messy stirring jobs, like beeswax and oils.

you know that it leaves the sides of the hole compacted and slick, which roots will find difficult to penetrate. "My solution is to carry an old dinner fork with me," Coston says. "A couple of slashing jabs at the sides of the hole loosen the soil just fine."

## Just-Right Shovel I

Just about every gardener has a tool they wouldn't be without, and extension horticulture agent Sydney Park Brown is no exception. When she heads toward her perennial beds, she's usually carrying her favorite implement: an irrigation shovel (also known as a trenching shovel). No, Park Brown has no need to dig water ditches in her Tampa, Florida, garden; she just finds this short-handled, narrow-bladed shovel ideally suited for a woman. Its long, narrow blade is perfect for controlling the size of the holes she digs, and because the blade doesn't hold much soil, it never gets too heavy to lift. The D-shaped handle and short shaft give her just enough leverage to transplant perennials or root up weeds and yet still allow her to work easily in a small space.

## Just-Right Shovel II

The gracefully curved raised beds in Bruce Gleeman's backyard provide an abundance of fresh flowers and herbs to enhance many of his culinary creations. To tend his diverse backyard plot, this Philadelphia-based baker and caterer relies on one garden tool over all others—a war-surplus entrenching tool. Gleeman finds this compact shovel excellent for getting into tight spaces as he works his compost-enriched loam. The spade head folds and locks in different positions, so he can also use this tool as a lightweight pick for busting up clods or removing a stray tree root. Plus, when folded, it takes up little room in his crowded tool shed.

## Fake Flowers Mark the Spot

Linda Howard, a home gardener from Evansville, Indiana, was new to gardening when she hit upon an idea for marking planting spots that also makes her garden look pretty. "In the spring, I keep an eye out for artificial flowers at yard sales, the kind with a stiff wire single stem. I use them to mark where I've planted daffodils and other bulbs, and in the vegetable garden, I use them at both ends of the row. So I don't forget what I planted there, I poke the wire through the seed packet to keep it in place. My flowers are easy to spot at a glance, so even the kids don't go trampling the rows I've planted."

The fake flowers stay in place through wind and rain. When the plants are up and growing, Howard pulls out the fake flowers, snips off the wire stems to use as twist-ties in the garden, and tosses out the faded blooms.

## It's Time for Daffodils

Daffodil lover Sally Roth of New Harmony, Indiana, often stops at other people's gardens to ask about unusual varieties that catch her eye. Yet by the time daffodil-planting time rolls around, she says, "I've either forgotten the name or lost the paper I'd written it on, or even worse, I've forgotten to order the bulbs and the mail-order companies have sold out."

"I've tried pinning my notes to a bulletin board and sticking them on the refrigerator, but that doesn't work either. By fall, I'm so used to seeing that important reminder that I never even notice it," she says. So she turned to a thoroughly low-tech gadget—the calendar on her kitchen wall.

"In April, when I have the name of a new daffodil I want to try, I flip to the August page—when it's time to start buying daffodils—and make a note on any date, saying 'Buy daffodil 'Halesa', or whatever it is I want to try." Roth says she also jots down a few words about good companion plants and what she likes about the flower: its color, height, fragrance, and overall look, in case her landscaping designs have changed by the time it's time to order.

This reminder system works well for other plants whose planting time is different than

### Recycle It!

***On hand:*** Plastic-foam packing peanuts

***Turn them into:*** Pot drainage assistant

***How to do it:*** Layer plastic-foam packing peanuts about 1 inch thick in the bottom of small pots, or up to 3 inches deep in larger pots, for perfect drainage with no weight. It's especially good for hanging containers, says Irv Breber of Bensalem, Pennsylvania.

"I've also tilled them 7 to 8 inches deep into hard-packed soil areas where nothing much would grow, which increased the drainage enough to turn the soil into a successful planting area."

bloom time, says Roth, who uses the same system to make note of bearded irises and daylilies she likes.

## Little Red Wagon Is a Big Help

"My 3-year-old, Erica, isn't very good at weeding the garden or planting seeds," says Gretel Hartman of the Boston area, "but she does love to help. So I give her things that she can handle, and that's where her little red wagon comes in handy. It's great for moving around the small pots of plants I start indoors or buy at the garden center, or for moving transplants."

In fact, says Hartman, the wagon is so useful that she has adopted it even when Erica isn't helping. She uses it to hold weeds for transport to the compost pile, and she has even used it to give away extra bearded irises, sundrops (*Oenothera* sp.), mint, and other prolific growers, as well as her extra ripe tomatoes and zucchini. The wagon is narrower than her wheelbarrow, she notes, so it fits in tight quarters in the garden without damaging nearby plants.

"The first time I used it as a plant stand, I piled it with irises when I thinned out my beds and put a sign on it that said 'Free plants—please help yourself!'" says Hartman. The freebies were snapped up within a couple of hours by passersby in the neighborhood, who tell Hartman that they can't wait for the next appearance of the little red wagon.

## Perfect Potting Table

If you have an old dresser, sideboard, or vanity, then you have an instant potting table. All you have to do is set the piece of furniture outside. The drawers make great storage and the top is a perfect surface for puttering with plants or stacking pots. If the design permits, add hooks for hanging hand tools.

## PVC Marks the Spot

Can't figure out a use for those short pieces of PVC pipe? Turn them into planting markers. Push pipe pieces into flowerbeds to mark locations of dormant bulbs or wildflowers, or use

Recycle It!

***On hand:*** Plastic pots

***Turn them into:*** Handy scoops

***How to do it:*** "Save all your sturdy 3-, 4-, and 6-inch plastic pots. When you aren't using them for repotting, they make excellent scoops for potting soil, mulch, pet food, and bird seed," says Linda Harris of Fulton, Kentucky. Simply wash and dry them, and stick a little tape over the holes to keep scoop from leaking.

# Build It!

## Planting Compass

If you want to plant your seedlings the exact same space apart, Jeff Ball's garden compass may be just the gadget you need. Ball, a garden writer from West Chester, Pennsylvania, says it was his idea and his father's ability to manufacture it. "This compass is modeled on the compasses we used in grade school to draw circles on the blackboard," says Ball. My father and I devised it to be used when planting a vegetable garden with the intensive planting method. We wanted to place each plant exactly within its tolerance in terms of distance from another plant in 360 degrees of direction. It's also handy when you simply need to plant 20 seedlings 5 inches apart."

To make the compass, use a couple pieces of scrap wood. Hardwood like oak or maple will last longer, but use whatever you have on hand. You can buy threaded rod already cut, or you can simply hacksaw the head off a machine bolt.

### Materials

Two 1½ × 18-inch pieces of ½-inch-thick hardwood

1½-inch length of ¼-inch threaded rod

Two washers for ¼-inch bolt

Two ¼-inch wing nuts

Band saw, saber saw, or handsaw

Drill

### Directions

1. Cut the wood to about 18-inches long. Make a pattern for a long, tapered shape, based on the illustration at left. Mark the pattern on each piece of wood and cut to shape. (A band saw or saber saw would be helpful, but a handsaw will work as well.)
2. Cut the narrow ends to form a point on each piece, round the corners on the thicker end of each piece, and sand the rough edges.
3. Drill a ¼-inch hole ¾ inch from the rounded ends of each piece.
4. Thread the rod through the two wood strips and attach with a washer and wing nut on each side. Tighten the nuts to hold the compass securely. Loosen the nuts to adjust the angle as needed.

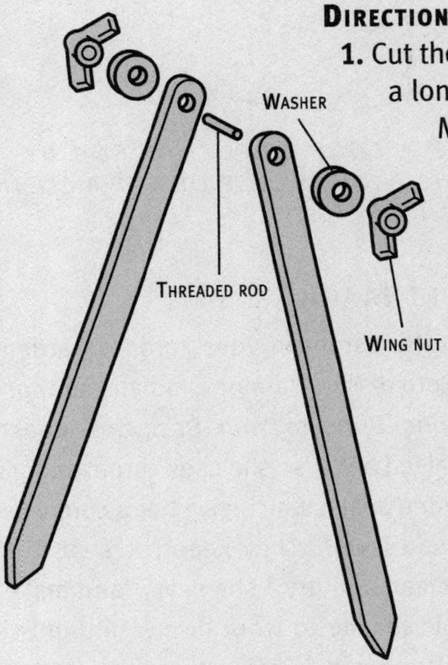

**Recycle It!**

***On hand:*** Broken metal or plastic miniblinds

***Turn them into:*** Plant labels

***How to do it:*** Sally Cummings of Albany, New York, clips labels to length with a sturdy scissors, making one end of the label pointed. Then she uses a permanent marker or a laundry marker to write pertinent information on the label.

them as row markers in the vegetable garden. You can easily write notes on them with a marking pen.

## Here's the Scoop

Here's a gadget that comes in handy when you need a scoop of potting soil or peat moss. All you need to make your own is a clean, empty plastic bottle with a handle and a pair of craft or kitchen scissors, says Judy Glattstein of Frenchtown, New Jersey. Just lay the bottle on its side, with the handle on top. Make a partial cut as for a funnel, more than one-third but somewhat less than one-half the circumference of the bottle, starting just below the handle. Then, from each end of that cut, make an angled cut along the body of the cylinder down to the base, narrowing gradually toward the base. Join the cuts just before you reach the bottom of the bottle, as shown, to make a handy, all-purpose scoop.

*Get the scoop on potting soil by making a soil scoop out of a clean plastic bottle.*

## Carpet Magic

Try a little carpet in your garden. Gardener Sally Roth of New Harmony, Indiana, author of *Attracting Birds to Your Backyard*, doesn't have raised beds, so she uses carpet samples for garden seats, which give her a comfy seat at ground level. "They keep the seat of my jeans clean and dry," she says, "and make it possible for me to work in my garden even right after a rain." Roth asks at carpet stores for outdated samples.

# Build It!

## Holding Bed for Potted Plants

Have you ever gone plant shopping and brought home lots of great treasures, only to realize you don't have a place ready for them in the garden? Ernest Heintzelman of Kempton, Pennsylvania, certainly knows what that's like! He was lucky enough to snap up 12 pine seedlings for only $5, but he needed time to prepare a good planting site for them. Heintzelman knew that keeping all those small pots upright and watered could be a real challenge, so he decided to create a holding bed where they would be safe until he was ready to plant them.

Heintzelman built a simple frame from scrap lumber, and then filled it with chipped hardwood mulch (free from many local townships) and sunk his potted trees to their rims in the mulch. The mulch drains well but also reduces water loss from evaporation, so the pots don't need frequent watering. "You can hold most woody plants in a nursery for several years, with periodic feedings of fish emulsion or compost tea," he says.

### Materials

- 16 feet of 1 × 8 or 2 × 8 lumber
- 12 penny nails (or 2- to 3-inch galvanized deck screws)
- Potted seedlings
- Hardwood mulch
- Circular saw or handsaw
- Hammer or a cordless drill with both drill-bit and driver attachments
- Framing square or measuring tape

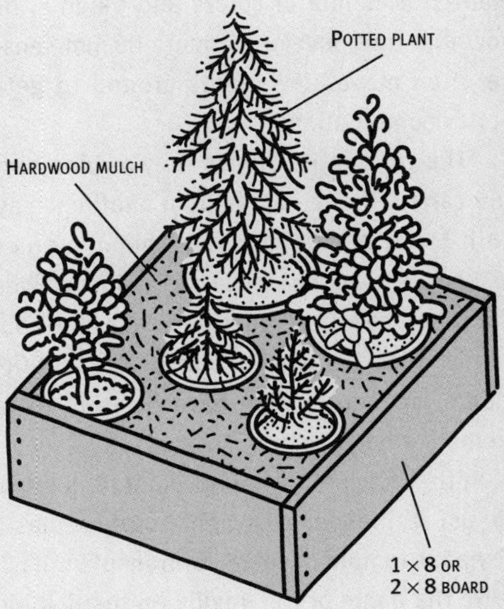


### Directions

**1.** Cut the lumber into four 4-foot sections using a circular saw or handsaw. (If you want a smaller or larger bed, adjust the lengths accordingly.)

**2.** Nail each corner together with two to four nails, or drill pilot holes with a cordless drill, and then use a driver attachment to drive in galvanized deck screws. Make sure the corners are square with a framing square, or measure across the diagonals (they should be equal).

**3.** Position the nursery frame in an out-of-the-way spot, set in your potted plants, and then fill in around them with mulch.

***On hand:*** A plastic kitty litter jug

***Turn it into:*** Plant markers

***How to do it:*** Using a pair of heavy-duty scissors, cut out strips of jug the length and width you need. Use a permanent marker to write on them.

## Walk the Plank!

Donna Armstrong of Harleysville, Pennsylvania, remarks, "The old ways are often the best!" She and others who garden at Heckler Plains Farmstead, an 18th-century German kitchen garden located in Harleysville, use long wooden planks, just as their historical counterparts did years ago. Laying the plank over a raised bed (the hallmark of the kitchen garden) creates a wonderful, clean platform from which to plant, weed, or cultivate. The edge of the plank is an excellent marker for sowing precise, straight rows, too. Plank criteria? Something that is long enough to lay on top of the raised bed. After all, the gardeners of yore would have recycled what was available. So don't sweat dimensions.

## Flatware for Your Flowers

Sturdy plastic flatware is ideal for labeling outdoor plantings. Use a #2 pencil to write information on the blade of the knife or bowl of the spoon—ink (even from indelible markers) doesn't usually hold up. Push the flatware handle into the soil until only the top inch of the utensil is showing. Rest assured the marker will be there next spring to warn you before digging into lilies, hibiscus, and other late-emerging perennials! To make shorter labels for small pots, snip plastic flatware in half.

## Dishpans for Daylilies

Try a daylily dishpan trick to keep yourself organized at planting time, says teenager David Roth-Mark of New Harmony, Indiana. Roth-Mark has been a daylily enthusiast since he planted his first garden. At first he planted a jumble of colors and heights, but now that he's developing more design sense, he often moves the plants around to get a better combination.

"The trouble is, unless they're blooming, you can't tell one daylily from another," says Roth-Mark. He depends on plant markers to keep the names straight in his garden, but when it's time to transplant, he commonly ends up with a pile of unidentified plants, no matter how hard he tries to remember what's what.

Roth-Mark has solved his plant ID dilemma by using inexpensive light-colored plastic dishpans to hold daylilies for transplanting. "I write the name of the daylily on the dishpan with a black marker before I even put the

# Build It!

## A Very Able Label

Midwestern winters are tough on a lot of things—people, animals, and even plant labels. Frost heaves them out of the ground and severe weather beats off any writing on them in just a few months.

So Lee and Ruth White of Postville, Iowa, have come up with a super label that handles even what the harshest weather dishes up.

**Materials**

- Piece of 1 × 3-inch wood, ½ inch thick
- Heavy-duty aluminum foil
- Drill
- 12-inch length #9 galvanized wire
- Heavy-duty stapler and staples
- Ballpoint pen
- Permanent marker (optional)

**Directions**

1. Cut the wood to size, and drill a hole in the center near the top.
2. Cut the foil to fit the front of the wood, and staple it in place.
3. Use a ballpoint pen to write the plant name on the foil, pressing firmly. If desired, trace over the writing with a permanent marker.
4. Loop the wire through the hole as shown.

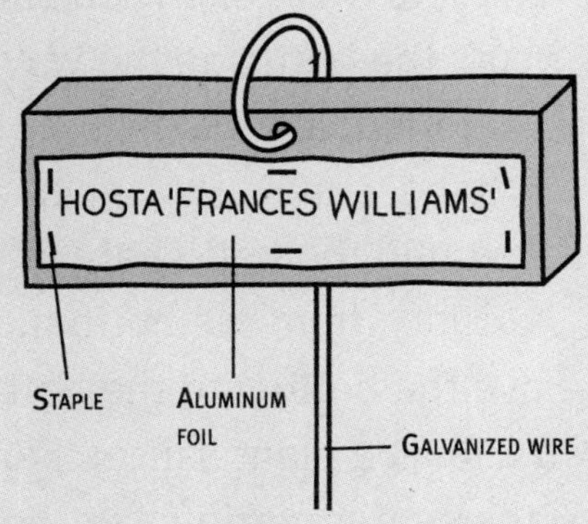


plants in," he says. "The dishpan makes it easy to cart the plants around, it holds them securely, and, with a little water in the bottom, it keeps them fresh until I can get them into the ground."

## Classy Labels

Fancy copper plant labels look great, but they cost a fortune and are often so undersize that they give you just an inch or two to insert them into the soil. Make your own elegant copper labels by purchasing sheets of thin copper at a crafts store. Just cut into the size and shape desired with a pair of craft or kitchen scissors. Label by pressing firmly with a dull pencil.

## Extra-Large Labels

Most store-bought plant labels are too narrow to hold much more than a plant's name. That can be a problem if you want to include additional information for vegetable crops,

### Recycle It!

***On hand:*** Bleach bottle

***Turn it into:*** Plant marking stakes and plant saucer

***How to do it:*** Lois Stringer of Bellefonte, Pennsylvania, rinses empty bleach bottles and lets them dry. Then she cuts the bottle all the way around, just below the handle, and cuts again around the bottle, about ½ inch from the bottom. Save the bottom of the bottle to use as a plant saucer. From the center portion, cut the circle apart so you can flatten out into a panel. (You may need to roll in the opposite direction of how it's curved to get it to lie flat.) Cut it across the short width to make ¾-inch strips for plant markers, which take permanent marker or crayon very well.

such as planting date, expected harvest date, and so on. Frustrated by narrow commercial plant labels, Cheryl Coston of Fairdealing, Missouri, came up with a way to make extra-large labels. "First, I bought an inexpensive package of wooden skewers," she says. "They were about 12 inches long, with 20 in a package for $1. Then I stuck them in a piece of plastic foam and spray painted them white." That created attractive and durable stakes.

For the labels themselves, Coston cut 4 × 6-inch rectangles from a white bleach bottle, made five evenly spaced, horizontal slits across each one, and wove the skewers through them. She uses a Sharpie pen to write all the notes she needs to make on the rectangles and sets them out in the garden. "I thought they might look tacky but figured they would do until I could figure out an alternative," Coston says. "But they don't look tacky or like bleach bottles at all, and I'm still using them. Best of all, I can read them without even bending over!"

## Color Them Pretty, Color Them Right

Raising seedlings is a passion for Caroline Whitenack of Doylestown, Pennsylvania. She raises hundreds of flower seedlings every year to plant her dozen different gardens and local church gardens and to supply neighbors and family with plants.

To keep her seedlings identified so they don't get mixed up, she buys 12-inch plastic stakes and cuts them into thirds, then uses stick-on color dots in various colors (available in office-supply stores) to color-code the seedlings. She uses the color-coding system for the seedlings until they are transplanted into their final setting. Whitenack says she never has unwelcome surprises when the plants bloom!

## Glue Stick Saves Seeds at Planting Time

Have you ever spilled the excess seed from a seed packet all over a garden bed because the seed packet flap just wouldn't stay shut? Sometimes you don't want to plant a whole packet of lettuce, beans, or annual flowers at one time, but it's a problem to keep the opened seed packets securely shut.

"Some seeds don't come in resealable packets, and the ones that do often lose their stickiness after being opened a few times," observes gardener Cheryl Coston of Fairdealing, Missouri. "So I learned to carry a restickable-type glue stick along in my planting tote. The glue stick works perfectly for creating a good sticky seal on a seed packet flap."

Glue sticks are available at discount stores and office supply stores, and they cost less than $2.

***On hand:*** Plastic foam meat trays

***Turn them into:*** Foolproof tomato cage labels

***How to do it:*** It's impossible to find labels stuck in the ground once tomato vines sprawl. Instead, cut strips of plastic foam and punch a hole in one corner of each strip with a hole puncher. Write the ID on the label, then thread a twist-tie through the hole, and attach the label to the top of tomato cage where it's easily visible.

# Plant Protectors

Half of the gardening battle is over: Your seeds have finally sprouted! Now is the ideal time to protect your plants from the will of the weather. This section will suggest ways to keep your plants warm and safe without having to depend upon expensive commercial products.

## Bulb Defender

City dwellers often discover their freshly planted bulbs dug up and scattered about. Is the culprit a jealous neighbor? A pesky pooch? "It's most likely squirrels," says Judy Glattstein, author of *Flowering Bulbs for Dummies* and world-renowned bulb lecturer. "Squirrels may think that light, fluffy soil means something tasty has been buried by another squirrel and will dig up (but not eat) your tulips and daffodils." To keep these critters from excavating your bulb beds, Glattstein recommends dropping an old window screen or short lengths of thorny rose or bramble branches over the site. Once the ground firms up or freezes, you can remove these defenses and wait for your spring show.

## Tomato Protection

Laurie Kendrick of Hooper, Utah, protects tender tomato seedlings with pieces of 4-inch-wide PVC pipe cut into 12- to 14-inch lengths. After she has planted the seedlings, she carefully puts a piece of PVC pipe over the top of each one and pushes it into the ground. Laurie leaves the PVC on all growing season to protect the tomatoes from cutworms and to provide support.

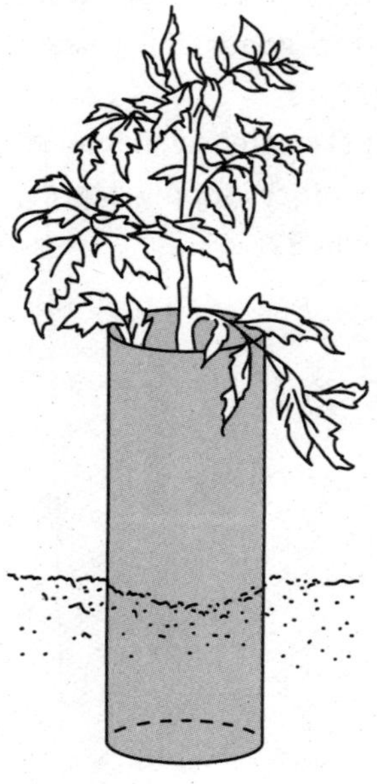

*Keep cutworms from damaging your tomatoes and support the plants at the same time.*

## Wall of Plastic

Vincent Norris of State College, Pennsylvania, has invented his own tomato plant protectors that he says outperform commercial water-filled cloches. All it takes to protect a plant from cold weather is a 1-gallon plastic milk jug and an empty 6-gallon plastic bucket (check with local contractors for drywall buckets).

Norris plants his tomatoes as soon as the morning soil temperature reaches 55°F. (That's still several weeks before the last frost date in his area.) He places a water-filled jug next to each plant at planting time. Then every evening, he inverts a bucket over each tomato plant and the jug beside it. "The water in the jug keeps the temperature inside the bucket well above the outside air temperature." he says. "By the time the tomato plants become too large to fit inside a bucket, they no longer need the covers," he says. "I've never lost a single tomato plant to frost," he adds.

**Recycle It!**

***On hand:*** Odd pieces of PVC pipe and an old bedsheet

***Turn them into:*** Shade cover for transplants

***How to do it:*** Stick pipe pieces into the ground among plants and spread the sheet over them. Weight the corners with bricks.

## Plant Protection Cubed

Cool-climate gardeners know the value of water-filled containers for insulating their vegetable crops from the cold. Kelly Winterton of Mountain Green, Utah, works in a high-volume, photo-finishing lab and has access to used 4- and 5-gallon, flexible, collapsible plastic containers in which the photo chemicals are shipped. (He calls them "cubitainers.") Winterton recognized their garden potential and turned them into season extenders.

"I rinse the cubitainers out well," he explains, "and then fill them with water and place them around plants that are sensitive to cold. They hold much more water than similar commercial products and the plants never outgrow them. I leave them in place all growing season," Winterton continues. "In the summer, they tend to moderate the extreme heat, so they work well with plants that need a little relief from the heat in the middle of the day, such as broccoli and cauliflower. When the cooler weather of the fall arrives, the cubitainers are still there, doing their job. I can easily overwinter my cole crops here in Zone 4. And as soon as the snow melts, they resume growing to give me a spring crop way before the cabbageworms become active."

Winterton points out that because of their size, the cubitainers also serve as a mulch to moderate soil and air temperature. He suggests that you can enhance the insulating power of the cubitainers even more by covering them and the plant with floating row covers or ventilated clear plastic. The secret is volume and mass. "Getting 30 gallons of water around each plant makes all the difference in the world," Winterton says.

### Cloche Security Flap

A lot of you probably cut the bottoms off of gallon milk jugs and place the jugs over plants as cloches. These individual plant shelters can speed early growth. Using them also helps prevent cool-season crops such as cabbage, cauliflower, and broccoli from going to seed prematurely. Only trouble is, the empty jugs are lightweight and not very secure. There's a simple way to correct the problem: Instead of cutting the entire bottom from the jug, make a large flap by cutting along three sides of the bottom. Then bend the flap out 180 degrees and cover it with soil or large rocks to hold the jug in place. What a simple solution!

### Fig Protection

If you're growing fig trees anywhere cooler than Zone 7, you have to nurse the trees through the winter, and that can be a big job. "I used to wrap my fig tree with burlap," says Joseph Schlien of Baltimore, Maryland, "but it was a lot of work, and the wraps kept coming apart." Since then, he has found the perfect wrap: tubular foam insulation that slips over water pipes. Schlien has found that it fits perfectly over the trunk and branches of his fig tree! He simply slips it over and tapes it with electrical black tape. He bought all he needed for $5 and says he can use it over and over again, year after year.

### Homemade Hot House

"I'm a tomato fanatic!" says Linda Monier of Olive Branch, Mississippi. "And I want them early!" Monier makes the most of her growing season by creating a special solar-heated bed for her tomatoes. About 6 weeks before last frost—that's April 15 in her area—she covers a 4 by 8-foot bed with black plastic mulch and then sinks 6- to 7-foot-tall rebar stakes

**Recycle It!**

***On hand:*** Old sheets and mangled paper clips

***Turn them into:*** Shade cover for transplants

***How to do it:*** Cover newly planted shrubs, perennials, and other transplants by cutting a section of sheet to drape over the tops and sides of the plant. If necessary, secure the cloth to the soil by bending a few of the clips into U-pins. Remove after 1 or 2 days.

1 or 2 feet deep every 30 inches or so just outside the long edges of the bed. When the last frost date has passed, she digs a planting hole to the inside of each stake and plants her tomatoes.

To create a low-tech drip-watering system, she cuts off the bottom of 2-liter soda bottles, drills a couple of holes in each lid with a cordless drill, and then buries them about 6 inches deep, top-end down—one beside each plant. "When I need to water, I just fill up the upside-down bottles," she says.

Even in her southern garden, late spring can throw in a few chilly days, so Monier has come up with some clever insulation ideas to keep her tomato seedlings warm and cozy. "I take empty milk jugs, fill them with water, and place them around the plants," she says. "I use as many milk jugs as will fit into the bed without crowding the plants too much—and that's a lot! Then I take 4-mil-thick clear plastic sheeting and wrap it around the stakes on the outside, completely enclosing the bed in a mini greenhouse." (The top is left open to avoid overheating.) "The plants get off to a great start!" Monier claims.

Once the days are dependably warm and night temperatures remain at least 60°F, she removes the clear plastic. And when it gets really hot, she removes the water jugs and covers the black plastic with straw to keep the roots from cooking. "I have tomatoes by June 1 every year!" she says.

## Keeping Kitty In

Most of us put up fences to keep critters—rabbits, raccoons, and deer—out of our yards. But some of us need fences to keep critters—especially our feline friends—in, to keep them safe and prevent them from digging in our neighbors' yards.

Cats, of course, are climbers, so it takes a little ingenuity to build a fence to contain them. Nancy Milligan of Lemon Grove, California, has found the answer. She simply installed V-shaped, 45-degree brackets near the top along the inside of the existing 6-foot-tall fence that surrounded her yard. (To make these brackets, she purchased metal

### Recycle It!

***On hand:*** Half-gallon plastic juice bottles

***Turn them into:*** Tomato plant insulators

***How to do it:*** After planting tomato seedlings, surround each one with six juice bottles filled with water, and then wrap the whole thing in bubble wrap. The bottles insulate the plants during cold nights. As warmer weather arrives, unwrap the bubble wrap and remove the bottles.

shelving brackets and bent them from a 90-degree angle to a 45-degree angle. The brackets already have holes in them, so it's easy to attach them to a wooden fence using ½-inch screws.) Milligan then fastened a long strip of hardware cloth on top of the brackets with twist ties or wire to make an impenetrable cat barrier. Milligan points out that plastic netting or wooden lattice would also do the trick.

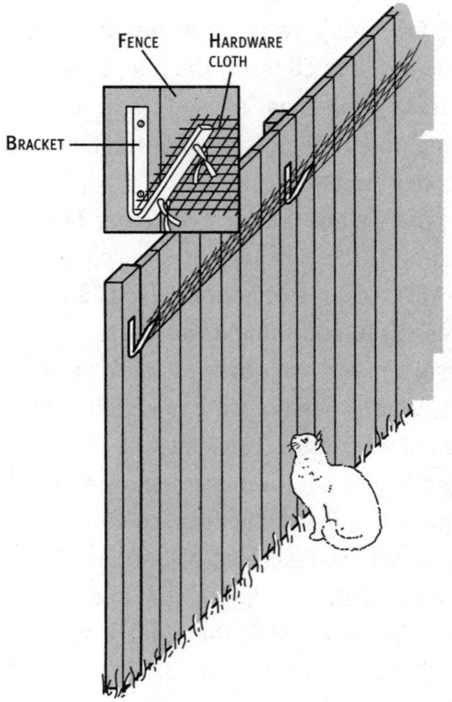


*KEEP YOUR CAT IN YOUR YARD—AND OUT OF THE NEIGHBORS'—WITH THIS SIMPLE HARDWARE-CLOTH BARRIER. BECAUSE IT ANGLES INWARD, KITTY CAN'T GET PAST IT.*

**Recycle It!**

***ON HAND:*** 2-liter soda bottles

***TURN THEM INTO:*** Plant protectors

***HOW TO DO IT:*** Scrape the label from a 2-liter soda bottle using a utility knife or a single-edge razor, and then cut the base off the bottle. Lower the bottle over a small plant, and twist it into the soil. Remove the cap to ventilate during the day, and replace the cap at night.

## RING AROUND THE TREE TRUNK

Ever drive up to your house just as the fellow who cuts your lawn was mowing down one of your newly planted saplings? Randy Myer of Hastings, New York, did and he wasn't amused. So he invented a perforated plastic tree collar that snaps around a young tree. As the trunk grows, the diaphragm opening expands to fit it, just as a camera lens opens to let in more light. The plastic surface is easy to conceal with mulch, thousands of tiny holes let plenty of water through to the roots, and best of all, the raised rim keeps lawn mowers at bay. (See "Resources" on page 344 for ordering information.)

*PROTECT YOUR TREE'S BARK FROM LAWN MOWER BITES WITH THIS TREE COLLAR FASHIONED FROM THE BOTTOM PART OF A PLASTIC NURSERY POT.*

If you're a do-it-yourselfer at heart, you can make a trunk protector from a 5-gallon or larger plastic nursery pot. Simply slice off the bottom, cutting through the container about 1 inch from the bottom edge. With a hammer and nail, poke holes in the bottom surface—the more the merrier. Then cut a hole with a craft scissors or utility knife in the center that's big enough to accommodate your sapling's trunk with a few inches to spare. Make a slit from the hole to the outer edge so the collar will open, slip it in place around the tree, and disguise the plastic surface with mulch. Keep an eye on the collar as your tree grows and remove it before the fit gets snug. By then, your tree should be big enough to catch someone's attention before it's too late.

**Recycle It!**

***ON HAND:*** Sheer white window curtains

***TURN THEM INTO:*** Row covers

***HOW TO DO IT:*** Drape old curtains over garden plants to protect them from insects or light frosts. They work great and hold up better than expensive spun garden fabrics. You can even throw them in the washer if needed!

# Seed-Starting Stuff

What do film canisters, hoes, rulers, forks, and cardboard toilet-paper rolls have in common? With a little gardening imagination and effort, they can make seed starting a snap. In the next few pages, you'll learn how to make homemade flat covers, planting boxes, mini greenhouses, and coldframes for your next seed-starting projects.

## Benchmarked Seed Storage

"Seeds from some trees and wildflowers germinate better when they get a good winter chill, but I don't like to put messy seeds planted in soil in my refrigerator," says gardener Barbara Pleasant, who's trying to reforest several acres of land in Alabama with native plant seedlings. Instead, Pleasant uses her outdoor potting bench as a storage site for seeds that need a cold treatment. After collecting the seeds, she sticks them in a small paper envelope. Then she tucks the envelope into a margarine tub filled with damp potting soil. She uses a marker to label the lid of the container about the contents. Then she stashes the containers in the pile of leaves that accumulates under her potting bench.

"By February, when I'm ready to plant the seeds in flats, they think they've been through winter. Sometimes they're already beginning to sprout when I take them out of the tubs," Pleasant says.

## Artistic Flat Covers

Most seeds crave light to help them germinate, but verbenas and some other flowers like to sprout in the dark. "When I sow flats of flower seeds that like to germinate in darkness, I cover them with pieces of illustration board cut slightly larger than the flats," says Alabama gardener Barbara Pleasant. "I use bricks to hold the board in place. The board keeps things dark and moist. Heavy cardboard will work, too, but it isn't as durable as illustration board," Pleasant says. You can buy illustration board at art-supply stores.

## Plant-in-a-Box

Each year, Delores and Dave Johnson of Golden Valley, Minnesota, start about 8,000 plants from seed—with no greenhouse. (Saying they know how to start seeds efficiently is an understatement.) How do they do it?

Dave says he likes to speed the process by not using little flats. Instead, he has built a large planting box (line with galvanized metal) about 3 × 2 feet and 4 to 6 inches deep. (You could make yours any dimensions you want.) He puts a layer of crushed rock on the bottom, topped by a little sand. The top 2 inches are filled with seed-starting mix. He hangs a cool, white four-bulb fluorescent light about 4 inches above the planting box.

You could plant seeds in the box just as it is, but Dave likes to further refine the process by cutting 2 × 4-inch dividers from strips of galvanized metal for his 3 × 2-foot box. He inserts those into the soil about 1 or 2 inches, just enough to keep the seedlings neatly apart.

Then Dave sows the seeds. He can get up to 60 different types of seeds in his box. And because of its size, the box has a more stable temperature and retains moisture better than smaller containers.

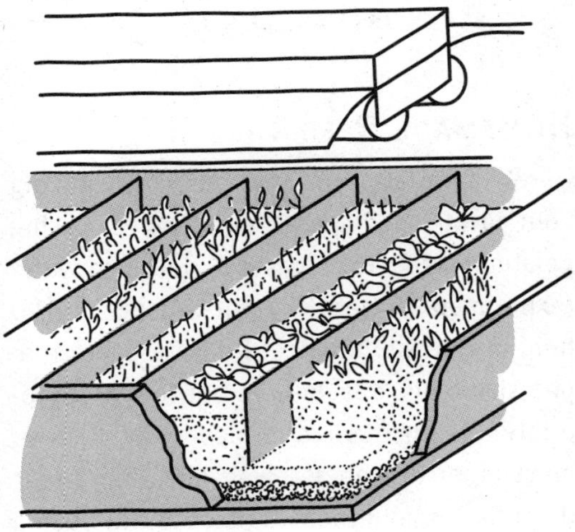

*MAXIMIZE LIMITED SPACE WITH THIS SEED-STARTING PLANTING BED.*

***ON HAND:*** A small plastic fork

***TURN IT INTO:*** A transplanting tool for small seedlings

***HOW TO DO IT:*** Break off the two outside prongs of the fork, leaving just two prongs. Slip the tines around an individual seedling and carefully lever it out of the seed-starting tray, roots and all.

## RULE IT OUT

Cut an old yardstick down to size—a tad shorter than the width of a seed tray, to be precise—and you're ready to fly through planting. Just fill the tray with your seed starting mix, level it off, and mark rows about $1\frac{1}{2}$ inches apart with the cut ruler's edge. You can easily control the depth this way, and keep rows straight.

If you have, say, several varieties of tomato plants you wish to try this year, mark many short rows width-wise across the flat. Then plant the seeds, skipping a row between varieties (don't forget to label each variety!). This system gets the seeds off to a great start and makes transplanting easy.

**Recycle It!**

***On hand:*** Clear plastic clamshell containers (the kind you get salads in at delis)

***Turn them into:*** A mini greenhouse for starting seeds

***How to do it:*** Just wash out the container, add your favorite seed-starting mix, and plant your seeds. Open container as needed to vent or water.

## Homemade Seed Tape I

Seed tapes make sowing and spacing seeds in the garden easy and precise. The problem is premade tapes are expensive, and you can't always get your favorite varieties on a tape. The solution is to make your own—it's a fun activity for a rainy day when you can't get out in the garden.

You'll need one package of gelatin (any type), one resealable plastic bag, a roll of paper towels, and your seeds. Make the gelatin in a bowl according to package directions and allow it to cool but not set. Pour the seed into the bowl of cooled gelatin and mix thoroughly.

Cut a hole, just large enough for a single seed to fit through, in one corner of the bottom of a plastic bag. Spoon the gelatin and seed mixture into the bag.

Cut paper towels into 1-inch-wide strips and squeeze the gelatin seed mixture onto the paper-towel strips, spacing seeds according to seed packet directions. Allow the strips to dry. Then roll them up loosely, and store for up to 2 days.

In the garden, unroll the seed strips in a furrow and cover with soil.

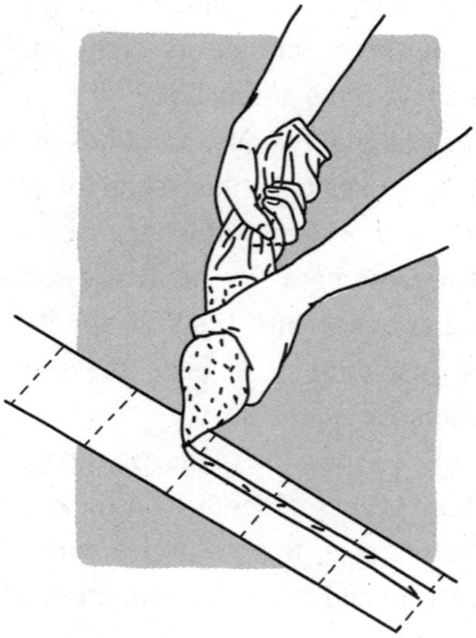

*Save money—and use the varieties you like best—by making your own seed tape instead of buying a commercial one.*

## Homemade Seed Tape II

Here's a variation on the theme of making your own seed tapes. Instead of using gelatin, make a thick paste of flour and water (experiment to get the right consistency) to hold the seeds in place. Roll the paste into pea-size balls, space them out to the appropriate distance on a 1-inch-wide strip of newspaper or paper towel, and then press them flat to hold them in place. Next, push a single seed into each spot of paste. After the paste dries, you can plant the entire "tape" in the garden.

## Homemade Seed Tape III

Toilet paper and glue are the basis of yet another gardener's method for making seed tape. Pat Patterson of Eugene, Oregon, finds that making her own seed tapes is a great winter-gardening activity. Patterson uses single-layer toilet paper and white glue to make the tape. She unrolls the paper and squeezes out two or more lines of glue on it. Then she places the seeds on the glue, spaced according to the seed packet directions. (Use a moistened toothpick or tweezers for tiny seed that are hard to hold.)

Pat lets the tape dry thoroughly, and then rolls it up and labels it until planting time. (When planting, be sure to cover the paper completely so it doesn't wick moisture.)

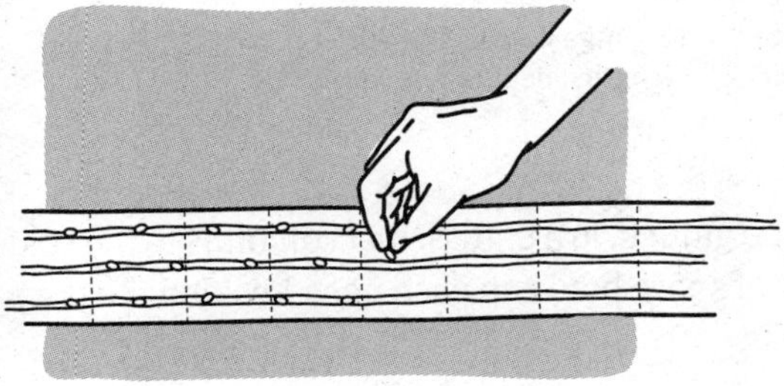

*A little glue and some toilet paper go a long way when making a seed tape.*

## Waterbed Germinator

Starting seeds indoors can save you plenty of dollars compared to buying plants at the garden center, but unless you keep the seeds warm enough, poor germination can be a problem. Commercial seed-starting mats are an option, but they can be expensive, too. For an inexpensive substitute that will provide *plenty* of well-heated space for seed starting, check yard sales and want ads for a single-size, waterbed mattress. To use the mattress for

***On hand:*** Butcher's twine, kite string, or cotton yarn

***Turn it into:*** Seed-starting tape

***How to do it:*** Head out to the garden armed with a pail of water, a 7- to 8-inch length of twine, seeds, and some old newspaper. Put the twine in the pail, and while it soaks, dig your planting furrow. By the time you do that, the twine should be saturated. Then sprinkle a row of seeds the same length on a sheet of the newspaper. Dip the twine in the seeds and plant the whole thing. As the seedlings germinate, the twine will degrade, giving a bit of organic matter to the soil. Says Sunnyvale, California, Master Gardener Dagmar Cechanek, "It's great for those almost-invisible seeds like carrots, lettuce, or nigella. I find it much easier than the classic method of mixing them with sand."

# Build It!

## Customized Hoop Coldframe

Professional gardener Gary Prochaska of Ames, Iowa, makes coldframes that fit over planting beds and crop rows using bits and pieces of materials he has around the garage. He customizes them for a wide variety of shapes and erects some long *after* the crop is planted. Prochaska, for example, uses his to extend the harvest of spinach, radishes, and turnips.

**Materials**

- At least six 12-inch lengths of 2-inch-diameter galvanized steel fence posts or similarly sized lengths of metal pipe
- 6-foot lengths of PVC flexible well pipe, one for each fence post
- Two 2-foot stakes
- Heavy string or cord
- 6-foot wide, 4-mil clear plastic
- Bricks or stones
- 12-gauge wire in 12-inch lengths, bent to form a U

**Directions**

**1.** Sink the fence posts or metal pipe into the ground, in a pattern that conforms to the coldframe's outline. Leave no more than 3 feet of space between each post. Position the posts so the tops are 2 to 3 inches above the soil.

bottom heat, spread the mattress out on the floor in a spot where it won't be in your way, and fill it with water. Lay slats over the mattress, spaced about 1 foot apart, and place flats of seed trays or seed pots right on the slats. Once the seeds germinate, move the flats under lights.

## A Cool Solution for Transplant Pots

Next time you indulge in a pint or half-pint of ice cream, be sure to save the paper carton it came in: These containers make great pots for seedlings! Wash the ice cream container and lid thoroughly, and line the lid with aluminum foil. Poke a drainage hole in the bottom of the container, then place the lid under the container as a saucer. Fill the container with sterile potting soil to 1 inch below the top. Transplant one seedling into each container, then place them under lights until it's time to move them out to the garden. At transplanting time, remove the lid from the bottom and cut several slits in the bottom and sides, up to but not through the top rim. Plant the entire pot, leaving the top inch extending above ground for a built-in cutworm collar.

**2.** Insert the flexible well pipe into the posts, pushing the pipe down as far as possible.

**3.** Pound the stakes about halfway into the ground at each end of the frame. Tie string to one stake and then stretch and loop the string across the hoops as shown. Tie the string to the stake at the opposite end. This stabilizes the hoops. Repeat with two more lengths of string.

**4.** Place the plastic over the hoops and string, using bricks or stones to hold down any corners that may flap.

**5.** Place a piece of the 12-gauge U-shaped wire in front of each post. Then, to prevent the plastic from flapping stretch a length of string over the hoops and secure the string by tying each end to the U-shaped wire.

**6.** When you want to give the covered plants some ventilation, simply roll up the sides slightly, tucking the plastic under the outside strings secured with the U-shaped wires.

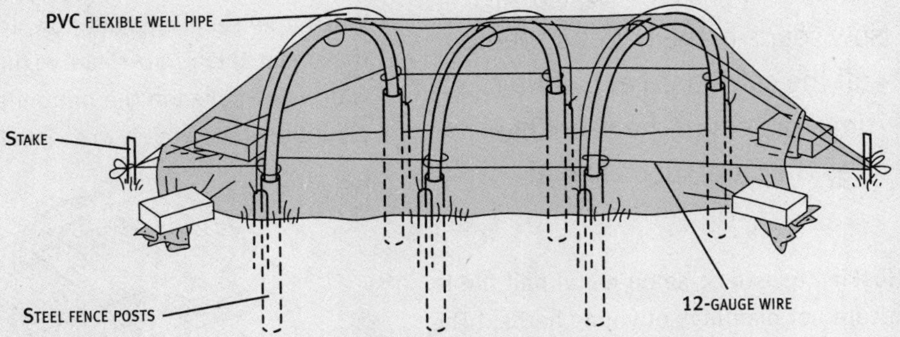


## Simple Seed Collectors

Cheryl Coston of Fairdealing, Missouri, used to use resealable plastic bags to collect seeds from her garden. It was never an easy process, though, trying to hold the bag open with one hand while collecting seeds with the other hand. Happily, she found a better alternative: Tupperware Hamburger Stackers. ("Finally a use for those things!" she says.) She carries a stack of them into the garden for collecting different types of seeds. And because one container serves as the lid for the next, there's no fumbling for separate covers.

## Manicure Your Herb Seedlings

Herb gardener Pat Hoskins of Evansville, Indiana, likes to try new herbs from seed, but she found weeding and thinning the plants a painstaking chore, until she found just the right tool for the trick.

"None of my tools was small enough to lift out herb seedlings or to get between the herbs to root out weeds," says Hoskins. "One day, I was walking around my yard with a nail file in hand, when I realized I had the perfect tool right in my fingers."

***On hand:*** Toilet paper tubes

***Turn them into:*** Seed-starting pots

***How to do it:*** Pack the tubes tightly into a seed-starting flat so that they stand upright. Fill them with potting soil, and sow seeds in them. Cut or peel off the cardboard at planting time, or set out the seedlings as they are, tubes and all.

Hoskins uses a common metal nail file to manicure her plantings of young herbs. "The pointed end is perfect for digging out weeds in those tight spaces. When I want to transplant herbs, I slip the file deep into the ground, round end first, to get below the roots and lift out the plant."

Hoskins gets double-duty out of her weeder, too. "When I'm done working in the herbs," she says, "I can clean my fingernails on the way to the house!"

## Easy Seed-Starting Cartons

If your family drinks lots of milk or juice, chances are you have an ample supply of half-gallon cardboard cartons. S. D. H. Wilson of Stratford, Connecticut, has found a great gardening re-use for these containers: "They make fantastic seed-starting trays!" she says.

She cuts the cartons in half lengthwise, and then staples shut the pour-spout on the one half. "Then I poke a lot of holes in the bottom of each carton with an ice pick, fill them with damp starting medium, and plant my seeds." She fits about a half-dozen of the half-cartons on a tray and slips a large plastic bag—with the end open for air circulation—over them. (If you want to give the seeds some bottom heat to speed germination, set the tray on a wire cookie rack over a commercial seed-starting mat.)

When the seeds sprout in a carton, remove it from the tray and place it under florescent lights. When the seedlings outgrow their cartons, transplant them into clean yogurt containers with holes poked in the bottom and let them grow until they're ready to go into the garden.

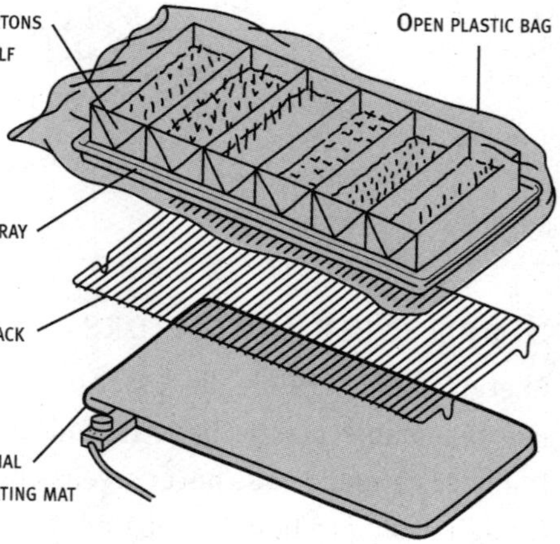


*Don't throw out those empty milk cartons. Instead, turn them into seed-starting trays.*

## Soda Bottle Greenhouse

With a few cuts and a little taping, Wanda Thomas of Wright City, Missouri, transforms a 2-liter soda bottle into a mini greenhouse for starting seeds. Here's how: First remove the labels from the bottle, and then cut a 2-inch-wide section out of the middle of the bottle, leaving the top and bottom intact. Take the 2-inch section you removed and cut it in half to form two C-shaped strips of plastic. Tape the ends of each segment together to form two half-dollar-size, 2-inch-tall cylinders.

Use a nail to tap a few drainage holes in the bottom of the soda bottle. Turn the bottom right side up, add a 1-inch layer of potting soil, and then settle the two cylinders into the soil so they're right next to each other. (When you look down on them, they should form a figure eight, dividing the bottom of the bottle into four compartments.) Add enough potting soil to reach the top of the cylinders. Moisten the soil thoroughly, and sow the seeds.

Tape the top of the bottle to the bottom, and place the whole setup under plant lights on a windowsill with lots of bright but indirect natural light, or in a sheltered location outdoors. Remove the top half of the bottle when you need to water; leave it off when you are ready to harden-off the seedlings before moving them outdoors.

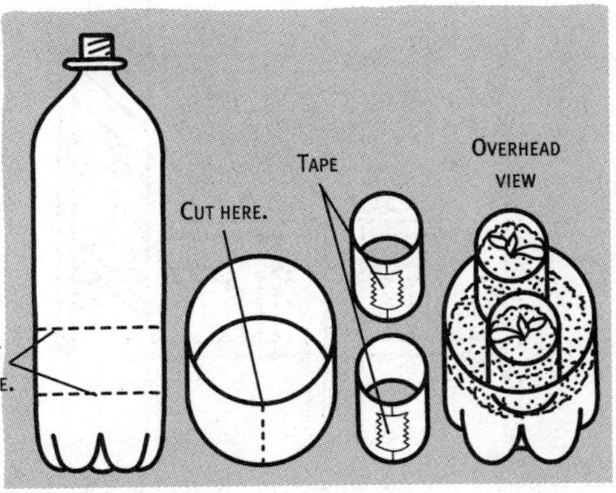


*A COUPLE OF CUTS AND A FEW PIECES OF TAPE TRANSFORM A SIMPLE SODA BOTTLE INTO A SUPER SEED-STARTING SETUP.*

**Recycle It!**

***ON HAND:*** Plastic film canisters

***TURN THEM INTO:*** Waterproof seed storage

***HOW TO DO IT:*** Wash the plastic canisters with soap and warm water to make sure there are no residual chemicals and label them with masking tape. Make sure both the containers and your seeds are perfectly dry before you snap on the lids for storage.

## KITTY'S CUSTOM TOMATO TRAYS

Seems like more and more things are packaged in plastic jugs, these days—even cat litter. That's the way Janelle Steckley of Sanford, Michigan, buys it, though she has always felt a little guilty about the plastic waste. "Even though I did put the jugs out in my recycling container when they were empty," she says, "it still somehow seemed wasteful." Not anymore, however. She has figured out how to reuse the containers by turning them into versatile plant pots for her seedlings. She just cuts off the top, pokes a few holes in the bottom for drainage using a nail, and then fills

### Recycle It!

**On hand:** Plastic film canisters

**Turn them into:** Space-saving seed stratifiers

**How to do it:** If you have seeds that need to be chilled (stratified) before sowing, put each type in a separate canister along with enough damp, sterile potting soil to fill the container. Snap on the lid, label with masking tape, and place in the refrigerator to chill.

the container with potting soil. "The beauty of these containers is that you can make them as deep as you like," she says. "I like to transplant my tomato seedlings into deep pots after they grow their first true leaves. I bury them right up to their top leaves so the roots develop all the way up the stem." With their extra-deep root systems, her tomato plants get off to a great start in the garden!

## Seeds Take a Seat

Those fancy seed-starting setups you see in catalogs are enticing—until you look at the price! "I really wanted one of those metal shelving units with adjustable plant lights, but they sold for up to $600," recalls Pat Hall Borow of Decatur, Georgia. So about 5 years ago, she developed her own method. "It works great and is a whole lot cheaper than those commercial seed-starting units," she says.

Here's how to make your own: Place two ladder-back chairs facing one another, with the seats touching. Sow your seeds in two seed-starting trays with clear tops and drainage holes. Place the flats on a drip tray and set the tray across the seats. Take two fluorescent light sticks and tie a loop of string to the end of each stick. Then tie each end of the light stick to the bottom rung of the ladder-back chairs. (Use a slip knot or other temporary knot.) Now you have a light stick suspended just over each seed tray.

Keep the lids on the trays until your seeds have sprouted. When leaves begin to form, remove the clear lids, and water and feed the seedlings as needed. As the seedlings grow, simply raise the light sticks by re-tying the strings on the next rung up.

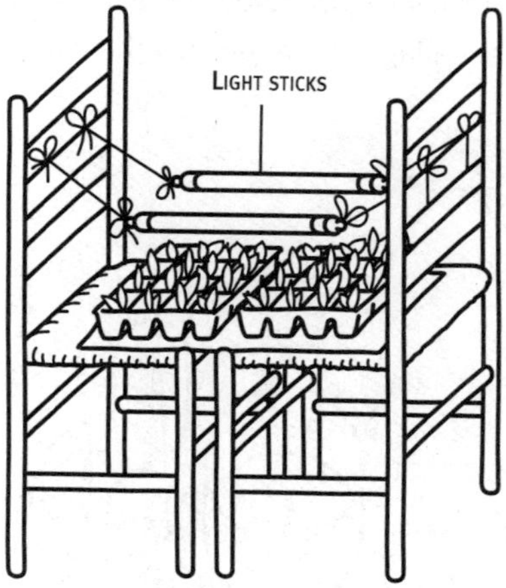


*PULL UP A COUPLE OF LADDER-BACK CHAIRS, HANG TWO LIGHT STICKS IN BETWEEN THEM, AND YOU HAVE A LOW-COST, NO-FRILLS, SEED-STARTING SETUP!*

# Build It!

## Adjustable Grow Lights

Fluorescent shop-light fixtures are invaluable for indoor seed starting, but the short hanging chains they come with can make adjusting their height a challenge. Don Engebretson, a Minnesota Master Gardener and avid seed-starter, uses a handy pulley system to make raising and lowering his lights a snap! "This setup produces thick and bushy plants every time," says Engebretson.

### Materials

Two U-hooks

2 clothesline pulleys

Two 10-foot clotheslines

4-foot fluorescent light fixture

2 S-hooks (usually supplied with fixture)

Two 1-foot lengths of light duty chain (usually supplied with fixture)

Heavy-duty alligator clips

Hammer or drill

### Directions

**1.** Install the U-hooks in your ceiling joists, spaced about 4 feet apart. Tap the end of each U-hook into the wood with a hammer (or predrill a hole if the wood is too hard), and then twist them until all the threads are in the wood.

**2.** Slip the ring on one pulley over the end of one U-hook. Repeat with the other pulley and U-hook.

**3.** Thread one end of each clothesline over each pulley. Tie one end of each clothesline to the end of a chain section.

**4.** Place the light fixture on the floor (if your seedlings will be sitting on the floor) or on your seed-starting bench. Hook one end of an S-hook onto the free end of the chain, and hook the other end of each S-hook onto the back of the fluorescent fixture.

**5.** Pull down on the free end of each clothesline to raise the light. Use the alligator clips to hold the ropes together when the lights are at the height you want (usually about 4 inches above the tops of the seedlings).

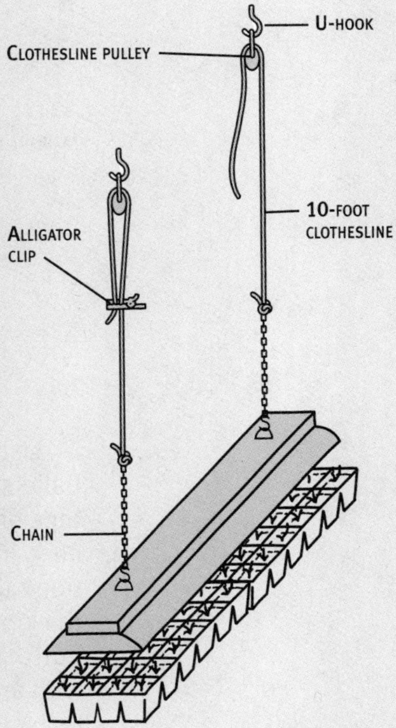

# Build It!

## A Pallet-Table Plant Bench

After Lisa Anne Haynes and her husband finished building a greenhouse for their Mahomet, Illinois, garden, they needed to furnish it with sturdy benches and tables to hold flats of seedlings and potted plants. Rather than buying benches, the Hayneses found a way to beat that expense by building plant benches out of wooden pallets. Those ubiquitous pallets are easy to come by, of course, and turning them into benches turned out to be a simple task, too.

### Materials

Used pallet

2 × 4, cut into four 3-foot lengths

Galvanized nails

Hammer

Saw

### Directions

**1.** Lay the pallet down flat on a work surface and nail one 3-foot-long 2 × 4 leg to each corner of the pallet, perpendicular to the pallet.

**2.** Depending on the construction of the pallet, you may need to cut off the ends of the bottom deck boards at the corner so the legs can butt against the main pallet skids. (See below for details.)

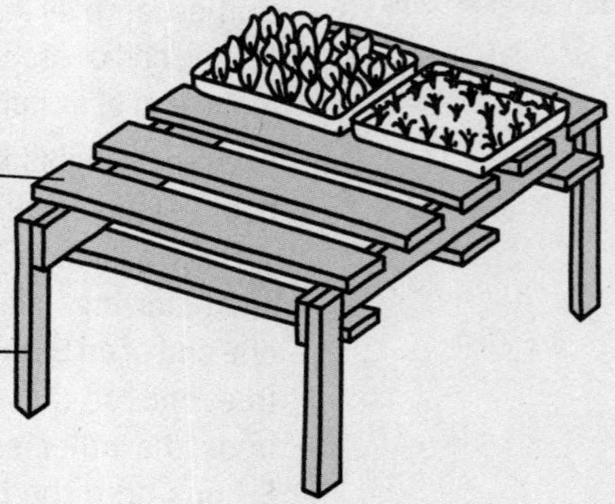


Lisa doesn't worry about the water that drips through the pallets when she waters her plants. In fact, she takes advantage of it by growing shiitake logs under the tables. However, early in the season, when she uses the benches as propagation tables, she covers the surface of the pallets with 3-mil-thick plastic, and places an electric space heater to provide bottom heat. After sowing her seed flats, she covers them with another sheet of plastic (over a bamboo frame) to keep the soil toasty and to encourage the seeds to pop up.

## Mini Shade House

When she has to harden-off a lot of seedlings, Caroline Whitenack of Doylestown, Pennsylvania, creates a temporary shade house in miniature. She builds four pillars by stacking three plastic milk crates for each pillar. Then, she uses four 2 × 4s to create a frame, using the milk crate pillars as the corners. Nail the 2 × 4s together. (The frame could be any size, and you can use whatever size 2 × 4 scrap pieces you have on hand.)

After Whitenack lays out the frame, she drapes plastic window screening over the top of the frame and uses a staple gun to attach the screening to the wooden frame. Allow the screening to extend almost down to the ground.

This mini shade house provides a large, sheltered area for flats of plants. "This works wonderfully for shading a large amount of tender seedlings for several days to a week. When that group is ready for transplanting, I bring out more plants to harden off," says Whitenack. When she's finished using the shade house, she just dismantles it and either uses the parts for something else or stores them away.

## No More Smashed Seedlings

Covering a seed-starting tray with plastic is a great way to provide emerging seedlings with a humid environment. Problem is, how do you keep the plastic off the seedlings? Lynn MacMahon, a gardener from Flushing, New York, came up with this resourceful way.

Heat an ice pick over the flame on a gas stove, and then use the pick to punch six holes in a plastic seed flat. (Wear heavy leather gloves while you do this to protect yourself from burns.) Punch one hole in each corner

### Recycle It!

***On hand:*** Paper cups

***Turn them into:*** Seed-starting containers

***How to do it:*** For an inexpensive alternative to peat or plastic pots, use small paper cups for indoor sowing of fast-growing plants, such as squash and melons. At planting time, it's easy to peel away the paper without damaging the roots.

### Recycle It!

***On hand:*** Used yogurt containers

***Turn them into:*** Seed-starting pots

***How to do it:*** Simply wash them out, poke a few small holes in the bottom, add seed-starting mix, and plant!

**Recycle It!**

***On hand:*** Opaque plastic sweater boxes

***Turn them into:*** Mini greenhouses for seed starting

***How to do it:*** Put small seed trays filled with sterile potting soil and your seeds inside these boxes, water from below, close the lid and set the boxes in a warm place until the seeds germinate. Then put the opened box under a set of fluorescent shop lights and watch the seeds grow.

and one in the middle of each long side of the flat. Cover the bottom of the tray with cat litter or perlite, and then put the pots in the tray.

Next, loop a piece of electrical wire from each corner hole to the opposite corner hole, and twist the ends in place to secure. Likewise, loop a piece through the two middle holes, and twist to secure. Finally, put a clear plastic bag over the entire setup, and tuck the bag under the tray or close it with a twist tie. The electrical wire frame will keep the plastic up off of the seedlings.

## Let There Be Light

Cuttings, germinating seeds, and indoor plants all benefit from direct light—something easily accomplished with an overhead lighting system. Here's how Lynn MacMahon of Flushing, New York, builds hers.

"I use a shop rack system and turn the steel shelving upside down, which makes a tray with a lip around it," MacMahon explains. "Then I line the shelf with heavy plastic and fill it with cat litter or perlite. I cover the shelf with nylon window screening and set the pots on top of the screening. The screening keeps the pots from sinking in and the cat litter keeps the environment humid. I hang shop lights for the bottom shelf from the shelf above and hang shop lights for the top shelf from the basement rafters." You could try this same set up in a garden shed or garage, as long as you have a source of electricity.

## Going to Great Lengths

All the seed packets give planting directions such as, "plant 2 to 3 inches apart," "plant in hills 2 to 3 feet apart," "plant 6 inches deep," and so on. But, how many gardeners do you know who carry yardsticks?

Use a permanent marker to mark off inches on your trowel, or inches and feet on the handle of your shovel or hoe. You can even mark off gallons on the inside of your bucket. Knowing how long your shovel is will also help you calculate heights of walls and trees and distances between objects. Even better, measure your body parts and memorize the lengths of your fingers, arms, reach, and height. You may forget your yardstick, but chances are good you won't go to the garden without your fingers!

# Build It!

## Dibble Board for Seed Trays

Once you've experienced the fun of growing plants from seed, it's easy to get carried away with indoor seed sowing. Dorothy Nichols, author of *Tips and Secrets for a Magnificent Garden*, knows all about that: Each year, she raises thousands of flower, herb, and ornamental grass seedlings for her Moscow, Idaho, all-organic, demonstration garden. To help speed up her sowings, she constructed a "dibble board" to create the proper size seed holes for her particular seed starter—an 8 × 12-inch Perma-Nest plant tray. You can make your own to fit your favorite seed-starting flat. Here's how:

**Materials**

Scrap piece of ¼-inch outdoor plywood

¾-inch galvanized roofing nails

Saw

Ruler or yardstick

Drill with 3/32-inch bit

Hammer

**Directions**

**1.** Measure your existing seed-starting flat and cut the plywood slightly smaller to fit just inside.

**2.** With the pencil and ruler or yardstick, draw lines 1½ inches apart across the plywood, lengthwise and widthwise. (This ensures that your dibble board will produce evenly spaced holes in the flat.) Drill a 3/32-inch pilot hole at each point where the lines intersect.

**3.** Drive the nails through the holes, all the way to the heads.

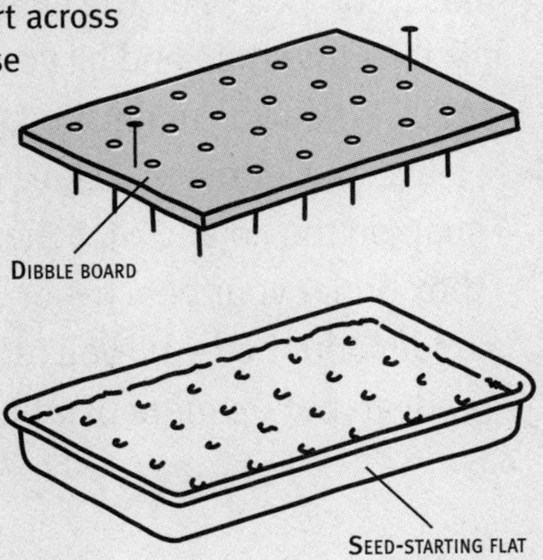


## Gadget Gold Mines

Do you have a sponge brush and hors d'oeuvre picks at home? Then you have some instant garden gadgets. Here's how you can use these items for your seed-starting efforts.

Hors d'oeuvre picks are handy for thinning out seedlings, suggests Chaz Macdonald of Center Valley, Pennsylvania.

Sponge paintbrushes with wooden handles are perfect for disinfecting the corners of six-pack pots, reports Macdonald.

**Recycle It!**

***On hand:*** Plastic, under-the-bed storage box

***Turn it into:*** Potting soil mixing bin

***How to do it:*** Put the box on your potting bench, tool bench, or kitchen table. Scoop in the ingredients of your potting medium (soil, peat moss, compost, and the like), mix it all together, and fill your pots. When you're finished, leave any leftovers inside, snap on the lid and tuck the box under your bench—or under your bed—till you're ready to pot up more plants.

## Good Night, Cozy Seedlings

Dyed-in-the-wool gardeners like to squeeze out as much growing season as they can. To do just that, Marina Wojciechowski of Lansdale, Pennsylvania, combines a raised bed coldframe with bricks to cheat the cold weather. Wojciechowski fills the frame with leftover bricks—the kind with three holes in them—spacing the bricks 2 inches apart. She pushes the bricks into the soil until the soil level is flush with the top of the bricks. Wojciechowski plants seeds in each hole and in the 2-inch spaces between the bricks.

During the day, the sun warms the bricks, which retain some of that heat during the cold overnights. Wojciechowski's brick trick helps her get an early jump on spring, starting zinnias and other semihardy plants this way. In about 2 weeks, or when the seedlings are abut 2 inches high, Marina gently lifts the bricks and pushes the seedlings out of their holes for transplanting or hardening-off. The seedlings in the 2-inch-wide spacer strips are easy to just lift up once the bricks have been removed.

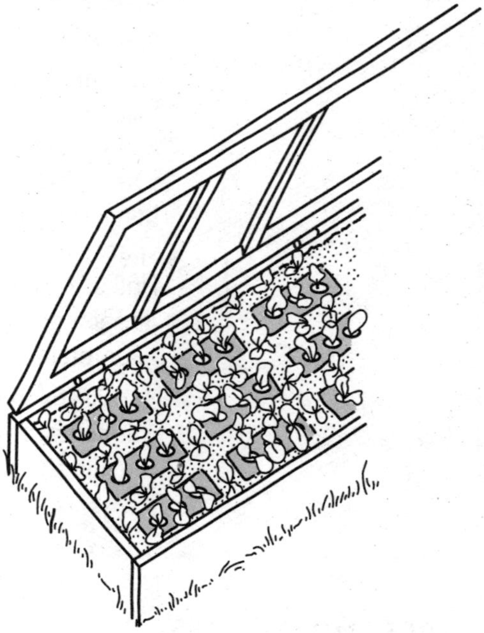

*Get a jump on spring by lining a coldframe with scavenged three-hole bricks. The bricks warm up quickly and make perfect seed "flats."*

# Storage Savers and Tool Organizers

Say good-bye to the days of lost garden gadgets. With a bit of brainstorming, storage will be a breeze and your seed, note, and tool-hunting days will be over. In this section, learn how to make your own "String Thing," "Plant Condo," seed recipe box, and tool caddy.

## File under "Salads"?

Keep your seed packets organized with the help of a recipe box. Label the dividers according to type of seed (annuals, perennials, greens, vegetables, and so on), and stash the seed packets there. For seed you've collected at home, put the seed in one of those tiny self-sealing plastic bags you can purchase at a jeweler, and label it with a permanent marker.

## Seeds on Ice

Andrea Ray Chandler, ace garden writer and photographer from Olathe, Kansas, stores all her seed packets in tight-sealing Tupperware containers. Before she shuts and "burps" the lid, she tosses in any desiccant packets that she finds in new shoe boxes. The boxes then go into her spare fridge, where the seeds will remain viable for several years.

## Safe for All Your Fine Herbs

Don't have room to hang your herbs to dry? Susan Albert, Texas author of the acclaimed China Bayles herbal mysteries, has found that the best way to dry her herb harvest is to use a portable sweater dryer. This simple device, available at many department stores, has a 2-foot-square mesh screen that's supported by 8-inch, foldable legs. Pick your herbs in the morning after the dew has dried off, then place them flat on the rack in the shade on a dry day. The rack works especially well for small-leaved herbs, such as thyme.

## Plant Condo

After remodeling her kitchen, Anne Cunningham, a writer for the Bay Area Gardener Web site, found herself with a number of white, plastic-coated wire storage baskets. The gardening lightbulb went off in her mind, and she envisioned these baskets as the perfect shelves for her numerous seedlings and transplants. Because these baskets stack, she could place the plants that require lots of sun on the top shelf and those that need shade underneath. The whole structure is very compact and looks quite colorful against the side of her house. Snails and slugs have trouble getting through the wire, but water gets through easily. If you can't find old wire baskets, you can buy new ones in all shapes and sizes at most home centers and hardware stores.

***On hand:*** Plastic strawberry flats

***Turn them into:*** Dahlia tuber holders

***How to do it:*** In early winter when frost has killed dahlia foliage, lift the tubers and shake off the soil. Then line each of the flat's compartments with a paper towel, set in the tubers—one per cubbyhole—and put the flat in a cool, dark place. The rectangular flats stack easily so they won't take up much space, and the ventilated sides will keep needed air circulating to the tubers all winter long.

## Well Noted

If you have trouble keeping track of your gardening notes and packets of leftover seeds, try using the binder system that Vermont garden writer Warren Schultz cooked up. Schultz admits he isn't the most organized gardener but says that his binder system is foolproof. To follow his example, you'll need a three-ring binder, four-pocket plastic photo sleeves, index cards, and a pen.

Schultz earmarks an index card for every pack of seeds, and after he sows the seeds, he writes all the relevant information on that card. When he's finished, he seals the seed pack with a piece of tape, then puts the pack and its index card into the same pocket of a photo sleeve. He inserts the sleeve into the binder and stores the binder on a shelf in a cool, not-too-sunny location.

Schultz takes the binder out into the garden with him to make notes on the cards, and then easily slips them back into the correct pockets. If he needs to make a second or third sowing of any variety, he knows right where to find the seeds. At the end of the gardening season, he slips a packet of silica gel or other desiccant into one of the pockets and stores the whole binder in a cool, dry place until the following year.

## String Thing

Gardeners go through a lot of string for tying, trellising, and marking out rows and beds. Those in the know realize that the large cones of cotton garden string are very cost-effective. But if you've ever tried to use one, you also realize that it's bulky and hard to handle and keep clean in the garden. What's more, you've probably longed for a third hand to help out—or at least a better way of managing the cone. Well, here's one! Using just a bleach bottle, Cheryl Coston of Fairdealing, Missouri, built her own "string thing," which makes dealing with these large cones easy.

To make a string thing, cut a flap in the side of a bleach bottle, making it large enough to slip the cone in. Then poke a hole in the cap with an ice pick. Set the cone inside the bottle and thread the end of the string through the cap. Stick a couple of pieces of Velcro on the flap so you can open and close it. Carry the string thing by the handle, and pull out the string as needed through the cap. All the while, the string stays clean and dry inside.

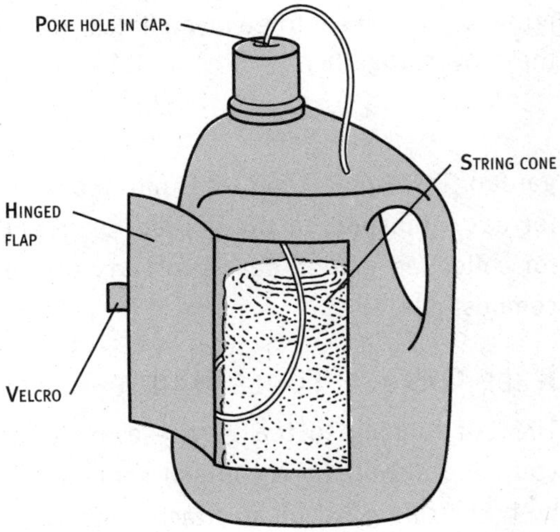


*WITH A FEW SIMPLE MODIFICATIONS, A BLEACH BOTTLE MAKES A HANDY CADDY FOR CARRYING STRING WHEREVER YOU NEED IT IN THE GARDEN.*

***ON HAND:*** Old filing cabinet

***TURN IT INTO:*** Tool storage chest

***HOW TO DO IT:*** An old metal or wooden file cabinet makes a great place to store hand tools, pruning tools, string, gloves, and all kinds of miscellaneous garden items.

## A Spicy Idea for Seed Storage

Viewing a herbarium at a seed laboratory gave Linda Harris, a Master Gardener from Fulton, Kentucky, a nifty idea for saving her own flower seeds from year to year. She uses an old wooden spice rack and recycled glass spice jars or pill bottles. The rack has three shelves and can hold about 15 bottles.

Linda collects seeds from faded garden flowers and lets them dry thoroughly. Then she pours the seeds into a clean, dry bottle and caps it. She says she also keeps leftover flower seeds from store-bought packets this way. (It's also good for herb seeds and small- to medium-size vegetable seeds.) "The bottles keep everything organized neatly and protect the seeds from humidity in the air," Linda says. "I use adhesive tape to label the bottles and write the flower name and

# Build It!

## Rust-and-Dirt-Defying Tool Bag

"I never used my fancy tool bags because I didn't want to get them dirty," says Carolyn Roof of Paducah, Kentucky. "Most hand-tool bags are heavy-duty canvas or lined with plastic. A wet tool left in the bag can easily rust, especially in our humid climate. The answer to wet tools and dirty bags came in the form of landscape fabric. You can buy it at any garden center; it comes in a roll about 45 inches wide, and it is available in various thicknesses. Choose the thickest fabric available for this project. It is soft, lets moisture out, is black, and is washable. Finally, I have a tool bag I really use."

**Materials**

- ½ yard of 45-inch-wide landscaping fabric
- Scissors
- Sewing machine and thread

**Directions**

**1.** Lay fabric out flat on cutting surface. Cut two 3-inch-wide strips from the short side for handles.

**2.** Fold each 18 by 3-inch strip in thirds lengthwise, to make it three layers thick. Stitch along the center of each handle, sewing all three layers together.

date on the tape with a ball-point pen." Her seed rack hangs on a hook in her mudroom, where the air is cool most of the time, and there's no direct sunlight. Once she's slipped on her gardening, the seeds are right there at her fingertips.

### A Peachy Carryall

If you enjoy buying peaches or other fruit direct from local orchards, you may have some extra peach baskets around your house or garage. Don't let them gather dust in a corner. They're a great lightweight carryall for the garden. Toss some hand tools into a basket for easy transport to the garden, or use it for collecting garden debris to carry to the compost pile.

### Keep Garden Tools Handy

Tired of running to the garage every time you need a tool? Save yourself some steps by trying this great idea: Attach a standard mailbox to a post right in your garden and use it to store some of your most-used hand tools and gloves. If you're like most gardeners, every time you walk through the

**3.** Fold down 1 inch on each short side of the remaining fabric. Stitch the fold in place to create the top hem.

**4.** Stitch one handle to each hemmed edge of the bag, placing the ends of the handle about 6 inches in from each outer edge of the fabric. To secure the handles, stitch in a square and then reinforce it by stitching an X over the squares.

**5.** Fold the body in half with the top seam folds to the outside. Sew up each side, allowing ½-inch seam allowance (creating the bag). Stitch again ¼ inch from your first row of stitching to reinforce the seam.

**6.** Turn bag right side out, stuff with tools, and go.

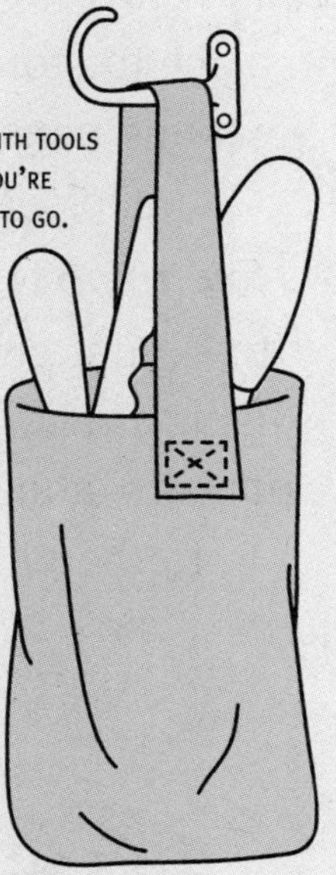

FILL WITH TOOLS AND YOU'RE READY TO GO.

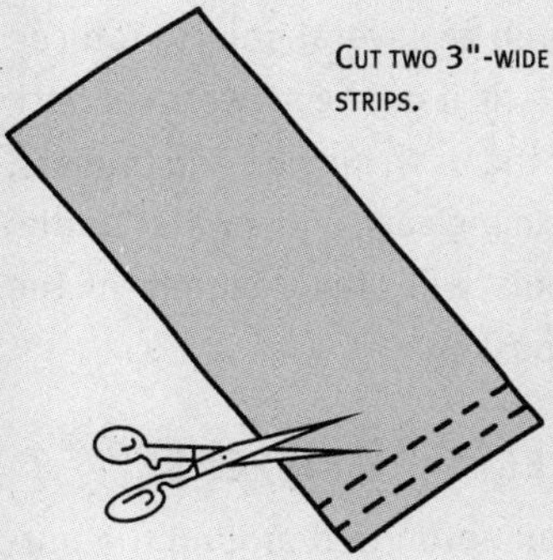

CUT TWO 3"-WIDE STRIPS.

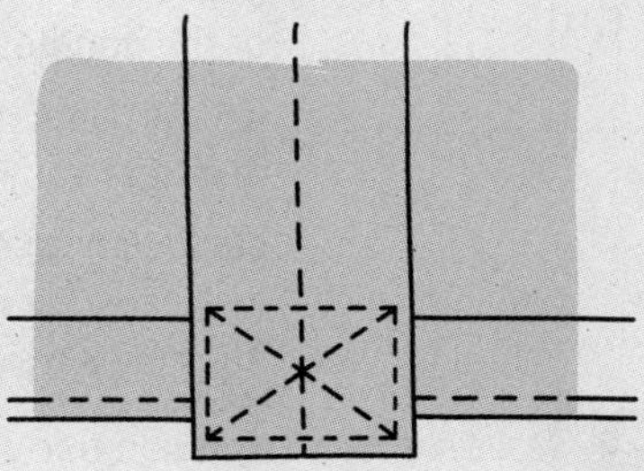

REINFORCE HANDLE BY STITCHING AN X OVER THE SQUARE.

yard, you find weeds to dig, spent flowers to snip, or branches to trim. Once you have a garden mailbox, your garden gloves, trowel, and pruners are handy whenever you need them!

## A Bucket Carryall

Old drywall-compound pails are free for the taking wherever you find drywallers and painters working. Warren Schultz of Essex Junction, Vermont, salvaged one and turned it into a garden carryall. Here's how to make your own: Wash and dry the bucket. Heat the end of a screwdriver over a fire or with a blow torch, and melt holes just below the lip of the bucket, spaced every 4 inches. Tie a nail apron (available from a hardware store) around the lip of the bucket with the pockets on the outside. Poke holes through the fabric to correspond to the holes in the bucket. Lace a leather shoelace through the holes to fasten the apron to the bucket. Put your seeds, notepaper, and pencils in the pockets and your hand tools in the bucket, and you have a handy way to carry all your gardening stuff wherever you need it!

Recycle It!

***On hand:*** A fishing vest

***Turn it into:*** A convenient place to store labels, marking pens, tissues, and seeds

***How to do it:*** Nothing to it. Just put on the fishing vest, pack the pockets, and head out to the garden.

Recycle It!

***On hand:*** A carpenter's belt

***Turn it into:*** A tool caddy

***How to do it:*** Strap on the belt, insert your tools, such as a trowel and pruners, and you're all set.

## Mower Caddy

"When mowing, I always seemed to find a twig that needed cutting, but it didn't get cut because the pruners were hanging in the house. The pruners just won't stay in my pocket," says Carolyn Roof of Paducah, Kentucky. "I came up with a simple solution. A carpenter's cloth apron is a wonderful hand-tool carrier that you can wear for either riding or push mowing."

She recommends making this modification to hold the tools in place in the apron: Cut a piece of 1-inch-wide elastic so it's slightly longer than the width of the apron pocket. Pin the elastic along the top edge of the pocket, stretching to fit. Anchor stitch at each end, and then sew the elastic to the apron at several points. You can wear the apron, or tie it on the mower seat back or the handles of the push mower. Add pruners, a sharpener, a pruning saw, and a water bottle, and go. Your tools will stay securely in the elastic-snugged pocket.

## The Gardener's "Briefcase"

You can use a nail apron tied around the outside of a 5-gallon plastic bucket for holding seeds, pruners, and tools. Fill the bucket with larger tools or garden supplies when going to and from the garden. Attach the lid to the bucket with a duct-tape hinge to create a waterproof supply trunk, or seat. Commercial garden tool buckets include inner, stacking trays, but resealable plastic bags work fine for thrifty gardeners.

## Dry Soak

You really can recycle anything. Case in point: Turn that old foot soaker into a tool or weed caddy. Bring it along to the garden and put

# Build It!

## Old-Time Tool Caddy

If you want the look of a weathered oldie without the antique-shop price tag, do what Juneau, Alaska, gardener Natasha Zahn Pristas did: Build your own. Here's how she did it.

### Materials

Two 1-inch-thick boards for ends, each 9 × 7¼ inches

Finish nails

Three 1-inch-thick boards for bottom and sides, each 19½ × 7½ inches

1½-inch-diameter dowel, about 19 inches long

Paint or stain (optional)

Saw

Drill

Hammer

### Directions

**1.** Cut the two rectangular end pieces so their sides angle to a top width of 3½ inches, as shown in the illustration below.

**2.** Predrill the nail holes, and nail the bottom and side panels together.

**3.** Predrill nail holes for the angled end pieces, and nail them to the sides and bottom of the box.

**4.** Measure the dowel for a tight fit, and cut it to the inside length of the box (it will be roughly 18½ inches). Predrill nail holes in ends of caddy. Make pilot holes in dowel.

**5.** Nail the dowel/handle in place.

**6.** Paint or stain the box, or leave it to weather naturally.

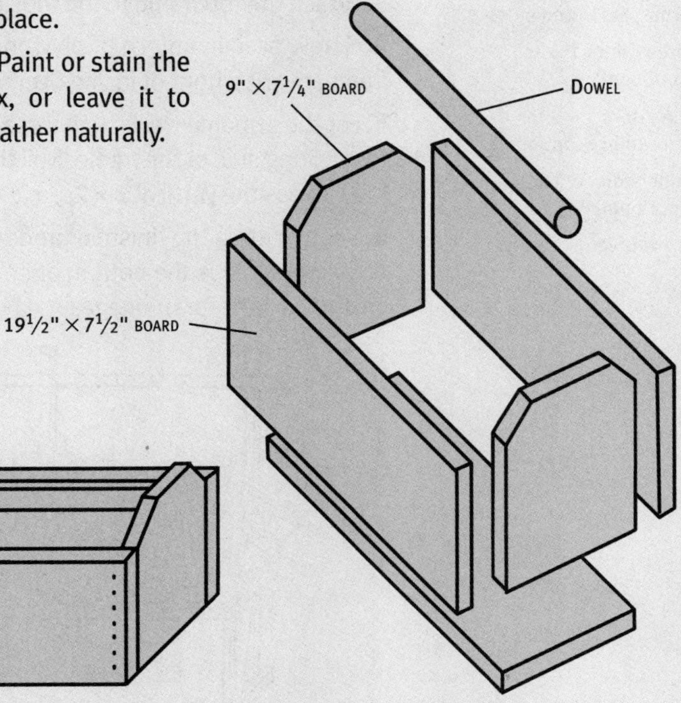

# Build It!

## Container Corral

If you garden in containers on a roof deck or wind-swept terrace, or—as Victoria Hawley does in Portland, Oregon—on a houseboat, this bottomless frame could save your prized plants from taking to the sky in a stiff breeze.

### Materials

You can use whatever lengths of materials suit your needs. This size is designed to use five office-sized plastic garbage cans for containers.

Four 6½-foot 1 × 2s

Eight 10-inch 1 × 2s

Screws or galvanized nails

Eight 16-inch 1 × 2s

¼-inch plywood to form the front, back, and sides

Three 4-foot 1 × 2s (optional)

One 7-foot 1 × 2 for crosspiece (optional)

Paint, stain, or varnish (optional)

Screwdriver or hammer

### Directions

**1.** Screw or nail two 6½-foot 1 × 2s and two 10-inch 1 × 2s together to form a rectangle. Screw or nail two 10-inch 1 × 2s 27 inches in from each end to form a reinforcement large enough for the center container (this will be the bottom part of the frame). Make a second rectangle the same way (this will be the top part of the frame).

**2.** Screw or nail one of each of the 16-inch 1 × 2s to a corner of the bottom frame, including the center rectangle, so that the 1 × 2s are vertical.

**3.** Attach the top frame to the tops of the vertical 1 × 2s.

**4.** Screw or nail a piece of plywood facing to each side of the frame; overlap front of facing over sides of facing.

**5.** For the optional trellis, nail three 4-foot-long 1 × 2s vertically to one long side of the frame. Nail the 7-foot-long 1 × 2 horizontally across the vertical 1 × 2s, a few inches from their tops.

**6.** Paint or stain the finished product as desired and set in your containers. Leave the bottom open for drainage. Place the pots on 1 × 2 scraps for drainage.

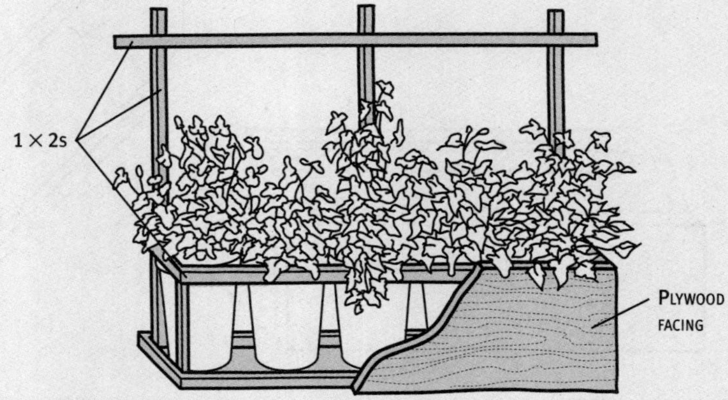

weeds in it as you pull them out, or fill it with tools before you head out to the garden so you can carry everything you need at once.

## A Tisket, a Tasket

A totable basket! Made from three used coffee cans, this nifty flower-collecting tote is the ultimate in recycling. Linda Harris of Fulton, Kentucky, says that she finds it's best to use coffee cans of the same size to keep the tote balanced. It's also a nice touch to spray paint the cans to add an artistic touch.

After the paint is dry, set the first can on a level surface. Wrap and tie one end of a ball of twine around the can. Wrap the twine around the can several times, then wrap it around a second can, pulling the second can close to the first one. Wrap the twine around the second can several times, then repeat the wrapping for a third can. The cans will form a triangle. Wrap the twine all the way around the outside of the three joined cans until the cans are tightly lashed together. Knot the twine securely in the wrapping on one side.

To make a comfy twine handle, cut three lengths (or six for a wider handle) of twine about 36 inches long. Holding the twine lengths together as if they were one, knot them to the twine on one side of the can tote. Braid or twist the lengths, then knot them to the twine on the opposite side of the tote.

Keep flower cutters or hand pruners in one of the cans, and fill the two other cans with water to take to the garden when cutting flowers. The water-filled cans will keep your cut flowers fresh and wilt-free until you get back to the house to arrange them.

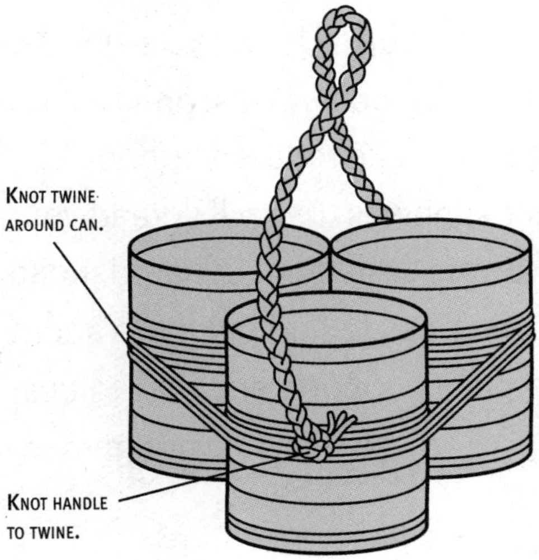


*Tie metal coffee cans together for a handy cut-flower tote.*

# Trellises and Supports

Running out of room in your garden? Think "up"! Use bicycle wheels, chopsticks, baby gates, and tomato cages to make trellises, arbors, and other supports that will spread your plants upward instead of outward. Read the following tips to find out more about creating plant supports and how to best use them in your garden.

## GORGEOUS GARAGES

The front of most garages are pretty stark, but they don't have to be that way. You can dress up your garage door with perennial twining vines—good choices are kiwis (*Actinidia* spp.), five-leaved akebia (*Akebia quinata*), Dutchman's pipes (*Aristolochia* spp.), bittersweets (*Celastrus* spp.), sweet autumn clematis (*Clematis terniflora*), jasmine, and pyracanthas. Other vines are suitable also, as long as they won't grow taller than 20 to 30 feet.

On either side of the garage door plant your vine of choice (just be sure it won't grow taller than 20 to 30 feet). Install galvanized eye screws in regularly spaced intervals up the sides of the door and above the door. (Do this so you can thread the wire in a zigzag pattern.) For larger vines, install the screws all the way up to the roof. Then thread galvanized wire through each eye, looping it around the eye screws at least once—and, voilà, you have a sturdy wire trellis, and within a year or two, that baked stretch of garage front will be a sea of greenery. (Give the vines a good pruning two or three times a year to keep them in check.)

*USE AN ON-THE-WALL VINE TRELLIS TO TURN A DULL GARAGE FRONT INTO A SEA OF GREEN.*

## CHICKEN OUT YOUR VINES

Each time a heavy wind whips up, Tucson, Arizona, gardener Sue Giles can expect to see some of the mature vines that cloak her neighbor's adobe house flopping in the yard. That's because twining-type vines don't cling well to adobe without a trellis, and many homeowners don't want to install supports, fearing they'll damage the adobe. But Giles came up with a novel solution to the problem at her own home. She nailed chicken wire to unseen portions of her roof, allowing the vines to secure themselves to the wire.

This method works best if you have a flat roof where you can install the chicken wire out of sight. But small amounts of chicken wire could be nailed to angled roofs, too, especially if the wire is spray painted first in a color that matches the roof.

## Fishing for a Trellis

Clear monofilament fishing line makes one of the fastest, lowest-maintenance, and most invisible trellises there is. Simply hammer in a pattern of nails into your house where you want vines to grow, adding a dab of paint to conceal the nails. Then twist and tie on the fishing line.

*Create an invisible trellis in minutes using fishing line.*

## Wine and Roses

Part of the fun of gardening is finding new uses for unusual items. Martha Neal always keeps her eyes peeled for interesting objects to complement her many beds and borders on her 10 acres in Hamden, Connecticut. When she spotted several nifty copper-colored promotional wine racks in her local liquor store, she knew right away how lovely her morning glories would look twining up the curved metal sides. After a few well-placed "bribes" of cookies and coffee to the store staff, they gave the racks to her when the promotion was over. Neal set the 6-foot-high, freestanding racks in her gardens and weighted the bases down with some of the ever-present rocks from her New England soil. All her vining annuals and perennials enjoy the spirited supports, and Neal enjoys the classy look they lend to her winter landscape.

## Caged Beauties

Few garden sights are as sad as beautiful peony blooms sprawling face down in the mud. But if you've ever priced those commercial peony hoops, you're likely looking for a less expensive staking solution. Jan Hale Barbo, the garden columnist for the *Santa Fe New Mexican,* has the answer!

After planting 50 peonies around her Espanola, New Mexico, home, Barbo tried using those inexpensive, cone-shaped, 3-foot-high tomato cages that are sold at most hardware stores. However, once the cages were installed, she noted that "the bare metal looked horrible and shiny and detracted from the graceful beauty of my peonies." Barbo solved this problem by grouping all the cages together in the back of an old trailer and spraying them with hunter green paint. Now she has perfect flower supports:

**ON HAND:** Siberian iris leaves

**TURN THEM INTO:** Organic twine

**HOW TO DO IT:** Use Siberian iris leaves instead of garden twine or plastic wire twist-ties for tying up tomato bushes, staking lilies, or any taller veggie or perennial. This material is very durable, says Minnesota gardener Don Engebretson, and it turns a pleasant golden brown, giving your garden a kind of country look.

"They blend and disappear into the landscape even before the foliage emerges enough to hide them." She also finds that these colored cages work great for other tall and floppy flowers such as Oriental poppies (*Papaver orientale*).

## UNDERWIRE SUPPORT

Those plant supports you see in the catalogs are neat, but they're also expensive. So why not build your own? That's what Master Gardener Bob Mortiz of Sioux City, Iowa, does. He bends a 72-inch length of #9 galvanized wire into a circle, leaving about 30 inches on one end vertical. Then he sticks the straight end of the wire into the soil—and, voilà, an instant plant support. Mortiz notes that this support works great by itself, or you can make a bunch of supports and place them in a circle, which he says works wonders holding up peonies in bloom.

*SAVE MONEY BY MAKING YOUR OWN PLANT SUPPORTS OUT OF WIRE.*

## SAFE AND STRETCHY PLANT TIE

When it's time to trellis her vegetable plants, Cheryl Coston of Fairdealing, Missouri, raids the clothes drawer. "I use old T-shirts and socks cut into strips as plant ties," she says. "They're very strong and stretchy, so they give as the plant grows. Dark colors, except red, blend in with the foliage and aren't noticeable after a week or so, when the color fades."

## WINDOW FRAME TRELLIS

Nothing conveys the romance of a cottage garden quite as well as a window surrounded by clematis, roses, or other flowering vines. Caroline Jumper of San Jose, California, has developed a very simple and inexpensive way to get that look. Using a few simple materials, she and her husband have constructed removable supports for vining flowers all around their house (and along a fence as well).

All it takes is some 12- to 14-gauge wire, four 2- to 3-inch-long eye screws, and a turnbuckle for each window trellis. Install the eye screws into the side of the house at the corners of the window (or wherever desired). Run a length of wire through all four eye screws, then attach the free ends to the turnbuckle (position this wherever you can reach it easily). "The eye screws keep the wire a few inches from the house, which is enough room for good air circulation," Jumper says. "And the turnbuckle allows us to tighten the wire as needed or remove it easily when it's time to paint or take the roses down for serious pruning."

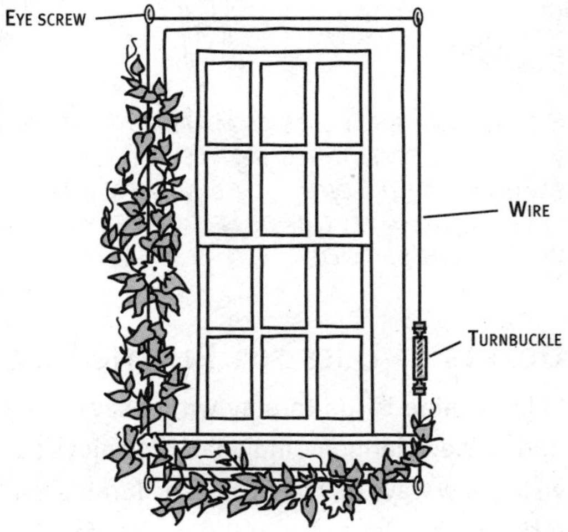


*GIVE YOUR HOME A COTTAGE-GARDEN LOOK BY CREATING WINDOW TRELLISES FOR FLOWERING VINES.*

**Recycle It!**

***ON HAND:*** Old tent frame parts

***TURN THEM INTO:*** Garden trellis

***HOW TO DO IT:*** Put together the tent frame or frames—without the tent—then place in a sunny location in your garden. Cut pieces of heavy string long enough to reach your plants. Tie one end of each string to the top of the frame and gently wrap the free end around the stem of tomatoes, peas, or other vines to guide them upward.

## REBAR TO THE RESCUE

Climbing roses and flowering vines add a touch of country charm to any garden. To show off his climbers, Bill Robinson of Sierra Madre, California, prefers arbors and teepee-shaped support structures, but he found that commercial trellises were quite expensive. So he decided to make his own, and he found the perfect material to make them: concrete reinforcing metal, or rebar. "You can buy a 20-foot length of ¼-inch rebar at a home-supply store for a couple of bucks," Robinson says. "It's very strong but relatively easy to work with, and it turns a lovely shade of rust after being exposed to the elements, which blends in with the stems."

To make a rebar teepee, take a 20-foot length of ¼-inch rebar, grab it firmly by one end, and enlist a friend to do the same at the other end. Place the center point of the bar against a strong post, then walk toward each other until the rebar is bent into a U. Repeat with a second piece of rebar. Carry the bent rebar to the garden and push the ends of one U into the ground as far as you can. Prop a length of 2 × 4 against it if needed to hold it upright while you get the second piece in position. Place the second U over the first, oriented in the opposite direction to create a cross pattern at the top. Push the second U into the ground until the arches meet at the top center, then fasten them together with wire. "I train all kinds of climbers to grow up and through this simple structure, and it looks lovely," Robinson says.

To make a rebar arbor, bend two 20-foot pieces of rebar as you would for a teepee, but don't make the bend so sharp: You want the ends to be 5 to 6 feet apart. Push the ends of the first length of arch into the ground enough to stabilize it. Place the second arch parallel to the first arch, 1 to 2 feet away, and push the ends into the ground. Cut five or six crosspieces of rebar to length with a hacksaw—they should overlap the arches a couple inches on each end. Fasten the crosspieces to the arches by wrapping wire in an X pattern around each intersection.

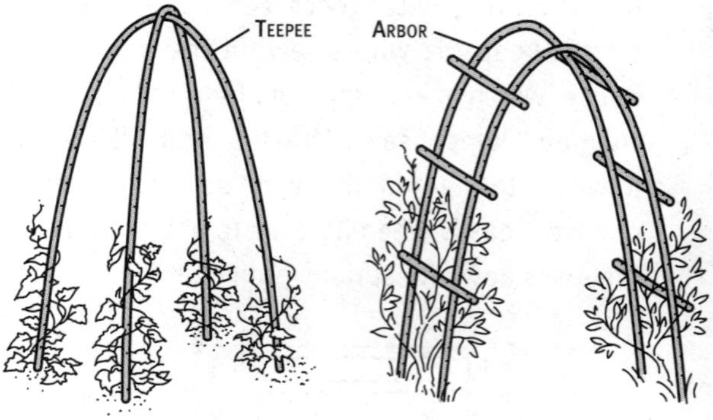


*REBAR MAKES A GREAT MATERIAL FOR A VARIETY OF VINE SUPPORTS. BOTH TWINING AND TENDRIL-CLIMBING VINES FIND IT EASY TO GRAB. IT'S LOVELY WITH ROSES, TOO!*

**Recycle It!**

***ON HAND:*** Old Christmas tree

***TURN IT INTO:*** Pole bean trellis

***HOW TO DO IT:*** "Replant" the old tree by sinking it into a hole deep enough to keep it upright. Then plant your pole beans around the bottom but away from the trunk a bit so they get enough light.

## DOZENS OF USES FOR PLASTIC PIPE

"Plastic pipe is fun to play with," says Sally Roth of New Harmony, Indiana, who enjoys devising new ways to use the cheap, durable material. So far, she has used PVC pipe to fashion trellises, make columns to hold butterfly feeders and birdbaths, to support floppy plants, and to predator-proof her birdhouse posts. "I never work from a pattern or plan," she says. "I just figure it out as I go along. I've only had two problems with it so far: First of all, that white pipe sticks out like a sore thumb, so I paint it a dark color that blends in better. (See "Build It!" on page 317 for de-

# Build It!

## Bicycle-Wheel Trellis

Frank Fowlie, a Master Gardener from Mountain View, California, turned an old bicycle wheel into a unique trellis for his runner beans and erected it in a raised bed. Here's how to do it.

### Materials

- 1 metal pipe, slightly smaller in diameter than the hole in the wheel
- Three lag bolts
- 28-inch bicycle wheel
- Nails or tent pegs
- Twine
- Drill
- Hammer

### Directions

**1.** Drill three holes 1 inch down from the top of the pipe, and insert the bolts so they stick out about an 1 inch to support the wheel.

**2.** Pound the pipe into the ground and set the wheel in place over the pipe.

**3.** Hammer a nail into the edge of the raised bed directly under each spoke. If you don't have a raised bed, you can use tent pegs pounded directly into the soil.

**4.** Attach one end of a piece of twine to each nail, run the twine up over the spoke above the nail, and back down again, and attach this end of twine to the nail. Repeat this process for each nail.

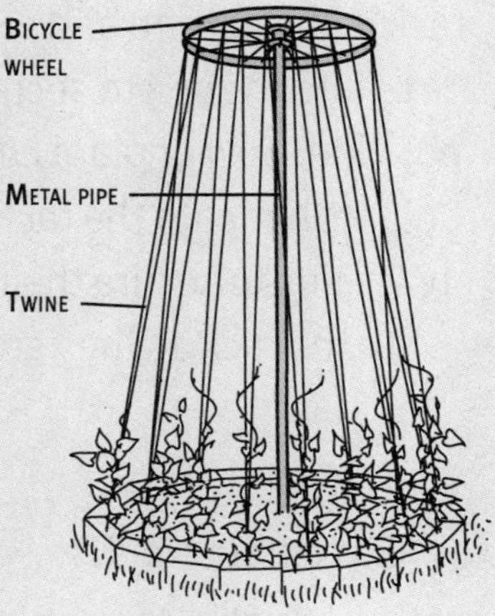


tails.) Second, raffia and wire slip off the pipe, so when I want to make trellises, I use duct tape to fasten the ends, then wrap with raffia to hide the tape."

## Help Young Vines Climb

To help tiny vining plants—such as sweet peas, morning glories, and thunbergias—find their way to a trellis, tie string around the head of a long nail. Sink the nail into the ground next to the seedling and tie the string onto the trellis. Attach the vine (gently!) to the string with a twist-tie.

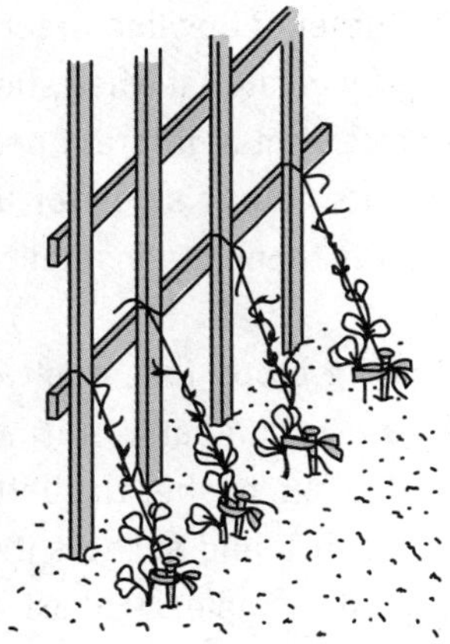

*Give small vining plants a sense of direction by guiding them toward the trellis.*

**Recycle It!**

***On hand:*** A wooden clothes-drying rack

***Turn it into:*** A trellis

***How to do it:*** Simply unfold the rack in the garden and push the legs into the soil to secure it in position. Sow or plant creeping plants beneath the rack. Use twist-ties to secure their vines to the rack as they grow.

## Baby Gates Grow Up

Inexpensive, versatile, and storable: Those are the qualities that most of us look for in trellises. Becky Turner of Bowling Green, Indiana, found the perfect material when she viewed a common object from a different perspective. Now she haunts garage sales for used baby gates, and turns them into instant trellises in her garden.

For sprawling crops that don't climb too tall, such as cucumbers, Turner simply stretches a gate out, pushes the bottom 1 or 2 inches into the dirt, and anchors it with 5- to 6-inch-long garden staples. (For extra stability, hammer two 1 × 2 posts into the ground at each end of the gate and attach them with cord, wire, or reinforced packing tape.) As your crops grow, help their vines climb over the support. For climbing plants like morning glories, Turner stands a gate on end beside a wall or post and anchors the bottom to the ground with garden staples. She then expands the gate and, using heavy-duty twist-ties, fastens the other end with screws or nails driven into the wall or post.

Don't have a baby gate available for trellising? The sturdy metal springs from an old crib make a good substitute! For a freestanding trellis, sink two 5-foot-tall, 2 × 2 posts about 1 foot deep into the soil and as far apart as the width of the springs. Stand the springs on end between the posts, and lash the springs securely to the posts using wire or rope. To use the springs against a wall or fence, screw four eye screws into the wall or fence, conforming to the dimensions of the spring frame, and fasten the springs to it using wire or rope. Sow or set climbing plants at the base.

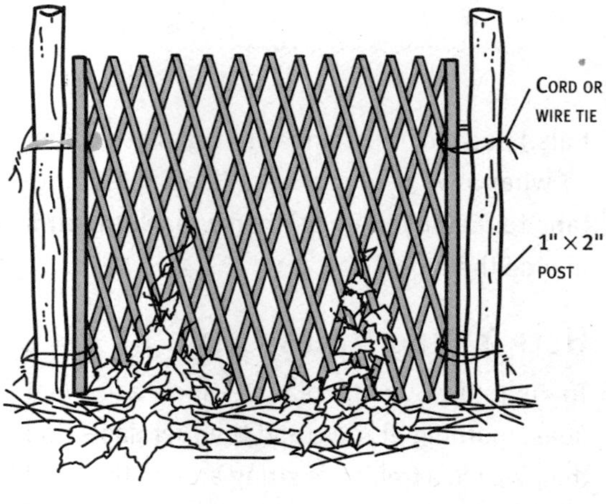


*Just because your kids are grown doesn't mean you have to throw out that baby gate; transform it into a garden trellis.*

# Build It!

## Steel Cable Spool Trellis

Spent steel cable spools are commonly free for the hauling and offer tempting design possibilities despite their rough appearance. With a little ingenuity, you can create a beautiful trellis that you won't need to hide in the back lot. (If you can't find an abandoned spool by the side of the road, call your local telephone or cable TV company.)

### Materials

- Empty wooden steel cable spool
- Three $1\frac{1}{2}$-inch wood screws
- 6- to 8-foot-long wood pole ($1\frac{1}{2}$-inch dowel or hand-rail stock)
- 2-inch galvanized roofing nails
- Big ball of heavy-duty string
- Seeds
- Screwdriver
- Hammer
- Ax or saw

### Directions

**1.** Prepare a level site for the trellis by clearing an area about 3 feet wider than the actual spool. Position the spool so it's stable—use wood shims to level if necessary.

**2.** Insert the three $1\frac{1}{2}$-inch screws at even intervals around the pole about 1 inch below the top end. Place the other end of the pole through the middle of the spool and hammer it into the ground until it is secure—about 1 foot deep is good. (Use an ax or a saw to shape a point on the end of pole if the soil is hard.)

**3.** Hammer galvanized roofing nails spaced 3 inches apart around the base and top of spool, leaving $\frac{1}{2}$ inch of the nail head exposed.

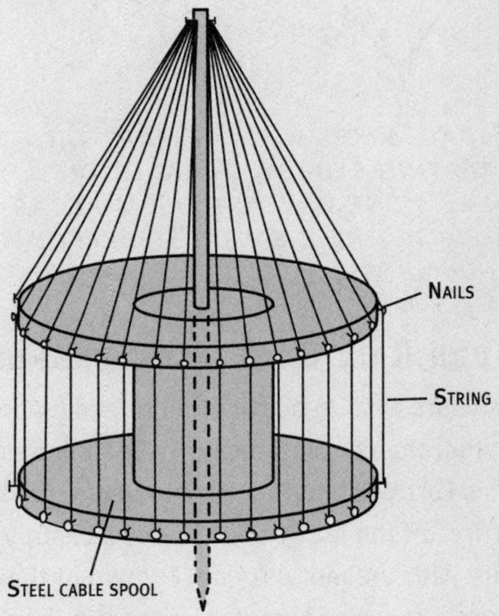


**4.** Tie strong string securely to a nail at the base of the spool. Run the string up to the top of the spool and twist it around a nail once or twice, and then run the string to the top of the pole and twist it around a screw. Then run the string down to the base of the spool and begin again. Repeat the process until all the nails are strung and the trellis is complete. If you run out of string, simply tie a new piece of string to the nail and begin threading the string again.

**5.** Plant seeds or transplants around the base of the trellis. If needed, train young vines to the string by securing them with twist-ties. Before long, that old spool will be hidden behind a glorious display!

## Rebar the King

One of the great quests for gardeners, especially vegetable gardeners, is the search for the perfect staking material. Linda Monier of Olive Branch, Mississippi, believes she's found the right stuff: concrete reinforcing metal, commonly known as rebar.

"I thought of it when we were building a new garage next to our house and had to go buy rebar for the foundation," says Linda. Admiring the 20-foot-long metal rods for their strength and durability, she realized they would make perfect, indestructible trellises. But first, the rebar had to be cut down to size. "I just had my husband, Marty, buy a few extra 4-gauge rods, the thickest diameter, and cut them into thirds with an acetylene torch." Marty suggests you could instead cut them with a hacksaw, or have the concrete supply house cut them to your specifications. "I use them for staking tomatoes, beans, or whatever needs it," Linda says.

That's not all. "We also cut some in half and used them to create an A-frame with plastic netting on both sides for my cucumbers. The fruits grow straighter and longer, and I have a great place to get out of the summer sun in the garden! I can also plant my summer lettuces under the A-frame to keep the intense heat off of them."

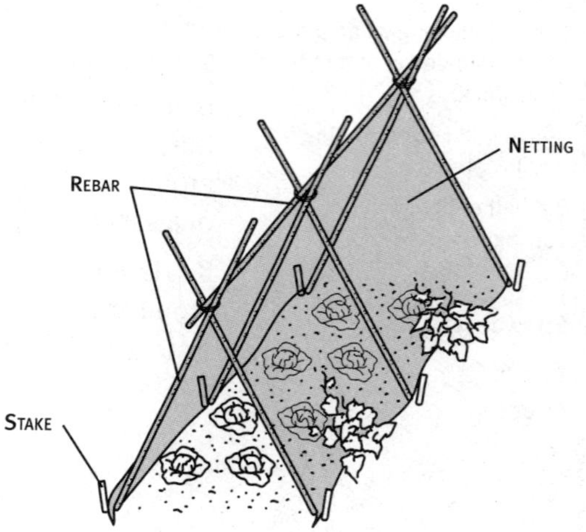


*Rebar makes a great material for creating sturdy, durable trellises. Here's one way to build a rebar A-frame trellis that's perfect for cucumbers.*

***On hand:*** Old chopsticks

***Turn them into:*** Houseplant supports

***How to do it:*** Dig those old chopsticks out of your kitchen drawer and put them to good use as a support for tall, floppy, or twining houseplants.

## Turn Rain Gear into Sunshine

Not sure what to do with that ripped umbrella? Rather than throw it away, try Bea Kline's trick. This Fort Washington, Pennsylvania, gardener strips off the fabric and creates a canopy topiary with the metal frame. Try two of these at the entrance of a garden or even in your vegetable bed for a striking, formal look.

## Living Garden Art

Create a sure conversation piece with a worn-out lawn chair! Simply remove the tattered webbing from a metal lawn chair, and secure the chair frame to the ground with U-shaped metal pins over the bottom bars. According to Bea Kline, of Fort Washington, Pennsylvania, you can create an interesting, large-scale topiary. A fast-climbing vegetable like scarlet runner beans is all you need. Plant seeds or transplants around the base of the chair—and, voilà, your "living" chair will be a definite ice breaker for your next garden party.

# Build It!

## PVC Garden Entry Posts

Before Sally Roth of New Harmony, Indiana, uses any PVC in her garden, she gives it a quick spritz of spray paint. "I usually use matte-finish black or very dark green-black," she says, "which practically disappears among the greenery. One of my favorite projects was a pair of simple PVC gateposts that defined the entrance to a hot-colored butterfly garden of orange, yellow, and red flowers. I sprayed those pipes bright cobalt blue. It made me feel as if I were in Mexico."

### Materials

Spray paint in your choice of color

Two 7-foot sections of 5- to 6-inch-diameter PVC pipe

Two PVC end caps, to fit pipe, and glue

Gallon bucket of ordinary soil (for each pipe)

Level

Funnel

Shovel or post-hole digger

### Directions

**1.** Spray paint pipes and caps. If coverage is spotty, let dry and apply a second coat of spray paint.

**2.** Dig a 2-foot-deep hole for each post, using a shovel or post-hole digger. Have a helper hold the pipe in place while you backfill. Use a level to keep the posts plumb. Tamp thoroughly with feet. While the helper supports the pipes, pour a bucket of soil into each, using the funnel to weight the bottom ends.

**3.** Attach end caps to one end of each pipe section with glue, as per supplier's instructions. Let dry. Touch up with spray paint if needed.

# Build It!

## Twig Trellis

"When I moved to a new home where the electric meter was situated in an extremely unattractive place on the house wall facing the swimming pool, I built a decorative twig trellis to hide it," says Barbara Reese Yager of Charlotte, North Carolina. She collected branches until she had enough for the design, and then used supplies she had on hand to complete it. "The result was a perfectly lovely focal point against the wall, which also cleverly screened the meter from view." Yager built this trellis to fit a specific wall space. You can adjust the dimensions of your trellis to fit any area you like by selecting longer or shorter branches. Train a vine on the trellis (clematis would be very attractive in a sunny location) or just let it stand decoratively.

**Materials**

- 4 attractive tree branches, 8 to 10 feet long and 1 to 1½ inches in diameter
- 6 to 8 attractive tree or shrub branches, 5 to 6 feet long and ½ to 1 inch in diameter
- Baling twine or rawhide strips
- Mounting nails or mortar pins (depending on the surface to which you're attaching it)
- Pruners

**Directions**

**1.** Collect the branches. If you have woods on your property, you can gather them there. If not, call a local tree-trimming service to see if they can provide what you need.

### Raising the Stakes

If you love reusing cast-off items, try these tips from Charles Cresson, horticulturist, garden consultant, and author from Swarthmore, Pennsylvania. Broom handles, mop handles, and such make sturdy, nicely finished stakes for garden use. He also adds old galvanized water pipes (no lead, please) for staking taller plants and young trees. The shorter pipes make good markers for small trees and shrubs. Simply drive three short pipes in a protective triangle around the young plant. The pipes protect from trampling and mower damage, he notes. Cresson also likes concrete rebar for tall perennials and young trees. "The natural color blends well with the landscape, rebar lasts forever, and it never breaks as other stakes often do with time," he says. "If you don't have any lying around from that last foundation or driveway project, many home centers sell short lengths or will cut long pieces to any length you need," Cresson remarks.

**2.** Lay the four longer branches (the uprights) on a flat surface such as a floor or patio, spacing them about 12 inches apart. Use the larger-diameter ends as the bottom, lining them up so the base will be even.

**3.** Lay the smaller branches (the crosspieces) across the uprights in a pleasing pattern. They can be spaced equidistantly, as shown here, or placed against the uprights in any pattern you like. Leaving a stub, start lashing a crosspiece to an upright, wrapping twine in an X. Several wraps for each side of the X should be sufficient. Cut and fasten off the twine.

**4.** Repeat for each joining, until every joint is lashed and fastened.

**5.** Using pruners, shape and finish off the ends of the uprights and the stubs of the crosspieces so they are eye-pleasing to you.

**6.** Lash the finished trellis to nails, mortar pins, or fence posts.

**7.** Plant a vine at base, if desired.

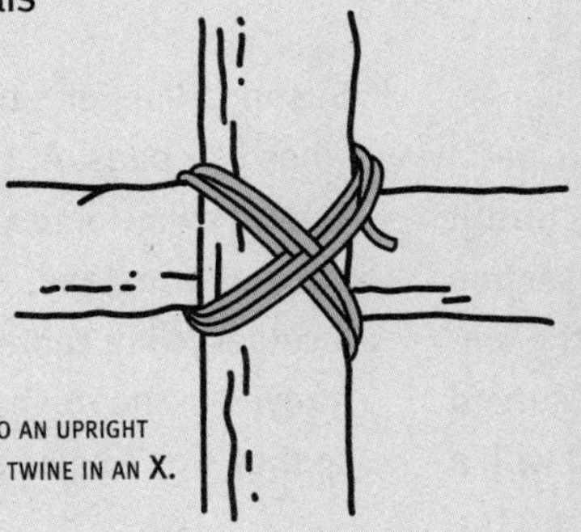

LASH A CROSSPIECE TO AN UPRIGHT BRANCH BY WRAPPING TWINE IN AN X.

## FUN FENCE-POST FINIALS

"I wanted a pretty finishing touch for the handmade wooden fence my neighbor crafted for me, but didn't want to spend a fortune on fancy carved finials," says Caroline Whitenack of Doylestown, Pennsylvania. "So I got the idea to use 4-inch clay flower pots to top the fence posts."

Whitenack painted the pots to match the fence, using outdoor latex paint. If your pots fit snugly over the fence post, there's no need to secure them further. If the pots wiggle and slide off the fence posts, Whitenack has an ingenious trick for keeping them in their place: For each fence post, cut a short piece of 1/4-inch wooden dowel the same height as each pot, and then drill a 1/4-inch-diameter × 3/4-inch-deep hole in the top of each fence post. Glue the dowel in place. When the glue dries, set the pots upside down over the top end of the fence posts. Whitenack said that the pots looked so cute that she received many compliments. And the pots wintered well outdoors to boot!

# Build It!

## Cucumber Ladder

Frank Fowlie, a Master Gardener from Mountain View, California, says cukes grow better on this sturdy, slanted trellis than on any other support he has found. His leans up against a wall of a three-bin composter, but yours could find a home on any sunny patch of garden beside your garage, a tool shed, or a fence.

**Materials**

Two 4-foot 2 × 4s for the runners

Seven 5-foot 1 × 2s for the risers

Nails

Hammer

Saw

**Directions**

**1.** Saw one end of each 2 × 4 at an angle. (This will allow the finished ladder to sit flush against its support wall.)

**2.** Starting at soil level, nail both ends of the 1 × 2 risers to the 2 × 4 runners at 6-inch intervals to form a ladder.

**3.** Lean the finished ladder against its support wall, plant your crop, and let 'er rip.

## Undressed Umbrella

So a recent windstorm de-frocked your patio umbrella? Don't throw it out. Instead, turn it into a topiary frame. Here's how. Sink a section of PVC pipe into the ground and pop in the umbrella shank. (If your umbrella has a curved handle, you may have to cut that off first with a saw.) Plant ivy at the base, and train it up the shaft and then later out across the spokes.

## Soda Pop Six-Pack Trellis

Here's a creative way to get a second use out of plastic six-pack holders: Turn them into a trellis. All you need besides the holders are some twist-ties and either dowels or 2 × 4s. Simply fasten the six-hole plastic rectangles together with twist-ties to make a trellis of any size and shape you want. Thread dowels through the top and bottom rows of holes and fasten the top dowel to a wall or hang it between 2 × 4s sunk into the ground. Portland, Oregon, gardener Susan LeMaster says, "It's perfect for annual vines like peas. At the end of the summer you stash it away for next year." If you decide to dispose of it instead, check to see whether your local recycling center will accept it. If you must throw it in the trash, cut all the rings apart first so they won't be a hazard to wildlife."

## Stake Your Claim

When it comes to plant staking, Chela Kleiber, director of education at Tyler Arboretum near Media, Pennsylvania, takes full advantage of recycling. She scours her property for well-forked fallen branches, then uses them to support asters in an unobtrusive way. "It's a very British practice," she says, "and a nice, natural look." These won't work for large heavy plants like hollyhocks, but for midsize clumps like asters they're great, like a cupping hand. Besides fallen branches, you can save prunings, too, for this naturalistic—and free—way to stake floppy plants.

# Build It!

## Portable Bamboo Arbor

When you want shade and privacy in a hurry without the expense, bother, and long-term commitment of a construction project, try this fast alternative from Marianne Lipanovich, who gardens in Redwood City, California. It costs a pittance, goes together fast, and—best of all if you're a gardener on the go—you can pack it up in a snap and move it to another area of your garden.

Adjust the size and the number of support rails to suit your space and the weight of the vines the arbor will support. Lipanovich designed hers to be 12 × 6 × 8 feet. Single crosspieces on three sides provide stability and growing space for lightweight vines.

### Materials

- Four 8-foot bamboo poles, 1½ inches in diameter
- Four sturdy terra-cotta pots, 18 to 20 inches in diameter
- Sand and stones
- Potting soil
- Four 12-foot bamboo poles, 1½ inches in diameter
- Four 6-foot bamboo poles, 1½ inches in diameter
- Nylon cord or rope
- Seeds or plants
- Twine or nylon netting, if desired
- Utility knife or scissors

### Directions

1. Set four 8-foot bamboo poles into the pots, and anchor the poles with sand and stones. Pour potting soil on top of the sand and stones to further steady the poles.
2. Fasten two 12-foot bamboo poles and two 6-foot bamboo poles to the tops of the upright poles with nylon cord or rope, using the lashing technique shown in the illustration below.
3. Add two more 12-foot poles and two more 6-foot poles as supports midway up the upright poles using the same lashing technique.
4. Sow seeds or set plants into the pots.
5. Tie twine or nylon netting to the top and sides if your vines need added support.

Use this lashing technique for poles.

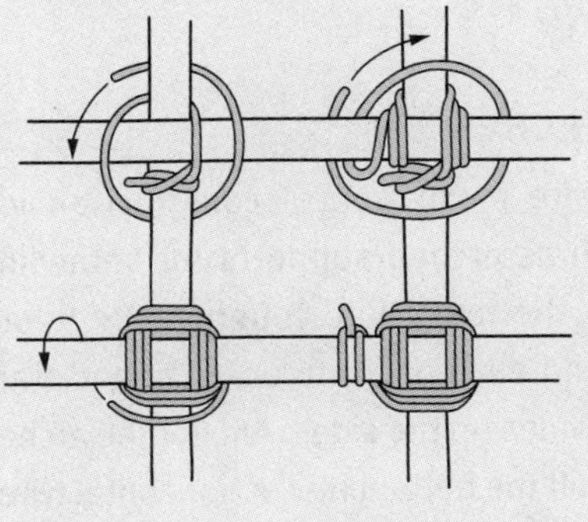

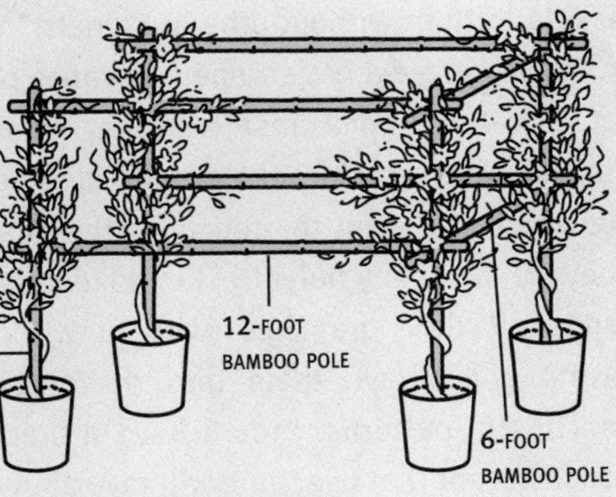

***On hand:*** Willow and alder prunings

***Turn them into:*** Unobtrusive plant supports

***How to do it:*** Simply bend them into arches and push the ends into the soil around plants that tend to flop.

## Romantic Woven Branches

Mimi Hoag of San Leandro, California, uses twigs and branches for many garden projects. "I use long, slender twigs (such as forsythia and willow) to make hoop supports for perennial plants and pea vines. The twigs blend in so well, the supports are completely unnoticeable. Sometimes they even take root! Honeysuckle vines are great for weaving into baskets, with or without other materials."

There's also every gardener's favorite project—the twig fence. Insert strong, shorter branches vertically into the ground along the line where you want the fence for the posts. (They can be of any height.) Then take longer, slender, flexible branches (with or without leaves) and weave them into the vertical branches in patterns. "You'll have a unique garden accent that everyone will rave about," assures Hoag.

## Self-Centering Tree Stakes

Generally, young trees don't need staking, but if your site is windy or has loose, sandy soil or if the tree is particularly top heavy, you may need to stake it for the first growing season. But excessive or uneven pressure on a young tree trunk is just as bad as no support at all. Bungie cords take all the trouble and guesswork out of the job. Simply drive the stakes equidistant from the tree trunk. Then wrap one or more bungie cords around each stake and the tree and hook their ends together. Use the same number and size cords on each side. For best results, remove stakes once the tree is strong enough to support itself.

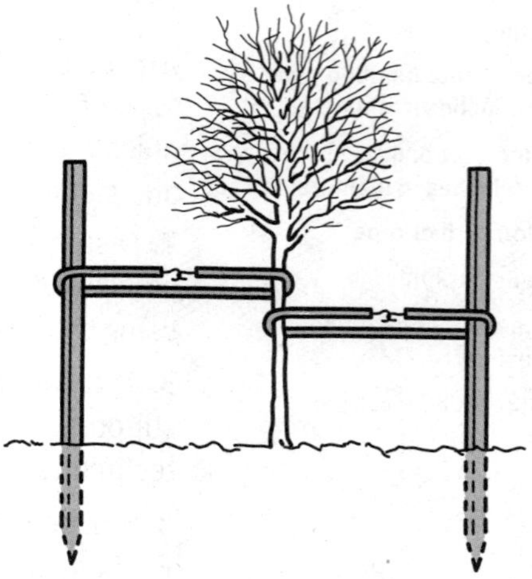

*A couple of stakes and bungie cords provide excellent support for young trees.*

## Wire Arches

Leftover wire mesh from a construction job works well as arched supports for sprawling vines. Cut the mesh into roughly 3 × 5-foot pieces, bend each one into an arch, and train the young vines up the sides. Anchor the arches by cutting off the bottom row of horizontal wires and sinking the vertical wires into the ground.

# Build It!

## Plastic, Fantastic Trellis

Ed Bender of Carlsbad, California, wanted to grow peas, beans, and flowering vines along a 5-foot-high white fence that surrounds his backyard. "And I wanted a trellis that would be both portable and good-looking," he says. Bender realized that PVC pipe would make perfect trellis material. "It's more durable than wood, and less noticeable against the white fence." And he soon found out that building a trellis from PVC was an easy job.

### Materials

- Two ½-inch PVC elbows
- Clear PVC glue
- ½-inch-diameter, schedule 40 PVC pipe cut into the following lengths:
  - 3 sections cut to 5 feet
  - 4 sections cut to 3 feet
  - 2 sections cut to 3 inches
- Four ½-inch PVC Ts
- 1-inch-diameter PVC pipe cut into two 6-inch lengths
- Two #6 hooks
- 1-inch-gauge chicken wire or nylon netting

### Directions

**1.** Working on a solid, flat surface, glue a PVC elbow to the top of two of the 5-foot lengths of PVC.

**2.** Glue a PVC T to the top of the remaining 5-foot length.

**3.** Making sure that they're square and level, glue a 3-foot length of PVC into each of the horizontal openings of the T.

**4.** Glue the other end of the 3-foot lengths into the elbows to form an M-shape frame as shown.

**5.** Glue a T to the bottom of the center 5-foot length, as shown.

**6.** Glue a T to the bottom of each of the outside 5-foot lengths as shown, and glue a 6-inch length of PVC into the bottom of those two Ts.

**7.** Glue the remaining 3-foot lengths into the horizontal openings of the Ts.

**8.** Stand the trellis up against the fence, and mark the ground where the feet hit.

**9.** Sink the two lengths of 1-inch PVC into the ground, at those marks against the fence.

**10.** Screw two hooks horizontally into the fence about 3 feet apart with the open end of the hooks oriented up.

**11.** Hang the top part of the trellis on the hooks and slide the trellis legs into the PVC anchors.

**12.** Fasten chicken wire or nylon netting over the frame to complete the trellis.

# Weed Control

Weeds are one curse that afflicts the lowly gardener. One day the weeds are gone, the next, they're back. But weeding doesn't have to feel like a bad case of the plague. With the right weeding tools and preventive techniques, the road to weed-free living is fairly smooth. Read on to find out how to "'Hoe' Happy as a Clam."

## "Hoe" Happy as a Clam

Whether you live near the seashore or not, a short-handled clam rake can be the perfect thing for cultivating and freshening a garden bed. The rake's slender tines penetrate the ground deeply, bringing up rhizomes of grasses and other invasive weeds in large pieces that are easy to pick out of the soil. Market gardener George DeVault lives and farms in Pennsylvania, but he swears by his clam rake. "It's a lot less work than chopping away at weeds or hardened soil with a hoe," DeVault says.

If you don't live near the seashore, you may wonder where to buy a clam rake. One option is to order a clam rake especially designed for gardeners by Real. (See "Resources" on page 344 for ordering information.)

## Weeder Extraordinaire

Uncle Paul's J-hook weeder is Pennsylvania gardener Melanie DeVault's favorite homemade tool. "It was great for getting in under my climbing rose bushes and hosta and even shrubs to clear out the scraggly weeds without bending over, or sticking a hand in and fearing encountering a garden snake or something," DeVault says with a laugh. DeVault inherited the original J-hook weeder from her Uncle Paul, whom she remembers as a great gardener.

The tool was simply an old J-hook screwed into a wooden handle. When the old handle broke, she was heartbroken. Her husband saved the day by heading out to the supply shed and fashioning a replacement by screwing another large J-hook into a hoe handle. (J-hooks are cheap at hardware stores.)

## Easy Kneeling Pad

Gardeners of any age can benefit from some knee protection, but there's no need to spend money on a fancy commercial kneeling pad.

Barth Getto, a longtime gardener who lives outside of St. Louis, Missouri, suggests checking with your local carpet store for old carpet samples. Getto happens to be in the carpet business himself, so he has ready access to 36 × 16-inch carpet samples, and he says they make great pads for kneeling in the garden. "I often double the samples up in the early spring to keep my knees warm and dry," he says. For a really cushy experience, "I scrounge up a piece of foam and sandwich that between two carpet samples. These pads are best-sellers at our neighborhood garage sales!"

## Super Hoe I

Faced with weeding his 1½-acre pumpkin patch, Steve Hammerstone of Easton, Pennsylvania, took a look at his hoe and knew he needed a more comfortable and durable implement. "Why not make myself a tool that not only holds up to heavy hoeing but also fits my body better?" mused Hammerstone, a metal sculptor and market gardener. When he next visited his hardware store, he spotted an inexpensive ice chopper and knew he could convert it into his own personalized weeding machine.

Hammerstone put the head of the ice-chopper into a strong vice with the handle pointing straight up. He carefully heated the neck with a propane torch until it was not quite red hot, and then bent the handle down to form an almost 90-degree angle. (To be safe, be sure to wear eye protection and heavy leather gloves while using the torch.) After the tool cooled, he painted the metal to prevent rusting. Hammerstone now has a custom hoe with a head heavy enough to chop up the toughest weeds and a handle long enough to let him stand up straight while doing so.

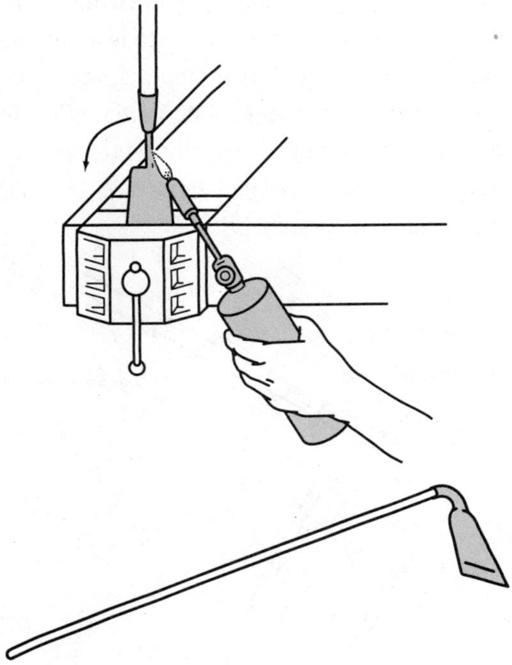

*It's easy to convert an inexpensive ice chopper into a sturdy, long-handled hoe. Just heat the neck of the chopper to soften the metal, then bend down the handle!*

## Super Hoe II

Champion recycler and Philadelphia gardener Will Anderson grew up across the street from a large vegetable plot tended by an older Italian gentleman. This sturdy gardener walked for miles to come hand-tend his garden, and he always arrived shouldering an equally sturdy handmade tool that he used to break, lift, and cultivate the heavy clay soil. When Anderson and his dad expressed interest in his Old World creation, the old man pantomimed how he heated the tang of a large flat-tined garden fork, bent it at a right angle, and then mounted it onto a longer, straight shovel handle. He wielded the tool by swinging it down from overhead and using the long handle to lever up the skewered earth. Anderson and his dad made their own version and used it to great effect in their own garden. It especially works well for pulling up sod, but "you better watch your toes!" adds Anderson.

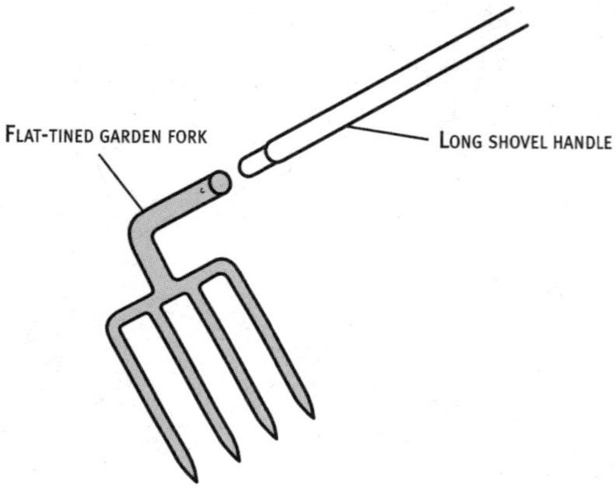


*TAKE TWO TRADITIONAL TOOLS—A FORK AND A SHOVEL—AND PUT THEM TOGETHER, AND YOU HAVE A SUPER NEW TOOL THAT'S GREAT FOR A VARIETY OF GARDEN TASKS!*

## Tree Rake

Living in Bertram, Texas, means living with bindweed. It grows everywhere—even up into the trees! Bill Albert, noted author of the Robin Paige Victorian mysteries, found that a potato rake is the finest bindweed removal tool in the business. This cross between a hoe and a pitchfork has three very sharp tines that easily snare the bindweed and bring it down for disposal. This rake is also useful for dragging piles of thorny clippings or for pulling compost out of a bin.

## Basic Black for Herbs

Gardeners everywhere know that black plastic is great for suppressing weeds, warming the soil, and conserving water. But don't think its use is limited to just the vegetable garden! Jim Weaver, a market gardener in Bowers, Pennsylvania, finds this material is perfect for his cut-your-own herb beds. "I've had fantastic success with sages, thymes, lavenders, and especially basils, which love the extra heat. I've even overwintered common rosemary!" he exclaims.

Weaver lays the plastic mulch down in the spring, punches holes in it, and plants the herbs in a staggered double row. As the closely spaced plants grow, their leafy canopies prevent the soil from getting too hot. The shade also protects the plastic, so Weaver can reuse the same sheets for up to three seasons. Another bonus? Weaver rarely has to water his rows of herbs. They grow all by themselves, ready for his customers to harvest their favorites.

## Never-Die Denims

The knees may be shot, or they may no longer fit, but you just can't kill an old pair of denim blue jeans, says Joan Janssen, editor of *Sage Leaves*, the newsletter of the Wisconsin unit of the Herb Society of America. She transforms her old jeans into durable kneeling pads. She cuts the leg portions into 12- to 14-inch lengths and stuffs them with rubber carpet pads, old soft sponges, bed pads, or even folded copies of the *Wall Street Journal*. Then she folds the edges and secures them with duct tape, string, or clothespins.

If you cut a longer piece, you can simply tuck the ends inside without fastening. Or, if you're feeling domestic, stitch the ends closed with a large needle and heavy thread, and add a denim loop to hang or carry them about. The jean-pads last for years, are recycled, free, and easy to clean (just unstuff and throw in the washer).

## Weed Isolators

If you find weeds poking up through your groundcovers, don't fret about how to dig them out. Here's a trick for dealing with the problem quickly and effectively without digging. First, cut the bottom one-third or one-half off a 1- or 2-liter plastic soda bottle. Then gather the weed's leaves into the bottle bottom, place the spray nozzle of an organic herbicide such as Weed-aside into the neck, and give the weed a blast. The bottle concentrates the deadly spray onto the weed and spares the groundcover from any damage.

*Don't let organic herbicides drift onto desirable plants! Keep their spray where you want it by isolating weeds with a soda-bottle shield.*

### Recycle It!

***On hand:*** Old straight or Phillips-head screwdriver whose tip has become dented or mangled

***Turn it into:*** Precision weeder

***How to do it:*** Just stick it in between pavers, flagstones, or cracks in your sidewalk and gouge out the weeds.

## Curtain Rod Weeder

Do sore muscles, a stiff back, or other aches and pains keep you from tending your garden? This simple tool may help. Thea Steinmetz, a Cleveland garden writer, recalls meeting an elderly, severely handicapped gardener who had made a nifty weeder from an old curtain rod (the two-piece rectangular type that expands). With a tin snips, she cut a V-notch in the end of the straight length of one piece. (The shorter bent section makes a perfect built-in handle.) She would wait until after a rainfall when the ground was wet, and then push the notched end into the earth right next to a weed. With a slight twist of the wrist, the weed would pop right out!

# Build It!

## Easy Kneeler

Aging joints won't stop 87-year-old Harvey DiGiorgio of Pittsburgh from tending his heirloom tomatoes and peppers. "At my age, the hardest part is getting down to the soil and then back up again." DiGiorgio's solution was to build a simple kneeler with side grips to steady him when getting up and down in the garden. The pipes that form the bottom help to keep the kneeler stable and prevent it from getting stuck in the mud. Below are the directions for reproducing DiGiorgio's kneeler, but feel free to experiment with the size to make the kneeler most comfortable for you. Be sure to use ¾-inch PVC, not ½ inch, which would be too weak.

**Materials**

- ¾-inch PVC pipe, cut with hacksaw as follows:
  - Two 20-inch pieces
  - Four 12-inch pieces
  - Four 8-inch pieces
  - Four 2-inch pieces
- Eight ¾-inch L-fittings
- Four ¾-inch T-fittings
- PVC primer and cement
- ½-inch exterior plywood (about 18 × 24 inches)
- Four ¼ × 1½-inch carriage bolts and nuts
- Old carpet or foam padding, heavy plastic, or sturdy cloth (optional)
- Staple gun and staples (optional)
- Drill with ¼-inch drill bit
- Nail or awl (optional)
- Handsaw

### Directions

**1.** Fit the PVC pipe pieces together, as shown in the diagram. Don't use the adhesive at this point; you just want to make sure all the parts fit together.

**2.** When you're ready to permanently assemble your kneeler, start with the rectangular base first, gluing each joint together one at a time. Follow the instructions that came with the PVC cement. (Typically, you prime each part of the joint first, apply the glue, and then squeeze the parts together.) Make sure the four T-fittings are all pointing directly upward, perpendicular to the base.

**3.** Glue together the parts that form the upright supports.

**4.** Drill four ¼-inch holes into the long pipes of the base, near the corners (see diagram). It may help to start the holes by nicking the surface of the pipe with a nail or awl.

**5.** Cut the plywood to fit the kneeler frame. Position the plywood on the frame and mark the location of the mounting holes. Drill the four holes with the ¼-inch bit. Attach the plywood with the carriage bolts and nuts.

**6.** To make the kneeler easy on your knees, use a loose piece of old carpet or foam padding on top of the plywood. To make the padding a permanent part of the kneeler, cover the foam with heavy plastic or sturdy cloth secured to the underside of the plywood with staples.

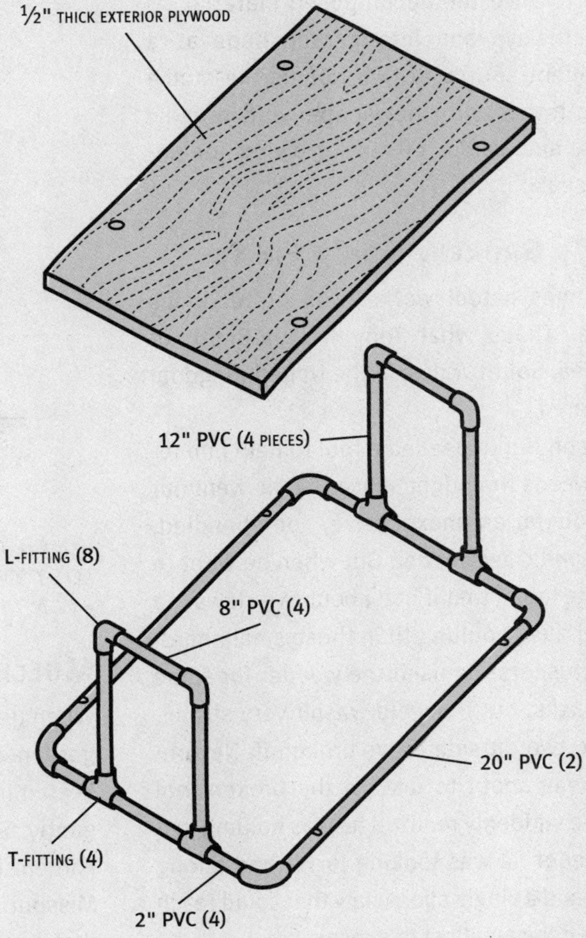

## Double-Duty Mulch for Pathways

Here's a way to have your mulch and sheet compost too! In spring, cover garden pathways with newspaper or cardboard. Spread straw, grass clippings, weeds, and other biodegradable material over the newspaper to hold it in place. Enjoy weed-free paths all season long. The following spring, use a spade to slice the decomposed material off the pathways and into garden beds as a convenient source of rich humus. Re-mulch the pathways with newspaper and organic debris, and you're off and growing for another season.

## If It's Broken, Don't Fix It

Sometimes a tool works even better if it's broken! That's what Tony Nelson-Smith of Swansea, South Wales, in the United Kingdom discovered.

Nelson-Smith needed a tool to help him remove weeds from tight spaces, so he went out and bought an inexpensive, long-handled, three-toed claw weeder. But when he went to work, he found that it had about two claws too many; it just wouldn't fit in those small, hard-to-reach spots. He used the weeder for some other tasks, but the weld wasn't very strong, and the two outside claws broke off. Nelson-Smith was about to discard the broken tool when he suddenly realized he was holding just the weeder he was looking for! It had a long handle and a single sharp claw that could reach into even the smallest of spaces.

"Now I use it for hoeing in very constricted spaces (like between rows of seedlings in a nursery bed), for clearing between rocks or paving slabs, and for uprooting individual weeds," Nelson-Smith says. "It does jobs for which most other tools are too clumsy. I regard it as quite essential."

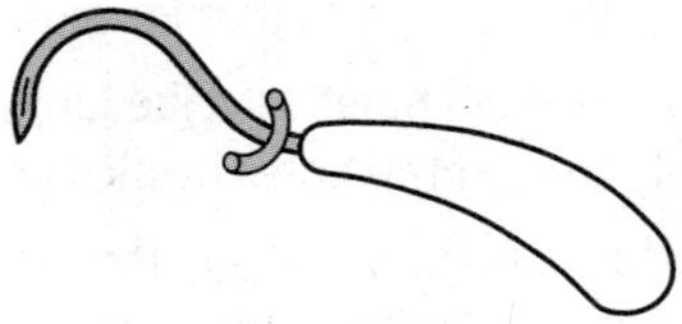

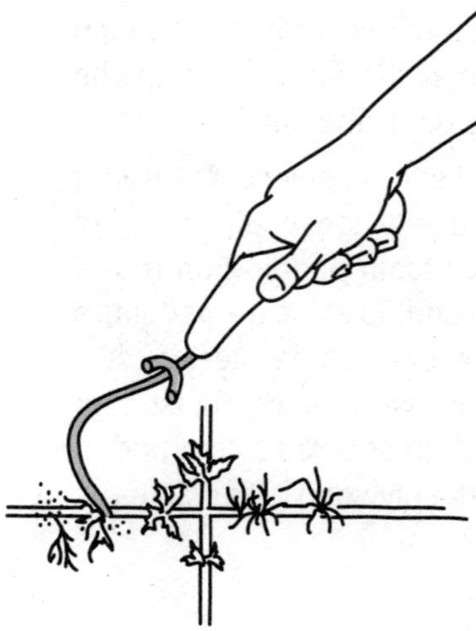

*When this three-clawed weeder lost two of its claws, it became an even more valuable tool.*

## Mulch Magic

When using plastic mulch or landscape fabric, gardeners face the eternal problem of how to keep it in place easily, inexpensively, and elegantly. Sure, you can use those ready-made garden staples, but Mike Coston of Fairdealing, Missouri, invented a new and improved staple that beats the store-bought ones in several ways. Coston's stakes cover more ground, cost next to nothing in materials, and are so easy to make that he can put together two or three of them per minute.

# Build It!

## Weed Scraper

If you grow corn, you know how important weed control is for getting a good harvest. Kris Lopez Fitzgerald and Shawn Fitzgerald of Stillwater, Oklahoma, raise native varieties for seed for a local seed conservancy, so they spend a lot of time caring for their corn crop, and they just weren't satisfied by conventional hoes and hand weeders. Unless used very carefully, the broad blades endangered the small sprouting corn plants. With a little ingenuity, Shawn came up with a perfect corn-weeding tool. It worked so well, it even earned a name: the "Weed Scraper!"

### Materials

- Wooden broom or mop handle
- Brass strip, 1⁄16 inch × 3⁄4 inch × 10 inches
- 1⁄8-inch bolt and nut
- Stainless steel lashing cable
- Hacksaw
- Drill with 1⁄8-inch steel bit

### Directions

**1.** Cut the wooden handle to a 12-inch length with the hacksaw.

**2.** Again using the hacksaw, cut a 1-inch-deep notch across the center of the flat end of the handle.

**3.** With a 1⁄8-inch drill bit, drill a hole through the end of the handle, perpendicular to the notch, 1⁄2 inch from the end.

**4.** Bend the brass strip into a flattened loop, bringing the two ends together to form a tab.

**5.** Insert the tab into the notch, and mark drill holes on the tab through the holes in the handle.

**6.** Remove the tab and drill holes at the mark with the drill bit.

**7.** Reinsert the tab into the notch, slip a bolt through the holes, and secure it with a nut.

**8.** Wrap the lashing cable around the notched end of the handle to hold the tab in place and prevent the blade from wiggling.

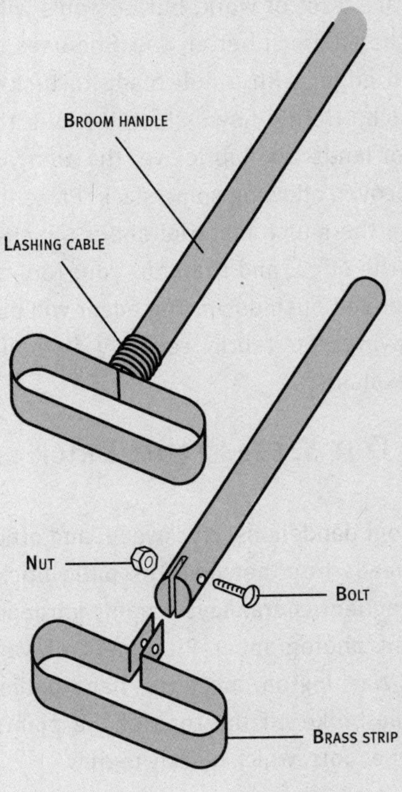


Kris says the Weed Scraper works especially well on young weed and grass seedlings, and it's most effective when the soil is moist but not soggy. "Our corn seedlings were already up when I weeded with the tool, and I found I had great control in tight places using it."

### Recycle It!

***On hand:*** Newspaper and shredded paper

***Turn it into:*** Mulch, compost, and plant protection

***How to do it:*** Use newspaper as a mulch by laying four to six sheets down over garden paths. Scatter grass clippings over the newspaper to make it a little more attractive. Shredded household mail, bills, and other paper can also be added to your compost pile, says Irv Breber of Bensalem, Pennsylvania.

Caroline Whitenack of Doylestown, Pennsylvania, uses sheets of newspaper as plant protection when nights get chilly. She places a flat upside down over her plants, and then covers it with a few sheets of newspaper until morning.

To make the staples, start with a coil of 12-gauge galvanized wire (similar to that used for coat hangers). Cut the wire into 21-inch lengths. Using pliers, bend about 7 inches on each end downward to form two legs. Then, bend the middle down about 1 inch so that the wire forms a capital M. That leaves a 7- to 8-inch-wide staple. Because these are so much wider than store-bought staples, you won't need very many. "For a 4 × 16-foot bed, I use one at each corner and two or three down each long side," Coston says.

Do you prefer to hold plastic mulch or landscape fabric in place by burying the edges in the soil? Traditional wisdom advises digging a trench around the mulched area, tucking in the edges, and backfilling with soil. That's a lot of work, but Coston's wife, Cheryl, has a much better way. She uses an old lawn edger with a dull blade to tuck in the mulch. Here's how: "Just lay out the plastic or landscape fabric over the area you want to cover, allowing some slack. Place the edger on the mulch material about 6 inches in from the edge, and then put your foot on the edger and push down. The edger will pull out, leaving the fabric securely in soil," Cheryl explains.

## Drive Out Weeds from Brick Paths

Getting out dandelions, chickweed, and other pesky weeds from between the patio bricks was a frequent chore, says organic gardener and plant photographer Rick Mark of Vancouver, Washington, because hand-pulling commonly broke off the tops of the plants, leaving the roots, which quickly regrew.

"I tried a trowel and a dandelion digger," says Mark, "but they were too big to fit between the bricks," which were laid in a sandy base atop gravel and soil. "So I dug out the longest, strongest flat-head screwdriver I could find. Its shaft was just the size I needed to slip between the bricks and pry out dandelions and other deep-rooted weeds."

The screwdriver makes quick work of less tenacious weeds and weed seedlings, too, says Mark. "I can drag it down a row between the bricks in less than a minute, and uproot everything in its path." When he's done getting out the weeds, he shakes off the soil, piles the weeds for compost, and sweeps loose soil and sand back into the cracks.

***On hand:*** A mason's trowel

***Turn it into:*** A weeding tool

***How to do it:*** Put the trowel in a vise and bend the blade to a 90-degree angle. To use the trowel, stick the blade into the soil and pull the trowel toward yourself. "It does the job just as well as the expensive weeders in the garden catalogs, at about one-sixth of the price," says Jerry Anderson, a Master Gardener from Portland, Oregon.

## Poison Ivy Barrier

Carolyn Roof of Paducah, Kentucky, advises, "If you need an impervious barrier between you and poison ivy, try this: Put a plastic newspaper sleeve bag over your hand and arm like a glove before pulling out that piece of poison ivy. After you've pulled it out, peel the 'glove' inside out while you're still holding the weed. Then you can throw the whole thing away safely." There's no danger of spreading the plant oils as there is when you use garden gloves for the task. Bread bags work well for this, too. (You knew you were saving them for something!)

## Fork It Over

A table fork is great for unearthing the roots of smaller weeds such as chickweed and knot weed. For bigger weed problems, try spreading roofing tar paper over the problem area for several weeks to smother weeds.

## A Carpet of Tomatoes

Rolling out the carpet is exactly what home gardener Deborah Burdick of Mt. Vernon, Indiana, does when it's time to plant tomatoes. "When I wanted to expand my garden to make more room for tomatoes, my lawn care helpers suggested I try their technique: They unrolled an old piece of wall-to-wall carpet onto their lawn, cut holes in it, and planted their tomatoes in the holes. The carpet blocks

# Build It!

## Mrs. Berry's Favorite Weeder

The Berry Botanic Garden in Portland, Oregon, started its life as the cherished home turf of renowned plantswoman Rae Selling Berry. She designed and made a number of these weeders, several of which are still in use at the garden.

**Materials**

- A sturdy branch or an old tool handle, about 6 inches long
- 2-foot piece of ¼-inch baling wire
- Drill
- Vise
- Pliers
- Metal file

**Directions**

**1.** Drill a ¼-inch hole through each end of the branch or tool handle.

**2.** Put the baling wire into the vise, and bend the center portion into a D shape using the pliers.

**3.** Push the long ends of the wire through the holes in the handle, bending the tips tight against the end to fasten.

**4.** Bend the D-shaped opening to an angle of about 45 degrees.

**5.** With the file, sharpen the lower edge of the baling wire.

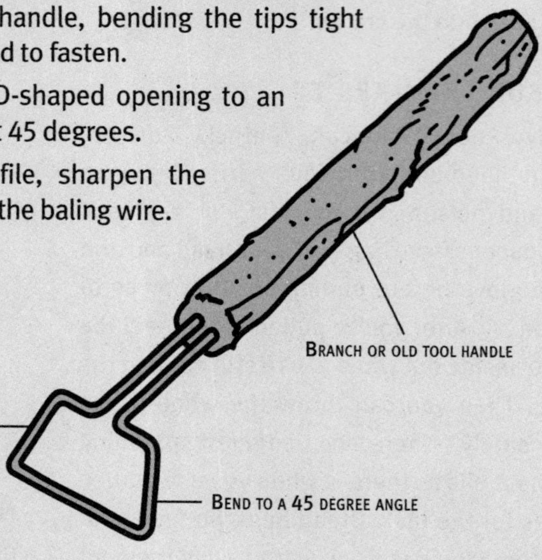


weeds, keeps the soil moist, and encourages earthworms."

Burdick finds carpet pieces at her local thrift shop, or begs them from friends, who are glad to oblige. She searches for natural-looking colors, such as browns and greens. After planting her patch, she covers the carpet with grass clippings all summer to hide the carpet. "You should see all the worms when I peel up a corner!" she exclaims. "No wonder my tomatoes do so well."

## THROW IN THE TOWEL

"I love new, fluffy towels," says gardener Gretel Hartman of the Boston area. "I used to take the old thin ones to the thrift shop, until one day I realized they were all cotton—just another plant fiber that would gradually turn back to soil."

At first Hartman planned to tear the towels into strips and add them to her compost pile, but then she had an even better idea. "I had a roll of weed-blocking landscape fabric in my hand, ready to buy," she says, "when I remembered the towels. That's when I began using them as mulch around my shrubs and perennials. I lay them out as flat as possible, snipping here and there if I have to, and cover them with wood chips or grass clippings or compost, whatever beautifier mulch I happen to be using at the time."

Hartman says her old bath towels do an efficient job of smothering existing weeds and blocking new ones. And she noticed a bonus: "When Baltimore orioles came back in spring, they spied a piece of towel sticking out from the garden and went to work unraveling it for their nest."

Vegetable gardener Linda Howard of Evansville, Indiana, uses the same technique with old rag rugs that she scoops up at country auctions or thrift shops, or donates from her own house once they're past their prime. "They last 2 to 3 years," she notes, "and work better at blocking weeds and smothering grass than any other mulch I've tried."

# Pest Identification Guide

*Not sure what insect is snacking on your tomatoes or nibbling on your roses? This handy guide to 31 common garden pests will help you recognize the bad guys—and then tells you how to give them the old heave-ho the organic way.*

| Pest | Description | Damage | Organic Control |
|---|---|---|---|
| APHID  | Adults: 1/16"–3/8" long; pear-shaped; have 2 tubes on rear of abdomen and long antennae. May be winged or wingless; green, pink, black, gray, or white. Nymphs: resemble adults. Common in North America. | Nymphs and adults suck sap from vegetable crops, small ornamentals, and fruit or shade trees; if severe, leaves and flowers may drop. Cause plant distortion. Secrete honeydew, which helps sooty mold to grow. Feeding may spread plant viruses. | Plant pollen and nectar plants. Release aphid midges, lady beetles, lacewings, or parasitic wasps. Spray plants with water to knock aphids off. Use garlic spray, summer oils, or insecticidal soap. |
| APPLE MAGGOT  | Adults: 1/4" long; dark-colored flies; yellow legs; transparent wings patterned with dark, crosswise bands. Larvae: 1/4" long, white, develop inside fruit. Found in eastern United States and Canada; also in northern California. | Maggot larvae tunnel through apples, blueberries, and plums, leaving brown winding trails behind. Often, infested fruit will drop prematurely. Thin-skinned and early-maturing cultivars are most affected. | Plant late-ripening cultivars. Plant white clover groundcover to attract pupae predators. Hang traps in trees from mid-June until fruit colors. Pick up and destroy dropped fruit daily until September; collect fruit twice a month in fall. |
| ARMYWORM 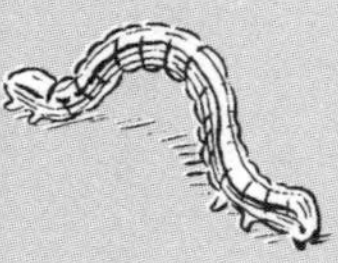 | Adults: pale, gray-brown moths with 1½"–2" wingspans. Have a white dot in the center of each forewing; active at night. Young larvae: smooth and pale green. Older larvae: reach 1½"; greenish brown with white side stripes and dark or light back stripes. Eggs: greenish white; on lower leaves. Found east of the Rockies, southeastern Canada, New Mexico, Arizona, and California. | Will feed on lawn grass, corn, and other field crops, especially asparagus, beans, beets, cabbage, cucumbers, lettuce, spinach, and tomatoes. Will move en masse to a new location when food supplies become limited. Larvae can consume entire plants in 1 night. First-generation larvae cause the most damage. | Attract native predators, including parasitic wasps and flies. Spray *Bacillus thuringiensis* var. *kurstaki* (BTK) to kill larvae. In July, spray superior oil to kill eggs of second generations. Cultivate the soil after harvest to expose pupae to predators. |

| Pest | Description | Damage | Organic Control |
|---|---|---|---|
| **BLACK CHERRY APHID**  | Adults: 1/8" long; winged or wingless. Nymphs: smaller than adults but are otherwise identical. Both adults and nymphs are black. Commonly found wherever black cherries are grown in North America. | Adults and nymphs feed by sucking sap from black cherry leaves and tender shoots. Feeding curls leaves and can stunt growth in leaves and stems. Heavy infestations may kill young trees. Aphid honeydew spots foliage and fruit and promotes the growth of sooty fungus. | Plant pollen- and nectar-producing flowers to attract native predators. Release purchased aphid midges, lacewings, lady beetles, or parasitic wasps. Spray insecticidal soap, though sparingly because it may damage cherry leaves. |
| **BLACK VINE WEEVIL**  | Adults: up to 1/3" long; oblong; flightless; brownish gray or black with dirty yellow back patches. Larvae: 1/2" long, white grubs with yellowish heads. Eggs: in soil around host plants. Found in northern United States and southern Canada. | Both adults and larvae feed on broad- and narrow-leaved evergreen trees and shrubs, fruits, and ornamentals. Adults chew along leaf edges, though damage is rarely severe. Larvae can stunt plant growth by feeding on roots, potentially resulting in plant death. | At night, shake weevils onto a sheet and destroy them. Release parasitic nematodes into the soil by applying a liquid solution. Catch adult weevils on shrubs by tying a 6" band of plastic wrap around the shrub trunk and painting the plastic with Tanglefoot. |
| **CABBAGE LOOPER**  | Adults: gray-brown moths with a silvery spot in the middle of each forewing; 1 1/2" wingspans; active in late evening. Larvae: green with two white or light yellow lines down their backs and sides. Eggs: on the undersides of leaves. Common in the United States and southern Canada. | Larvae chew large holes in leaves of cabbage-family plants, as well as beets, celery, lettuce, peas, spinach, tomatoes, carnations, nasturtiums, and mignonette. They cause the most damage during their last few days of development. May destroy entire plants. | If the infestation is small, handpick caterpillars several times weekly. Attract native predators and parasites by planting pollen and nectar plants. Bury cabbage crop residue to destroy cocoons before adults emerge in spring. Spray BTK. |
| **CODLING MOTH** 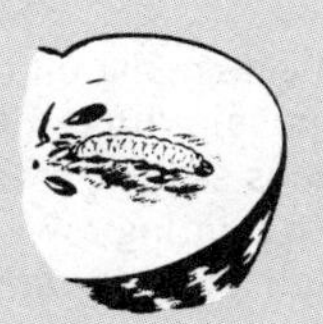 | Adults: gray-brown with 3/4" wingspans. Wings have wavy, coppery brown patterns; forewings have brown tips. Larvae: up to 3/4" long, brown-headed, pinkish white caterpillars. Found throughout North America. | Larvae tunnel through and ruin apples, apricots, cherries, peaches, pears, and plums. Tunneling begins at the base of the fruit and usually ends at the core. Dark castings may be found at the base of the tunnel, although this may not be noticed until the fruit is cut open. | Trap caterpillars by tying sticky tree bands around trunks as they leave to pupate. Destroy all trapped larvae and pupae. Attract ground beetles. Use pheromone traps. In late winter, remove cocoons from tree bark by scraping, and spray dormant oil. |

*(continued)*

# Pest Identification Guide—Continued

| Pest | Description | Damage | Organic Control |
|---|---|---|---|
| COLORADO POTATO BEETLE  | Adults: 1/3" long; yellowish orange; 10 long black stripes on their wing covers; black spots on their thoraxes. Larvae: 1/16"–1/2" long, humpbacked, dark orange grubs with a row of black side dots. Eggs: bright yellow ovals that stand in clusters on the undersides of leaves. Found throughout North America. | Adults and larvae feed on potatoes and other related plants. They both chew on leaves and stems, resulting in severe defoliation of older plants, or death of young plants. Mature plant yields may be reduced due to feeding. | Mulch plants with deep straw; cover plants with floating row covers. Destroy adults, eggs, and larvae on sight. Shake adults from older plants onto a sheet and destroy them. Spray *Bacillus thuringiensis* var. *san diego* when eggs are present. In fall, kill beetles by tilling the soil. |
| CORN EARWORM  | Adults: yellowish tan moths with a wingspan of 1½"–2". Larvae: 1"–2" long, have yellow heads, black legs, white and dark side stripes; green, pink, or brown. Eggs: round, ribbed and light green; on undersides of leaves or on corn silks. Found throughout North America. | Larvae enter corn ears from the tips, feed on corn silks and kernels, and leave excrement trails. Will chew tomato flower buds and leaves and will burrow into ripe fruit. Also known to attack peppers. Mostly affects early and late corn cultivars. | Plant corn cultivars with tight, long husks. Attract native predators by interplanting with pollen and nectar plants. Keep outdoor lights off at night. Once corn silk starts to dry, apply BTK, parasitic nematodes, or mineral oil to ear tips. Time sprays so they coincide with egg hatches. |
| CUCUMBER BEETLE, SPOTTED  | Adults: 1/4" long; greenish yellow with 12 black spots on wing covers. Larvae: up to 3/4" long, white grubs with reddish brown heads; brown patches on first and last segments. Found throughout the United States and southern Canada east of the Rockies. | Larvae feed on roots of cucumber and corn plants by tunneling into the base of stems. Adults chew fruit skin, leaves, and sometimes petals of squash family plants, or other crops and flowers. Adults may transmit cucumber mosaic virus and bacterial wilt. | Plant squash family cultivars resistant to wilt and cucumber mosaic virus. Cover small and low plants with floating row covers; you may have to hand-pollinate the plants. Apply parasitic nematodes to soil around corn plants. Remove and destroy crop residue after harvest. |
| CUCUMBER BEETLE, STRIPED  | Adults: 1/4" long; yellow; have black heads and three black stripes on wing covers. Larvae: 3/4" long grubs, white with reddish brown heads. Found west to Colorado and New Mexico; in Canada, west to Saskatchewan. | Larvae feed on roots of squash family plants, sometimes stunting or killing plants. Adults feed on squash, bean, corn, and pea seedling leaves and shoots; flowers of older plants; and fruit. Adults may transmit bacterial wilt and mosaic viruses. | Plant cultivars resistant to wilt and mosaic viruses. If infestation is severe, cover plants with floating row covers. Mulch plants with deep straw. Apply parasitic nematodes to soil around plants. |

| Pest | Description | Damage | Organic Control |
|---|---|---|---|
| **CUTWORM** 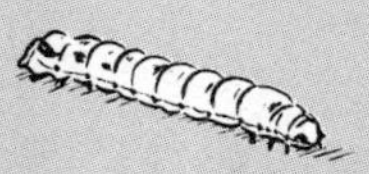 | Adults: large, brownish gray moths with $1\frac{1}{2}$" wingspans. Larvae: 1"–2" long, fat, greasy gray or brown caterpillars with shiny heads. Most species are in soil, some climb plants. Found throughout North America. | Larvae are night feeders and will cut the stems of seedlings, shoots, and transplants of early vegetables and flowers at or below the soil line, injured plants may fall over. If plants are small, they may be eaten entirely! Adults do not damage plants. | Plant later in the season. Use cutworm collars around stems of plants. Dig around damaged plants and destroy worms. Sprinkle bran mixed with BTK and molasses a week before planting. |
| **EUROPEAN CORN BORER**  | Adult females: pale yellow-brown moths with dark wing zigzags and 1" wingspans. Males: darker and smaller. Larvae: 1" long; grayish beige with brown heads and dots on segments. Found in northern and central United States, central and eastern Canada. | Larvae may attack beans, peppers, potatoes, tomatoes, and small grains. Find young larvae on corn tassels, beneath ear husks, and on the first whorl of leaves. Older larvae feed on stalks, tassels, and ears. Weakened stalks may break. Larvae overwinter in crop residue. | Plant strong-stalked and tight-husked cultivars. Attract native predators. If infestation is severe, detassel two-thirds of corn plants before pollen sheds. Apply BTK or mineral oil to ear tips. If on leaves, spray BTK. After harvest, shred and compost, or bury stalks immediately. |
| **FLEA BEETLE**  | Adults: $\frac{1}{10}$" long; black, brown or bronze; large hind legs used to jump like fleas when disturbed. Larvae: up to $\frac{3}{4}$" long, white grubs with brown heads; live in soil. Found throughout North America. | Adults chew small holes in leaves of cabbage-family plants, potatoes, and spinach, with most damage in early spring. Seedlings may be killed, larger plants usually survive. Larvae feed on plant roots and may cause large losses. Adult flea beetles may spread viruses. | Delay planting to avoid population peak; cover seedlings and shoots with floating row covers or fine mesh until beetles die. Interplant crops to create shady conditions, which deter flea beetles. |
| **GREEN FRUITWORM** 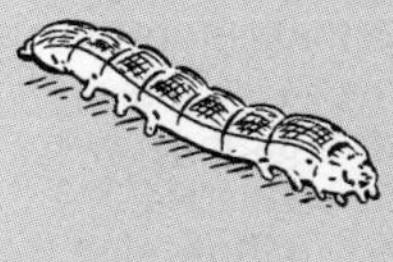 | Adults: Grayish pink forewings, each with two purplish gray spots. Larvae: $1\frac{1}{4}$" long; pale green with narrow white stripes. Eggs: white with grayish tinge and many ridges. Found throughout North America. | Larvae feed on leaves of deciduous fruits. They usually do not cause serious damage to leaves but later bite into fruit and may completely consume it. | Where infestations are heavy, spray BTK as soon as leaf damage is noticed. |

*(continued)*

# Pest Identification Guide—Continued

| Pest | Description | Damage | Organic Control |
|---|---|---|---|
| IMPORTED CABBAGEWORM 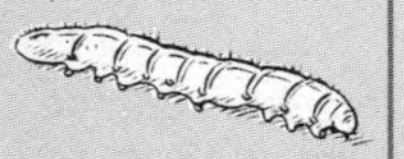 | Adults: White-winged butterflies with black wing tips and 2 or 3 spots on forewings; 1½" wingspan. Larvae: green with a light yellow back stripe. Eggs: tiny yellow cones on leaf undersides. Found throughout North America. | Larvae feed on leaf undersides of all cabbage-family plants, eventually leaving ragged holes in cabbage leaves and florets of cauliflower and broccoli. Soils leaves with dark green pellets. | Plant purple cabbage cultivars; protect and attract natural enemies, including yellow jacket wasps. Handpick caterpillars and eggs. Cover plants with floating row covers. Use yellow sticky traps. Spray BTK. |
| JAPANESE BEETLE  | Adults: ½" long; blocky; metallic blue-green; bronze wing covers; white abdomen hair; long legs with large claws. Larvae: up to ¾" long, fat, dirty white grubs, found in soil. Found in all states east of the Mississippi River. | Adults feed on many vegetables, especially asparagus, beans, corn, okra, onions, rhubarb, and tomatoes. In warm weather, they eat flowers and cause leaves to drop by skeletonizing them. May defoliate plants completely. Larvae feed on roots of lawn turf and other grasses. | Cover small or valuable garden plants with screens or floating row covers. Handpick or vacuum beetles or shake beetles off plants and destroy. Dry out lawn between waterings and aerate the turf in late spring and early fall. |
| LEAFHOPPER 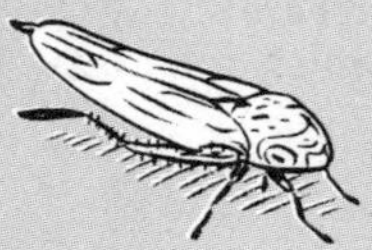 | Adults: 1/10"–½" long; wedge-shaped; broad triangular head; brown or green; color bands on wings; use strong hind wings to jump into flight. Nymphs: similar to adults but paler and wingless; hop rapidly. Found throughout North America. | Adults and nymphs suck juice from stems and leaf undersides of flowers, fruit trees, and vegetables, especially apple trees, beans, eggplant, grapes, peanuts, potatoes, and squash-family plants. Plants may develop tipburn and yellowed, curled leaves with white spots, or warty, crinkled and rolled edges. | Encourage parasitic flies, lady beetles, lacewings, spiders, and other native predators. Spray strong streams of water to wash nymphs from plants. Spray dormant oil to kill overwintering adults. Spray neem or insecticidal soap while nymphs are small. |
| MEXICAN BEAN BEETLE  | Adults: ¼" long; yellowish brown with 16 black spots on wing covers. Larvae: ⅓" long, yellowish grubs with spines. Eggs: bright yellow, laid in clusters on leaf undersides. Found east of Mississippi River, Texas, Arizona, Utah, Colorado, and Nebraska. | Both larvae and adults skeletonize leaves of cowpeas, lima beans, snap beans, and soybeans. They feed from underneath leaves, creating a lacy pattern. Infestations may decrease pod production or kill plants. | Plant resistant cultivars; plant early; cover young plants with floating row covers. Attract native predators with flowering weeds; plant soybeans as a trap crop—destroy them once they're infested with larvae. Handpick larvae and adults. |

| Pest | Description | Damage | Organic Control |
|---|---|---|---|
| PEAR PSYLLA 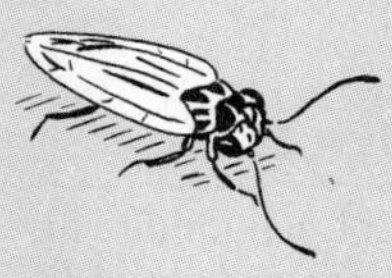 | Adults: 1/10" long; dark red-brown; green or red marks; transparent wings (like roofs) over their backs. Nymphs: small, oval, yellow with red eyes and no wings. Eggs: yellow and oval. Found in eastern United States and Canada; also in Pacific Northwest and California. | Saliva causes pear and quince leaves to yellow. If infestation is severe, leaves will brown and drop; fruit will drop prematurely or be stunted. Honeydew supports growth of sooty mold. May spread diseases and viruses by sucking juices. | Encourage native predators. Spray dormant oils after fall leaf drop and before bud swell in spring. Spray insecticidal soap or summer oil during growing season. |
| PLUM CURCULIO  | Adults: 1/5" long; brownish gray; warty wing covers; white hair. Larvae: 1/3" long, white grubs with brown heads. Eggs: round, white, laid singly under crescent-shaped cuts in fruit skin. Found in eastern North America. | Adult feeding and egg-laying leaves half-circle scars in fruit skin of apples, blueberries, and most tree fruits. Larvae tunnel and feed near fruit pits, causing fruit to rot or prematurely drop. | Collect and destroy fallen fruit daily. Knock curculios from trees onto a ground sheet by sharply tapping tree with a padded stick; drown the curculios in soapy water. |
| ROSE CHAFER  | Adults: 1/3" long; reddish brown with yellow hairs on wing covers; black underside. Larvae: small white grubs in soil. Found throughout North America. | Adults chew on flowers, leaves and fruit of blackberries, grapes, raspberries, strawberries, tree fruits, garden vegetables, dahlias, hollyhocks, irises, peonies, poppies, and roses. Serious damage occurs when numbers are high. Larvae feed on grass and weed roots. | Control is usually not needed. Handpick if necessary. With severe infestations, protect plants with floating row covers. Cultivate soil to kill pupae. |
| SLUG  | Adults: 1/8"–1" long; gray, tan, green or black with dark spot patterns; exude a slimy mucus. Eggs: clear; oval or round; found in jellylike masses under stones, twigs, logs, or other garden debris. Found throughout North America. | Feeds on decayed plant matter. Will chew large holes in bulbs, stems, and plant foliage. May completely destroy seedlings; young shoots and plants may be severely damaged. May climb trees and shrubs to feed. Will attack any vegetable; can decimate citrus and tender plants. | Encourage birds, snakes, toads, lizards, ground beetles, and fireflies. Repel slugs with copper strips on tree trunks or shrubs. Edge gardens with copper flashing. Use commercial slug tape. Spread cinders or wood ash to protect seedlings. Set out small dishes of beer to drown slugs. |

*(continued)*

# Pest Identification Guide—Continued

| Pest | Description | Damage | Organic Control |
|---|---|---|---|
| SPIDER MITE  | Adults: 1/75"–1/50" long; eight legs; reddish, pale green or yellow with fine hairs. Nymphs: like adults; six legs. Spins fine webs on leaves and shoots. Found throughout North America. | Adults and nymphs feed by sucking juice from plant cells on leaf undersides. Will attack vegetables, ornamental trees, fruit trees, berries, herbs, annuals, perennials, shrubs, vines, and houseplants. Feeding weakens plants, causes leaf drop, and stunts fruit. Look for yellow-speckled or bronze leaves and webbing. | Maintain high humidity in greenhouses and around houseplants. Release predatory mites. Spray dormant oil on fruit trees; minimize pesticide use to protect predatory mites. Spray neem or insecticidal soap. Spray summer oil on tolerant woody shrubs and trees. |
| SQUASH BUG 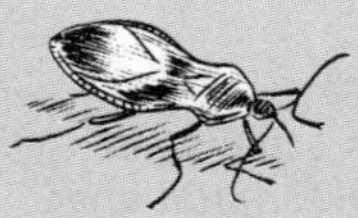 | Adults: 5/8" long; oval; dark brown to black; flat abdomen with fine, dark hair. Nymphs: pale green. Older nymphs: reddish thorax and abdomen; sometimes looks like they've been rolled in gray powder. Found throughout North America. | Adults and nymphs suck plant juice from pumpkins, squash, or other squash-family plants. May cause leaves and shoots to turn black and die. Severe infestations may limit fruit production. Damage mimics wilt disease. | Plant resistant cultivars. Use floating row covers over young plants—you may have to hand pollinate. Handpick bugs from leaf undersides. Place boards on the ground next to plants; in the morning, destroy adults found under the boards. |
| SQUASH VINE BORER 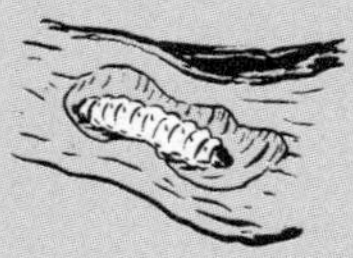 | Adults: moths with brownish olive forewings; clear hind wings; fringed hind legs; and a red abdomen with black rings; 1"–1½" wingspan. Larvae: 1" long, white grubs with brown heads. Found throughout most of North America. | Larvae burrow into vines of squash-family plants, but especially those with thick stems like gourds, pumpkins, and squash. While boring, the larvae chew inner vine tissue and leave slimy castings behind. Attacked vines will wilt and girdled vines will rot. May also feed on fruit. | Plant early; promote vigorous and fast growth. Cover young plants with floating row covers—you may have to hand pollinate. |
| STINK BUG  | Adults: ½"–5/8" long; five-sided, shield-like body; green, tan, brown or gray. May have bright red or black harlequin markings. Will emit a foul smell if disturbed. Nymphs: wingless, oval, similar to adults. Eggs: barrel-shaped, underneath leaves. Found throughout North America. | Adults and nymphs suck sap from leaves, flowers, fruit and seeds of beans, cabbage, corn, okra, peas, squash, soybeans, tomatoes, peaches, and forage crops. Leaves may wilt, turn brown, or have brown spots. Feeding on fruit causes scarring. Legume pods may drop or have deformed seeds. | Encourage native predators; control garden weeds; remove crop residue in fall. Handpick all stages; crush eggs; shake plants over a container of soapy water. Spray insecticidal soap. Till garden at end of growing season. |

| Pest | Description | Damage | Organic Control |
|---|---|---|---|
| TARNISHED PLANT BUG  | Adults: 1/4" long; oval; light green to brownish copper, top of each wing has black-tipped triangle; back half of wings slant to the rear. Nymphs: wingless; yellow-green; five black dots on body; similar to adults. Found throughout North America. | Adults and nymphs suck juice from leaves, buds, and fruit of a wide variety of flowers, fruit, vegetables, and weeds. Toxic saliva causes plants to drop buds and pods; will also distort leaves and shoots. Sometimes plants will wilt or be stunted. Branch tips blacken and die back. | Avoid legumes as cover crops in orchards. Encourage native predators. If infestation is severe, cover small plants with floating row covers. Mow weeds and decrease crop debris. Spray summer oil on tolerant plant species. |
| TOMATO HORNWORM 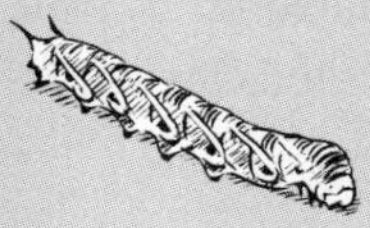 | Adults: narrow-winged, gray moths with 4"–5" wingspans. Larvae: up to 4 1/2"; green with large black horn on tail; diagonal side marks. Found throughout North America. | Larvae chew holes in leaves of tomatoes, eggplants, peppers, potatoes, and tobacco, leaving the midribs. Young plants may be completely defoliated. If infestation is severe, may chew on stems and fruit. | Handpick and destroy caterpillars. Spray BTK or neem if caterpillars are small. Till garden soil in early spring and fall. |
| WATER LILY BEETLE 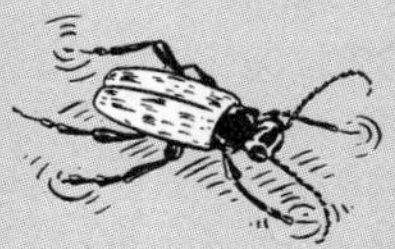 | Adults: 1/4" long; blocky wing covers; yellow legs; brown joints; long antennae; dark, rusty brown. Larvae: small white grubs. Found in North America where waterlilies and smartweed grow. | Chews holes in leaves and flowers of water lilies, smartweeds, purple loosestrife, and water chestnut. Will leave stippling on plant leaves. | Clean up dead plant foliage, especially from the water's edge. Wipe off eggs from underneath leaves. Handpick larvae from leaves. If infestation is severe, though limited to one plant, remove infested plant from garden. |
| WHITEFLY  | Adults: 1/20" long; powdery-white. Nymphs: 1/30" long; flat; legless; translucent and scaly. Eggs: gray or yellow pinpoint-sized cones on leaf undersides. Found in North American greenhouses and in warm regions of California, Florida, the Gulf states, and West Coast areas. | Nymphs and adults suck plant juice from citrus, ornamentals, annuals, rhododendrons, azaleas, grapes, and vegetables (especially squash- and tomato-family plants), causing plants to weaken. May spread viruses; honeydew supports sooty mold. | Encourage native predators. Capture adults on yellow sticky traps. Vacuum adults from leaf undersides. Spray neem, insecticidal soap, or summer oil on oil-tolerant plants. |

# Resources

To help you find great plants, garden supplies, and even more ingenious gardening ideas, we've compiled the following list of plant associations, gardening organizations, mail-order nurseries, garden suppliers, and product manufacturers. When you contact associations or specialty nurseries by mail, please enclose a self-addressed, stamped envelope with your inquiry. Notes in italics indicate particular products, plants, or services offered.

## Associations and Organizations

**American Dianthus Society**
Rand B. Lee
P.O. Box 22232
Santa Fe, NM 87502-2232

**American Horticultural Therapy Association**
909 York Street
Denver, CO 80206-3799
Phone: (303) 331-3862
Web site: www.ahta.org

**American Iris Society**
Ada Godfrey
9 Bradford Street
Foxborough, MA 02035
Web site: www.irises.org

**American Rose Society**
P.O. Box 30000
Shreveport, LA 71130-0030
Phone: (318) 938-5402
Fax: (318) 938-5405
Web site: www.ars.org

**Backyard Wildlife Habitat Program**
National Wildlife Federation
8925 Leesburg Pike
Vienna, VA 22184-0001
Web site: www.nwf.org/habitats

**Bio-Dynamic Farming and Gardening Association**
Bldg. 1002B, Thoreau Center, The Presidio
P.O. Box 29135
San Francisco, CA 94129-0135
Phone: (888) 516-7797
Fax: (415) 561-7796
E-mail: biodynamic@aol.com
Web site: www.biodynamics.com

**California Certified Organic Farmers**
1115 Mission Street
Santa Cruz, CA 95060
Phone: (831) 423-2263
Fax: (831) 423-4528
E-mail: ccof@ccof.org
Web site: www.ccof.org

**The Lady Bird Johnson Wildflower Center**
4801 La Crosse Avenue
Austin, TX 78739-1702
Phone: (512) 292-4100
Fax: (512) 292-4627
E-mail: wildflower@wildflower.org
Web site: www.wildflower.org

**The Maine Organic Farmers and Gardeners Association**
P.O. Box 2176
Augusta, ME 04338
Phone: (207) 622-3118
Fax: (207) 622-3119
Web site: www.mofga.org

**National Gardening Association**
180 Flynn Avenue
Burlington, VT 05401
Phone: (802) 863-1308
Fax: (802) 863-5962
Web site: www.garden.org

**North American Butterfly Association (NABA)**
4 Delaware Road
Morristown, NJ 07960
Phone: (973) 285-0907
Fax: (973) 285-0936
E-mail: naba@naba.org
Web site: www.naba.org

**North American Fruit Explorers (NAFEX)**
1716 Apples Road
Chapin, IL 62628
Phone: (217) 245-7589
Fax: (217) 245-7844
E-mail: vorbeck@csj.net
Web site: www.nafex.org

**Northeast Organic Farming Association (NOFA)**
Web site: www.nofa.org
*An affiliation of seven state chapters—CT, MA, NH, NJ, RI, VT. Check Web site for state contacts*

**Rodale Institute Experimental Farm**
611 Siegfriedale Road
Kutztown, PA 19530
Phone: (610) 683-1400
Fax: (610) 683-8548
E-mail: info@rodaleinst.org
Web site: www.rodaleinstitute.org

**Seed Savers Exchange**
3076 N. Winn Road
Decorah, IA 52101
Phone: (319) 382-5990
Web site: www.seedsavers.org

**Seeds of Diversity Canada**
P.O. Box 36
Station Q
Toronto, Ontario M4T 2L7
Canada
Phone: (905) 623-0353
E-mail: sodc@interlog.com
Web site: www.seeds.ca

**Wild Ones—Natural Landscapers, Ltd.**
P.O. Box 23576
Milwaukee, WI 23576
Web site: www.for-wild.org

## Beneficial Insects

**Bountiful Gardens**
18001 Shafer Ranch Road
Willits, CA 95490-9626
Phone: (707) 459-6410
Fax: (707) 459-1925
E-mail: bountiful@sonic.net
Web site:
www.bountifulgardens.org

**Gardens Alive!**
5100 Schenley Place
Lawrenceburg, IN 47025
Phone: (812) 537-8651
Fax: (812) 537-5108
Web site: www.gardensalive.com

**Gurney's Seed and Nursery Co.**
110 Capital Street
Yankton, SD 57079
Phone: (605) 665-1671
Fax: (605) 665-9718
Web site: www.gurneys.com

**Harmony Farm Supply and Nursery**
P.O. Box 460
Graton, CA 95444
Phone: (707) 823-9125
Fax: (707) 823-1734
Web site: www.harmonyfarm.com

**The Natural Gardening Co.**
P.O. Box 750776
Petaluma, CA 94975-0776
Phone: (707) 766-9303
Fax: (707) 766-9747
Web site:
www.naturalgardening.com

**Peaceful Valley Farm Supply**
P.O. Box 2209
Grass Valley, CA 95945
Phone: (530) 272-4769
Fax: (530) 272-4794
Web site: www.groworganic.com

**Territorial Seed Co.**
P.O. Box 157
Cottage Grove, OR 97424-0061
Phone: (541) 942-9547
Fax: (888) 657-3131
E-mail: tertrl@srv1.vsite.com
Web site:
www.territorial-seed.com

## Bulbs

**Breck's**
6523 N. Galena Road
Peoria, IL 61632
Phone: (800) 804-6742
Web site: www.brecks.com

**Brent and Becky's Bulbs**
7463 Heath Trail
Gloucester, VA 23061
Phone: (804) 693-3966,
(877) 661-2852
Fax: (804) 693-9436
E-mail:
store@brentandbeckysbulbs.com
Web site:
www.brentandbeckysbulbs.com

**Bundles of Bulbs**
PNB 349
1498 M Reisterstown Road
Baltimore, MD 21208
Phone: (215) 581-2188
Fax: (215) 862-3696

**Dutch Gardens**
P.O. Box 2105
Lakewood, NJ 08701
Phone: (800) 818-3861
Fax: (732) 780-7720
E-mail: info@dutchgardens.nl
Web site: www.dutchgardens.nl

**McClure and Zimmerman**
P.O. Box 368
108 W. Winnebago
Friesland, WI 53935-0368
Phone: (800) 883-6998
Fax: (800) 374-6120
E-mail: info@mzbulb.com
Web site: www.mzbulb.com

**Van Bourgondien Bros.**
P.O. Box 1000
Babylon, NY 11702-9004
Phone: (800) 622-9997
Fax: (800) 327-4268
E-mail: blooms@dutchbulbs.com
Web site: www.dutchbulbs.com

## Flowers

**Abundant Life Seed Foundation**
P.O. Box 772
Port Townsend, WA 98368
Phone: (360) 385-5660
Fax: (360) 385-7455
E-mail: abundant@olypen.com
Web site:
http://csf.Colorado.edu/perma/abundant

**Kurt Bluemel, Inc.**
2740 Greene Lane
Baldwin, MD 21013-9523
Phone: (800) 248-7584
Fax: (410) 557-9785
E-mail: kbi@bluemel.com
Web site: www.bluemel.com

**Bluestone Perennials**
7211 Middle Ridge Road
Madison, OH 44057
Phone: (800) 852-5243
Fax: (440) 428-7198
E-mail: bluestone@bluestoneperennials.com
Web site:
www.bluestoneperennials.com

**Bountiful Gardens**
18001 Shafer Ranch Road
Willits, CA 95490-9626
Phone: (707) 459-6410
Fax: (707) 459-1925
E-mail: bountiful@sonic.net
Web site:
www.bountifulgardens.org

**Burns Water Gardens**
R.R. #2
Baltimore, Ontario K0K 1C0
Canada
Phone: (905) 372-2737
Fax: (905) 372-8625
E-mail: wtrgdn@eagle.ca
Web site: www.eagle.ca/~wtrgdn

**W. Atlee Burpee and Co.**
300 Park Avenue
Warminster, PA 18974
Phone: (800) 888-1447
Fax: (215) 674-4170
Web site: www.burpee.com

**Busse Gardens**
17160 245th Avenue
Big Lake, MN 55309
Phone: (800) 544-3192
Fax: (320) 286-6601
E-mail: customerservice@bussegardens.com
Web site: www.bussegardens.com

**California Carnivores**
7020 Trenton-Healdsburg Road
Forestville, CA 95436
Phone: (707) 838-1630
Fax: (707) 838-9899
E-mail: califcarn@aol.com
Web site:
www.californiacarnivores.com
*Commercially propagated pitcher plants* (Sarracenia *ssp.*)

**Carroll Gardens**
444 E. Main Street
Westminster, MD 21157
Phone: (800) 638-6334
Fax: (410) 857-4112
Web site: www.carrollgardens.com

**Collector's Nursery**
16804 N.E. 102nd Avenue
Battle Ground, WA 98604
Phone: (360) 574-3832
Fax: (360) 571-8540
E-mail:
dianar@collectorsnursery.com
Web site:
www.collectorsnursery.com

**Daydreamer Aquatic and Perennial Gardens**
225 Rumsey Road
Columbus, OH 43207
Phone: (614) 491-2978
E-mail: dowatdpg2@aol.com
Web site:
www.daydreamergardens.com

**Daylily Discounters**
6212 W. SR 235
Alachua, FL 32615
Phone: (904) 462-1539
Fax: (904) 462-5111
E-mail:
support@daylilydiscounters.com
Web site:
www.daylilydiscounters.com

**Ferry-Morse Seed Co.**
P.O. Box 488
Fulton, KY 42041-0488
Phone: (800) 283-3400
Fax: (800) 283-2700
Web site: www.ferry-morse.com

**Flowery Branch Seed Co.**
P.O. Box 1330
Flowery Branch, GA 30542
Phone: (770) 536-8380
Fax: (770) 532-7825
E-mail:
seedsman@mindspring.com
Web site: www.flowerybranch.com

**Forestfarm**
990 Tetherow Road
Williams, OR 97544-9599
Phone: (541) 846-7269
Fax: (541) 846-6963
E-mail: orders@forestfarm.com
Web site: www.forestfarm.com

**Fragrant Farms, Inc.**
413 Woods Lane
New Harmony, IN 47631
Phone: (888) 814-4665
Fax: (812) 682-4577
E-mail: mark@fragrantfarms.com
Web site: www.fragrantfarms.com

**The Fragrant Path**
P.O. Box 328
Fort Calhoun, NE 68023
*Seeds of fragrant, old-fashioned, and rare plants*

**Goodwin Creek Gardens**
P.O. Box 83
Williams, OR 97544
Phone: (800) 846-7359
Fax: (541) 846-7357
E-mail: info@goodwincreek gardens.com
Web site: www.goodwincreek gardens.com

**Greer Gardens**
1280 Goodpasture Island Road
Eugene, OR 97401-1794
Phone: (541) 686-8266
Fax: (541) 686-0910
E-mail: orders@greegardens.com
Web site: www.greergardens.com

**Heard Gardens Ltd.**
5355 Merle Hay Road
Johnston, IA 50131
Phone: (515) 276-4533
Fax: (515) 276-8322
E-mail: info@heardgardens.com
Web site: www.heardgardens.com

**Heronswood Nursery**
7530 N.E. 288th Street
Kingston, WA 98346
Phone: (360) 297-4172
Fax: (360) 297-8321
E-mail: orders@heronswood.com
Web site: www.heronswood.com

**J. L. Hudson, Seedsman**
SR 2, Box 337
LaHonda, CA 94020

**Jackson and Perkins**
P.O. Box 1028
Medford, OR 97501
Phone: (800) 292-4769
Fax: (800) 242-0329
E-mail: service@jacksonand perkins.com
Web site: www.jacksonand perkins.com

**Johnny's Selected Seeds**
RR 1, Box 2580
Foss Hill Road
Albion, ME 04910-9731
Phone: (207) 437-9294
Fax: (207) 437-2759
E-mail:
johnnys@johnnyseeds.com
Web site: www.johnnyseeds.com

**J. W. Jung Seed Co.**
335 S. High Street
Randolph, WI 53957-0001
Phone: (800) 297-3123
Fax: (800) 692-5864
E-mail: info@jungseed.com
Web site: www.jungseed.com

**Logee's Greenhouses, Ltd.**
141 North Street
Danielson, CT 06239-1939
Phone: (860) 774-8038;
(888) 330-8038
Fax: (888) 774-9932
E-mail: logee-info@logees.com
Web site: www.logees.com

**Dan Majeski Nurseries**
P.O. Box 674
117 French Road
West Seneca, NY 14224-0674
Phone: (716) 825-6410
Fax: (716) 827-8537
E-mail:
danjr@majeskinursery.com

**Midwest Wildflowers**
Box 64
Rockton, IL 61072
Phone: (815) 624-7040

**Milaeger's Gardens**
4838 Douglas Avenue
Racine, WI 53402-2498
Phone: (800) 669-1229
Fax: (262) 639-1855
E-mail: milaeger@execpc.com
Web site: www.milaegers.com

**The Natural Garden**
38W443 Highway 64
St. Charles, IL 60175
Phone: (630) 584-0150
Fax: (630) 584-0185

**Niche Gardens**
1111 Dawson Road
Chapel Hill, NC 27516
Phone: (919) 967-0078
Fax: (919) 967-4026
E-mail: orders@nichegdn.com
Web site: www.nichegdn.com

**Nichols Garden Nursery**
1190 N. Pacific Highway
Albany, OR 97321-4580
Phone: (541) 928-9280
Fax: (800) 231-5306
E-mail: customersupport@nicholsgardennursery.com
Web site: www.nicholsgardennursery.com

**Park Seed**
1 Parkton Avenue
Greenwood, SC 29647-0001
Phone: (800) 845-3369
Fax: (800) 275-9941
E-mail: info@parkseed.com
Web site: www.parkseed.com

**Pinetree Garden Seeds**
P.O. Box 300
New Gloucester, ME 04260
Phone: (207) 926-3400
Fax: (888) 527-3337
E-mail: pinetree@superseeds.com
Web site: www.superseeds.com

**Plant Delights Nursery, Inc.**
9241 Sauls Road
Raleigh, NC 27603
Phone: (919) 772-4794
Fax: (919) 662-0370
E-mail: office@plantdel.com
Web site: www.plantdel.com

**Prairie Moon Nursery**
R.R. #3, Box 163
Winona, MN 55987
Phone: (507) 452-1362
Fax: (507) 454-5238
Web site: www.prairiemoonnursery.com

**Prairie Nursery**
P.O. Box 306
Westfield, WI 53964
Phone: (800) 476-9453
Fax: (608) 296-2741
Web site: www.prairienursery.com

**Roslyn Nursery**
211 Burrs Lane
Dix Hills, NY 11746
Phone: (631) 643-9347
Fax: (631) 427-0894
E-mail: roslyn@roslynnursery.com
Web site: www.roslynnursery.com

**Seeds Blüm**
27 Idaho City Stage Road
Boise, ID 83716
Phone: (800) 742-1423
Fax: (208) 338-5658
E-mail: 103374.167@compuserve.com
Web site: www.seedsblum.com

**Seeds of Change**
P.O. Box 15700
Sante Fe, NM 87506-5700
Phone: (888) 762-7333
Fax: (888) 329-4762
E-mail: gardener@seedsofchange.com
Web site: www.seedsofchange.com

**Select Seeds Antique Flowers**
180 Stickney Hill Road
Union, CT 06076
Phone: (860) 684-9310
Fax: (800) 653-3304
E-mail: info@selectseeds.com
Web site: www.selectseeds.com

**Shepherd's Garden Seeds**
30 Irene Street
Torrington, CT 06790-6658
Phone: (860) 482-3638
E-mail: custsrv@shepherdseeds.com
Web site: www.shepherdseeds.com

**Stokes Seeds Inc.**
P.O. Box 548
Buffalo, NY 14240-0548
Phone: (716) 695-6980
Fax: (716) 695-9649
E-mail: Stokes@stokeseeds.com
Web site: www.stokeseeds.com

**Territorial Seed Co.**
P.O. Box 157
Cottage Grove, OR 97424-0061
Phone: (541) 942-9547
Fax: (541) 942-9881
E-mail: tertrl@srv1.vsite.com
Web site: www.territorial-seed.com

**Thompson and Morgan, Inc.**
P.O. Box 1308
Jackson, NJ 08527-0308
Phone: (800) 274-7333
Fax: (888) 466-4769
E-mail: tminc@thompson-morgan.com
Web site: www.thompson-morgan.com

**Van Ness Water Gardens**
2460 North Euclid Avenue
Upland, CA 91784-1199
Phone: (800) 205-2425
Fax: (909) 949-7217
E-mail: vnwg@vnwg.com
Web site: www.vnwg.com

**Wayside Gardens**
1 Garden Lane
Hodges, SC 29695-0001
Phone: (800) 845-1124
Fax: (800) 457-9712
E-mail: curator@waysidegardens.com
Web site: www.waysidegardens.com

**We-Du Nurseries**
Route 5, Box 724
Marion, NC 28752
Phone: (828) 738-8300
Fax: (828) 738-8131
E-mail: wedu@wnclink.com
Web site: www.we-du.com

**White Flower Farm**
P.O. Box 50
Litchfield, CT 06759-0050
Phone: (800) 255-2852
Fax: (860) 496-1418
E-mail:
custserv@whiteflowerfarm.com
Web site:
www.whiteflowerfarm.com

**Wildseed Farms**
P.O. Box 3000
425 Wildflower Hills
Fredericksburg, TX 78624-3000
Phone: (800) 848-0078
Fax: (830) 990-8090
E-mail: wsf@fbg.net
Web site:
www.wildseedfarms.com

**Woodlanders, Inc.**
1128 Colleton Avenue
Aiken, SC 29801
Phone/Fax: (803) 648-7522

## Fruits and Berries

**Adams County Nursery, Inc.**
26 Nursery Road
P.O. Box 108
Aspers, PA 17304
Phone: (717) 677-8105
Fax: (717) 677-4124
E-mail: acn@cvn.net
Web site: www.acnursery.com

**Bear Creek Nursery**
P.O. Box 411
Northport, WA 99157
Phone: (509) 732-6219
Fax: (509) 732-4417
E-mail:
info@bearcreeknursery.com
Web site:
www.BearCreekNursery.com

**Country Carriage Nurseries and Seed, Inc.**
P.O. Box 548
Hartford, MI 49057
Phone: (616) 621-2491

**Cummins Nursery**
18 Glass Factory Bay Road
Geneva, NY 14456
Phone: (315) 789-7083
E-mail: jmc1@epix.net
Web site: www.dabney.com/
cumminsnursery

**Edible Landscaping**
361 Spirit Ridge Lane
P.O. Box 77
Afton, VA 22920-0077
Phone: (804) 361-9134
Fax: (804) 361-1916
E-mail: el@cstone.net
Web site: www.eat-it.com

**Hartmann's Plant Company**
P.O. Box 100
Lacota, MI 49063-0100
Phone: (616) 253-4281
Fax: (616) 253-4457
E-mail: info@harmannsplant
company.com
Web site: www.hartmannsplant
company.com

**Hidden Springs Nursery**
170 Hidden Springs Lane
Cookeville, TN 38501
Phone: (931) 268-2592

**Indiana Berry and Plant Co.**
5218 West 500 South
Huntingburg, IN 47542
Phone: (800) 295-2226
Fax: (812) 683-2004
E-mail: berryinfo@inberry.com
Web site: www.inberry.com

**Raintree Nursery**
391 Butts Road
Morton, WA 98356
Phone: (360) 496-6400
Fax: (888) 770-8358
E-mail: customerservice@
raintreenursery.com
Web site:
www.raintreenursery.com

**Rocky Meadow Orchard & Nursery**
360 Rocky Meadow Road NW
New Salisbury, IN 47161
Phone: (812) 347-2213
Fax: (812) 347-2488
E-mail: rockymdw@netpointe.com

**St. Lawrence Nurseries**
325 S. H. 345
Potsdam, NY 13676
Phone: (315) 265-6739
E-mail: trees@sln.potsdam.ny.us
Web site: www.sln.potsdam.ny.us

**Southmeadow Fruit Gardens**
P.O. Box 211
10603 Cleveland Avenue
Baroda, MI 49101
Phone: (616) 422-2411
Fax: (616) 422-1464
E-mail: smfruit@aol.com

**Stark Bro's Nurseries and Orchards Co.**
P.O. Box 10, Dept. AB 1122 A9
Louisiana, MO 63353
Phone: (800) 478-2759
Fax: (573) 754-5290
E-mail: service@starkbros.com
Web site: www.starkbros.com

**Van Well Nursery**
P.O. Box 1339
Wenatchee, WA 98807
Phone: (509) 886-8189,
(800) 572-1553
Fax: (509) 886-0294
E-mail: vanwell@vanwell.net
Web site: www.vanwell.net

## Gardening Supplies and Tools

**Alsto's Handy Helpers**
Route 150 East
P.O. Box 1267
Galesburg, IL 61402-1267
Phone: (800) 447-0048
Fax: (800) 522-5786
E-mail:
customerservice@alsto.com
Web site: www.alsto.com

**The Beneficial Insect Co.**
137 Forrest Street
Fort Mill, SC 29715
Phone: (803) 547-2301

**Biocontrol Network**
5116 Williamsburg Road
Brentwood, TN 37027
Phone: (615) 370-4301
Fax: (615) 370-0662
E-mail: info@biconet.com
Web site: www.biconet.com

**BioSensory**
Windham Mills Technology Center
322 Main Street, Building 1,
2nd floor
Willimantic, CT 06226-3149
Phone: (860) 423-3009
Web site: www.biosensory.com

**Bountiful Gardens**
18001 Shafer Ranch Road
Willits, CA 95490-9626
Phone: (707) 459-6410
Fax: (707) 459-1925
E-mail: bountiful@sonic.net
Web site:
www.bountifulgardens.org

**W. Atlee Burpee and Co.**
300 Park Avenue
Warminster, PA 18974
Phone: (800) 888-1447
Fax: (215) 674-4170
Web site: www.burpee.com

**Charley's Greenhouse Supply**
17979 State Route 536
Mount Vernon, WA 98273-3269
Phone: (800) 322-4707
Fax: (800) 233-3078
Web site:
www.charleysgreenhouse.com

**Delgard Aluminum Ornamental Fencing**
Delair Group, Inc.
8600 River Road
Delair, NJ 08110
Phone: (800) 235-0185
Fax: (856) 663-1297
E-mail: info@delairgroup.com
Web site:
www.delairgroup.com/delgard

**Dripworks**
190 Sanhedrin Circle
Willits, CA 95490
Phone: (800) 616-8321
Fax: (707) 459-9645
E-mail: dripwrks@pacific.net
Web site: www.dripworksusa.com
*Drip irrigation products*

**Ehrlich Chemical Company**
Magic Circle Deer Repellent
Donna Zerbee
500 Spring Ridge Drive
Reading, PA 19612
Phone: (610) 372-9700

**agAccess/Fertile Ground Books**
3912 Vale Avenue
Oakland, CA 94619-2222
Phone/Fax: (530) 298-2060
E-mail: books@agribooks.com
Web site: www.agribooks.com

**Gardener's Supply Co.**
128 Intervale Road
Burlington, VT 05401-2850
Phone: (888) 863-1700
Fax: (800) 551-1412
E-mail: info@gardeners.com
Web site: www.gardeners.com

**Gardens Alive!**
5100 Schenley Place
Lawrenceburg, IN 47025
Phone: (812) 537-8651
Fax: (812) 537-5108
E-mail:
gardenhelp@gardens-alive.com
Web site: www.gardensalive.com

**Harmony Farm Supply and Nursery**
P.O. Box 460
Graton, CA 95444
Phone: (707) 823-9125
Fax: (707) 823-1734
E-mail: info@harmonyfarm.com
Web site: www.harmonyfarm.com

**Johnny's Selected Seeds**
RR 1, Box 2580
Foss Hill Road
Albion, ME 04910-9731
Phone: (207) 437-9294
Fax: (207) 437-2759
E-mail:
johnnys@johnnyseeds.com
Web site: www.johnnyseeds.com

**Kinsman Garden Co., Inc.**
P.O. Box 357
River Road
Point Pleasant, PA 18950-0357
Phone: (800) 733-4146,
(215) 297-0890
Fax: (215) 297-0450
E-mail: kinsmangarden@bux.com
Web site:
www.kinsmangarden.com

**Lehman's Catalog**
One Lehman Circle
P.O. Box 41
Kidron, OH 44636
Phone: (888) 438-5346
Fax: (330) 857-5785
E-mail: info@lehmans.com
Web site: www.lehmans.com

**A. M. Leonard, Inc.**
241 Fox Drive
P.O. Box 816
Piqua, OH 45356-0816
Phone: (800) 543-8955
Fax: (800) 433-0633
E-mail: info@amleo.com
Web site: www.amleo.com

**Max-Flex Fence Systems**
U.S. Route 219
Lindside, WV 24951
Phone: (800) 356-5458
Fax: (304) 753-4827
E-mail: mail@maxflex.com
Web site: www.maxflex.com

**The Natural Gardening Co.**
P.O. Box 750776
Petaluma, CA 94975
Phone: (707) 766-9303
Fax: (707) 766-9747
E-mail:
info@naturalgardening.com
Web site:
www.naturalgardening.com

**Natural Insect Control**
RR#2
Stevensville, Ontario
L0S 1S0 Canada
Phone: (905) 382-2904
Fax: (905) 382-4418
E-mail: nic@niagara.com
Web site: www.natural-insect-control.com

**N.I.M.B.Y.**
DMX Industries
6540 Martin Luther King
St. Louis, MO 63133
Phone: (314) 385-0076
Fax: (314) 385-0062
E-mail: dmxinds@aol.com

**Ohio Earth Food, Inc.**
5488 Swamp Street, NE
Hartville, OH 44632
Phone: (330) 877-9356

**Peaceful Valley Farm Supply**
P.O. Box 2209
Grass Valley, CA 95945
Phone: (888) 784-1722,
(530) 272-4769
Fax: (530) 272-4794
E-mail: contact@groworganic.com
Web site: www.groworganic.com

**Pinetree Garden Seeds**
Box 300
New Gloucester, ME 04260
Phone: (207) 926-3400
Fax: (888) 527-3337
E-mail:
superseeds@worldnet.att.net
Web site: www.superseeds.com

**Planet Natural**
1612 Gold Avenue
Bozeman, MT 59715
Phone: (406) 587-5891
Fax: (406) 587-0223
E-mail: ecostore@mcn.net
Web site: www.planetnatural.com

**Plow and Hearth**
P.O. Box 5000
Madison, VA 22727-1500
Phone: (800) 627-1712
Fax: (800) 843-2509
Web site: www.plowhearth.com

**Pond and Landscape Solutions, Inc.**
2899 E. Big Beaver, #238
Troy, MI 48083
Fax: (248) 524-9059
E-mail: sales@pondsolutions.com
Web site: www.pondsolutions.com

**Saratoga Rail Fence and Supply Co.**
P.O. Box 13864
Albany, NY 12212-9600
Phone: (800) 869-8703
Fax: (518) 869-8755
*PVC post and rail fencing*

**Seeds of Change**
P.O. Box 15700
Sante Fe, NM 87506-5700
Phone: (888) 762-7333
Fax: (888) 329-4762
E-mail:
gardener@seedsofchange.com
Web site:
www.seedsofchange.com

**H. B. Sherman Traps Inc.**
3731 Peddie Drive
Tallahassee, FL 32303
Phone: (850) 575-8727
Fax: (850) 575-4864
E-mail: traps@shermantraps.com
Web site: www.shermantraps.com

**Smith and Hawken**
2 Arbor Lane, Box 6900
Florence, KY 41022-6900
Phone: (301) 771-4542
Fax: (301) 986-4829
E-mail: smithandhawkencustomer service@discovery.com
Web site: www.smithandhawken.com

**The Tanglefoot Company**
314 Straight Avenue SW
Grand Rapids, MI 49504-6485
Phone: (616) 459-4139
Fax: (616) 459-4140
E-mail: tnglfoot@aol.com
Web site: www.tanglefoot.com

**Territorial Seed Co.**
P.O. Box 157
Cottage Grove, OR 97424-0061
Phone: (541) 942-9547
Fax: (541) 942-9881
E-mail: tertrl@srv1.vsite.com
Web site: www.territorial-seed.com

**Unilock New York, Inc.**
51 International Boulevard
Brewster, NY 10509
Phone: (800) 864-5625
Fax: (914) 278-6788
E-mail: unilock@unilock.com
Web site: www.unilock.com
*Paving stones, retaining walls, and curbing*

**Whatever Works**
Earth Science Building
74 20th Street
Brooklyn, NY 11232
Phone: (800) 499-6757
Fax: (718) 499-1005
Web site: www.whateverworks.com

**Worm's Way**
7850 N. Highway 37
Bloomington, IN 47404
Phone: (800) 274-9676
Fax: (800) 316-1264
E-mail: sales@wormsway.com
Web site: www.wormsway.com

## Herbs

**Fox Hollow Seed Co.**
P.O. Box 148
McGrann, PA 16236
Phone: (412) 548-7333
Fax: (412) 543-5751

**Gaia Garden Herbal Dispensary**
2672 West Broadway
Vancouver, BC V6K 2G3
Canada
Phone: (604) 734-4372
Fax: (604) 734-4376
E-mail: herbs@gaiagarden.com
Web site: www.gaiagarden.com

**Goodwin Creek Gardens**
P.O. Box 83
Williams, OR 97544
Phone: (800) 846-7357
Fax: (541) 846-7357
E-mail: info@goodwincreek gardens.com
Web site: www.goodwincreek gardens.com

**Horizon Herbs**
P.O. Box 69
Williams, OR 97544
Phone: (541) 846-6704
Fax: (541) 846-6233
E-mail: herbseed@chatlink.com
Web site: www.chatlink.com/~herbseed

**Johnny's Selected Seeds**
RR1, Box 2580
Foss Hill Road
Albion, ME 04910-9731
Phone: (207) 437-4357
Fax: (207) 437-2759
E-mail: customerservice@johnny seeds.com
Web site: www.johnnyseeds.com

**Long Creek Herbs**
Route 4, Box 730
Oak Grove, AR 72660
Phone: (417) 779-5450
Fax: (417) 779-5450
E-mail: jim@longcreekherbs.com
Web site: www.longcreekherbs.com

**Lunar Farms Herbals**
3 Highland-Greenhills
Gilmer, TX 75644
Phone: (800) 687-1052
E-mail: spritsong1@aol.com
Web site: www.herbworld.com/lunarfarms

**Nichols Garden Nursery**
1190 N. Pacific Highway
Albany, OR 97321-4580
Phone: (541) 928-9280
Fax: (800) 231-5306
E-mail: customersupport@ nicholsgardennursery.com
Web site: www.nicholsgardennursery.com

**Richters Herb Catalogue**
357 Highway 47
Goodwood, Ontario
L0C 1A0 Canada
Phone: (905) 640-6677
Fax: (905) 640-6641
E-mail: orderdesk@richters.com
Web site: www.richters.com

**Sage Mountain Herbs**
P.O. Box 420
E. Barre, VT 05649
Phone: (802) 479-9825
Fax: (802) 476-3722
E-mail: SageMtnHP@aol.com
Web site:
www.sagemountainherbs.com

**The Sandy Mush Herb Nursery**
Dept. OGRS
316 Surrett Cove Road
Leicester, NC 28748
Phone: (704) 683-2014

**Shepherd's Garden Seeds**
30 Irene Street
Torrington, CT 06790-6658
Phone: (860) 482-3638
E-mail:
custsrv@shepherdseeds.com
Web site:
www.shepherdseeds.com

**Well-Sweep Herb Farm**
205 Mt. Bethel Road
Port Murray, NJ 07865
Phone: (908) 852-5390
Fax: (908) 852-1649

## Soil Testing

**Cook's Consulting**
R.D. 2, Box 13
Lowville, NY 13367
Phone: (315) 376-3002
*Organic recommendations, free soil-testing kit*

**Peaceful Valley Farm Supply**
P.O. Box 2209
Grass Valley, CA 95945
Phone: (888) 784-1722,
(530) 272-4769
Fax: (530) 272-4794
E-mail: contact@groworganic.com
Web site: www.groworganic.com

**Timberleaf Soil Testing Services**
39648 Old Spring Road
Murrieta, CA 92563
Phone: (909) 677-7510
*Basic and trace mineral soil tests; organic recommendations provided*

**Wallace Laboratories**
365 Coral Circle
El Segundo, CA 90245
Phone: (310) 615-0116
Fax: (310) 640-6863
E-mail: contact@wallace-labs.com
Web site: www.wallace-labs.com

**Woods End Research Laboratory**
P.O. Box 297
Mt. Vernon, ME 04352
Phone: (800) 451-0337
Fax: (207) 293-2488
E-mail: weblink@woodsend.org
Web site: www.woodsend.org

## Trees, Shrubs, and Vines

**Carroll Gardens**
444 E. Main Street
Westminster, MD 21157
Phone: (800) 638-6334
Fax: (410) 857-4112
Web site: www.carrollgardens.com

**Forestfarm**
990 Tetherow Road
Williams, OR 97544-9599
Phone: (541) 846-7269
Fax: (541) 846-6963
E-mail: orders@forestfarm.com
Web site: www.forestfarm.com

**Greer Gardens**
1280 Goodpasture Island Road
Eugene, OR 97401-1794
Phone: (541) 686-8266
Fax: (541) 686-0910
E-mail: orders@greegardens.com
Web site: www.greergardens.com

**Gurney's Seed and Nursery Co.**
110 Capital Street
Yankton, SD 57079
Phone: (605) 665-1671
Fax: (605) 665-9718
E-mail: info@gurneys.com
Web site: www.gurneys.com

**Pickering Nurseries, Inc.**
670 Kingston Road
Pickering, Ontario
L1V 1A6 Canada
Phone: (905) 839-2111
Fax: (905) 839-4807
Web site:
www.pickeringnurseries.com

## Roses

**The Roseraie at Bayfields**
P.O. Box R
Waldoboro, ME 04572-0919
Phone: (207) 832-6330
Fax: (800) 933-4508
E-mail: zapus@roseraie.com
Web site: www.roseraie.com

**Roslyn Nursery**
211 Burrs Lane
Dix Hills, NY 11746
Phone: (631) 643-9347
Fax: (631) 427-0894
E-mail: roslyn@roslynnursery.com
Web site: www.roslynnursery.com

**Wayside Gardens**
1 Garden Lane
Hodges, SC 29695-0001
Phone: (800) 845-1124
Fax: (800) 457-9712
E-mail:
curator@waysidegardens.com
Web site:
www.waysidegardens.com

**White Flower Farm**
P.O. Box 50
Litchfield, CT 06759-0050
Phone: (800) 255-2852
Fax: (860) 496-1418
E-mail:
custserv@whiteflowerfarm.com
Web site:
www.whiteflowerfarm.com

**Woodlanders, Inc.**
1128 Colleton Avenue
Aiken, SC 29801
Phone/Fax: (803) 648-7522

## Vegetables

**Abundant Life Seed Foundation**
P.O. Box 772
Port Townsend, WA 98368
Phone: (360) 385-5660
Fax: (360) 385-7455
E-mail: abundant@olypen.com
Web site: csf.Colorado.edu/perma/abundant

**Bountiful Gardens**
18001 Shafer Ranch Road
Willits, CA 95490-9626
Phone: (707) 459-6410
Fax: (707) 459-1925
E-mail: bountiful@sonic.net
Web site:
www.bountifulgardens.org

**W. Atlee Burpee and Co.**
300 Park Avenue
Warminster, PA 18974
Phone: (800) 888-1447
Fax: (215) 674-4170
Web site: www.burpee.com

**Companion Plants**
7247 N. Coolville Ridge Road
Athens, OH 45701
Phone: (740) 592-4643
Fax: (740) 593-3092
E-mail: complants@frognet.net
Web site:
www.companionplants.com

**The Cook's Garden**
P.O. Box 535
Londonderry, VT 05148
Phone: (800) 457-9703
Fax: (800) 457-9705
E-mail:
gardener@cooksgarden.com
Web site: www.cooksgarden.com

**William Dam Seeds Ltd.**
P.O. Box 8400
Dundas, Ontario
L9H 6M1 Canada
Phone: (905) 627-6641
Fax: (905) 627-1729
E-mail: willdam@sympatico.ca

**Fedco Seeds**
P.O. Box 520
Waterville, ME 04903
Phone: (207) 873-7333
Fax: (207) 872-8317
E-mail: fedco@mint.net

**Ferry-Morse Seed Co.**
P.O. Box 488
Fulton, KY 42041-0488
Phone: (800) 283-3400
Fax: (800) 283-2700
Web site: www.ferry-morse.com

**Filaree Farm**
182 Conconully Highway
Okanogan, WA 98840
Phone: (509) 422-6940
E-mail:
filaree@northcascades.net
Web site: www.filareefarm.com

**Fox Hollow Seed Co.**
P.O. Box 148
McGrann, PA 16236
Phone: (412) 548-7333
Fax: (412) 543-5751

**Garden City Seeds**
778 Highway 93 N
Hamilton, MT 59840
Phone: (406) 961-4837
Fax: (406) 961-4877
E-mail: seeds@montana.com
Web site:
www.gardencityseeds.com

**Gurney's Seed and Nursery Co.**
110 Capital Street
Yankton, SD 57079
Phone: (605) 665-1671
Fax: (605) 665-9718
E-mail: info@gurneys.com
Web site: www.gurneys.com

**Henry Field's Seed and Nursery Co.**
415 North Burnett
Shenandoah, IA 51602
Phone: (605) 665-4491
Fax: (605) 665-2601
E-mail: info@henryfields.com
Website: www.henryfields.com

**Heritage Seed Co.**
HC 78, Box 187
Star City, AR 71667
Phone: (870) 628-4820
E-mail: questions@daylilies.net

**Ed Hume Seeds**
P.O. Box 1450
Kent, WA 98035
Fax: (253) 859-0694
E-mail: HumeSeeds@aol.com
Web site: www.humeseeds.com

**Irish Eyes with a Hint of Garlic**
P.O. Box 307
Thorp, WA 98926
Phone: (509) 964-7000
Fax: (800) 964-9210
E-mail: potatoes@irish-eyes.com
Web site: www.irish-eyes.com

**Johnny's Selected Seeds**
RR1, Box 2580
Foss Hill Road
Albion, ME 04910-9731
Phone: (207) 437-4357
Fax: (207) 437-2759
E-mail: customerservice@johnnyseeds.com
Web site: www.johnnyseeds.com

**Native Seeds/SEARCH**
2509 N. Campbell Avenue # 325
Tucson, AZ 85719
Phone: (602) 327-9123

**Nichols Garden Nursery**
1190 N. Pacific Highway NE
Albany, OR 97321
Phone: (541) 928-9280
Fax: (541) 967-8406
E-mail: info@gardennursery.com
Web site: www.gardennursery.com

**Park Seed**
1 Parkton Avenue
Greenwood, SC 29647-0001
Phone: (800) 845-3369
Fax: (800) 275-9941
E-mail: orders@parkseed.com
Web site: www.parkseed.com

**Pinetree Garden Seeds**
P.O. Box 300
616A Lewiston Road
New Gloucester, ME 04260
Phone: (207) 926-3400
Fax: (888) 527-3337
E-mail: superseeds@worldnet.att.net
Web site: www.superseeds.com

**Ronniger's Seed and Potato Co.**
P.O. Box 1838
Orting, WA 98360
Phone: (860) 893-8782
Fax: (360) 893-3492

**Seed Savers Heirloom Seeds and Gifts**
3076 N. Winn Road
Decorah, IA 52101
Phone: (319) 382-5990
Fax: (319) 382-5872

**Seeds Blüm**
27 Idaho City Stage Road
Boise, ID 83716
Phone: (800) 742-1423
Fax: (208) 338-5658
E-mail: 103374.167@compuserve.com
Web site: www.seedsblum.com

**Seeds of Change**
P.O. Box 15700
Sante Fe, NM 87506-5700
Phone: (888) 762-7333
Fax: (888) 329-4762
E-mail: gardener@seedsofchange.com
Web site: www.seedsofchange.com

**Seeds Trust, High Altitude Gardens**
P.O. Box 1048
Hailey, ID 83333-1048
Phone: (208) 788-4363
Fax: (208) 788-3452
E-mail: higarden@micron.net
Web site: www.seedsave.org

**Shepherd's Garden Seeds**
30 Irene Street
Torrington, CT 06790-6658
Phone: (860) 482-3638
Fax: (860) 482-0532
E-mail: custsrv@shepherdseeds.com
Web site: www.shepherdseeds.com

**R. H. Shumway, Seedsman**
P.O. Box 1
Graniteville, SC 29829-0001
Phone: (803) 663-9771
Fax: (888) 437-2733
Website: www.rhshumway.com

**Southern Exposure Seed Exchange**
P.O. Box 170
Earlysville, VA 22936
Phone: (804) 973-4703
Fax: (804) 973-8717
E-mail: gardens@southernexposure.com
Web site: www.southernexposure.com

**Territorial Seed Co.**
P.O. Box 157
Cottage Grove, OR 97424-0061
Phone: (541) 942-9547
Fax: (541) 942-9881
E-mail: tertrl@srv1.vsite.com
Web site: www.territorial-seed.com

**Tomato Growers Supply Company**
P.O. Box 2237
Fort Myers, FL 33902
Phone: (941) 768-1119
Fax: (888) 768-3476
Web site: www.tomatogrowers.com

**Vermont Bean Seed Co.**
Garden Lane
Fair Haven, VT 05743
Phone: (803) 663-0217
Fax: (888) 500-7333
E-mail: info@vermontbean.com
Web site: www.vermontbean.com

**Willhite Seed Inc.**
P.O. Box 23
Poolville, TX 76487
Phone: (817) 599-8656
Fax: (817) 599-5843
E-mail: info@willhiteseed.com
Web site: www.willhiteseed.com

**Wood Prairie Farm**
Jim and Megan Gerritsen
49 Kinney Road
Bridgewater, ME 04735
Phone: (207) 429-9765 or
(800) 829-9765
Fax: (800) 300-6494
Web site: www.woodprairie.com

## Wildflowers

Abundant Life Seed Foundation
P.O. Box 772
Port Townsend, WA 98368
Phone: (360) 385-5660
Fax: (360) 385-7455
E-mail: abundant@olypen.com
Web site: csf.colorado.edu/perma/abundant

**Clyde Robin Seed Co.**
P.O. Box 2366
Castro Valley, CA 94546
Phone: (510) 785-0425
Fax: (510) 785-6463
Web site: www.clyderobin.com

**Native Seeds/SEARCH**
2509 N. Campbell Avenue # 325
Tucson, AZ 85719
Phone: (602) 327-9123

**Plants of the Southwest**
Agua Fria Road
Route 6, Box 11A
Santa Fe, NM 87501
Phone: (800) 788-7333
Fax: (505) 438-8800
E-mail: contact@plantsofthesouthwest.com
Web site: www.plantsofthesouthwest.com

**Prairie Moon Nursery**
Route 3, Box 163
Winona, MN 55987
Phone: (507) 452-1362
Fax: (507) 454-5238
Web site:
www.prairiemoonnursery.com

**Prairie Nursery**
P.O. Box 306
Westfield, WI 53964
Phone: (800) 476-9453
Fax: (608) 296-2741
Web site: www.prairienursery.com

**Wildseed Farms**
P.O. Box 3000
425 Wildflower Hills
Fredericksburg, TX 78624-3000
Phone: (800) 848-0078
Fax: (830) 990-8090
Web site:
www.wildseedfarms.com

# Recommended Reading


## Composting and Soil

Appelhof, Mary. *Worms Eat My Garbage.* Kalamazoo, MI: Flower Press, 1982.

Greshuny, Grace. *Start with the Soil.* Emmaus, PA: Rodale, 1993.

Hynes, Erin. *Rodale's Successful Organic Gardening: Improving the Soil.* Emmaus, PA: Rodale, 1994.

Martin, Deborah, and Grace Gershuny, eds. *The Rodale Book of Composting.* Emmaus, PA: Rodale, 1992.

Martin, Deborah, and Karen Costello Soltys, eds. *Rodale Organic Gardening Basics: Soil.* Emmaus, PA: Rodale, 2000.

## General Gardening

Benjamin, Joan, ed. *Great Garden Shortcuts.* Emmaus, PA: Rodale, 1996.

Bradley, Fern Marshall, and Barbara Ellis, eds. *Rodale's All-New Encyclopedia of Organic Gardening.* Emmaus, PA: Rodale, 1992.

Bucks, Christine, ed. *Rodale Organic Gardening Basics: Vegetables.* Emmaus, PA: Rodale, 2000.

Coleman, Eliot. *The New Organic Grower.* White River Junction, VT: Chelsea Green Publishing, 1995.

Costenbader, Carol W. *The Big Book of Preserving the Harvest.* Pownal, VT: Storey Communications, 1997.

Cunningham, Sally Jean. *Great Garden Companions.* Emmaus, PA: Rodale, 1998.

Lanza, Patricia. *Lasagna Gardening.* Emmaus, PA: Rodale, 1998.

Logsdon, Gene. *The Contrary Farmer's Invitation to Gardening.* White River Junction, VT: Chelsea Green Publishing, 1997.

Stone, Pat. *Easy Gardening 101.* Pownal, VT: Storey Communications, 1998.

Swain, Roger. *The Practical Gardener.* Boston: Little, Brown and Company, 1989. Reprint, New York: Galahad Books, 1998.

## Fruits and Berries

McClure, Susan. *Rodale's Successful Organic Gardening: Fruits and Berries.* Emmaus, PA: Rodale, 1996.

Nick, Jean, and Fern Marshall Bradley. *Growing Fruits and Vegetables Organically.* Emmaus, PA: Rodale, 1994.

Reich, Lee. *Uncommon Fruits Worthy of Attention.* Reading, MA: Addison-Wesley Publishing, 1991.

## Herbs

Duke, James A. *The Green Pharmacy.* Emmaus, PA: Rodale, 1997.

Gladstar, Rosemary. *Herbal Healing for Women.* New York: Simon & Schuster, 1993.

James, Tina. *The Salad Bar in Your Own Backyard.* Reisterstown, MD: Gardening from the Heart, 1996.

Kowalchik, Claire, and William H. Hylton. *Rodale's Illustrated Encyclopedia of Herbs.* Emmaus, PA: Rodale, 1987.

Long, Jim. *Herbs, Just for Fun: A Beginner's Guide to Starting an Herb Garden.* Oak Grove, AR: Long Creek Herbs, 1996.

——. *Classic Herb Blends.* Oak Grove, AR: Long Creek Herbs, 1996.

McClure, Susan. *The Herb Gardener: A Guide for All Seasons.* Pownal, VT: Storey Communication, 1995.

Oster, Maggie. *Herbal Vinegar.* Pownal, VT: Storey Communication, 1994.

Oster, Maggie, and Sal Gilbertie. *The Herbal Palate Cookbook.* Pownal, VT: Storey Communications, 1996.

Smith, Miranda. *Your Backyard Herb Garden.* Emmaus, PA: Rodale, 1997.

Sombke, Laurence. *Beautiful Easy Herbs.* Emmaus, PA: Rodale, 1997.

Tourles, Stephanie. *The Herbal Body Book.* Pownal, VT: Storey Communications, 1994.

## Landscape and Flower Gardening

Bender, Steve, and Felder Rushing. *Passalong Plants.* Chapel Hill: The University of North Carolina Press, 1993.

Bradley, Fern Marshall, ed. *Gardening with Perennials.* Emmaus, PA: Rodale, 1996.

Byczynski, Lynn. *The Flower Farmer: An Organic Grower's Guide to Raising and Selling Cut Flowers.* White River Junction, VT: Chelsea Green Publishing, 1997.

Cox, Jeff. *Perennial All-Stars: The 150 Best Perennials for Great-Looking, Trouble-Free Gardens.* Emmaus, PA: Rodale, 1998.

D'Amato, Peter. *The Savage Garden: Cultivating Carnivorous Plants.* Berkeley, CA: Ten Speed Press, 1998.

DiSabato-Aust, Tracy. *The Well-Tended Perennial Garden: Planting and Pruning Techniques.* Portland, OR: Timber Press, 1998.

Ellis, Barbara. *Taylor's Guide to Growing North America's Favorite Plants.* Boston: Houghton Mifflin, 1998.

Harper, Pamela, and Frederick McGourty. *Perennials: How to Select, Grow and Enjoy.* Los Angeles: Price Stern Sloan, 1985.

McKeon, Judy. *The Encyclopedia of Roses.* Emmaus, PA: Rodale, 1995.

Phillips, Ellen, and C. Colston Burrell. *Rodale's Illustrated Encyclopedia of Perennials.* Emmaus, PA: Rodale, 1993.

Sombke, Laurence. *Beautiful Easy Flower Gardens.* Emmaus, PA: Rodale, 1995.

Taylor, Norman. *Taylor's Guide to Annuals.* Rev. ed. Boston: Houghton Mifflin, 1986.

Soltys, Karen Costello, ed. *Rodale Organic Gardening Basics: Roses.* Emmaus, PA: Rodale, 2000.

## Pest Management

Ellis, Barbara W., and Fern Marshall Bradley. *The Organic Gardener's Handbook of Natural Insect and Disease Control.* Emmaus, PA: Rodale, 1992.

Gilkeson, Linda, et al. *Rodale's Pest and Disease Problem Solver.* Emmaus, PA: Rodale, 1996.

Hart, Rhonda. *Bugs, Slugs, and Other Thugs.* Pownal, VT: Storey Communications, 1991.

## Season Extension

Colebrook, Binda. *Winter Gardening in the Maritime Northwest.* Seattle, WA: Sasquatch Books, 1989.

Coleman, Eliot. *Four-Season Harvest: How to Harvest Fresh, Organic Vegetables from Your Home Garden All Year Long.* White River Junction, VT: Chelsea Green Publishing, 1992.

## Seed Starting

Bubel, Nancy. *The New Seed-Starter's Handbook.* Emmaus, PA: Rodale, 1988.

Ondra, Nancy, and Barbara Ellis. *Easy Plant Propagation.* (Taylor's Weekend Gardening Guides.) Boston: Houghton Mifflin, 1998.

Powell, Eileen. *From Seed to Bloom.* Pownal, VT: Storey Communications, 1995.

## Weeds

Hynes, Erin. *Rodale's Successful Organic Gardening: Controlling Weeds.* Emmaus, PA: Rodale, 1995.

Pleasant, Barbara. *The Gardener's Weed Book.* Pownal, VT: Storey Communications, 1996.

## Magazines and Newsletters

*Avant Gardener, The,* P.O. Box 489, New York, NY 10028

*Common Sense Pest Control Quarterly,* Bio-Integral Resource Center (BIRC), P.O. Box 7414, Berkeley, CA 94707-0414

*Country Living Gardener,* 224 W. 57th Street, New York, NY 10019

*Growing for Market,* P.O. Box 3747, Lawrence, KS 66046

*Homesteader's Connection,* P.O. Box 5186, Cookeville, TN 38505

*HortIdeas,* 750 Black Lick Road, Gravel Switch, KY 40328

*Organic Gardening,* Rodale, 33 E. Minor Street, Emmaus, PA 18098

# Index

*Note:* Page references in *italics* indicate illustrations. Those in **boldface** indicate charts.

## A



## B

# D

# M

# Q



# R



# S

# USDA Plant Hardiness Zone Map

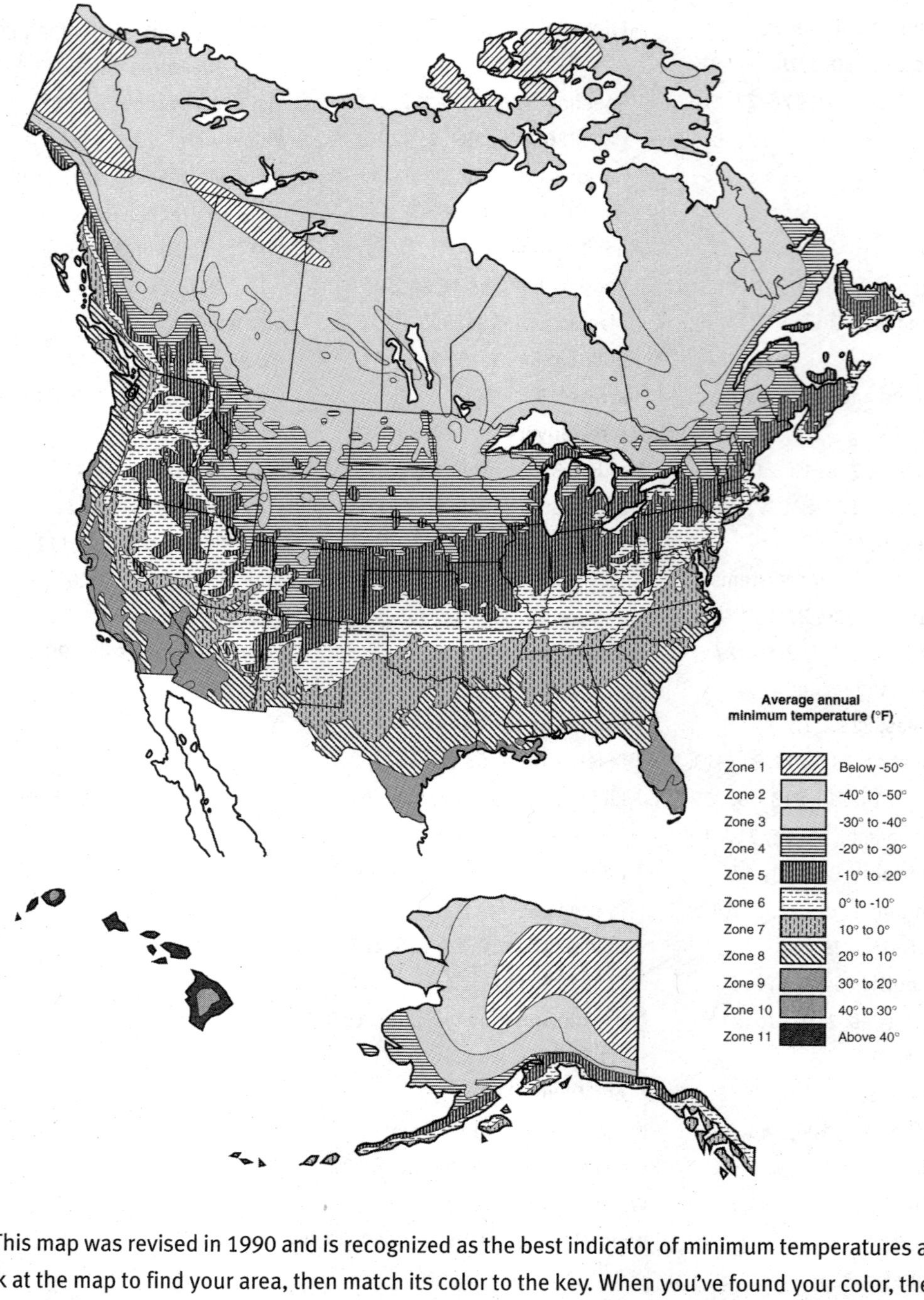


This map was revised in 1990 and is recognized as the best indicator of minimum temperatures available. Look at the map to find your area, then match its color to the key. When you've found your color, the key will tell you what hardiness zone you live in. Remember that the map is a general guide; your particular conditions may vary.